BROOKLANDS BOOKS

AUSTIN HEALEY 3000

Gold Portfolio

1959~1967

Compiled by
R.M. Clarke

ISBN 1 85520 049X

Distributed by
Brooklands Book Distribution Ltd.
'Holmerise', Seven Hills Road,
Cobham, Surrey, England
Printed in Hong Kong

BROOKLANDS BOOKS

BROOKLANDS ROAD TEST SERIES

AC Ace & Aceca 1953-1983
Alfa Romeo Alfasud 1972-1984
Alfa Romeo Alfetta Coupes GT. GTV. GTV6 1974-1987
Alfa Romeo Giulia Berlinas 1962-1976
Alfa Romeo Giulia Coupes 1963-1976
Alfa Romeo Spider 1966-1987
Allard Gold Portfolio 1937-1958
Alvis Gold Portfolio 1919-1969
American Motors Muscle Cars 1966-1970
Aston Martin Gold Portfolio 1972-1985
Austin Seven 1922-1982
Austin A30 & A35 1951-1962
Austin Healey 100 & 100/6 Gold Portfolio 1952-1959
Austin Healey 3000 Gold Portfolio 1959-1967
Austin Healey 'Frogeye' Sprite Col No.1 1958-1961
Austin Healey Sprite 1958-1971
Avanti 1962-1983
BMW Six Cylinder Coupes 1969-1975
BMW 1600 Col. 1 1966-1981
BMW 2002 1968-1976
Bristol Cars Gold Portfolio 1946-1985
Buick Automobiles 1947-1960
Buick Muscle Cars 1965-1970
Buick Riviera 1963-1978
Cadillac Automobiles 1949-1959
Cadillac Automobiles 1960-1969
Cadillac Eldorado 1967-1978
High Performance Capris Gold Portfolio 1969-1987
Chevrolet Camaro SS & Z28 1966-1973
Chevrolet Camaro & Z-28 1973-1981
High Performance Camaros 1982-1988
Camaro Muscle Cars 1966-1972
Chevrolet 1955-1957
Chevrolet Impala & SS 1958-1971
Chevrolet Muscle Cars 1966-1971
Chevelle and SS 1964-1972
Chevy Blazer 1969-1981
Chevy EL Camino & SS 1959-1987
Chevy II Nova & SS 1962-1973
Chrysler 300 1955-1970
Citroen Traction Avant Gold Portfolio 1934-1957
Citroen DS & ID 1955-1975
Citroen 2CV 1949-1988
Shelby Cobra Gold Portfolio 1962-1969
Cobras & Replicas 1962-1983
Corvair 1959-1968
Chevrolet Corvette Gold Portfolio 1953 1962
Corvette Stingray Gold Portfolio 1963-1967
High Performance Corvettes 1983-1989
Datsun 240Z 1970-1973
Datsun 280Z & ZX 1975-1983
De Tomaso Collection No.1 1962-1981
Dodge Charger 1966-1974
Dodge Muscle Cars 1967-1970
Excalibur Collection No.1 1952-1981
Ferrari Cars 1946-1956
Ferrari Cars 1973-1977
Ferrari Dino 1965-1974
Ferrari Dino 308 1974-1979
Ferrari 308 & Mondial 1980-1984
Ferrair Collection No.1 1960-1970
Fiat-Bertone X1/9 1973-1988
Fiat Pininfarina 124 + 2000 Spider 1968-1985
Ford Automobiles 1949-1959
Ford Bronco 1966-1977
Ford Bronco 1978-1988
Ford Cortina 1600E & GT 1967-1970
Ford Fairlane 1955-1970
Ford Falcon 1960-1970
Ford GT40 Gold Portfolio 1964-1987
Ford RS Escorts 1968-1980
High Performance Escorts Mk1 1968-1974
High Performance Escorts Mk II 1975-1980
High Performance Mustangs 1982-1988
Honda CRX 1983-1987
Hudson & Railton 1936-1940
Jaguar Cars 1957-1961
Jaguar Cars 1961-1964
Jaguar Mk2 1959-1969
Jaguar E-Type Gold Portfolio 1961-1971
Jaguar E-Type 1966-1971
Jaguar E-Type V-12 1971-1975
Jaguar XKE Collection No.1 1961-1974
Jaguar XJ6 1968-1972
Jaguar XJ6 Series II 1973-1979
Jaguar XJ6 & XJ12 Series III 1979-1985
Jaguar XJ12 1972-1980
Jaguar XJS Gold Portfolio 1975-1988
Jaguar XK120.XK140.XK150 Gold Portfolio 1948-1960
Jeep CJ5 & CJ6 1960-1976
Jeep CJ5 & CJ7 1976-1986
Jensen Cars 1946-1967
Jensen Cars 1967-1979
Jensen Interceptor Gold Portfolio 1966-1986
Jensen Healey 1972-1976
Lamborghini Cars 1964-1970
Lamborghini Cars 1970-1975
Lamborghini Countach Col No.1 1971-1982
Lamborghini Countach & Urraco 1974-1980
Lamborghini Countach & Jalpa 1980-1985
Lancia Stratos 1972-1985
Land Rover 1948-1973 - A Collection
Land Rover Series II & IIa 1958-1971
Land Rover Series III 1971-1985
Land Rover 90 & 110 1983-1989
Lincoln Gold Portfolio 1949-1960
Lincoln Continental 1961-1969
Lotus and Caterham Seven Gold Portfolio 1957-1989
Lotus Cortina Gold Portfolio 1963-1970
Lotus Elan Gold Portfolio 1962-1974
Lotus Elan Collection No.2 1963-1972
Lotus Elite 1957-1964
Lotus Elite & Eclat 1974-1982
Lotus Turbo Esprit 1980-1986
Lotus Europa 1966-1975
Lotus Europa Collection No.1 1966-1974
Lotus Seven Collection No.1 1957-1982
Marcos Cars 1960-1988
Maserati 1965-1970
Maserati 1970-1975

Mazda RX-7 Collection No.1 1978-1981
Mercedes 190 & 300SL 1954-1963
Mercedes 230/250/280SL 1963-1971
Mercedes Benz SLs & SLCs Gold Portfolio 1971-1989
Mercedes Benz Cars 1949-1954
Mercedes Benz Cars 1954-1957
Mercedes Benz Cars 1957-1961
Mercedes Benz Competion Cars 1950-1957
Mercury Muscle Cars 1966-1971
Metropolitan 1954-1962
MG TC 1945-1949
MG TD 1949-1953
MG TF 1953-1955
MG Cars 1959-1962
MGA Roadsters 1955-1962
MGA Collection No.1 1955-1982
MGB Roadsters 1962-1980
MGB GT 1965-1980
MG Midget, 1961-1980
Mini Moke 1964-1989
Mini Muscle Cars 1961-1979
Mopar Muscle Cars 1964-1967
Mopar Muscle Cars 1968-1971
Morgan Three-Wheeler Gold Portfolio 1910-1952
Morgan Cars 1960-1970
Morgan Cars Gold Portfolio 1968-1989
Morris Minor Collection No.1
Mustang Muscle Cars 1967-1971
Oldsmobile Automobiles 1955-1963
Old's Cutlass & 4-4-2 1964-1972
Oldsmobile Muscle Cars 1964-1971
Oldsmobile Toronado 1966-1978
Opel GT 1968-1973
Packard Gold Portfolio 1946-1958
Pantera Gold Portfolio 1970-1989
Plymouth Barracuda 1964-1974
Plymouth Muscle Cars 1966-1971
Pontiac Tempest & GTO 1961-1965
Pontiac GTO 1964-1970
Pontiac Firebird 1967-1973
Pontiac Firebird and Trans-Am 1973-1981
High Performance Firebirds 1982-1988
Pontiac Fiero 1984-1988
Pontiac Muscle Cars 1966-1972
Porsche 356 1952-1965
Porsche Cars in the 60's
Porsche Cars 1960-1964
Porsche Cars 1964-1968
Porsche Cars 1968-1972
Porsche Cars 1972-1975
Porsche Turbo Collection No.1 1975-1980
Porsche 911 1965-1969
Porsche 911 1970-1972
Porsche 911 1973-1977
Porsche 911 Carrera 1973-1977
Porsche 911 Turbo 1975-1984
Porsche 911 SC 1978-1983
Porsche 914 Gold Portfolio 1969-1976
Porsche 914 Collection No.1 1969-1983
Porsche 924 Gold Portfolio 1975-1988
Porsche 928 1977-1989
Porsche 944 1981-1985
Range Rover Gold Portfolio 1970-1988
Reliant Scimitar 1964-1986
Riley 11/2 & 21/2 Litre Gold Portfolio 1945-1955
Rolls Royce Silver Cloud 1955-1965
Rolls Royce Silver Shadow 1965-1981
Rover P4 1949-1959
Rover P4 1955-1964
Rover 3 & 3.5 Litre 1958-1973
Rover 2000 + 2200 1963-1977
Rover 3500 1968-1977
Rover 3500 & Vitesse 1976-1986
Saab Sonett Collection No.1 1966-1974
Saab Turbo 1976-1983
Shelby Mustang Muscle Cars 1965-1970
Stubebaker Gold Portfolio 1947-1966
Stubebaker Hawks & Larks 1956-1963
Sunbeam Tiger & Alpine Gold Portfolio 1959-1967
Thunderbird 1955-1957
Thunderbird 1958-1963
Thunderbird 1964-1976
Toyota MR2 1984-1988
Triumph 2000. 2.5. 2500 1963-1977
Triumph GT6 1966-1974
Triumph Spitfire 1962-1980
Triumph Spitfire Col No.1 1962-1982
Triumph Stag 1970-1980
Triumph Stag Collection No.1 1970-1984
Triumph TR4-TR5-TR250 1961-1968
Triumph TR6 1969-1976
Triumph TR6 Collection No.1 1969-1983
Triumph TR7 & TR8 1975-1982
Triumph Vitesse & Herald 1959-1971
TVR Gold Portfolio 1959-1988
Volkswagen Cars 1936-1956
VW Beetle Collection No.1 1970-1982
VW Golf GTi 1976-1986
VW Karmann Ghia 1955-1982
VW Kubelwagen 1940-1975
VW Scirocco 1974-1981
VW Bus. Camper. Van 1954-1967
VW Bus. Camper. Van 1968-1979
VW Bus. Camper. Van 1979-1989
Volvo 120 1956-1970
Volvo 1800 1960-1973

BROOKLANDS ROAD & TRACK SERIES

Road & Track on Alfa Romeo 1949-1963
Road & Track on Alfa Romeo 1964-1970
Road & Track on Alfa Romeo 1971-1976
Road & Track on Alfa Romeo 1977-1989
Road & Track on Aston Martin 1962-1984
Road & Track on Auburn Cord and Duesenburg 1952-1984
Road & Track on Audi & Auto Union 1952-1980
Road & Track on Audi 1980-1986
Road & Track on Austin Healey 1953-1970
Road & Track on BMW Cars 1966-1974
Road & Track on BMW Cars 1975-1978
Road & Track on BMW Cars 1979-1983

Road & Track on Cobra, Shelby & GT40 1962-1983
Road & Track on Corvette 1953-1967
Road & Track on Corvette 1968-1982
Road & Track on Corvette 1982-1986
Road & Track on Datsun Z 1970-1983
Road & Track on Ferrari 1950-1968
Road & Track on Ferrari 1968-1974
Road & Track on Ferrari 1975-1981
Road & Track on Ferrari 1981-1984
Road & Track on Fiat Sports Cars 1968-1987
Road & Track on Jaguar 1950-1960
Road & Track on Jaguar 1961-1968
Road & Track on Jaguar 1968-1974
Road & Track on Jaguar 1974-1982
Road & Track on Jaguar 1983-1989
Road & Track on Lamborghini 1964-1985
Road & Track on Lotus 1972-1981
Road & Track on Maserati 1952-1974
Road & Track on Maserati 1975-1983
Road & Track on Mazda RX7 1978-1986
Road & Track on Mercedes 1952-1962
Road & Track on Mercedes 1963-1970
Road & Track on Mercedes 1971-1979
Road & Track on Mercedes 1980-1987
Road & Track on MG Sports Cars 1949-1961
Road & Track on MG Sprots Cars 1962-1980
Road & Track on Mustang 1964-1977
Road & Track on Peugeot 1955-1986
Road & Track on Pontiac 1960-1983
Road & Track on Porsche 1961-1967
Road & Track on Porsche 1968-1971
Road & Track on Porsche 1972-1975
Road & Track on Porsche 1975-1978
Road & Track on Porsche 1979-1982
Road & Track on Porsche 1982-1985
Road & Track on Porsche 1985-1988
Road & Track on Rolls Royce & B'ley 1950-1965
Road & Track on Rolls Royce & B'ley 1966-1984
Road & Track on Saab 1955-1985
Road & Track on Toyota Sports & GT Cars 1966-1984
Road & Track on Triumph Sports Cars 1953-1967
Road & Track on Triumph Sports Cars 1967-1974
Road & Track on Triumph Sports Cars 1974-1982
Road & Track on Volkswagen 1951-1968
Road & Track on Volkswagen 1968-1978
Road & Track on Volkswagen 1978-1985
Road & Track on Volvo 1957-1974
Road & Track on Volvo 1975-1985
Road & Track - Henry Manney at Large and Abroad

BROOKLANDS CAR AND DRIVER SERIES

Car and Driver on BMW 1955-1977
Car and Driver on BMW 1977-1985
Car and Driver on Cobra, Shelby & Ford GT 40 1963-1984
Car and Driver on Corvette 1956-1967
Car and Driver on Corvette 1968-1977
Car and Driver on Corvette 1978-1982
Car and Driver on Corvette 1983-1988
Car and Driver on Datsun Z 1600 & 2000 1966-1984
Car and Driver on Ferrari 1955-1962
Car and Driver on Ferrari 1963-1975
Car and Driver on Ferrari 1976-1983
Car and Driver on Mopar 1956-1967
Car and Driver on Mopar 1968-1975
Car and Driver on Mustang 1964-1972
Car and Driver on Pontiac 1961-1975
Car and Driver on Porsche 1955-1962
Car and Driver on Porsche 1963-1970
Car and Driver on Porsche 1970-1976
Car and Driver on Porsche 1977-1981
Car and Driver on Porsche 1982-1986
Car and Driver on Saab 1956-1985
Car and Driver on Volvo 1955-1986

BROOKLANDS PRACTICAL CLASSICS SERIES

PC on Austin A40 Restoration
PC on Land Rover Restoration
PC on Metalworking in Restoration
PC on Midget/Sprite Restoration
PC on Mini Cooper Restoration
PC on MGB Restoration
PC on Morris Minor Restoration
PC on Sunbeam Rapier Restoration
PC on Triumph Herald/Vitesse
PC on Triumph Spitfire Restoration
PC on VW Beetle Restoration
PC on 1930s Car Restoration

BROOKLANDS MOTOR & THOROGHBRED & CLASSIC CAR SERIES

Motor & T & CC on Ferrari 1966-1976
Motor & T & CC on Ferrari 1976-1984
Motor & T & CC on Lotus 1979-1983

BROOKLANDS MILITARY VEHICLES SERIES

Allied Mil. Vehicles No.1 1942-1945
Allied Mil. Vehicles No.2 1941-1946
Dodge Mil. Vehicles Col. 1 1940-1945
Military Jeeps 1941-1945
Off Road Jeeps 1944-1971
Hail to the Jeep
US Military Vehicles 1941-1945
US Army Military Vehicles WW2-TM9-2800

BROOKLANDS HOT ROD RESTORATION SERIES

Auto Restoration Tips & Techniques
Basic Bodywork Tips & Techniques
Basic Painting Tips & Techniques
Camaro Restoration Tips & Techniques
Custom Painting Tips & Techniques
Engine Swapping Tips & Techniques
How to Build a Street Rod
Mustang Restoration Tips & Techniques
Performance Tuning - Chevrolets of the '60s
Performance Tuning - Ford of the '60s
Performance Tuning - Mopars of the '60s
Performance Tuning - Pontiacs of the '60s

BROOKLANDS BOOKS

CONTENTS

BROOKLANDS BOOKS

ACKNOWLEDGEMENTS

Our first volume about these Big Healeys came out several years ago and is now out of print. We felt, however, that the appeal of these cars has increased so much in recent times that readers would appreciate the more comprehensive coverage we can provide through our Gold Portfolio series. So this new volume is devoted to the 3000 models alone, and we have dealt with the earlier 100 and 100-Six models in a companion volume of their own.

None of the Brooklands Books could exist without the generous support of those who own the copyright to the original material they reproduce. For permission to reprint the articles in this volume, we are pleased to thank the managements of Autocar, Auto-Sport, British Car, Car and Car Conversions, Car and Driver, Cars Illustrated, Classic and Sportscar, Classic Car, Motor, Motor Life, Motor Sport, Motor Trend, Performance Car, Road & Track, Safety Fast, Special Interest Autos, Sporting Motorist, Sports Car Graphic, Sports Cars Illustrated and Sports Car World.

Finally, our thanks go to motoring writer James Taylor, who has once again kindly agreed to introduce this latest volume for us.

R.M. Clarke

By the time the Austin-Healey 3000 appeared in July 1959, the Big Healey was a familiar sight on British and North American roads. The new models were hard to distinguish from their forebears by a cursory visual examination, but they incorporated one very significant improvement. This was a big-bore 2912cc version of the BMC six-cylinder engine. Not only was this more powerful than its 2638cc predecessor, but it was also more torquey. The result was that the Healey 3000 was faster through the gears and had a higher top speed than all of its standard-production forebears.

In 1962, the triple-carburettor Mk.II version appeared, offering even more power but no real performance improvements from an engine that proved difficult to keep in tune. So the Mk.II convertible — with a proper soft top and 2+2 seating — reverted to twin carburettors, and the final Mk.III models introduced in 1964 looked to other means for their power increase.

In their final years, the works Healeys became respected rally machines, and thus remained desirable even in a market-place which had been their road performance out-classed by the likes of Jaguar's E-type. But the 3000, durable as it was, could not last forever: production came to an end late in 1967, largely because of the cost of modifying the car to meet safety and exhaust emissions regulations due to be introduced in the USA during 1968.

A Big Healey still has undeniable charisma, and these classic British sports cars of the 1960s are today much prized by enthusiasts all over the world. I hope those enthusiasts will join me in welcoming this latest excellent addition to the Brooklands Books Gold Portfolio series.

James Taylor   Woodcote, Oxon.

AUSTIN-HEALEY 3-LITER

On a jag in a Healey

A LL OF ROAD & TRACK's previous road tests of Austin-Healeys—there have been five, not counting this one r the Sprite, since 1954—have been performed in California under practically identical conditions. In the case of he new 3000 model a slight obstacle presented itself. This bstacle was some 2800 miles of road between New York where the only two 3000's in the country happened to be t the end of May) and California, where the test crew aited with anxious eyes on the deadline for this issue.

Quickly our small but enthusiastic New York staff,

consisting of Harvey B. Janes, Eastern Editor, and David E. Davis, Jr., Eastern Advertising Manager, offered a solution. They would drive one of the new cars nonstop from New York to the Road & Track offices in California. Thus we would have our test car in plenty of time and they would be firmly established as heroes, having set all sorts of new coast-to-coast driving records.

They got underway in the early evening on a Monday and, with the aid of a package of innocent-looking but highly potent pep pills, pulled up at the Road & Track

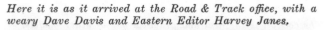

tock except for its Lucas road lights, the 3-liter looks much etter after a bath, even in Los Angeles water.

Here it is as it arrived at the Road & Track office, with a weary Dave Davis and Eastern Editor Harvey Janes,

With the hardtop, a comfortable all-weather town car . . .

And for traveling, better endowed than some sports cars.

offices a little over 57 hours later, full of praise for the car and for their own powers of endurance. When we informed them that a certain French economy sedan had covered the same distance in roughly 54 hours, they were only mildly impressed. The drivers of this French car, they told us, had cheated; they had not stopped to eat along the way. Of the total elapsed time of 57 hours in the Healey, at least three and a half hours had been consumed in various restaurants along the route. In addition, they had been forced to drive through a wild rainstorm and flood in Ohio and had wasted nearly an hour in a bootleg sports car garage just outside of St. Louis trying to replace a silly little rubber grommet that had fallen off the throttle linkage and into a sealed compartment under the instrument panel. In view of all this, our drivers steadfastly and with glassy eyes claimed the following coast-to-coast records: fastest trip in an English car; fastest in an Austin-Healey; fastest in a 3-liter car; fastest in a four-seater roadster with detachable hardtop; fastest by a bearded and mustachioed two-man crew. We might add that it was also the longest distance ever covered in the course of a Road & Track road test.

With the first part of our program successfully completed, we proceeded with the actual performance testing without so much as changing the oil or greasing the car.

When the Healey left New York, it had just under 500 mile on the odometer. We had hoped to be able to complete ou tests in California without tuning the engine in any way by the time the car arrived it was so well broken in an running so beautifully—in spite of having been drive hard—that this was entirely feasible.

The speedometer proved to be extremely accurate, whic helped our heroes keep up a good on-the-road average During the acceleration runs it seemed that the gearbox, sti somewhat stiff, might be adversely affecting the car's per formance; but when we checked the times against thos on the 100-6 last year they proved to be just about righ in view of the changes that have been incorporated in th new car. The engine of the 3000 is nothing more or les than a bored-out version of the 100-6 powerplant. Displace ment is now 2912 cubic centimeters, or roughly 10% larger than before.

On the other hand the rear-axle ratio has been change from 4.1 to 3.9, which would figure to knock about 5% off the performance all along the line. This leaves a ne improvement of 5%. In other words, the increase in engin displacement has more than made up for the change i axle ratio. Acceleration, pulling power on hills, etc., ar therefore improved about 5% over last year's car.

On long grades the car pulls beautifully in top overdriv

The cockpit is the neat and practical one of other models.

It looks the same, but it isn't: see text and performance dat

PHOTOGRAPHY: POOLE

During our top-speed runs we found that if the 3000 is held in 4th gear until about 100 miles per hour, it will fairly leap ahead when overdrive is engaged, and acceleration will continue smoothly and steadily up to better than 112 mph. All of our drivers agreed that in the matter of performance and smoothness the latest Austin-Healey was pleasantly similar to the original XK-120 Jaguar.

Previously, in all our tests on Austin-Healeys, we experienced considerable difficulty in getting the true ultimate top speed. The older models will over-rev in 4th, but when overdrive is engaged at about 100 mph, the car fails to respond. In other words, it takes several miles to obtain terminal velocity. The new car, with the larger engine and closer-ratio overdrive, still has lots of punch at 100 mph and accelerates from that speed to an indicated 120 mph in just over a mile. Tapley readings, for example, are almost exactly 5% better in each gear, as expected, but in overdrive the readings averaged 10% better. The 100-6 used a .778 overdrive ratio with a 4.10 rear axle; the 3000 employs a .820 overdrive ratio which, with the new 3.90 rear axle, gives the same over-all ratio as before in this gear. Here's how the production models compare:

		3000	MM	100-6	100-4
Time,	0-40	5.2	5.2	6.1	6.2
	0-60	9.8	10.4	12.2	11.7
	0-80	17.5	19.2	22.5	20.8
ss ¼		17.1	17.4	18.2	18.1
Top speed		112.5	109.0	105.0	102.0

For the performance tests we adhered to the red line on the tachometer (5200 revolutions per minute). Yet the 6-cylinder engine is very smooth, and it will run well past 5500 rpm with no complaint and no audible sign of valve clatter setting in. The indirect gears are quiet except for 1st, which growls a little. If you get tired of this, it's perfectly possible to forget it and use 2nd gear for starting up. The gearbox was still rather stiff and shifts were hard to make, a feature rather typical of British sports cars for the first few thousand miles. Obviously the gearbox hadn't been used much in the course of the cross-country run.

Handling characteristics are extremely friendly once you get used to the automobile. The steering is quite sensitive to throttle opening—too little produces oversteer, especially on fast bends that have been entered a bit too quickly. Adding more throttle will give fairly constant understeer all the way up to the breakaway point. From there, too much throttle will produce oversteer again, although this can be used to advantage to flick the tail out in tight corners.

Considering the softness of the suspension the ride is surprisingly firm at lower speeds, but above 60 mph it smoothes out considerably and the adhesion seems actually improved, even on rough surfaces. The Dunlop RS-4 tires give excellent traction and on the cross-country trip proved themselves, happily, to be far better on wet roads than previous Dunlops. The 3000 has disc brakes in the front and finned drums in the rear. There is no booster for these brakes, and at speeds below 30 mph the pedal pressure required to stop the car within a comfortable distance is noticeably greater than with the all-drum brake system on the 100-6. At the equivalent of racing speeds the braking is smooth and powerful, with a minimum of nose dive. Even when slight fade is finally produced, after several panic stops from 100 mph, recovery is extremely quick.

The best way to describe the new Austin-Healey 3000 is to say that it is a real enthusiasts' sports car: fun to drive, with lots of performance and good handling and braking characteristics. It could have better cockpit ventilation and seating position, and we still wish that the manufacturer would return to the cleaner styling of the older 4-cylinder cars, but these are only minor grievances. Dollar for dollar this is still one of the top sports cars on the market. ⊛

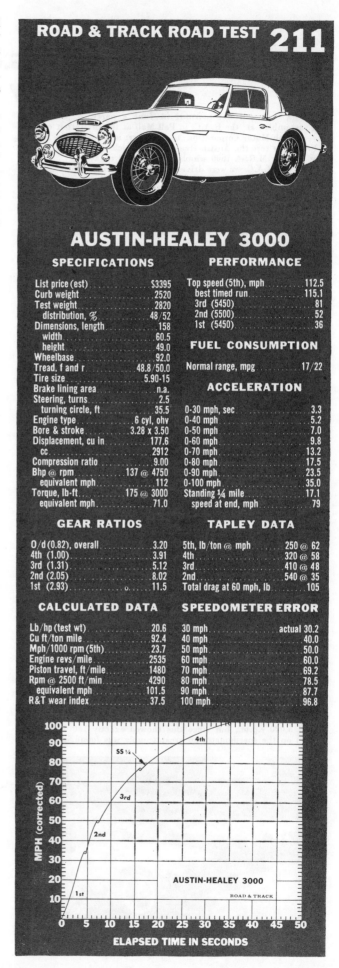

AUSTIN-HEALEY 3000

SPECIFICATIONS

List price (est)	$3395
Curb weight	2520
Test weight	2820
distribution, %	48/52
Dimensions, length	158
width	60.5
height	49.0
Wheelbase	92.0
Tread, f and r	48.8/50.0
Tire size	5.90-15
Brake lining area	n.a.
Steering, turns	2.5
turning circle, ft	35.5
Engine type	6 cyl, ohv
Bore & stroke	3.28 x 3.50
Displacement, cu in	177.6
cc	2912
Compression ratio	9.00
Bhp @ rpm	137 @ 4750
equivalent mph	112
Torque, lb-ft	175 @ 3000
equivalent mph	71.0

PERFORMANCE

Top speed (5th), mph	112.5
best timed run	115.1
3rd (5450)	81
2nd (5500)	52
1st (5450)	36

FUEL CONSUMPTION

Normal range, mpg	17/22

ACCELERATION

0-30 mph, sec	3.3
0-40 mph	5.2
0-50 mph	7.0
0-60 mph	9.8
0-70 mph	13.2
0-80 mph	17.5
0-90 mph	23.5
0-100 mph	35.0
Standing ¼ mile	17.1
speed at end, mph	79

GEAR RATIOS

O/d (0.82), overall	3.20
4th (1.00)	3.91
3rd (1.31)	5.12
2nd (2.05)	8.02
1st (2.93)	11.5

TAPLEY DATA

5th, lb/ton @ mph	250 @ 62
4th	320 @ 58
3rd	410 @ 48
2nd	540 @ 35
Total drag at 60 mph, lb	105

CALCULATED DATA

Lb/hp (test wt)	20.6
Cu ft/ton mile	92.4
Mph/1000 rpm (5th)	23.7
Engine revs/mile	2535
Piston travel, ft/mile	1480
Rpm @ 2500 ft/min	4290
equivalent mph	101.5
R&T wear index	37.5

SPEEDOMETER ERROR

30 mph	actual 30.2
40 mph	40.0
50 mph	50.0
60 mph	60.0
70 mph	69.2
80 mph	78.5
90 mph	87.7
100 mph	96.8

AUSTIN-HEALEY 3000
ROAD & TRACK

ELAPSED TIME IN SECONDS

7

In the Alps with the M.G.-A 1600 and the Austin-Healey 3000

ON a cold and wet morning in June a party of journalists assembled at the R.A.C. in Pall Mall at the invitation of the British Motor Corporation to take part in a trip to the South of France to test the Austin-Healey 3000 which was announced in July and the M.G.-A 1600 which is announced today.

From the R.A.C. we were driven to Gatwick Airport where a chartered Transair Viscount waited to transport us in silence and comfort to Lyon where six M.G.s and six Healeys awaited our attention. There was little time to examine the cars as the 300-mile drive to Cap d'Antibes near Cannes had to be completed in time for dinner. I selected a red M.G.-A and like everyone else spent some time trying to open the boot to stow some luggage, but once the hidden catch behind the seats had been located the boot opened easily enough. A route had been selected by B.M.C. avoiding the N.7 and going via Grenoble, Gap, Digne, and Grasse along the N.85 known as the *Route des Alpes* but as much of this would have to be covered in darkness I decided to head the M.G. along the almost deserted N.7 in company with Gregor Grant of *Autosport* who had selected an Austin-Healey.

At the first of several stops for liquid refreshment we examined the specifications of the new cars and found that the major changes occurred in the engine and braking departments. On the M.G.-A 1600 the "B" Series engine has been bored out to a capacity of 1,588 c.c. (the same as the Twin-cam) and with an 8.3 : 1 compression ratio now gives 79.5 b.h.p. at 5,600 r.p.m. as compared with the 72 b.h.p. of the previous model. Following the general trend the M.G. 1600 is fitted with disc brakes on the front wheels combined with drums at the rear. Lockheed discs have been chosen for the M.G. while improved linings are used at the rear. Externally the only differences are the use of sliding sidescreens as standard equipment and a slight re-styling of the rear lights to accommodate separate flasher lamps.

Turning to the Healey we found that the "C" type engine has been enlarged to 2,912 c.c. and now develops 130 b.h.p. (gross), 124 b.h.p. net at 4,600 r.p.m., on a compression ratio of 9.03:1. This increase in capacity has been obtained by the use of a new cylinder block casting with a bore of 83.36 mm. and a stroke of 89 mm. The torque has gone up to 175 lb./ft. at 3,000 r.p.m. from its previous 149 lb./ft. and a strengthened gear cluster has been designed to cope with the increased power. The 3000 is the first model to be equipped with Girling disc brakes on the front wheels as standard equipment. The rear drums brakes have dimensions of 11 in. x 2¼-in.

This then is the sum total of noticeable changes to these two cars. The pleasing note for potential M.G.-A buyers is that prices remain the same—£940 7s. 6d. for the open model and £1,026 15s. 10d. for the coupé. The Healey 3000 is only a matter of £10 dearer than the 100-Six at £1168 9s. 2d. for the two-seater and £1,175 10s. 10d. for the occasional four-seater.

Having discovered these differences we headed the cars out on to the N.7 once more. All the cars were French-registered left-hand drive models destined for the Paris distributor and were brand new, some of them not having been fully run-in owing to the short notice given for the trip. Nevertheless the M.G.-A 1600 had a smooth flow of power and lost surprisingly little ground to the Healey on acceleration. The orange band on the rev.-counter runs from 5,500 to 6,000 r.p.m. and the red band from 6,000 to 7,000 r.p.m. In the lower gears the needle could be pushed well into the orange section without trouble but in top gear the engine could not be made to exceed 5,000 r.p.m., but since this showed exactly 160 k.p.h. (99 m.p.h.) on the speedometer no great trouble was found in keeping the Healey in sight. The steering of the M.G. is commendably light whilst gear changes can be made almost as quickly as the hand can move, although the synchromesh can be beaten if very fast changes are made.

The run to Cannes was uneventful, stops being made in Montelimar for the inevitable *Nougat* and at Avignon for petrol. The route from Aix-en-Provence to Cannes runs over some bumpy roads with enough mountain corners to test the suspension and roadholding of any car.

The M.G. survived the test with flying colours. If a corner was taken too ambitiously the rear end would slide out most controllably and could always be corrected with ease while the disc brakes could be relied on in an emergency and no trace of fade was noticed at any time. The pedal pressure required was higher than that needed for drum brakes but this was amply compensated for by the complete lack of fade which would have certainly been apparent with drums all round.

Next day a gastronomic expedition was planned to Vence which included some more mountain driving and for this trip I selected an occasional four-seater Healey fitted with overdrive. The transition from the fleet M.G. to the rather ponderous Healey is rather startling at first as all controls are much heavier than those fitted to the M.G. Owing apparently to carburation difficulties the car proved rather difficult to start at times, the engine having to be "caught" with the throttle. The throttle pedal itself was not above criticism as on all cars at least two inches of lost motion was apparent before the revs. began to rise. It was also placed higher than the brake pedal making heel-and-toe gear changes out of the question, but this fault should be merely a matter of adjustment. The gear-lever is bent sharply backwards about 2 inches from its base in order to bring the knob near the driver's hand and combined with a gearbox which was still rather stiff gear changing was nothing like as easy as on the M.G. This spoilt the otherwise excellent characteristics of the car because on mountain roads one had to be sure that the car was in gear before taking a bend at any speed and very often the gearbox would find neutral instead of the required gear. I arrived at a compromise by using third and overdrive third for much of the journey. Overdrive third was useful for the few straights encountered and by flicking the dashboard-mounted switch third gear was easily obtained. On corners up to around 50 m.p.h. the Healey could be slid quite comfortably and appeared to be very stable. The 3-litre engine of the Healey is of course given a much easier time than that of the M.G., and this aspect undoubtedly appeals to a great number of sports car buyers. In overdrive top at 4,000 r.p.m. the theoretical speed is 92.4 m.p.h., going up to 115.5 m.p.h. at 5,000 r.p.m. Owing to the stiffness of the gearbox we felt it unfair to take performance figures but the manufacturers claim that the car will reach 60 m.p.h. from a standstill in under 11 seconds and 100 m.p.h. in 31 seconds.

In the two days which followed we were able to thrash the cars about in the mountains or on shopping expeditions at will and most of the cars stood up to the test very well. Pottering through towns one's leg becomes rather weary if the brakes have to be used much because of the traditional reluctance of disc brakes to operate at low speeds.

Just as several journalists were becoming proficient at water-skiing the time came for us to return to England and leave the sunshine of the Riviera. The cars were driven to Nice Airport for the last time and we embarked on an Air France flight for London having a healthy respect for the latest versions of the M.G. and Austin-Healey. Full marks to the manufacturers for organising this rigorous test.—M. L. T.

The latest Austin-Healey can be recognized by the type number on the radiator grille and a glimpse of the disc brakes through the wheel spokes

IN general appearance the larger Austin-Healey has changed but little, since its successful Earls Court debut in 1952. Most of the changes made have been mechanical, and particularly in respect of the power unit. Three years ago the original 2.6-litre four-cylinder engine was replaced by a six-cylinder, and this has now been developed to its present size of 2.9 litres. Girling brakes again deal successfully with the higher speed capabilities of the latest model, and now 11in diameter discs at the front enable faster average speeds to be maintained without the bogey of brake fade to worry the driver.

These cars always have had a capacity for covering long distances in an effortlesss manner. Improved acceleration, particularly above 70 m.p.h., and appreciable increases in maximum speeds have resulted from the use of the larger engine. Compared with the last Road Test of a six-cylinder Austin-Healey which was fitted with a 4.1 to 1 axle ratio—than of the 3000 is 3.9 to 1—there is a cut of 4.9sec in the time from 0 to 100 m.p.h. Acceleration in the gears pays more generous dividends from the 50-70 m.p.h. range and upwards; over that range, in overdrive third, top and overdrive top, there are reductions of 0.7, 0.6 and 1.3sec on the last model's times. As the engine speed rises the times are cut further, and in the same gears between 70-90 m.p.h. the times come down by 1.1, 1.0 and 3.2sec. In the 80-100 m.p.h. range in top gear and overdrive top improvements of 4.1 and 3.4sec are recorded.

A noteworthy achievement is the gain in maximum speeds. In overdrive top there is an increase of 5 m.p.h. to 116 m.p.h., while in normal top the speed has gone up from 100 m.p.h., recorded by the 100-Six in May 1958, to no less than 110 m.p.h. for the new 3000 model. These figures are a good indication that the 2.9-litre engine is well able to deal with the extra weight and higher final drive gearing of the latest Austin-Healey.

None of the low-speed characteristics of the engine has been lost, and it pulls well on a light throttle; in town traffic the car can be driven quite comfortably in overdrive third and top gears, when low engine speeds are accompanied by an unobtrusive exhaust note. Most starts from rest can be made in second gear, even when fully loaded, and first is required only on gradients to get the car rolling.

Well-mannered as the car is when hemmed in by brick and concrete canyons, it makes a driver impatient to be outside city limits where the full performance can be savoured. Cruising speeds are entirely dependent upon road conditions, and on a Continental motorway 100 m.p.h. can be main-

tained without any mechanical distress. If time is a factor on a cross-country route, the engine responds willingly to every demand from the driver and it can be taken up to the normal limit mark for engine speed of 5,200 r.p.m. time after time without protest. Above 3,000 r.p.m. there is a fair amount of intake roar and fan noise.

The new engine has a compression ratio of 9.03 to 1, compared with the previous 8.25 to 1, and it does not take kindly to the premium grade petrol available on the Continent. Pinking when pulling at low engine speed, and excessive running on when the engine was switched off were evident during the testing abroad. The engine operated satisfactorily on British premium fuel, although care was needed to avoid pinking when pulling hard in top gear; many owners will prefer to use super premium grade. The fuel tank holds only 12 gallons and so refuelling stops are fairly frequent.

One of the optional extras fitted to the test car was a Laycock-de Normanville overdrive operating on third and top gears. This works with the efficiency and silence one has come to expect of the unit, and it is a valuable adjunct to the normal transmission. Its use keeps engine speed down, not only assisting economical fuel consumption but minimizing use of a revolution range where the exhaust note may become tiring to the occupants of the car. A control switch is placed on the right of the facia where it is quickly reached. Changes into and out of overdrive are snatch-free and immediate, and

Accessibility of all units likely to require routine attention is good. A single reservoir feeds fluid to the brake and clutch operating cylinders. A gauze air filter is fitted to each carburettor

9

Both sidescreens are secured to the doors by strong wing nuts: the screens are a good fit, and the windscreen pillars cause a minimum of obstruction

Austin-Healey 3000...

the whole of the transmission unit stands up well to full throttle test requirements. A larger clutch has been fitted to deal with the extra power of the 2.9-litre engine, and the gear teeth have been strengthened.

Clutch operation is light and there is a smooth take-up, with no slip evident during standing start acceleration tests. There is no doubt that the times taken for these tests, up to 70 m.p.h. at least, could have been improved upon if the gear change had not been so stiff, and if the rear wheels had maintained contact with the ground on initial take-off. As soon as the clutch was fully home and power applied, each time a test start was made, it was difficult to avoid axle hop.

The new gear ratios are well suited to the performance of the engine and car. Third and top, with their overdrive ratios, are pleasantly close, but not too much so, and acceleration in second and third is of the "kick-in-the-back" variety, care being necessary on wet roads to avoid wheel spin with full throttle.

Little difference has been made to the steering or suspension of the car by the extra weight compared with that of the previous model. The greater percentage is still on the rear axle and the car handles well. On wet roads, with the Dunlop Road Speed tyres inflated to 20 lb front and 23 lb rear, the back of the car is apt to swing when cornering. Steering characteristics in all normal circumstances are neutral; self-centring action is adequate without being forceful. In general the car is directionally stable providing a guiding hand rather than a firm grip is kept on the steering wheel; there is no sign of instability at maximum speed. On bad road surfaces there was some kick-back reaction at the steering wheel.

Tyre pressures are quite critical and the car handles best, two-up, with 23 lb sq in front and 26 lb rear—an increase of 3 lb on the makers' recommendation. For the high speed runs on an *autoroute* these pressures were increased by a further 6 lb front and rear.

The suspension is well damped, and firm enough to ensure that the car does not roll when cornering fast. Continental pavé can be uncomfortable if the tyre pressures are set only a few pounds above the lowest recommended. Ground clearance is limited, and "colonial" sections of road must be tackled with caution.

It was said of the drum brakes fitted to the last Austin-Healey tested that they proved entirely suitable. This may be repeated for the front disc, rear drum equipment of the 3000 model. The total test mileage amounted to over 1,500 miles, and at all times the brakes were excellent. On several

occasions when they were applied very hard at speeds in excess of 100 m.p.h. they retarded the car safely and surely.

For maximum results pedal pressures are rather high; normal check braking, however, is well within the capability of a woman driver. Servo assistance is not fitted, and providing the pedal pressures do not increase with use and wear it would not be necessary. The hand brake is efficient and the lever, between the driving seat and propeller shaft tunnel on right-hand drive cars, is easy to operate.

A number of points criticized on earlier models remain unchanged and, therefore, appear perhaps even more prominent and undesirable in a car which is basically very good. Driver comfort, for example, is marred by lack of room around the pedals; it is difficult to clear the throttle pedal when braking. The seat adjustment, pedal travel and steering wheel position suit a long-legged driver but not one of smaller stature who, in order to reach the pedals, must sit much too close to the wheel. The seat back rests, which tip forward to give access to the rear cockpit, are well raked and comfortable, but are not laterally stable. The seat cushions become "thin" after more than a 100-mile drive, and a tall driver lacks support under the thighs.

Most of the test driving was done with the hard top in position, and the performance figures were taken with the car so equipped. It is certainly a very desirable, if somewhat expensive piece of equipment; in some ways it improves the appearance of a car which is good-looking without it; it provides a warm, snug interior at night, and proved to be watertight. It is light in weight and is easily fitted to or removed from the car; there are four securing points.

The conventional folding hood, which is standard equipment, provides almost equally good protection, at the cost of more wind noise when driving fast. In order to make it neat and well fitting, no more material has been used than was necessary, and erection during a sudden rainstorm proved to be neither quick nor simple to an admittedly inexperienced crew. The same sliding Perspex side screens are used in conjunction with either hard top or hood; they are strong and well made, and fit well in the door apertures. There is no means of locking the car, and if it is left unattended for any length of time, valuables must be removed or locked in the boot.

Visibility in all directions from the driving compartment is good, the screen pillars are commendably thin, the top of each wing can be seen, and head room with hard top or hood erected is not stinted for driver or passenger. It is not really practicable for an adult to sit in the rear cockpit of the closed car, as even a child is not comfortable in this position, with its restrictions on height and leg room.

In comparison with photographs of the Austin-Healey 100 road tested by *The Autocar* in September 1953, there is very little difference to be seen in the layouts of the original production car and the latest version—another indication that the general design was satisfactory from the start. Leathercloth covers the facia, and the instruments are grouped in pairs on each side of the steering column. At night the panel lighting is sufficiently bright without causing dazzle, although there is no rheostat control. Recessed in the lower centre of the panel are the heater and demister controls.

In rain the screen of the closed car fogs up quickly, but the blower fan deals effectively with this without a great deal of noise. Self-parking screen wipers work well, and are helped by a simple form of screen washer. The water container for this is located in a hole in the shelf below the facia, where it not only occupies valuable space but is awkward to replace after filling. There is a strong grab handle in front of the passenger seat, and an ashtray sunk into the top of the propeller shaft tunnel has a sensible lid to prevent ash being blown about the car. Tucked away underneath the left side of the facia is the choke control. The bonnet release is even more elusive, to the right of the steering column behind the panel.

Powerful head lamps are essential for a fast car, and the 3000 is well equipped. There is a foot-operated dip switch which is easy to reach. Flashing direction indicators are combined with the parking and brake lights so that they are white and red, a system which does not find favour in many

European countries where amber coloured flashers are preferred.

Luggage accommodation is very limited, as the spare wheel and the battery take up a large proportion of the space in the locker. Normally, with the car used as a two-seater the space behind the front seats can be used for stowage. When the optional extra rear seats are not fitted two 6-volt batteries are placed forward of the rear axle beneath the floor and the spare wheel fits into a recess, leaving more room for luggage. A battery master switch is a useful item of standard equipment; it is in the right-hand corner of the luggage locker and provides a measure of security when the car is left unattended.

Roadside wheel changing involves the use of an old-fashioned screw-type jack, whose tedious operation would be annoying on a wet dark night. Every 1,000 miles 14 chassis points require grease gun lubrication, in addition to the checking of various oil levels.

The latest Austin-Healey maintains the reputation of a good quality, fast sports-touring car which its predecessors established; its original styling has not dated and the new performance will make it even more competitive.

AUSTIN-HEALEY 3000

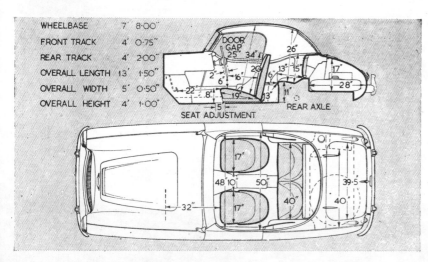

WHEELBASE	7' 8·00"
FRONT TRACK	4' 0·75"
REAR TRACK	4' 2·00"
OVERALL LENGTH	13' 1·50"
OVERALL WIDTH	5' 0·50"
OVERALL HEIGHT	4' 1·00"

Scale ¼in to 1ft. Driving seat in central position. Cushions uncompressed.

PERFORMANCE

ACCELERATION (mean):
Speed Range, Gear Ratios and Time in sec.

M.p.h.	3.21 to 1*	3.91 to 1	4.2 to 1*	5.12 to 1	8.03 to 1	11.45 to 1
10—30	—	—	—	5.4	3.6	2.8
20—40	9.0	6.8	6.5	5.1	3.5	—
30—50	9.0	6.8	6.5	5.2	—	—
40—60	9.0	7.1	6.6	5.6	—	—
50—70	9.5	7.3	7.0	6.1	—	—
60—80	10.3	8.4	8.2	—	—	—
70—90	13.0	10.4	9.9	—	—	—
80—100	16.7	13.9	—	—	—	—

*Overdrive.

From rest through gears to:

30 m.p.h.	..	..	3.5 sec.
40		..	5.6
50		..	8.0
60		..	11.4
70		..	14.3
80		..	18.9
90		..	24.8
100		..	32.8

Standing quarter mile, 17.9 sec.

MAXIMUM SPEEDS ON GEARS:

Gear			m.p.h.	k.p.h.
O.D.	(mean)		114.0	183.3
	(best)		116.0	186.5
Top	(mean)		108.0	173.6
	(best)		110.0	177.0
O/D 3rd	..	..	98.0	157.7
3rd	..	..	78.0	125.5
2nd	..	..	49.0	78.8
1st	..	..	34.0	54.7

TRACTIVE EFFORT (by Tapley meter):

			Pull (lb per ton)	Equivalent Gradient
O.D.	..	..	240	1 in 9.3
Top	..	..	316	1 in 7.0
O/D 3rd	..	..	325	1 in 6.8
3rd	..	..	424	1 in 5.2
2nd	..	..	625	1 in 3.6

BRAKES (at 30 m.p.h. in neutral):

Pedal load in lb	Retardation	Equivalent stopping distance in ft
25	0.22g	135
50	0.38g	79
75	0.60g	50
100	0.76g	39
120	0.90g	33.6

FUEL CONSUMPTION (at constant speeds):

Speed	Direct Top	O.D. Top.
30 m.p.h.	30.5 m.p.g.	35.4 m.p.g
40	27.5 ,,	33.0 ,,
50	23.2 ,,	29.8 ,,
60	21.0 ,,	25.0 ,,
70	19.6 ,,	22.4 ,,
80	18.3 ,,	20.5 ,,
90	16.6 ,,	18.6 ,,
100	—	16.4 ,,

Overall fuel consumption for 1,200 miles, 20.0 m.p.g. (14.12 litres per 100 km).
Approximate normal range 17—25 m.p.g. (16.6—11.3 litres per 100 km.)
Fuel: Premium grade.

TEST CONDITIONS: Weather: dry, cloudy. 10-20 m.p.h. wind. Air temperature, 65-70 deg. F.

STEERING: Turning circle:
Between kerbs, 33ft 11in R.H.; 36ft 11in L.H.
Between walls: 35ft 2in R.H.; 38ft L.H.
Turns of steering wheel from lock to lock, 3¼.

DATA

PRICE (basic), with four-seater body, £829.
British purchase tax, £346 10s 10d.
Total (in Great Britain), £1,175 10s 10d.
Extras (with tax): Radio £34, Heater £21 19s 2d, Overdrive £66 8s 2d, Wire wheels £35 8s 4d, Hard top £85.

ENGINE: Capacity: 2,912 c.c. (177.7 cu. in).
Number of cylinders: 6 in line.
Bore and stroke: 83.36 × 88.9 mm (3.3 × 3.5in).
Valve gear: overhead, pushrods and rockers.
Compression ratio: 9.03 to 1.
B.H.P. nett 124 at 4,600 r.p.m. (B.H.P. per ton laden 97.4).
Torque: 175 lb ft at 3,000 r.p.m.
M.P.H. per 1,000 r.p.m. in top gear, 18.94.
M.P.H. per 1,000 r.p.m. in O D top, 23.1.

WEIGHT: (with 5 gals fuel), 22.5 cwt (2,513 lb).
Weight distribution (per cent): F, 47.3; R, 52.7.
Laden as tested: 25.5 cwt (2,849 lb).
Lb per c.c. (laden): 0.97.

BRAKES: Type: Girling, disc front, drum rear.
Method of operation: hydraulic.
Drum dimensions: R, 11in diameter; 2.25in wide.
Disc diameter: F, 11.25in;
Swept area: F, 228 sq in; R, 155.5 sq in (301.5 sq in per ton laden).

TYRES: 5.90×15in Dunlop Road Speed.
Pressures (lb sq in): F, 20; R,23 (normal); F, 20; R, 26 (with full load).

TANK CAPACITY: 12 Imperial gallons.
Oil sump, 12 pints.
Cooling system, 20 pints.

DIMENSIONS: Wheelbase: 7ft 8in.
Track: F, 4ft 0.75in; R, 4ft 2in.
Length (overall): 13ft 1.5in.
Width: 5ft 0.5in.
Height: 4ft 2in with hood up.
Ground clearance: 4.5in.
Frontal area: 16.7 sq ft (approximately).

ELECTRICAL SYSTEM: 12-volt; 5*l* ampère-hour battery.
Head lights: Double dip; 50-40 watt bulbs.

SUSPENSION: Front, independent coil springs, wishbones and stabilizing bar. Rear, half-elliptic leaf springs and Panhard rod.

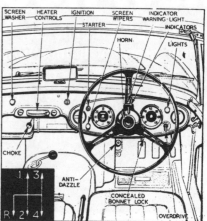

Bigger engine, higher compression, disc brakes

NEW AUSTIN HEALEY 3000

MORE POWER. The big Austin Healey keeps its dynamic lines, but there's a new growl of higher power from under the bonnet. The 6-cylinder engine is now bigger at 2912 cc. Compression is up to 9.03:1. With 130 brake-horsepower, top speed is well over 110 mph. DISC BRAKES on the front wheels are now regular equipment. OPTIONS: overdrive, heater, radio, hardtop, wirewheels. TRIM: 2-seater or occasional 4-seater. PRICE: from £824 plus £344.9.2 purchase tax.

THE AUSTIN MOTOR COMPANY LIMITED, LONGBRIDGE, BIRMINGHAM   **AUSTIN LOOKS YEARS AHEAD**

Bigger Brother for Austin-Healey

*New 130-hp model boasts 3-liter engine,
front disc brakes, optional hard top*

*Hard top gives new 3-liter Healey a brutish
look, but it still keeps refined profile.
Entry, however, requires some squirming.
All changes to engine are internal—bore
has been increased to 3.28 in. Girling
11¼-in. discs at front brake extra speed.*

by Len Griffing

SINCE ITS INCEPTION the Austin-Healey—
first the 100-4, later the 100-6—has held
a comfortable niche between the bigger
Jaguar and the smaller MG. Its popularity is
easy to understand. Its body lines are handsome, and the engine—even in absolutely
factory tune—develops enough suds to get off
briskly from a stoplight with stockers from
Detroit. Handling, though not flashing in
true stock condition, is fair, and very responsive to minor modification. All the elements
are there, including a Panhard rod at the
rear and a stabilizer bar at the front.

But, of course, times change. The Plymouth Fury and the Pontiac Bonneville not
only dragged away from stock 100-6'ers, but
did it ignominiously. It was no contest. Something had to be done.

Fast the in-line six might not have been,
but durable and sturdy it most assuredly was.
The hundred-plus-a-few horses extracted from
its 2639cc did not represent fabulous output,
so why not take out a few more? But how to
go about it?

To begin, the stroke/bore ratio was 1.12:1
(3.50 in. x 3.125 in.). There seemed to be
only one way to go. Besides, the modern trend
is toward shorter strokes—shorter, that is, in
relation to the bore. The cylinder was opened
up to 3.282 in., giving a new stroke/bore
ratio of 1.064:1.

The result is a new displacement of 2912cc
(171.7 cu. in.), and a new power rating of
130 hp, peaking at 4750 rpm. Compression
ratio is now 9.03 to 1.

To accommodate the new power, higher
rear end gears are fitted, which give higher
mph at equal rpm. Without the Laycock de
Normanville overdrive unit, standard gearing
is 3.55, producing 20.9 mph/1000 in top
gear. If ordered with overdrive, a lower 3.91
gearing is standard. Coupled with the .822:1
speed step-up, overdrive top produces 23.1
mph/1000 rpm. This is a net reduction of
10.6 per cent over the smaller-engined car.
Transmission ratios also have been altered
in the new model.

Because of the added displacement, the
torque factor is substantial. It's no problem
to pull a hill at 1000 rpm in fourth over-

ACCELERATION

0-45	7.0 secs.
0-60	12.6
¼-mile	18.8 & 75 mph

PASSING SPEEDS

30-50	6.4
45-60	5.5
50-80	13.4

drive. And the engine really doesn't appear to
be working, even though we certainly don't
recommend this kind of lugging.

As a companion to the bigger engine, a
10-inch clutch replaces the nine-inch disc,
and 11¼-inch disc brakes are fitted to the
front wheels (which do most of the stopping), while 11-inch x 2½-inch drums are
retained at the rear. As to stopping power,
well, you just can't fade a disc brake. Fade is
caused by friction heat expanding the friction-
producing components away from each other.
A disc brake expands the friction pads into
the disc; the hotter they get the better they
work.

In the appearance department, a new glass-
reinforced resin roof is available. This roof
is identical to the roofs installed on the cars
at Sebring (a touring car must have a roof),
except that the finish and the appointments
are lush. It stands as an example of what
can be done if someone puts his mind to
making a luxury accessory for a luxury car.
Roof interior is finished in a leather-like
perforated material, padded at the front end
for safety and appointment value. It looks
good, though on the pilot models fit was a bit
vague around the edges.

Test car was equipped with Dunlop R-4
tires, an excellent choice. Weight, with full
tank of gasoline, was 2580 lbs. Suspension
seemed a bit soft, but it was a road machine.
Besides, anybody knows how little you have
to do to make a street Austin-Healey handle
like a race car.

► "I don't know how the man does it. Every time he makes a change it's a winner and this one is the best of the lot."

This was an executive of a huge imported car firm talking. The reference was to Donald Healey and his Austin-Healeys. The allusion to winning was not made to races but to public acceptance of the product although in truth he could have said the same thing in that context.

When it comes to designing a car that will have people standing in line to buy, Mr. Healey ranks with the great men of the day — the likes of the Porsches, father and son — and very few others.

The reasons for this, at least as far as the American market is concerned, are far from complex. Each version from the BN-1 to the newest BN-7, subject of this test, has been a *sports* car in every sense of the word. Second, they have from the beginning been priced within reason; in fact it's hard to see how one can buy more car for the money. Finally, Healey has used his knowledge of the American likes and dislikes to full advantage. We Americans, he knows, are used to sheer, solid torque and a wide power range in our cars, giving gobs of acceleration off the mark or away from a stoplight. Every Austin-Healey built has, for its displacement, been a draggin' fool, especially the later six-cylinder versions. The final American preference is for a car that will cruise effortlessly at fairly high and steady average speeds over superhighways and freeways. Healey offers an overdrive to provide this aspect and the proof of the thinking is shown by the fact that by far the largest slice of the A-H pie sold in the U.S. is overdrive equipped.

The latest Austin Healey embodies all of these factors and carries them to a new high. There are 26 more pounds/feet of torque and 15 more horses, the figures being 149 lbs/ft at 3000 rpm and 130 bhp at 4750 rpm respectively. This has been accomplished by the simple expedient of increasing the bore to 3.282 inches which brings the displacement out to 171 cubic inches or 2912 cc and as an added bonus also ups the compression ratio to 9.03 to 1 since the same head is used. The stroke remains the same at 3.5 inches

This is the major change and it can be felt in the seat of the pants by those familiar with earlier models. The main effect is that low rpm performance is increased tremendously. The new A-H 3000 can be lugged from a standstill in second gear with no effort and will muddle through five mile-an-hour traffic all day in that gear without protest. Ten miles an hour is no particular strain in third and fourth gear can be used for anything from a shade under 20 mph to top speed. Another effect is that rapid acceleration is done in that tremendous rush-without-clamor that marks the American V8, the only noises being a low booming exhaust note and an unobjectionable buzz from the gearbox in the two lower gears. Torque is such that on a really rapid take-off there is a chirp from the rear tires every time a gear is changed except into fourth.

For a sports car, the revs are not high. This is not a "winding" type of engine, being red-lined at 5200 rpm, but it doesn't

ROAD TEST AUSTIN HEALEY 3000

U.S. Importer . . . . Hambro Automotive Corp.
27 W. 57th St., New York 22, N. Y.

PERFORMANCE

ACCELERATION:

From zero to	seconds
30 mph	3.4
40 mph	5.3
50 mph	7.3
60 mph	10.9
70 mph	14.2
80 mph	19.2
Standing ¼ mile	17.8
Speed at end of quarter	78 mph

SPEED RANGES IN GEARS: (5300 rpm max)

I	7-38
II	10-54
III	16-85
IV	21-top

SPEEDOMETER CORRECTION:

Indicated Speed	Timed Speed
30	28
40	39
50	49
60	60
70	70
80	80

SPECIFICATIONS

POWER UNIT:

BN7 engine . . . . Water-cooled, in-line Six
Valve Operation . . . . Pushrod ohv
Bore & Stroke . . 3.282x3.50 in (83.36x89 mm)
Stroke/Bore Ratio 1.07/1
Displacement . . . . 171.7 cu in (2912 cc)
Compression Ratio 9.03/1
Carburetion by . . . . Two SU H.D. 6
Max. Power . . . . . . 130 gross bhp @ 4750 rpm
(124 net @ 4600)
Max. Torque . . . . 175 lbs-ft @ 3000 rpm

DRIVE TRAIN:

Transmission ratios		overall ratio
I	2.93	(10.38)
II	2.05	(7.27)
III	1.31	(4.64)
IV	1.00	(3.54)
Final drive ratio	3.54	(3.91)

with 0.822 O.D.
Axle torque taken by leaf springs

RATING FACTORS:

Specific Power Output (net) . . . 0.72 bhp/cu in
Power to Weight Ratio (as tested) 22.1 lbs/hp
Piston speed @ 60 mph . . . . 1675 ft/min
Speed @ 1000 rpm in top gear . . . . . . 20.9 mph

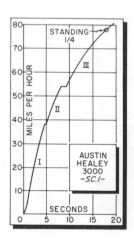

AUSTIN HEALEY 3000 -S.C.I-

Above: Top is erected by first plugging bows into place then fastening fabric to windshield.
Below: Sticker on speedo indicates overdrive model.

Above: Engine looks exactly like previous six-cylinder but has more punch.

Left: The three liter stays flat in the corners, really storms out.

need to wind. It builds car speed through sheer *push*. This steam-engine-like torque is coupled to high enough gear ratios so that the Healey 3000 engine is loafing where others are buzzing their hearts out. An engine that doesn't need to be twisted to high rotational speeds doesn't tend to wear which may give a clue as to why there are so many early BN-1 and BN-4 units in everday use. It also shows why the Healey is one of those cars that can be race-prepared at home, driven to the track, raced and then, barring accidents, driven home again. Under normal use the damn' things just don't wear out. The bodies may rattle after a few years and a few haybales and the plastic trim may peel off in time but they keep running like the tractors their engine characteristics resemble.

To take advantage of the added power here are a host of other minor changes, some apparent and some not so noticeable. The first and most noticeable change is a switch to Girling disc (segment type) brakes on the front wheels. The back wheels retain the 11 by 2¼ inch drums. Stopping power is, though quite smooth, of the *right now* variety. Not nearly as much pedal pressure is required as with the racing-option full disc set-up nor, for that matter, as with the earlier drums. No matter how we pounded it we could not induce fade or more than a tiny fraction of pedal loss. This tiny loss could probably be traceable to lining wear in the rear drum brakes which were kept working overtime to keep up with the discs. Stops were almost as powerful as with the full Dunlop racing disc layout on the Sebring Healey.

Another change, which will probably be noticed only by those familiar with the BN-cars, is found in the gearbox. Low gear has been raised to 2.93 to 1 as opposed to 3.076 in the earlier box. Second has been dropped in ratio to 2.053 as opposed to 2.913 and third has been raised to 1.309, replacing the former 1.333. The effect is a

bit disconcerting at first to a BN-6 driver due to the close spacing of first and second gears and the wide jump into third. We fail to see the reason for increasing this spread unless it is to produce that second gear lugging ability mentioned earlier. It's nice to have but it was also nice to be able to wind it up in second in the older versions. It's sort of a personal choice and not an easy one.

The overdrive unit, too, has been changed. It's less radical now with a 0.822 step-up instead of the 0.778 ratio used formerly. This has the favorable result that the engine can now peak in OD, formerly virtually impossible. Also the step up or down is not nearly as violent as in former models. The rear end ratio in non-OD cars is 3.545 instead of the 3.91 to 1 gears used before. The latter ratio is used in the AH 3000 when equipped with overdrive, replacing the 4.1 to 1 unit used earlier.

Another apparent change doesn't show up in the specification but can be felt. Exactly *what* was done is hard to place but the handling of the car is even better than before. Healeys are noted for their handling qualities — it takes a pretty major goof to make one come loose — but the new one has much of the feel of the competition prepared version but without the rock-hard feel of the race car. It shares with the competition car the feeling that you couldn't turn it over with a derrick. Spin it out, yes, Turn it over, no.

It is hard to truly judge the handling characteristics of the new Healey but from a few hurried laps around the course at Lime Rock Park with ordinary tires, it would seem to be a mildly final oversteering car. For a while, of course, one must turn *in* to the corner. Then for a noticeable period, long or short depending on the radius and speed of the bend, the car can be held in its drift with the wheels pointed dead ahead, steering done by throttle. Finally and fairly gently, more and more reverse lock must be ap-

plied, particularly if the corner is fairly tight. In this respect it resembles the competition BN-6 with which this writer has had some personal experience in over-cooking on a corner — twice to be exact. In each case the end result was that the car went off to the inside with the tail leading the way. This fits the classic, if oversimplified, description of oversteer which holds that if the car goes through the fence nose first you're understeering; if it goes out tail first, you have oversteered.

The final piece of improvement may seem relatively minor to all but other Healey owners. This one involves the top. Personally and collectively the staff of SCI has cursed the top used on the BN-6 which takes two strong men and a very agile boy to put up. The bows were stiff and almost impervious to coaxing and the front bow almost impossible to fasten. Once fastened it became a matter of dislocating fingers and thumbs to fasten the back curtain down. The new top has removable bows that can be unfolded first and then stuck into a pair of sockets and a front bow that will attach to the windshield frame without hammering. The back of the top now fits and can be fastened reasonably easily. True, it's still not a one-handed operation and it still takes time but one man *can* do the job without breaking a finger in the process. For those who still don't want to struggle we can only suggest the hard-top. In fact we'll suggest it anyway since it's far and away the best looking and best engineered fiberglas top in the industry. Used in conjunction with the Healey aluminum rimmed side curtains it makes the car as weather tight as any roadster can possibly become — and some coupes too for that matter.

Summing up: The new Austin Healey 3000 is a comfortable car, a fast car and a very quick car. Above all it is an eminently safe car. Even more important it's a good *sports* car.

Just about the only thing that'll beat camshafts is cubic inches, muses GORDON WILKINS

HEALEY 3-LITRE:
FORBIDDEN FRUIT

THE Austin Healey, which began in 1952 with a 2.6 litre four-cylinder engine and became the 100-Six with a full-throated six-cylinder power unit on a longer wheelbase in 1956, now enters a third phase of its career as the Austin Healey 3000 with an enlarged engine of 2.9 litres and Girling disc brakes on the front wheels.

The power unit is developed from the well-known B.M.C. C-type and is unchanged in its main design features. By enlarging the bores from 79.4 to 83.36 m.m., swept volume has been bumped from 2,641 to 2,912 c.c. Maximum power is up to 124 b.h.p. at 4,600 r.p.m. on the testbed and maximum torque rises to 167 lb. ft. at 2,700 r.p.m.

An increase of 10 per cent in swept volume has therefore produced a rise of 9 per cent. in maximum power and a bigger increase of 11½ per cent. in torque, which promises outstanding flexibility and effortless acceleration.

The clutch is a single-plate 10 in. and the four-speed gearbox, with short lever offset to the left side, now has a stronger gear cluster to cope with the higher torque.

Normal axle ratio of 3.545 to 1

gives a road speed of 20.9 m.p.h. per 1,000 r.p.m., but as usual the Laycock de Normanville overdrive is available at extra cost. It operates at a flick of the switch on third and top gears. When overdrive is fitted, the axle ratio is changed to 3.91 to 1 and overdrive top gives an overall ratio of 3.214 to 1. This produces a road speed of 23.1 m.p.h. per 1,000 r.p.m., so that in overdrive top the engine is doing only 3,470 r.p.m. at a steady 80 m.p.h.

The Girling disc brakes now standard at the front have discs of 11¼ in. diameter. At the rear are drum brakes 11 x 2¼ in. General chassis design is unchanged. Front suspension is by coil springs with wishbones and anti-roll bar and piston-type dampers act as pivots for the upper wishbones. Rear suspension is by half-elliptic springs with a Panhard rod for transverse control, and piston-type dampers.

External appearance is practically unchanged save for a flash with the figure 3,000 on the grille. There is a choice of two-seater or occasional four-seater body with small rear seats for children.

Both are similar in outward appearance. On the two-seater the spare wheel lies flat on a shelf above the rear axle projecting into the rear of the cockpit where it is enclosed in a plastic cover and two six-volt battery units are coupled together below it, leaving the whole trunk free for luggage. On the occasional four-seater, the spare wheel lies flat on the floor of the trunk and a single 12-volt battery is placed at one side, so that space for luggage is limited. A master switch is provided in the trunk, which can be locked to prevent anyone tampering with ignition, starter, lights or radio.

I tried one of the new models over 100 miles on the French Riviera and in the Maritime Alps. Although it had done only 1,000 miles and was still not fully free, the Healey's performance was impressive. This car was fitted with overdrive and the 3.214 to 1 axle. Although bigger, the new engine can run safely to higher revs than the old one thanks to lead indium bearings. Recommended limit is 5,250 r.p.m. instead of 4,800 and at these revs maximum speeds on gears are approximately: 1st 34 m.p.h., 2nd 49 m.p.h., 3rd 76 m.p.h., overdrive 3rd 93 m.p.h. The car went soaring on past 100 m.p.h. in top but I had no opportunity to time the all-out maximum, which should be about 115-116 m.p.h.

After correcting for a speedometer optimism of 3-4 per cent., acceleration figures were: 0-30 in 3.6 sec., 0-50 in 7.8 sec., 0-60 in 11.0 sec., 0-80 in 19.5 sec.

After another couple of thousand miles the car should certainly improve on these figures.

Running with the car open, air eddies around the cockpit began to affect acceleration at higher speeds and it would presumably need a fully broken-in car with folding top and screens erected to

Engine, naturally incorporating latest six-port head, looks the same from outside. Changes are in bore (now 83.36 mm.) and bearings. Rev limit is now well over 5,000.

achieve the excellent figure of 0-100 m.p.h. in under 31 sec. claimed by the makers. There was no time to check fuel consumption, but I would expect 17-24 m.p.g. according to driving methods.

Driving with six speeds, four on the lever and two on the switch, calls for some sort of routine if you are not to get tired of juggling with the controls. My method is to accelerate using first, second and direct third, then use the switch to make one of those magnificent instantaneous full-throttle shifts into overdrive third which only the Laycock de Normanville overdrive can produce. This takes the car up to 80 or 90 and I then pull the lever back into overdrive top. Slowing down I flick the switch with the throttle open to get a smooth shift into direct top (which gives a performance range quite close to overdrive third) and I then come down

through the direct gears using the lever. When motoring in the mountains, second, third and O/D third leave you happy in most situations.

The new power unit soars sweetly up to high revs with a deep-throated snarl from the exhaust. It is very flexible, so you don't have to be forever changing gears when touring. In overdrive top, for example, it would accelerate from 40 to 60 m.p.h. in 9.4 sec. and in direct top it took 7.0 sec., but a drop down to direct third would send the car to sixty in 5.4 sec.

The brakes are excellent and seem well able to cope with the new urge. If used hard at high speeds, they seem softer on the pedal than all-disc, servo-assisted installations but they do get results and repeated stops from 80 and more produced no fade.

WILKINS TESTS THE HEALEY 3-LITRE

All the same, the performance should be used with reasonable discretion. If you slam the throttle open in the lower gears it is easy to set the tail sliding, especially on loose gravel or wet surfaces, and smart corrective action is called for. The quick steering helps — it needs only 3¼ turns from lock to lock. The ride is unusually comfortable by sports car standards, even over rough mountain tracks.

The seats, upholstered in foam rubber with hide facings, are well tailored to give comfortable support when cornering fast and the centre armrest is useful. Drivers of average height who like to drive with their arms well extended may find that the pedals, especially the clutch, are rather far away. Unfortunately it is almost impossible to use heel and toe on brake and accelerator, so that clean downshifts are not easy to achieve when braking hard for a corner which turns out to be sharper than expected.

In all, I tried three cars and on each of them there was a two-inch dead area in the accelerator pedal before anything began to happen. This made progress rather jerky in traffic and it was difficult to give the right amount of throttle opening when double declutching a quick down shift. In view of the high performance of which this Healey is now capable, this should be cured without delay. Compression ratio is up from 8.25 to 9.03 to 1 and on French premium fuel there was some running-on after switching off. Steering was light and responsive, and the central handbrake lever is very handily located but the minor controls might be better placed. You switch on the ignition with one hand then feel for the starter with the other, and the choke is cunningly concealed below the instrument panel. Finish and all-weather equipment are up to usual good Austin Healey standards.

Single or duo-tone paintwork is standard; so are vinyl cockpit cover, windshield washer and Dunlop Road Speed tyres.

On the instrument panel are speedometer with trip and total distance recorders, tachometer. fuel gauge, oil pressure gauge and thermometer, with warning lights for dynamo charge. headlamp main beam and direction indicators. Clip-on rigid-frame side screens are carried in an envelope in the trunk when not in use. Besides overdrive. optional extras include an effective heater and demister, centre lock wire wheels, detachable hard top.

Current production of six-cylinder Austin Healeys is about 175 a week. Since the first model was introduced in 1952 93 per cent. of all production has been exported and exports are at present taking 97 per cent. of output. Although not by any means a sports racing car, the Austin Healey is a fast, well equipped and moderately priced road car which handles nicely, is fun to drive, and gives a comfortable ride even over quite bad surfaces. It can also be used with success in rallies and other sporting events. The latest improvements bring considerable extra performance with braking to match. British home market price is £824 for the two-seater before tax. This is a rise of £7 on the basic price. The four-seater is priced at £829.

(B.M.C. Australia say current Tariff Board quarrels make it unlikely that sportsmen here will see the new Healey before next year. —Ed.) #

Latest Healey interior is as attractive as ever. Extra seats are optional, but without them luggage room is greater. No 3,000s will reach Australia before 1960, say B.M.C.

Performance (car run 1,000 miles only; open, with top down):—

Acceleration through gears:

0-30 m.p.h.	3.6 sec.
0-45 m.p.h.	6.5 sec.
0-50 m.p.h.	7.8 sec.
0-60 m.p.h.	11.0 sec.
0-80 m.p.h.	19.7 sec.

Acceleration in gears:

2nd gear,	
20-40 m.p.h.	3.4 sec.
3rd gear,	
20-40 m.p.h.	4.8 sec.
30-50 m.p.h.	5.3 sec.
40-60 m.p.h.	5.4 sec.
Overdrive 3rd,	
20-40 m.p.h.	6.4 sec.
30-50 m.p.h.	6.7 sec.
40-60 m.p.h.	6.9 sec.
50-70 m.p.h.	7.1 sec.
60-80 m.p.h.	8.5 sec.
Top,	
20-40 m.p.h.	6.9 sec.
30-50 m.p.h.	6.9 sec.
40-60 m.p.h.	7.0 sec.
50-70 m.p.h.	7.4 sec.
60-80 m.p.h.	9.1 sec.
Overdrive top,	
40-60 m.p.h.	9.4 sec.
50-70 m.p.h.	9.8 sec.
60-80 m.p.h.	10.7 sec.
Standing ¼ mile	17.8 sec.

#

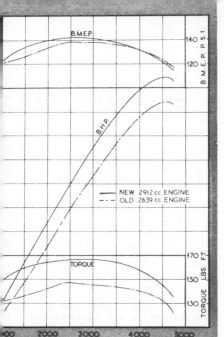

Net performance curves for the new engine compared with those for the previous one

Austin Healey 3000 with 2.9-litre Engine

cylinder unit was substituted, the car then being designated the 100-Six.

Towards the end of 1957 a new cylinder head, having separate ports and fed by a separate, light-alloy inlet manifold was introduced, and the improved gas flow increased power output from 102 b.h.p. at 4,600 r.p.m. to 117 b.h.p. at 4,750 r.p.m. The C-series B.M.C. engine has now been increased in capacity from 2,639 to 2,912 c.c. by enlarging the bores, and the net power output goes up to 124 b.h.p. at 4,600 r.p.m. This increase in engine capacity will be welcomed by competition-minded owners since the make will now be able to compete on more favourable terms in the international class D for cars having an engine swept volume up to 3,000 c.c.

A new casting has been designed for the combined cylinder block and crankcase; the cylinder bores have been increased from 79.4 to 83.36 mm, while the crankshaft stroke remains unchanged at 89 mm. To accommodate this increase in bore size the coolant passages between numbers 1 and 2, 3 and 4 and 5 and 6 cylinders are siamesed. At the same time the crankcase has been stiffened at the flywheel end by the addition of external webs. Flat-topped pistons are fitted, and the compression

ratio is raised from 8.5 to 1 to 9.0 to 1.

In addition to these changes, the C-series engines have been improved in detail since our last description, published on 29 November, 1957. Among modifications which have occurred at intervals since that date have been alterations to the crankshaft damper, elimination of a reduced diameter section of the inlet valve stems, and the use of a gear-type oil pump in place of the previous rotor-type.

Main differences between the engine as used in the Austin Healey 3000 and those for other six-cylinder B.M.C. models are the six-port cylinder head, used in conjunction with separate inlet manifold, and semi-downdraught HD6 S.U. carburettors.

A thermostatically controlled auxiliary carburettor for cold starting is fitted; polythene hose is used for sections of the fuel pipe line, and an S.U. electric pump feeds the carburettors from a 12-gallon tank.

To cope with the extra torque from the new engine, stronger transmission gears are fitted, as well as a new 10in diameter single-plate Borg and Beck clutch which has a friction area of 78 sq in, compared with 66 sq in of the previous 9in-diameter unit.

D ESIGNED by Donald Healey, the larger Austin Healey sports car has enjoyed continuous success since its introduction in 1952. First models were fitted with a four-cylinder, 2.6-litre Austin engine; four years later, the B.M.C. C-series six-

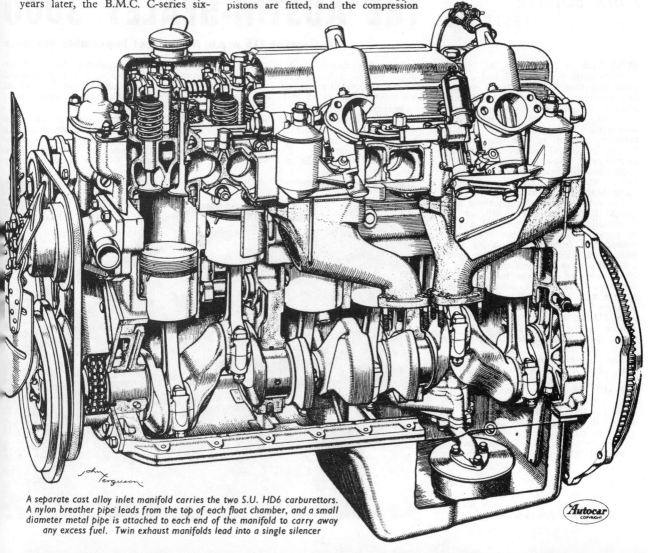

A separate cast alloy inlet manifold carries the two S.U. HD6 carburettors. A nylon breather pipe leads from the top of each float chamber, and a small diameter metal pipe is attached to each end of the manifold to carry away any excess fuel. Twin exhaust manifolds lead into a single silencer

A TYPICAL British sports .car, the Austin-Healey 3000 retains its position as one of the most attractive-looking machines in its class.

fitted to the test car, and this has a rather smaller step-up ratio than before. A short open Hardy Spicer propeller shaft conveys the drive to the hypoid axle.

The body is a very handsome open two-seater of the individual shape which we have come to associate with the larger Austin-Healey. The body fitted to the test car had the optional two children's seats which actually render it an occasional four-seater in effect. This model has a fair-sized luggage boot, but it is largely occupied with the spare wheel, tools and battery. A very neat hard top with excellent lines was fitted to the test car, and the sidescreens had sliding panels for signalling and ventilation.

The driving position is comfortable, though the adjustable steering wheel is rather close to the driver even in its most forward position. The seats give good support to the back, and if the cushions are not particularly soft, this is an advantage for a fast sports car. It is necessary to criticize the pedals rather strongly, for the clutch and brake are

JOHN BOLSTER TESTS THE

THE AUSTIN-HEALEY 3000

A Genuine 115 m.p.h. Machine of Impeccable Manners

Way back in 1952, when AUTOSPORT was quite a pup and I had a little more hair than I have now, I was the first journalist ever to drive an Austin-Healey. Belgium was the country where my secret tests were conducted, and subsequently, in 1956, I tried the six-cylinder version of the car around Europe in general and the Nürburgring in particular. Now, a bigger six-cylinder engine and disc brakes have come along, and so once again I have been enjoying some Austin-Healey motoring.

The new 3000 can be described as a typical British sports car with an exceptionally large and powerful engine. A conventional box-section frame has independent front suspension by wishbones and helical springs. There is an anti-roll torsion bar, and the steering is by a cam and peg type box. Behind, the hypoid rear axle is on semi-elliptic springs with a Panhard rod for lateral location. The Girling hydraulic brakes have 11¼ ins. discs in front aad 11 ins. drums at the rear. The 5.90-15 ins. Road Speed tyres may be on disc or wire wheels to choice.

The big six-cylinder engine has a cast iron block and head, the latter having six inlet ports. Carburation is by twin SU HD6 instruments, and there is a dual exhaust system. The crankshaft runs on four main bearings and the chain driven camshaft operates the valves by pushrods and rockers. The exhaust valves are in KE965 steel, and the solid-skirt aluminium pistons are tin

plated. The capacity of this nearly square unit is 3 litres, and it develops 130 b.h.p. at 4,750 r.p.m. on a compression ratio of just over 9 to 1.

Compared with previous Austin-Healeys, a larger clutch has had to be fitted to take the formidable torque of the engine, and the four-speed gearbox has wider pinions. The optional Laycock-de Normanville overdrive was

much too close together. The gear lever is also badly placed for a right-hand drive car, and tends to be stiff in action, but the synchromesh on the upper three speeds is excellent.

On moving off, one is at once impressed by the sheer power of the big engine, and this feeling persists after hundreds of miles of driving. The Austin-Healey 3000 is a wonderfully

DRIVING POSITION is comfortable, but clutch and brake pedals are rather too close together and the gear lever is badly placed for right-hand drive.

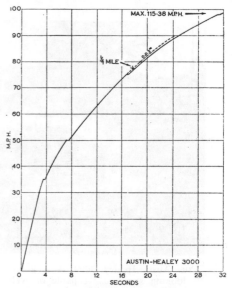

effortless car, and even if it is driven mostly on top gear it will fly past all the usual opposition. If the lower gears are used, real kick-in-the-back acceleration is available. Tried against other genuine 100 m.p.h. sports cars, the 3000 simply leaves them standing, its acceleration being really fierce.

· In the past, I have sometimes criticized B.M.C. engines for their lack of "bottom end" performance. The designers have now found the trick, and this new big six has all the torque in the world almost down to zero revs. It does tend to pink, and runs on when the ignition is switched off, which makes one hope that an aluminium head may later be offered as an extra. It is a power unit which joins in the fun when hard driving is afoot, and though it is fairly audible inside the small car, it never becomes rough however hard it is driven.

The ride is quite soft, and the urge of the engine enables the sharper curves to

DISTINCTIVE FLASHES on the front and rear of the car distinguish it from the successful 2.6-litre machine.

be slid under power when the cops are looking the other way. Driven as a fast touring car, this Austin-Healey is very controllable, and cruising at considerable speeds is all the more enjoyable because there is always more power available under the right foot. On a racing circuit, rather firmer suspension would be appreciated. The car remains controllable during fast cornering, but there is some pattering of the front wheels when racing techniques are employed. Similarly, the back axle can be made to hop during violent acceleration. It would be fair to say that the present suspension set-up is ideal for 90 per cent. of customers, but the remainder would applaud a little stiffening up here and there.

The brakes are powerful and do not fade. They do require a somewhat

heavy right foot, but the ability to stop is always there if one really presses. The clutch is also a little heavier than some, but one forgives all because it really grips at once and never slips or becomes fierce—even during the rigours of acceleration testing. The gears are commendably quiet, and can be snatched through really quickly when the rather unusual movement of the lever has been mastered.

Both for high speed work and touring the overdrive is a splendid device. On a winding road, third and overdrive third are the gears to use, and instantaneous up and down changes may be made without recourse to the gear lever. For fast cruising, one uses the overdrive top, flicking down to the direct drive for curves or overtaking. The ratios of the gearbox, rear axle and overdrive allow the potent engine to give of its best under all conditions.

The general finish of the car is pleasing and the appearance wholly delightful. The bonnet is rather full of engine, but normal maintenance is not unduly difficult. In spite of its impressive length of bonnet, the machine feels quite small and compact to drive and park. It has impeccable manners in traffic, and is a perfectly practical shopping car. When driven flat out, the big engine consumes a modicum of petrol, but at fast cruising speeds a praiseworthy 20 m.p.g. may be expected.

The Austin-Healey 3000 is a genuine 115 m.p.h. car which will yet appeal to many drivers who never exceed "eighty". It gives a wonderful feeling of reserve power which is perhaps one of motoring's greatest enjoyments. A touch of the pedal sends it flying uphill, and one never seems to be overdriving it. In spite of its great performance, the car employs no unusual components, and there is nothing to worry the most remote country garage. For the driver who enjoys horsepower and who finds the smaller sports cars a little too "gear-happy", this 3-litre speed model is just the job.

SPECIFICATION AND PERFORMANCE DATA

Car Tested: Austin-Healey 3000 occasional 4-seater. Price £1,175 10s. 10d. (including P.T.). Extras on test car: Hard top, £85; overdrive, £66 8s. 2d.; wire wheels, £35 8s. 4d.; heater, £21 19s. 2d.; radio, £34 (all including P.T.).

Engine: Six-cylinders 83.36 mm. x 88.9 mm. (2,912 c.c.). Pushrod operated overhead valves. 9.03 to 1 compression ratio. 130 b.h.p. at 4,750 r.p.m. Twin SU HD6 carburetters. Lucas coil and distributor.

Transmission: Borg and Beck 10 ins. clutch. Four-speed gearbox with synchromesh on upper three gears with central gear lever, ratios 3.214 o/d., 3.91, 4.207 o/d., 5.118, 8.026, and 11.456 to 1. Laycock-de Normanville overdrive. Open Hardy Spicer propeller shaft. Hypoid rear axle.

Chassis: Box-section pressed-steel frame. Independent front suspension by wishbones and helical springs with anti-roll torsion bar. Cam and peg steering gear. Rigid rear axle on semi-elliptic

springs with Panhard rod. Piston-type dampers. Girling hydraulic brakes with 11¼ ins. discs in front, 11 ins. drums behind. Knock-on wire wheels fitted 5.90-15 ins. Road Speed tyres.

Equipment: 12-volt lighting and starting. Speedometer, rev. counter, oil pressure, water temperature and fuel gauges. Windscreen washer. Flashing indicators. Extra: Heater, radio.

Dimensions: Wheelbase, 7 ft. 8 ins. Track, front 4 ft. 0¾ in., rear 4 ft. 2 ins. Overall length, 13 ft. 1½ ins. Width, 5 ft. 0½ in. Turning circle, 34 ft. Weight, 22½ cwt.

Performance: Maximum speed, 115.38 m.p.h. Speeds in gears, direct top 98 m.p.h., overdrive 3rd 90 m.p.h., 3rd 75 m.p.h., 2nd 50 m.p.h., 1st 35 m.p.h. Standing quarter-mile 17.6 secs. Acceleration: 0-30 m.p.h., 2.8 secs.; 0-50 m.p.h., 7.2 secs.; 0-60 m.p.h., 10.8 secs.; 0-80 m.p.h., 19.2 secs.; 0-100 m.p.h., 36 secs.

Fuel Consumption: 20 m.p.g.

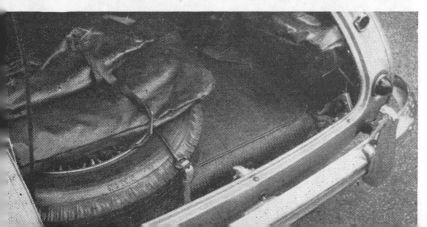

BOOT is of sufficient size for practical touring, though it contains battery, spare wheel and tools.

COMPACT and shapely, the Austin-Healey has a comparatively lazy engine which has now been tuned to realize its full potential.

will ever exceed 120 m.p.h., but above that speed he would be well advised to exercise some caution. The machine is short and has a rather conventional chassis, which becomes a little lively at the top end even in this improved form. Bumps or gusts of wind tend to deflect the car somewhat, but under suitable conditions it is safe to attain 125 m.p.h.

The Ruddspeed Austin-Healey is a car that will appeal to many because of the glorious sensation of sheer power that it gives. I was able to pass some very expensive speed models, particularly up hills, where this car really shines. There is some increase in the noise over the standard model, but the deep, powerful note is generally rather pleasing.

JOHN BOLSTER TRIES

THE RUDDSPEED AUSTIN-HEALEY 3000
A Good Looking Car of Really Fierce Performance

THE Austin-Healey 3000 is a good-looking sports car capable of well over 100 m.p.h. which combines exceptional flexibility with real acceleration. At its price, it is almost unbeatable as a practical high-performance sports-touring car. Yet, the temptation to develop that relatively lazy 3-litre, 6-cylinder engine is strong, and Rudds of Worthing have now made it possible to turn the big Healey into a real fire-eating monster.

The first essential is to modify the cylinder head, and the ports are opened up, valve seats modified, combustion chambers matched and polished, and the compression ratio is raised to 9.7 to 1. This work costs £25 including fitting charge. For another £25, Rudds will fit a special camshaft, and a triple inlet manifold plus a third S.U. carburetter can be installed for £39.

This work really allows the hefty power unit to realize its full potential, and in the compact and well-shaped sports two-seater, the performance cannot help being immense. However, such an engine is far too powerful for the roadholding afforded by the standard chassis, and a great deal of work has been carried out in rendering the performance usable.

The front shock absorbers and springs must be replaced by competition-type equipment, at a price of £25. New rear springs are £12, and a servo is fitted to the disc brakes at £19 10s. All these prices include fitting, and in certain instances an allowance is made for returned equipment. In addition, the test car had Michelin X tyres of 6.40-15 ins. size, for which a small body modification was required to give adequate clearance.

On the road, the performance is really fierce. Unfortunately, the Austin-Healey gearbox has a slow change from second to third which cannot be hurried. In spite of this considerable disadvantage, the following somewhat startling figures were recorded. Standing quarter-mile 16.8 secs.; 0-30 m.p.h., 2.8 secs.; 0-50 m.p.h., 5.8 secs.; 0-60 m.p.h., 9.4 secs.; 0-80 m.p.h., 14.8 secs.; 0-100 m.p.h., 21.6 secs. Driven hard, the fuel consumption is 17 m.p.g., which is not unreasonable for a 3-litre car. In spite of its high compression ratio, the engine pinks less than the standard power unit.

IMMENSE performance has been achieved by these Rudd modifications but the power gained by this very potent engine must be matched by improved roadholding.

The maximum speed is 125 m.p.h. with hood and sidescreens in position. The hood stands up to this great velocity remarkably well, but the sidescreens tend to bulge outwards. The work on the suspension eliminates the flap and patter of the front wheels, and the rear axle does not bounce during acceleration. The ride is firm but by no means unpleasantly so.

It is unlikely that the average owner

After prolonged slow-speed work in traffic, the engine tended to run unevenly, but cleared itself at once when the open road was reached. Starting was always instantaneous and the top gear flexibility was surprisingly good. As a practical sports-touring car for everyday use, yet with a capacity to flash past the "hundred" at the drop of a hat, this good-looking two-seater must represent exceptional value for money.

A Healey for Hurrying

Ruddspeed conversion makes a fast sports car phenomenally potent

WHEN the Austin-Healey was changed from a four- into a six-cylinder machine many enthusiasts were not entirely happy with the resultant performance. Since then the six-port head has rendered an improvement and the engine size has been increased to three litres from the original 2.6. In this form the car is now really fast enough to meet the needs of most drivers, but for those who are suitably experienced and wish to turn their Healey into something quite remarkable, or possibly to use it in competitions, Rudds of Worthing offer for well under £200 a conversion which not merely improves but rather transforms an already good sports car.

Far from being merely an engine conversion, the whole car has been modified, including the brakes and suspension, so that not only is performance increased but also it is made if anything more usable, some caution however being necessary on wet roads. It must be remembered, however, that the car is still comparatively cheap and so the general feeling of control is not the same as that of a highly expensive specialist-built machine. This results in the Healey being somewhat tiring to drive over long distances, but this is largely due to the fact that with the rev. counter at 3,000 r.p.m. and the speedometer needle at about 80 m.p.h., one feels that the car is waffling along so slowly that one really ought to get a move on and so a very few seconds later is travelling at over 100 m.p.h., at which speed a certain amount of concentration becomes desirable. Also tiring is the exhaust noise, which was sufficient to make the police look decidedly interested even if they did not essay a chase. However for everyday use the standard exhaust system can be used, presumably with some loss of power.

Our last road test of a standard Austin-Healey Six covered the smaller-engined version, so figures are not accurately comparative. Nevertheless, a Maximile speed which has risen from 103.9 m.p.h. to 113.1 m.p.h. mean, and acceleration which has enabled the Ruddspeed car to better standing quarter and 0-100 m.p.h. times by 2.0 and 11.9 seconds respectively, cannot to any great extent be due to an extra 273 c.c. of engine. Overall fuel consumption has, however, dropped by some 5 m.p.g. as might be expected when the additional carburetter is considered, although steady speed consumptions are not greatly different and at some speeds actually better.

For all the performance the car does not suffer unduly from temperament, starting being of the first time variety without

the need of any choke after a night in the open. Driving can be done almost exclusively in direct top with commendable smoothness if desired, whilst starts can be made in second gear without protest. Slight pinking could, however, be provoked even on 100 octane petrol on occasion, and after hard driving there was a tendency to run on.

Not every owner would, one feels, wish to convert his Healey to give the exceptional standard of performance offered by the Rudd conversion, but for those who wish to own a car which will reduce any road to a series of curves, all the straights having mysteriously disappeared and all other cars having stopped, this is a way in which such a vehicle can be acquired without enormous expense.

PERFORMANCE DATA; RUDDSPEED AUSTIN-HEALEY 3000

WEATHER
Dry with light wind (temperature 40°–44°F.; Barometer 29.4 in. Hg.).

"Maximile" Speed. (Timed quarter mile after one mile accelerating from rest.)

Mean of four opposite runs	113.1 m.p.h.
Best one-way time equals	113.9 m.p.h.

FUEL CONSUMPTION

Overdrive top m.p.g.	Direct top m.p.g.	
29½	26½	At constant 30 m.p.h. on level.
30	26½	At constant 40 m.p.h. on level.
27	24	At constant 60 m.p.h. on level.
23½	21	At constant 80 m.p.h. on level.
17½	—	At constant 100 m.p.h. on level.

Overall fuel consumption for 926 miles, 60.65 gallons, equals 15.3 m.p.g.

ACCELERATION TIMES (from standstill)

0–30 m.p.h.	3.1 sec.	0–70 m.p.h.	11.4 sec.
0–40 m.p.h.	4.7 sec.	0–80 m.p.h.	14.3 sec.
0–50 m.p.h.	6.4 sec.	0–90 m.p.h.	18.2 sec.
0–60 m.p.h.	8.8 sec.	0–100 m.p.h.	24.47 sec.

Standing quarter mile: 16.2 sec.

Acceleration times on upper ratios

	O/D top gear sec.	Direct top gear sec.	Direct third gear sec.
10–30 m.p.h.	8.8 ..	7.1 ..	5.3
20–40 m.p.h.	9.3 ..	7.4 ..	5.3
30–50 m.p.h.	9.5 ..	7.0 ..	4.9
40–60 m.p.h.	9.2 ..	7.0 ..	4.3
50–70 m.p.h.	9.5 ..	6.6 ..	4.6
60–80 m.p.h.	9.7 ..	6.3 ..	—
70–90 m.p.h.	9.8 ..	7.3 ..	—
80–100 m.p.h.	13.0 ..	10.1 ..	—

Brakes from 30 m.p.h.
0.93 g retardation (equivalent to 32½ ft. stopping distance) with 70 lb. pedal pressure.
0.80 g retardation (equivalent to 37½ ft. stopping distance) with 50 lb. pedal pressure.
0.49 g retardation (equivalent to 61½ ft. stopping distance) with 25 lb. pedal pressure.

RUDDSPEED AUSTIN-HEALEY 3000 MODIFICATIONS

	£	s.	d.
Modified cylinder head 9.7/1 compression ratio	25	0	0
Special camshaft	25	0	0
Triple inlet manifolds and two extra S.U. carburetters ..	39	0	0
Large bore exhaust system with chromed tail pipes ..	14	0	0
Stronger front springs and competition shock absorbers ..	25	0	0
Modified rear springs	12	0	0
Brakes modified to servo assistance	19	10	0
Michelin X 640×15 tyres on exchange for new tyres	15	0	0
(including modifying body to give wheel clearance)			
Oil temperature gauge and ammeter	12	10	0
Extension pedals (for short drivers)	1	0	0
Gear lever extension with wooden knob	1	15	0
Total	**189**	**15**	**0**

Allowances when a new car is modified:

	£	s.	d.
For shock absorbers and springs	7	10	0
For camshaft	2	0	0
For cylinder head and manifold	2	0	0

All charges include fitting.
Suppliers: K. N. Rudd (Engineers), Ltd., 41, High Street, Worthing.

Mighty powerhouse. Three carburetters at once distinguish the engine compartment of this tuned Austin-Healey, but a specially modified cylinder head, different camshaft and special exhaust system also help to raise the power output.

The Motor Road Test No. 25/60

Make: Austin-Healey Type: 3000 Hardtop (B.T.7.) With overdrive
Makers: The Austin Motor Co., Ltd., Longbridge, Birmingham

Test Data

CONDITIONS: *Weather : Dry, wind 5-15 m.p.h. (Temperature 70°-75°F., Barometer 29.7 in. Hg.) Surface : Dry tarmacadam. Fuel : 100 octane pump petrol.*

INSTRUMENTS

Speedometer at 30 m.p.h.	19% fast
Speedometer at 60 m.p.h.	10% fast
Speedometer at 90 m.p.h.	9% fast
Distance recorder	2% slow

WEIGHT

Kerb weight (unladen, but with oil, coolant and fuel for approx. 50 miles)	22 cwt.
Front/rear distribution of kerb weight	50/50
Weight laden as tested	25¾ cwt.

MAXIMUM SPEEDS

Flying Mile

Mean of six opposite runs	115.0 m.p.h.
Best one-way time equals	116.9 m.p.h.

"Maximile" Speed. (Timed quarter mile after one mile accelerating from rest.)

Mean of opposite runs	107.1 m.p.h.
Best one-way time equals	108.4 m.p.h.

Speed in gears

Max. speed in Direct Top gear	98 m.p.h.
Max. speed in Overdrive 3rd gear	92 m.p.h.
Max. speed in 3rd gear	75 m.p.h.
Max. speed in 2nd gear	48 m.p.h.
Max. speed in 1st gear	33 m.p.h.

FUEL CONSUMPTION

(Overdrive top gear)

35½ m.p.g. at constant 30 m.p.h. on level.
35 m.p.g. at constant 40 m.p.h. on level.
32 m.p.g. at constant 50 m.p.h. on level.
29 m.p.g. at constant 60 m.p.h. on level.
23½ m.p.g. at constant 70 m.p.h. on level.
20½ m.p.g. at constant 80 m.p.h. on level.
19 m.p.g. at constant 90 m.p.h. on level.
16 m.p.g. at constant 100 m.p.h. on level.

(Direct top gear)

31 m.p.g. at constant 30 m.p.h. on level.
29½ m.p.g. at constant 40 m.p.h. on level.
26½ m.p.g. at constant 50 m.p.h. on level.
23½ m.p.g. at constant 60 m.p.h. on level.
20½ m.p.g. at constant 70 m.p.h. on level.
18 m.p.g. at constant 80 m.p.h. on level.
16½ m.p.g. at constant 90 m.p.h. on level.

Overall Fuel Consumption for 1,632 miles, 86.8 gallons, equals 18.8 m.p.g. (15.0 litres/100 km.)

Touring Fuel Consumption (m.p.g. at steady speed midway between 30 m.p.h. and maximum, less 5% allowance for acceleration). 21.6 m.p.g.

Fuel tank capacity (maker's figure) 12 gallons.

STEERING

Turning circle between kerbs :

Left	33¾ ft.
Right	33¼ ft.

Turns of steering wheel from lock to lock 3

BRAKES from 30 m.p.h.

0.93 g retardation (equivalent to 32 ft. stopping distance) with 75 lb. pedal pressure.
0.67 g retardation (equivalent to 45 ft. stopping distance) with 50 lb. pedal pressure.
0.27 g retardation (equivalent to 111 ft. stopping distance) with 25 lb. pedal pressure.

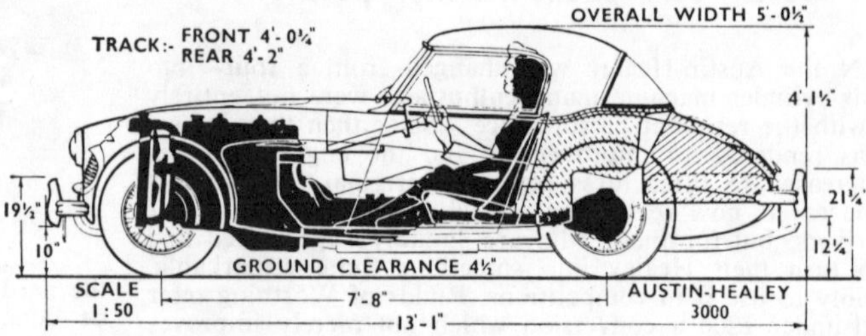
OVERALL WIDTH 5'-0½"
TRACK:- FRONT 4'-0½"
REAR 4'-2"
4'-1½"
19½"
10"
21¼"
12¼"
GROUND CLEARANCE 4½"
SCALE
1:50
7'-8"
13'-1"
AUSTIN-HEALEY
3000

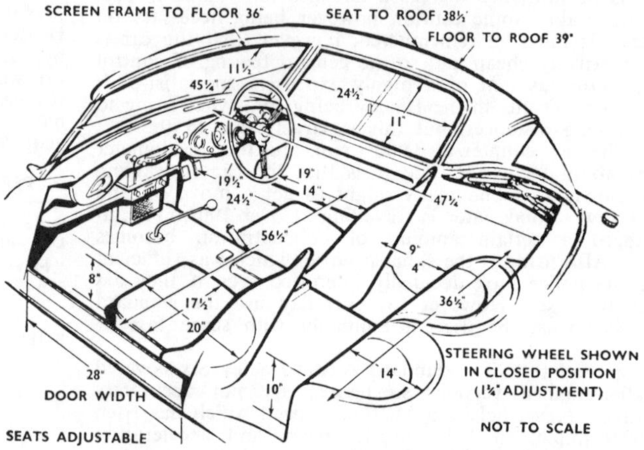
SCREEN FRAME TO FLOOR 36"
SEAT TO ROOF 38½"
FLOOR TO ROOF 39"
11½"
45¼"
24½"
11"
19"
19½"
14"
24½"
47¼"
56½"
9"
4"
8"
17½"
20"
36½"
28"
DOOR WIDTH
10"
14"
STEERING WHEEL SHOWN
IN CLOSED POSITION
(1¼" ADJUSTMENT)
NOT TO SCALE
SEATS ADJUSTABLE

ACCELERATION TIMES from standstill

0-30 m.p.h.	3.4 sec.
0-40 m.p.h.	5.7 sec.
0-50 m.p.h.	8.5 sec.
0-60 m.p.h.	11.7 sec.
0-70 m.p.h.	15.5 sec.
0-80 m.p.h.	19.9 sec.
0-90 m.p.h.	27.2 sec.
0-100 m.p.h.	39.3 sec.
Standing quarter mile	17.7 sec.

ACCELERATION TIMES on Upper Ratios

	Overdrive top gear	Direct top gear	3rd gear
10-30 m.p.h.	—	6.8 sec.	5.0 sec.
20-40 m.p.h.	8.6 sec.	6.6 sec.	5.1 sec.
30-50 m.p.h.	9.0 sec.	6.8 sec.	5.0 sec.
40-60 m.p.h.	8.9 sec.	6.6 sec.	5.5 sec.
50-70 m.p.h.	10.1 sec.	7.6 sec.	7.0 sec.
60-80 m.p.h.	11.7 sec.	8.7 sec.	—
70-90 m.p.h.	16.5 sec.	12.4 sec.	—
80-100 m.p.h.	20.0 sec.	—	—

HILL CLIMBING at sustained steady speeds

Max. gradient on overdrive top gear	1 in 8 (Tapley 280 lb./ton)
Max. gradient on direct top gear	1 in 6.2 (Tapley 355 lb./ton)
Max. gradient on overdrive 3rd gear	1 in 5.9 (Tapley 375 lb./ton)
Max. gradient on direct 3rd gear	1 in 4.8 (Tapley 460 lb./ton)
Max. gradient on 2nd gear	1 in 3.2 (Tapley 665 lb./ton)

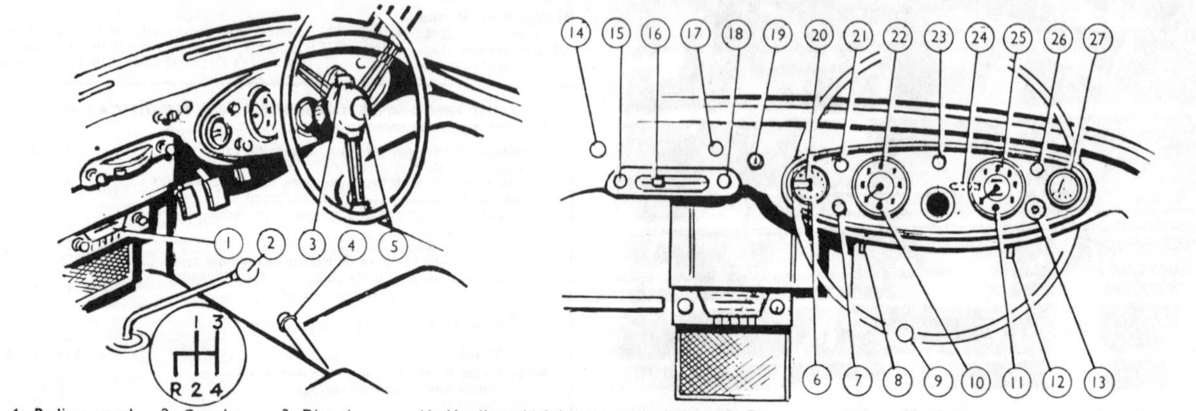
1
2
3
4
5
1 3
R 2 4
14
15
16
17
18
19
20
21
22
23
24
25
26
27
6
7
8
9
10
11
12
13

1. Radio controls. 2. Gear lever. 3. Direction indicator switch. 4. Handbrake. 5. Horn button. 6. Water thermometer. 7. Windscreen wipers control. 8. Panel light switch. 9. Dip-switch. 10. Dynamo charge warning light. 11. Headlamp high beam warning light. 12. Trip resetting knob. 13. Overdrive switch. 14. Screenwasher button. 15. Cold air control. 16. Heater control and fan switch. 17. Choke control. 18. Hot air control. 19. Ignition switch. 20. Oil pressure gauge. 21. Starter. 22. Tachometer. 23. Direction indicator warning light. 24. Bonnet catch release. 25. Speedometer. 26. Lights switch. 27. Fuel contents gauge.

The Austin-Healey 3000 Hardtop

An Occasional Four-seater Tested in Overdrive Form

SINCE the Austin-Healey "Six" was last tested, numerous small changes have been made in both the mechanical and body specifications. In conjunction with a 10% increase in engine size, bringing the capacity to just over 2.9 litres, the final drive gearing has been raised by 5%, a closer ratio overdrive fitted, and disc brakes have been adopted on the front wheels only. The particular car tested had the occasional four-seat body that now supplements the two-seat version and the well designed hardtop that effectively converts it to a closed car when the weather makes this expedient. All performance figures were taken with this fitted.

An unexpected by-product of these changes, which may be indicative of carburetter modifications, was the 5 to 15% improvement found in the overdrive top gear fuel consumption at speeds below 70 m.p.h. Less surprising, in view of the very smooth shape of the new hardtop, is the increase of 7 m.p.h. in maximum speed to the creditable figure of 115 m.p.h. It is probable that even better figures for acceleration and speed might have been obtained from a well-used model as the car tested

had done only 2,500 miles at the time and both engine and gearbox were relatively stiff.

In order to depress fully a long-travel clutch, it is necessary for the driver to sit quite close to the steering wheel, and for a person of average height the extended-arm steering position is out of the question, in spite of an adjustable steering column which allows the wheel to be moved quite near to the facia. The close conjunction of windscreen and driver is reminiscent of older sports cars and, despite a low seating position and a long broad bonnet, provides excellent visibility and a view of the road surface surprisingly close ahead. In addition, dirt or rain on the glass reduce visibility much less than with a distant screen and better protection is obtained

from the wind when the car is open; in this form the Austin-Healey is a very pleasant machine, and with the side-screens erect it is possible to cruise at speeds in the region of 80 m.p.h. without undue buffeting or turbulence, although with considerable wind noise as must be expected in an open car.

The small bucket seats give unusually good lateral support but have very upright backs and almost horizontal seat cushions. Many people would prefer to have the seats tilted bodily backwards with some extra padding to support the small of the back which tends to ache on long journeys.

With standard tyre pressures, the car is perhaps a little heavy to drive on slow, twisty roads, and although the wheels adhere firmly to the ground, hard driving

TOP REMOVED.—The aluminium-framed detachable sidescreens have sliding Perspex windows, and the self-parking wipers do not obstruct the view from the low driving position. The knock-off wire wheels are an optional extra.

In Brief

Price (including overdrive and hardtop as tested) £935 17s. 6d., plus purchase tax £391 1s. 6d., equals £1,326 19s.
Price without overdrive and hardtop (including purchase tax), £1,175 10s. 10d.
Capacity ... ... 2912 c.c.
Unladen kerb weight ... 22 cwt.
Acceleration:
  20-40 m.p.h. in top gear ... 6.6 sec.
  0-50 m.p.h. through gears 8.5 sec.
Maximum direct top gear gradient 1 in 6.2
Maximum speed ... 115.0 m.p.h.
"Maximile" speed ... 107.1 m.p.h.
Touring fuel consumption ... 21.6 m.p.g.
Gearing: 19.0 m.p.h. in top gear at 1,000 r.p.m. (overdrive, 23.1 m.p.h.); 32.5 m.p.h. at 1,000 ft./min. piston speed (overdrive, 39.6 m.p.h.).

is mild pinking at full throttle using ordinary premium grade fuel. This disappears with the use of 100 octane fuel or if the lowest part of the r.p.m. range is avoided by means of the gearbox. At the other extreme, the engine runs quickly and smoothly up to the limit of 5,200 r.p.m. which is marked with a red line on the tachometer.

Mechanically, this is a very quiet unit, but this advantage is rather negatived by a hard and purposeful exhaust note from the twin pipes which, although intrinsically pleasing, attracts a lot of attention and raises the internal noise level to a point where it can become tiring on a long, fast journey, particularly with the hardtop in use. The small "pancake" air filters do little to eliminate carburetter intake roar, and sudden throttle opening is accompanied by a pronounced gasping noise.

The quiet gearbox has very satisfactory close ratios, but at first it was not found light to operate. To some extent this was caused by the stiffness that is common with new boxes, and later in the test it became freer to the extent that leisurely changes slipped through very easily, but to force through a really quick change against the effective synchromesh still called for some effort.

The amount of gear changing required, of course, is greatly reduced by the wide torque range of the engine and by the optional Laycock overdrive fitted to the car submitted for test and which provides an immediate 18% reduction in engine speed. Operated by a facia switch, which is most convenient for finger-tip operation without moving the right hand from the wheel, this overdrive is very smooth in action. Available on top and third gears only, an interconnection prevents engagement on the overrun with a completely closed throttle, whilst full power changes were perceptible by little more than the change of exhaust note.

The AUSTIN-HEALEY 3000 HARDTOP

produces some scream from the Dunlop Road Speed tyres. With the extra 6 lb./sq. in. all round which is recommended for prolonged driving at speeds over 85/90 m.p.h., tyre noise is very hard to provoke, the steering is light, roll negligible and wheel adhesion and behaviour of the Panhard-rod-located back axle on bumpy roads remains extremely good. Quite heavy use of the throttle induces very mild oversteer and enables a series of bends to be negotiated very fast with relatively small movements of the steering, so that the close driving position necessitates little passing of the wheel from hand to hand. On wet and slippery roads, however, the accelerator must be treated with some discretion to avoid sudden breakaway at the back.

Although the steering displays very little feed-back from bumps and camber changes, the driver is aware of continual movement of the wheel in his hands due to a slight lateral shake from which the scuttle suffers on bad roads, and which also causes some bonnet movement and chattering from the sidescreens in open form, particularly with the high tyre pressures. Comfortable riding qualities, however, have not been sacrificed to gain good roadholding and the notable freedom from roll; although fairly hard

when travelling slowly, the ride flattens out at high speed to give an excellent compromise, free of pitch, too well damped for float, and transmitting sharp vertical movements only on substantial irregularities when the suspension approaches the end of its fairly limited travel.

Very easy to start from cold, the engine is rather slow to warm up and tends to spit back through the carburetters for the first mile or two unless the choke, which has a fast idling interconnection with the throttle, is pulled out slightly; thereafter it is notable for the effortless ease with which it produces a very impressive performance. Tuned for high torque in the low and medium speed ranges, it will pull strongly and smoothly from very low speeds although, driven in this unusual way, there

VISIBILITY.—A very large plastic window in the smooth and elegant hardtop affords an excellent rear view. The sidescreens close on to very effective rubber seals.

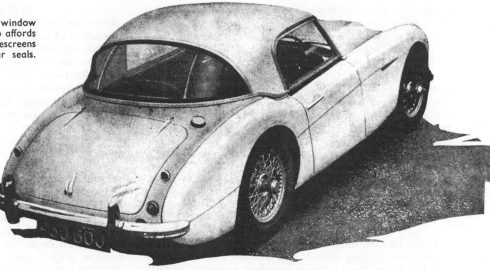

First impressions of the Girling brakes (disc front) suggested that a servo might be desirable to reduce the pedal pressures. It soon appeared, however, that a little warming up of the linings improved the efficiency very considerably and normal fairly hard driving keeps them at a temperature where they are pleasantly light to operate. As with many disc systems, gentle use sometimes caused a high-pitched squeal, but much more important was the fact that the heaviest operation in road use never produced any loss in braking power or balance.

Pedal Points

On a car of this sort, heel and toe operation of the accelerator and brake is a most useful facility which the Austin-Healey layout did not permit; the operation of the accelerator could be improved by elimination of initial free play together with more progressive opening thereafter. Other minor points which the driver may criticize include a mirror mounted too near the windscreen so that it chatters against the glass when correctly adjusted, and a fuel gauge which is extremely sensitive to acceleration or gradient.

A spell of warm weather which coincided with our test revealed that ventilation, even with the sliding windows open, is not adequate for these conditions. However, in the circumstances most owners would remove the hardtop, which is a very rapid and simple process involving two quick-action toggles and two wing nuts. Refitting is almost equally easy, and it is probably quicker to fit or remove the hardtop than it is to raise or lower the hood which, although quite straightforward, necessitates some care in stowing the fabric to ensure that it folds neatly into the space allotted. The doors rise as they open to avoid high kerbs and have been fitted with rather stiffly set friction hinges to hold them at any position. When closed, the side windows seat on soft rubber seals which are effective in excluding rain and draughts.

Although the occasional back seats look small, they are in fact adequate for two adults sitting rather high in the airstream when the car is open, but with the hardtop fitted, headroom is enough only for small children. In many cases this space will be used for carrying extra luggage as the boot itself is fairly small. A most useful feature is the fitting of a battery master switch inside the boot, which is the only part of the car which can be locked, so that valuable articles can be left in the boot and the whole car immobilized when it is parked.

A little attention to seating comfort and a few modifications to some of the minor controls would still further improve a car which now offers quite extraordinary performance in relation to its cost, taking performance in its broadest sense to include acceleration, maximum speed, roadholding and braking. The winning of the team award, amongst other striking successes, in the recent Alpine Rally, shows that durability is another attribute that must be added to this list.

Specification

Engine

Cylinders	6
Bore	83.36 mm.
Stroke	88.9 mm.
Cubic capacity	2,912 c.c.
Piston area	47.1 sq. in.
Valves	Pushrod o.h.v.
Compression ratio	9/1
Carburetter	Two S.U. H.D.6
Fuel pump	S.U. electric
Ignition timing control	Centrifugal and vacuum
Oil filter	Tecalemit full-flow
Max. power (net)	124 b.h.p.
at	4,600 r.p.m.
Piston speed at max. b.h.p.	2,680 ft./min.

Transmission

Clutch	Borg and Beck s.d.p. 9 in.
Top gear (s/m)	3.91 (overdrive, 3.20)
3rd gear (s/m)	5.12 (overdrive 4.19)
2nd gear (s/m)	8.02
1st gear	11.45
Reverse	14.78
Overdrive	Laycock-de Normanville
Propeller shaft	Hardy Spicer open
Final drive	Hypoid 11/43
Top gear m.p.h. at 1,000 r.p.m.	19.0 (Overdrive, 23.1)
Top gear m.p.h. at 1,000 ft./min. piston speed	32.5 (overdrive, 23.1)

Chassis

Brakes	Girling disc front. Girling drum rear
Brake diameters	Discs 11¼ in. dia. Drums 11 in. dia.

Friction areas: 112 sq. in. of friction surface working on 383 sq. in. of rubbed area.
Suspension:
  Front: Independent by coil springs and wishbones.
  Rear: Rigid axle with semi-elliptic leaf springs and panhard rod.
Shock Absorbers:
  Front: Armstrong hydraulic lever-type.
  Rear: Armstrong hydraulic lever-type.
Steering gear ... Cam and peg
Tyres ... 5.90-15 Dunlop Roadspeed

Coachwork and Equipment

Starting handle	Yes
Battery mounting	Off-side of boot
Jack	Screw type
Jacking points	Under front and rear suspension.

Standard tool kit: Jack and handle, starting handle, plug spanner and bar, ignition combination tool, valve key, copper hammer.
Exterior lights: Two head, two side/indicator, two tail/stop/indicator, rear number plate.

Number of electrical fuses	2
Direction indicators	Flashing, self-cancelling
Windscreen wipers	Lucas single speed self-parking
Windscreen washers	Tudor Manual
Sun visors	None

Instruments: Speedometer with decimal trip distance recorder, revolution counter, fuel gauge, oil pressure and water temperature gauge.
Warning lights: Dynamo and headlamp main beam.

Locks:	
With ignition key	Boot
With other keys	None
Glove lockers	None
Map pockets	One in each door
Parcel shelves	One below facia
Ashtrays	One on transmission tunnel
Cigar lighters	None
Interior lights	None

Interior heater: Optional extra. Smiths fresh air type with demisters.
Car radio: Optional extra. H.M.V. Push button.
Extras available: Hard top, overdrive, wire spoked wheels, heater, radio.

Upholstery material	Hide
Floor covering	Rubber-backed carpet
Exterior colours standardized: 6 single, 5 two tone.	
Alternative body styles	Open 2-seater

Maintenance

Sump 11¾ pints, S.A.E. 30 (including filter)
Gearbox: 5 pints, S.A.E. 30 plus 1½ pints for overdrive.

Rear axle	3 pints, S.A.E. 90
Steering gear lubricant	S.A.E. 90
Cooling system capacity	19 pints (2 drain taps)

Chassis lubrication: By grease gun every 1,000 miles to 14 points.

Ignition timing (static)	5° b.t.d.c.
Contact-breaker gap	.014-.016 in.
Sparking plug type	Champion N.3
Sparking plug gap	.025 in.

Valve timing: Inlet opens 5° b.t.d.c.; Inlet closes 45° a.b.d.c. Exhaust opens 40° b.b.d.c.; Exhaust closes 10° a.t.d.c.
Tappet clearances (Hot):

Inlet	.012 in.
Exhaust	.012 in.
Front wheel toe-in	¹⁄₁₆-⅛ in.
Camber angle	1°
Castor angle	2°
Steering swivel pin inclination	6½°

Tyre pressures: Front 20 lb. Rear 23 lb. (or 26 lb. with full load).

Brake fluid	Girling

Battery type and capacity: 12 volt, 57 amp. hr.

▶ In the engine conversion specialists' book, a *dernier cri* never remains *dernier* for long. Almost before the ink was dry on last summer's announcement of the Austin-Healey six's rerating from 2639 to 2912 cc, with a resulting gain of 7 bhp and 26 pound-feet of torque, British tunesmiths were in quest of further performance bonuses for the hottest edition of BMC's C-series engine. First to yell Eureka, to the best of our knowledge, was K. N. Rudd (Engineers) Ltd., of Worthing, Sussex, England, a firm with a reassuring racing background, e.g., the Rudd Racing Team's 2-liter class win at Le Mans last year with a stock but exquisitely prepared AC Ace. The standard BN7 Austin-Healey 3000, as road-tested in SCI's August, 1959 issue, gives 130 bhp gross at 4750 rpm and 175 pound-feet of torque. With the Ruddspeed condiments added, corresponding figures are 178 bhp at 6000 rpm — a 36.2% power increase — and 192 pound-feet of torque.

VISIBLE CHANGES

There isn't anything startling about the means used to achieve this startling end. It just adds up to the old story of fuller filling plus a hoist in compression ratio that's little more than nominal. Star dish on the menu, which is also the most expensive single item, is conspicuous as soon as

OTHER RUDD OPTIONS

Rudd also markets the makings of certain chassis modifications aimed at improved safety and roadability. These are all listed separately, so you can opt for some and skip the others, or skip the lot if you like. Items under this head are harder front springs and competition shock absorbers, reset rear springs (with the incidental benefit of a slight increase in clearance under the 3000's inconveniently low belly), and a vacuum servo assist for the existing Girling disc brakes on the front wheels. Source of this boost is the Clayton Dewandre Mot-A-Vac unit, which tucks away tidily within the right-side front fender and derives its vacuum from one of the induction balance pipes. The car we tested also had racing front disc pads.

Further Rudd options are two additional dash instruments — ammeter and oil thermometer — and a set of modified brake, clutch and throttle pedal pads. Former are matched, calibrated in white on black dials (which incidentally doesn't match the rest of the instruments, which have black figures on white faces).

Purpose of the pedal modification is twofold: first, to increase the normally-marginal lateral clearance between all three controls; second, to do something to correct an inherent

HOTTEST HEALEY 3000

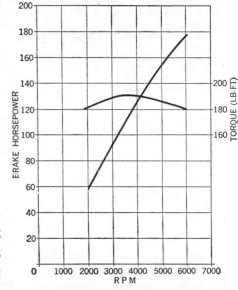

by Dennis May

You'd think most buyers of the spirited Healey 3000 would be sated by its standard tune, but Ken Rudd supplies a power pack that pumps in 48 extra bhp. Rudd isn't resting here; he has plans for a new version that will endow the 3000 with 200 horses!

the hood is lifted. This is a completely original intake system with triple HD6 SU carbs mounted on separate semi-down-draft manifolds, cast in aluminum alloy and finned on their upper faces. (The normal setup, of course, is dual HD6's on a common gallery.) Large-diameter copper balance pipes connect the three Rudd manifolds, which, though closely-neighbored to the two exhaust collectors, have no direct-contact hotspots. Lack of space under the adjoining fender precludes the fitting of air filter/silencers, so the SU intakes are left agape. The standard twin-pipe exhaust plumbing is retained, but a shorter system of larger bore, terminating just ahead of the left-side rear wheel, is available to special order.

The invisible end of the engine deal comprises a Rudd-speed camshaft, designed for extra power without loss of flexibility, and a reworked cylinder head with matched and polished combustion chambers, enlarged and highly-fettled ports, modified valve seats. Work on the head puts the compression up from 9.03 to 9.7 to 1. Purpose of the valve seat sculpture is to maintain clearance between the valves at full lift and the adjacent edge of the cylinder block.

deficiency in the 3000's range of driving positions. The BN7, of course, lacks a telescopic steering column, and with the seat set far enough back for comfortable arm reach a driver of average build finds himself short on leg length. Incidentally, medium-height drivers can't easily see over the steering wheel, and the seat has no vertical adjustment, only fore-and-aft. Rudd's brake and clutch pedal pads are bolt-on fittings and do their dual job very well, with the reservation that the brake pad still doesn't give a lineup permitting heel-and-toe gear changes. The alteration to the throttle consists of welding an extra section onto the arc of the standard pad; this gives an ampler foothold and also provides a built-in stop at the full-noise position, relieving the linkages of brunts they shouldn't be expected to bear.

In upping the output of the C-series engine from 130 to nearly 180 bhp — in fact an actual 180 if the shorter, freer and doubtlessly ruder exhaust system is specified — the Ruddspeeders might be supposed to have turned over a new leaf to end new leaves. But this, says Ken Rudd, is not necessarily so. On paper, or maybe only in their heads, they have conceived further tuning stages, mainly matters

Rudd-converted Healey sports third SU carburetor and special finned aluminum manifold.

The Managing Director of K. N. Rudd Engineering smiles his satisfaction after a trial run in a Rudd-prepared A-H 3000. His back-room boys have increased horsepower from a stock 130 to 178.

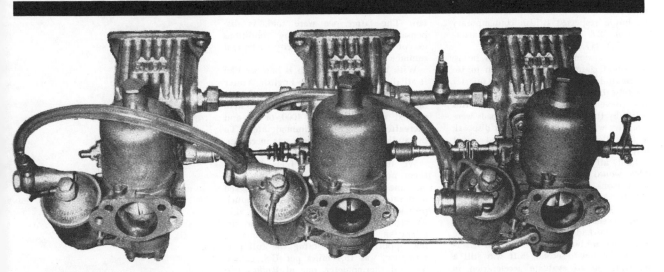

Three SU HD6 carburetors are mounted on separate stub manifolds machined from aluminum casting. Copper tubing joins all three stubs to balance intake. All three SUs are run sans silencers and filters due to lack of room under fender. Author May reports, however, that they are not terribly noisy.

of cam form, conservatively calculated to lift the bhp ceiling above two centuries. This becomes more feasible than it sounds when we add that the current Rudd camshaft gives no increase in valve lift. But it's emphasized that the reliability factor at upwards of 180 horsepower would be conjectural, and the requisite practical development work has not yet been essayed and won't be in the foreseeable future.

DELIVERY AND PRICES

As far as the U.S. market is concerned, Rudd has two types of customers in view. If for instance you're planning to buy a new 3000 through normal trade channels, you can specify the Ruddspeed treatments — as many or as few as you please — when placing your order. When this is received at BMC, the car is built to stock specification, turned over to Rudd's firm for modification, returned to BMC, finally shipped to your U.S. dealer. In such a case there is no direct transaction between you and Rudd, though he does pride himself — and this can be important — on dealing scrupulously and punctually with epistolic queries from users of his products in all parts of the world.

If on the other hand you already own a 3000 and aspire to extra poop, you write directly to K. N. Rudd (Engineers) Ltd., High Street, Worthing, Sussex, England, state your exact requirements and solicit quotations. Distances from port of entry to ultimate destination introduce a considerable variable, so it's difficult to simplify the cost factor adequately. As a rough guide, though, the basic price of the three special intake manifolds, one additional SU to supplement an existing pair of carbs, and all the necessary control apparatus, is approximately $105.00; Rudd camshaft, $50.00; hard front springs and shocks to match, $58.00; Mot-A-Vac brake servo unit and pipework, around $40.00. If you buy the camshaft or the gasworks set, something that comes for free is a drawing and a detailed sheet of instructions for modifying the head and porting to Rudd's recipe.

WHAT IT WILL DO

In road performance language, the improvement wrought by the protraction of the Ruddspeed Healey's power curve is what you'd expect. When you hit the throttle at anything above about 3000 rpm, things really happen. The

HOTTEST HEALEY 3000

demonstration car we borrowed had the same 3.91 to 1 axle ratio as the standard model SCI tested last year, the only discrepancy being in the overdrive ratios — 0.778 to 1 on the Ruddspeeder, 0.822 in the other case. Acceleration comparisons are therefore legitimate, though it's probable the stock sample had had a better break-in; Rudd's engine had done 21 hours on the bench and practically nothing on the road when we took his car over.

Here, then, are some specimen acceleration times, taken on surfaces that were perceptibly damp after recent rains but of inherently good traction properties (figures in brackets are from SCI's regular road test report): 0 to 50 mph, 6.2 seconds (7.3); 0 to 60, 9.3 (10.9); 0 to 70, 11.9 (14.2); 0 to 80, 15.4 (19.2); 0 to 100, 25.8 (not recorded for the standard car by SCI but a respected British contemporary made it 32.8 seconds); standing quarter-mile, 17.0 (17.8).

More accustomed to the car, as he is, Ken Rudd claims he can get down to 16-and-small-decimals for the standing quarter any time he likes on a dry road, and was only prevented from demonstrating this ability by the fact the available roads were never dry while the car was at our disposal. In equivalently expert hands, and under fully dehydrated conditions, it follows that probably all the acceleration figures quoted above would take a shave. As tested, with two persons aboard, the car weighed 2786 pounds.

STARTS AND TOP SPEED

Unlike the engine, the converted A-H's transmission had a reasonable road mileage on it when we borrowed the car, but nevertheless the low-to-second shift was still a bit stiff. So to evaluate acceleration in terms that would be unaffected by this, we clocked her over these gaps in normal top, giving 20 mph per thousand rpm: 50 to 80 mph, 9.5 seconds; 60 to 80, 6.0 seconds. A standard 3000 takes 2.4 seconds longer through the latter band.

Reverting to standing starts, two comments are relevant. First, the enlarged clutch (up from 9 to 10 inches in diameter) introduced concurrently with last year's bigger engine, showed no sign whatever of fatigue or resentment when subjected to a series of fairly brutal takeoffs. Second, the Rudd-modified rear springs had an unmistakably beneficial effect under these conditions; you just couldn't produce axle dance or related misconduct at the back end.

Circumstances made it impossible to confirm, by timing, Rudd's claim that this 178 bhp Healey is good for approximately 130 mph. On Britain's one and only motorway, the much-publicized M1, full-stick in overdrive top produced a fast and rather noisy rush to the equivalent of an indicated 126 mph on a speedometer that was actually calibrated to only 120. M1 being designed as a series of gently merging curves rather than linked straights, and our fellow travelers being seemingly in concerted rebellion against lane discipline, we never did hold the pedal against the floor until the needle's movement finally desisted.

Leaving out bottom and overdrive top gears, the mathematical equivalents to 6000 rpm on the remaining four ratios are 64 mph in second, 92 in third, 119 in overdrive third, 123 in normal top, and we repeatedly ran her up to the 6000 mark on each of these gears. If the C-series engine suffered any pain in the course of these exertions, it didn't let on, except maybe once, when we inadvertently went a shade past 6000 in second and floating valves yammered a word of warning. This particular engine, Mr. Rudd told us, had been run at 5500 rpm for three hours in a row on the bench, with no resulting valve stretch or other measurable ill effect.

SMOOTH UNDER THE HOOD

In what might be considered the problematical sector of the rpm range, between 5250 (where the tach is redlined on standard 3000's) and 6000 per minute, this engine isn't a degree less smooth than at more habitual turnovers. Whizzing around at its Ruddspeed peak, it merely produces more din from two sources, exhaust and fan. The latter, we were told, is dispensable under virtually any conditions except stop-start running in city traffic and summer temperatures.

With the top up — which is how we had it all the time, to keep the English Winter out and in the belief it would cut drag — noise from the twin-pipe exhaust system seemed moderate up to 4000 or so and thereafter increasingly immoderate. To bystanding ears, immoderacy sets in earlier.

MILEAGE IN A MALE CAR

We used two different fuels, both of them putatively 100 octane, in the A-H; on one of them the engine knocked moderately but distinctly without much provocation, on the other it never did. Average consumption, excluding the acceleration timings but otherwise missing few opportunities for using the full performance, was 15.4 miles per U.S. gallon. The oil thermometer, one of Rudd's two instrument options, is graduated to 230° F and redlined at 212. The highest reading we saw, right after the acceleration timings, was around 180 degrees.

The test car had the suspension and brake modifications listed earlier, and if we were buying a 3000 there isn't one we'd voluntarily forego. Good as the braking is on the standard car, the servo improves it, cutting pedal pressures wholesale without any loss of sensitivity.

On good surfaces, the balance and feel of the car didn't appear to be altered one way or the other by the non-standard suspension features. The overall effect of the competition dampers at the front and modified spring rates at both ends was to subdue cornering roll very markedly. Naturally, a fairly considerable loss of riding comfort is involved, particularly at low speeds and on bad surfaces, and in time, we suspect, this might have an indirect payoff by breeding body rattles and creaks. But Rudd is advisedly catering for a clientele that's male in the wider sense of the word, and specially for males who rate the delights of competition and really fast highway travel above self-featherbedding. —DM

PUT YOUR FOOT DOWN—AND LIVE!

The new Austin Healey '3000' is for those who love the feel of the sun and the wind. This car is alive. It responds in a flash. Accelerates with surging power. Corners like a polo pony. Disc brakes for sure, straight-line stops. It's the fabulous successor to the famous Austin Healey 100-Six which has dominated competition in its class. Top speed, a breathtaking 115 m.p.h. It's built for the track, yet takes to pleasure driving beautifully. For as low as $3051 p.o.e. (2- or 4-seater).

FACTS FOR THE SPORTS CAR CONNOISSEUR: 1. A 2912 cc engine with twin carburetors. 130 b.h.p. at 4750 r.p.m. 2. DISC BRAKES on front wheels for smooth, straight-line stops even at racing speeds. 3. GEARBOX. 4-speeds (6 with overdrive). Synchromesh on 2nd, 3rd, and top speeds. 4. INDEPENDENT FRONT SUSPENSION, with hydraulic shock absorbers and stabilizing bar; semi-elliptic leaf spring rear suspension, with hydraulic shock absorbers and panhard rod. 5. BODY. Steel/aluminum, adjustable bucket seats trimmed in leather. 6. AVAILABLE in either 2- or 4-seater, standard or deluxe models; detachable hardtop optional.

A product of THE BRITISH MOTOR CORPORATION LTD., makers of Austin Healey, Austin, MG, Magnette, Morris and Riley cars. Represented in the United States by Hambro Automotive Corp., Dept. 7, 27 W. 57th St., New York 19, N.Y. Sold and serviced in North America by over 1000 distributors and dealers.

Austin-
HEALEY

3000

Road Test

For the true dyed-in-the-wool motoring enthusiast of the old school, the three-liter Austin-Healey has preserved all of the sports car qualities once associated with the goggle-wearing, scarf-trailing-in-the-wind driver who likes to imagine he is Nuvolari while driving to the market.

A high-revving six-cylinder engine of nearly 178-cubic-inch displacement and a muffler that lets you know the engine is turning are great contributors to making the most of the Healey's low-speed torque. With two persons aboard it leaves a nice pair of rubber streaks while digging out, but from there on the wind buffeting and exhaust noise give the impression of a great deal more acceleration than 0-60 mph in 12.5 seconds.

Under the hood, which has twin safety catches and a metal rod to hold it open, is a snug-fitting, big by small-car standards, in-line ohv six, with twin side-draft SU carburetors angle-mounted to a six-port cast aluminum log-type intake manifold. These carburetors have jet-adjusting screws instead of the old-style nuts underneath and can be easily set with a screw driver. The latest models are coming through with thermo-electric chokes eliminating manual control for cold starts. On the other side, plugs are a cinch and the uncluttered valve cover requires only the removal of breather pipe and securing nuts to allow valve rocker adjustment. Distributor points can be set easily as they are in a

RUGGED BRITISH CONSTRUCTION AND A 3-LITER POWER-PLANT PRESERVE THE TRUE SPORTS CAR TRADITION

od location for two-handed use of eler gauge and screw driver, and e advance adjustment is by knurled ob and vernier scale.

The Healey, like many other Engh makes, is designed for easy, rmal maintenance by the owner ho can make the regularly required ljustments without a set of master echanics' tools, a grease rack, or pair of grimy coveralls. While oil vel check of the differential does quire jacking or crawling under, e transmission has a dipstick under e bell housing tunnel floor covering, d the brake fluid reservoir is as sy to fill as the radiator. More bitious owners might even tackle

relining the slip-in pad-type Girling disc brakes supplied as standard on the front wheels. Rear brakes are also Girling but are conventional 11-inch diameter by 2¼-inch-wide drums. Combined with the discs in the front, they provide consistent fade-free stopping for the Healey's dry weight of 2393 pounds.

The Healey 3000 is a real compact package, with a minimum of excess space, and the nomenclature, "occasional four-seater," does not really apply to four adults, no matter how occasional or brief the ride might be. Twin bucket seats for driver and passenger have good contours for comfort on easy-sliding tracks that

give full adjustment range for the short- or long-legged; but the two upholstered indentations behind them are a side-saddle, leg-cramping ride for one adult, only adequate for two pre-teen children.

Further compactness will be noticed when stowing luggage, as the rear compartment houses a 12-volt battery, spare tire and tools, the tonneau cover and removable side windows, leaving room only for small bags or parcels. In lieu of badly needed windwings of some sort to keep side air from screaming around the edge of the windshield and into one's ear, the sliding-pane, aluminum-framed side windows provide a great deal of comfort for highway cruising without destroying the pleasure of top-down driving. Besides, a lot of luggage space is gained in the rear compartment when it is not occupied with these side windows, and this combined with space under the tonneau in the "occasional" seat provides room enough for the baggage neeeds of two persons for week-long trips.

For the pure enthusiast, the Healey 3000 is an exciting cross-country touring car. Good passing power, open-air cockpit, a handy center-position stick shift, bucket seats and a great big tachometer endow it with the sports car "basics."

An electric-control overdrive, with switch conveniently located on the dash just under the right fingers as they rest on the steering wheel, is one of the finest "extra gear" units we have used in a long time. While made to give more miles per hour per thousand rpm's at cruising speeds in 3rd or 4th gear, the overdrive switch can be manipulated to provide two 3rd-gear and two 4th-gear ratios. In conventional 3rd, for example, a flip of the control switch changes the ratio from 14.47 mph per thousand rpm's to 17.65 mph per thousand. In 4th it jumps from 18.94 mph to 23.1 mph. The change is smooth and noiseless and requires no clutching or reaching for inaccessible knobs. It also saves a lot of unnecessary downshifts, especially in top gear, as a flick of the switch and slight throttle pressure produce an instant downshift for lower traffic speeds or passing acceleration. Rear-axle ratio furnished with overdrive is 3.91-to-1, as compared to the higher 3.54-to-1 for conventional transmissions. The lower ratios allow lugging down when not in overdrive and there is no trouble pulling out from 15 mph in top gear without a protest from the engine.

Premium fuel is recommended with the 9.03-to-1 compression ratio, although we did try a tank of regular grade for one stretch of highway cruising and found it was adequate for this purpose without changing the timing. While it is possible to make the engine ping at low speeds on this grade of fuel, we kept the rpm's high enough to avoid this condition and logged just about the same mpg highway mileage as with the premium-grade fuel over similar stretches of road.

STURDY aluminum-framed side windows have one fixed and one sliding clear plastic panel, fit well at top and sides and seal along lower edge with rubber strip. Generous chrome-plated wing nuts ease fastening to threaded studs front and rear on door panel. A vinyl case is provided to protect them when not in use but stowage is a problem in luggage area.

Fuel consumption of the three-liter Healey test car was not exactly in the compact-car class. The overdrive unit does save gasoline over long hauls where there is a chance to take advantage of higher cruising gear ratios, but normal driving conditions using minimum downshifts and staying on freeways as much as possible produced a rather disappointing 15.4 mpg, while road averages for 150-mile trips averaged 17.1 mpg. The red line of 5250 rpm's was never violated either through the gears in traffic or during acceleration test runs at the drag strip.

Healey suspension is on the firm side, and anything but smooth pavement is apt to annoy any but the real enthusiast. While the bucket seats give good support and legroom is generous, the firm ride and poorly ventilated area for the feet on either side of a rather generous bell housing and transmission hump are uncomfortable, and we were happy for the frequent stops we made to photograph or just plain cool off. *continued*

SEPARATE BOW (below) snaps into pocket of tonneau cover, prevents sagging. Flexible steel stays in rear section keep cover taut and wrinkle-free. In lower photos, folding tubular steel top bow fit into sockets in car body, fold to nest with vinyl top in neat compartment behind occasional seats. Full weather protection is provided. Top can be erected or removed by one person but the job is easier and quicker with an assistant.

GOOD LOW-END TORQUE OF HEALEY'S 6-CYL. ENGINE PROVIDES ENOUGH POWER TO SPIN THE WHEELS ON STANDING-START ACCELERATION.

Solid springing does not, however, endow the car with any superior handling qualities under hard cornering conditions. Despite a front stabilizer arm and a panhard rod in the rear, there is a pronounced sag of the outside rear end that seems to want to lift the diagonally opposite front wheel off the ground. Steering is positive under hard cornering, and control is easy to maintain but we made a special point to watch car attitude of stock production class Healeys in recent road races and observed the same tendency of the loaded rear corner to lean heavily while taking sharp bends at speed. Much of this leaning can be reduced by a heavier stabilizer arm such as used in the Sebring cars, and those who like to drive high-performance machinery on winding mountain roads such as we do would appreciate less tendency for the loaded rear wheel to feel as though a load of sandbags in the luggage compartment suddenly shifted to the outside of the curve.

Also observed at road races was the extreme ruggedness of the Healey. Pounding lap after lap on some of the rougher West Coast courses and at Sebring, the Healeys survived where more expensive machinery gave up with suspension and chassis components cracked or broken. It is not likely that even under the roughest treatment, the average driver will ever subject his car to the rigors of road racing, but it is nice to know that the car you own and drive was developed through tests of this kind.

As we have said, the creature comforts are a little on the severe side, but foul weather protection is not only adequate, it is attractive. A well-fitting vinyl top conforms well to the low-

REAR LUGGAGE compartment has limited space for baggage, as it houses spare tire, tools, 12-volt battery with acid-proof cover.

GIRLING disc brakes used on front wheels are easily serviced, adjust automatically.

THE HEALEY'S COCKPIT has all the niceties enjoyed by sportscar enthusiasts. Wheel has sliding adjustment, bucket seats are comfortable and well supporting, center stick shift is convenient, instrumentation is complete, and visibility is excellent.

"OCCASIONAL" seating for extra passenger is great for kids but is limited to one adult with legs extended over driveshaft tunnel. Top must be down as passengers' heads extend well above windshield level.

slung lines of the car, fits well around side windows, and seals perfectly with an overlapping lip on top of the windshield frame. Sliding plastic panes in the side windows allow added ventilation and provide enough room for hand signaling. It is difficult to design a pleasing top that stows in a small space without making some sacrifices. The Healey top does require time and care to raise or stow. Folding metal frame bows are separate from the top material itself and are best erected with the aid of two persons, especially in fitting the leading edge over the windshield lip.

For those who desire the cozy comfort of a coupe, there is an optional hard top with large rear window that really improves the appearance and comfort of the Healey.

While millions of car owners have gone the way of very high horsepower, arm-chair luxury and comfort, air conditioning, and huge barges 18 feet long, there is still a car for the enthusiast . . . the Austin-Healey 3000.　**—Charles Evans**

EXTRA-COST factory option hard top is well worth the price, as it provides snug and stylish comfort of a coupe, yet is quickly removable. Several American top makers offer fiberglass models to fit the Healey.

AUSTIN-HEALEY 3000
2-seater and occasional 4-seater

OPTIONS ON CAR TESTED: Overdrive, heater, wire knock-on wheels

ODOMETER READING AT START OF TEST: 8444 miles

RECOMMENDED ENGINE RED LINE: 5250 rpm

PERFORMANCE

ACCELERATION (2 aboard):

0-30 mph	4.2 secs.
0-45 mph	7.9
0-60 mph	12.4

Standing start ¼-mile . . . . 18.3 secs. & 73 mph

Speeds in gears @ 5250 rpm

1st	30 mph
2nd	46
3rd	75
4th	98

Speedometer Error on Test Car

Speedometer reading	34	48	55	65	75	85
Weston electric speedometer	30	45	50	60	70	80

Miles per hour per 1000 rpm in top gear (Tires 5.90 x 15)
18.94 mph . . . (Overdrive — 23.1 mph)

Stopping Distances: from 30 mph, 63 ft. — from 60 mph, 170 ft.

SPECIFICATIONS FROM MANUFACTURER

Engine
6-cylinder, in-line ohv
Bore: 3.282 ins. Stroke: 3.5 ins.
Displacement: 177.7 cu. ins.
Compression ratio: 9.03:1
Horsepower: 130 @ 4750 rpm
Ignition: 12-volt battery/coil

Gearbox
Manual 4-speed (synchro in top 3 gears); floor stick

Driveshaft
Open. Needle roller bearing U-joints

Differential
Conventional ring and pinion
Standard ratio 3.54:1
Overdrive ratio 3.91:1

Suspension
Front: Independent wishbones, coil springs, hydraulic lever-type shocks, stabilizer bar.
Rear: Semi-elliptic leaf springs, solid axle, hydraulic lever-type shocks, panhard rod

Wheels and tires
15-in. ventilated steel discs
15-in. knock-on wire spoke (optional)
5.90 x 15 in. Dunlop Road Speed tires

Brakes
Girling hydraulics
Front: 11¼-in. discs
Rear: 11-in. diameter x 2¼-in. wide drums

Body and frame
Heavy box-section frame, with aluminum and steel "roadster" body. Wheelbase 92 in.
Track, front 48¾ in., rear 50 in.
Overall length 157½ in.
Dry weight 2393 lbs.

The author and Bill Shepherd in their Austin-Healey 3000 on a typical loose Alpine col. Under these conditions crews have to average no less than 38 m.p.h.

Clean Sweep

by John Gott

With the outright BMC victory in the Liège–Rome–Liège Rally still very much in mind, the BMC Team Captain looks back to the 'Alpine' which preceded it, in which the Austin-Healey 3000s won every class and team award open to them

THE B.M.C. Competitions Department always supports the Coupe des Alpes (better known, perhaps, as the 'Alpine') in strength. Not only is it one of the top rallies, but it is a driver's event in which luck plays little part in the results and consequently much can be learnt about the mechanical weaknesses of the competing cars. This latter factor is, of course, one of the chief reasons why go-ahead manufacturers enter works cars in rallies; it is far better that a works driver should break down on some inaccessible mountain-top and point out the reason, which can then be put right, than that John Motorist should do so on his Continental tour.

As far as mechanical stress was concerned, the 1960 'Alpine' was one of the toughest of recent years. The course was the usual 2000-mile 'figure-of-eight' from Marseilles to Cannes via Monza, but it had only one night stop (at Chamonix) instead of the usual three, whilst the average speed was increased and the sections shortened. The Automobile Club de Marseille et Provence also reverted to a scheme they used some

years ago whereby the fastest car in the class set the 'bogey' time in the tests and any car was penalised if outside 5 per cent. of that time, and/or not within 10 and 7 per cent. of the times of the fastest cars in the Touring and G.T. Categories respectively. This meant, of course, that it was risky not to drive the tests 'flat', so that the cars got little respite.

It also called for much hard thinking by Marcus Chambers and myself as to the best cars to use, and the degree of tune for them. Eventually we concluded that, as an Austin-Healey '3000' had been 8th in the Tulip, 4th in the R.A.C. and 2nd in the Deutschland (with the class wins as a matter of course), it was about ripe for an outright win, although we appreciated that the 'Alpine' competition would be much tougher than in any of the other three events. Four '3000's were accordingly prepared with the emphasis on maximum performance, by the use of modified heads and manifolds with three S.U. carburetters. This naturally entailed a considerable 'calculated risk'. It is not too difficult

considerably to increase engine output, but only actual experience can show whether the other components will stand up to the increased strain. That we were going to find out!

The cars, incidentally, were two of last year's team and two new 1960 models; being a sentimentalist where cars are concerned, I was delighted to have the car which I had used in 1959 to finish 2nd in class and 7th in G.T. category.

To back up the Austin-Healey striking force there were three Mini-Minors and two Sprites. The Minis were driven by Gold/Hughes, Pitts/Ambrose and Jones/James, whilst the Sprites were handled by Tommy Wisdom/Jack Hay and John Sprinzel/Stuart Turner.

The '3000' crews were Pat Moss/Ann Wisdom, who are not only the fastest lady drivers in the game but are more than able to see off mere males, the Tulip-winning Morley twins, who have taken to the big Austin-Healey like ducks to water (they were 4th in the R.A.C. on their first outing in one), myself with Bill Shepherd (who had won a Coupe on a Healey in 1958), and Ronnie Adams with John Williamson, who had been Bill's partner in 1958. Ronnie was new to Healeys, but he is very experienced and won the 'Monte' in 1956. The 'Alpine', however, has not been his luckiest event, and 1960 was to prove no exception.

TOUGH OPPOSITION

On arrival at Marseilles we found that we were going to be up against some very tough opposition. There were full works teams from Citroën, Ford, Sunbeam, Triumph and Volvo, with works-prepared teams from Jaguar, Porsche and Renault. Even more formidable was the Alfa Romeo team on special S.S. Giuliettas, prepared and looked after by Conrero himself. And in case the works teams didn't keep us busy enough, there was a 250GT Ferrari to deal with. Another big headache was the Ford team, manned by the redoubtable Harrison family, Gerry Burgess, Anne Hall and Vic Preston, a Safari winner. These cars turned out to have three-carburetter, light alloy heads, disc brakes, gearboxes with overdrives giving five forward speeds, and much lightened coachwork; their b.h.p. was reputed to be 152, and they performed as though that estimate were about right.

The quality of the crews was as high as that of the cars. In addition to Britain's top rally drivers, the Continental rally stars were there in force. Amongst other famous names, France was represented by Paul Coltelloni and Annie Soisbault, reigning European Rally Champions, backed up by Roger de Lageneste, Henri Oreiller, Robert Buchet and José Behra (Jean's brother); Sweden had Ewy Rosqvist, the 1959 European co-champion, Gunnar Andersson, the 1958 Champion, and Erik Carlsson, the 1959 runner-up. Schock and Moll had entered, but they had so great a lead in the Championship that Mercedes had scratched them; however, they left in Bohringer and Socher, who had been second in the 'Monte'. Drivers of this calibre are only interested in cars and crews which, they think, have a good chance. At scrutineering we were therefore gratified to note their keen interest in our cars, but rather amused by their shrewd questions, designed to elicit details of the cars' performance and of our tactics.

These were, in fact, largely left to individual crews. At our final team conference where the route, the passes, the tests, the weather, the schedule and the opposition was carefully evaluated—we reckoned the Alfas and the Porsches were liable to give

Pat Moss and Ann Wisdom exuberantly collected together all the trophies won by the Austin-Healey team in the 'Alpine' and posed with them displayed on the dusty bonnet of their car

us the most trouble—Marcus had succinctly summed up by saying, 'We're here to win everything we can. You are all experienced enough to know how to do that without blowing up or crashing your cars. Good luck to us all'.

This gave us all a pretty free hand, and, at our private crew conference the night before the start, Bill and I decided that the rally would be won and lost on the Quatre Chemins section in the last 100 miles. We planned our drive, therefore, to make each section and test 'clean' by the barest margin, so that car and crew would be in as good a trim as possible for this all-important stage.

THE FIRST TEST

That others hadn't got quite the same plan of campaign was proved next morning. Within 20 miles of the start came the first test, a twisting 5¼-mile climb on the Col Ste. Beaume. The record (by a single-seater racing car) is 8 min. 15.2 sec. Oreiller's Alfa (a rally car, be it remembered) did 8 min. 17 sec., followed by our Miss Moss in 8 min. 27 sec. This blistering pace penalised all the cars in our class except the Austin-Healeys and the Ferrari, and obviously was a severe shock to the Ford team; more particularly to Edward Harrison, who was hoping for that coveted trophy, a Gold Coupe, awarded for unpenalised runs in three consecutive years. It was a little galling to be penalised within 20 miles, for, although the penalisation would be finally calculated upon the total times in all tests, the first climb is always a pointer to the ways things are likely to go.

The Ste. Beaume results were confirmed by the next test, 13½ miles on Mont Ventoux, one of the European Hill-Climb Championship courses. Having made second F.T.D. last year, I was pleased to return a time well below last year's F.T.D.— but that wasn't fast enough for 1960. Oreiller made F.T.D., and this time his Alfa team-mate, Roger de Lageneste, and the Ferrari managed to beat Miss Moss, but no other mere male could manage it. Oreiller's *average* for the climb to 6000 feet was, incidentally, just under 60 m.p.h., and on the lower stretches the Austin-Healeys were doing around 110 m.p.h.

So far it seemed as though the A.C.M.P. had adopted the Tour de France scheme of a leisurely tour from test to test, with the emphasis upon speed rather than reliability. The run to the Italian frontier at Mont Genèvre was, however, a really tough stage in the old 'Alpine' tradition; i.e., some very tight sections over poor road surfaces. The climb at dusk up and over the Col de Menée was particularly difficult, as it was only 28 km. (16½ miles) long, of which five kilometres were appallingly rough. This penalised most of the small cars, and, not long after, Les Leston slid off the road. As Slotemaker had earlier retired with axle trouble, the formidable Triumph team was no longer a threat.

Trouble, however, wasn't to be confined to the Triumph team. Apart from a tyre burst when the Morleys hit a rock which had rolled into their path on Mont Ventoux, the Austin-Healeys had been running like clockwork. But at the Mont Genèvre control the Morleys came in to report that they had lost third gear. This was dealt with by converting their gearbox to overdrive on all gears, which gave them overdrive second to replace the lost third gear. The conversion throws a terrific strain on the gearbox and is only to be recommended

39

as a temporary expedient—but they had 1500 tough miles to go. No sooner was this crisis dealt with than Ronnie came in to report that he had lost all gears except bottom and top. This meant his retirement, for although the car could be driven back to Cannes in this state, it could never have got over the passes ahead. Never before in either the 'Alpine' or Liège-Rome-Liège had we had gearbox trouble, but it was now obvious that the increased b.h.p. was proving too much for the old gearboxes. We had, of course, fulfilled one branch of our assignment (*i.e.*, trouble-shooting), but we hadn't expected trouble to strike quite as soon as this. Although we did our best to hide it from the other équipes, there was some gloom in the Healey team, and Bill and I spent the next few hours imagining noises in our own gearbox!

A HIGH-SPEED DEMONSTRATION

This gloom was somewhat dispelled by the test at Monza, where, in groups of ten, the cars had to cover four timed laps on the road circuit, of which the fastest alone counted. The Austin-Healeys being in the last group, we knew what we had to beat before going on the track. Oreiller had done just under 2 min. 17 sec. and the Ferrari 2 min. 20 sec. As the fastest Austin-Healey lap to date was 2 min. 19 sec. by Jack Sears, Marcus felt that 2 min. 20 sec. would be fair enough. We had other ideas, however. The three red Austin-Healeys streaked round in line ahead, opening out on the second lap to keep out of each others' way and closing in again on the last lap to finish in line astern. Pat did just under 2 min. 15 sec., Donald Morley did 2 min. 16 sec., and I did 2 min. 17 sec. Pat's average speed was just under

95 m.p.h., and all the Healeys were touching just on 122 m.p.h. by rev. counter on each straight. This high-speed demonstration put us in tearing spirits for the infamous Vivione and Gavia.

In fact, we managed these without undue difficulty. On the Vivione all three Healeys caught the Ferrari, which had started 2 minutes ahead of the Morleys. The Swiss Ferrari crew were real sportsmen, for they pulled right over to let us all past and, at the start of the Gavia, offered to leave a minute after the girls (and so lose 60 marks) to avoid holding them up. Needless to say, the girls did not accept this offer, but the Ferrari stopped to let them past as soon as the Austin-Healey hove in sight. We were all delighted to see these great sportsmen do so well later in the Six-Hour G.T. race at Clermont Ferrand.

The rest of the stage to Chamonix, apart from the passage of the Grand St. Bernard in cloud, was tiring rather than difficult motoring, so we managed to make up enough time to have a quick lunch and a refreshing swim in the lake at Lecco. The cars were not neglected either; they were carefully checked over and found to be in good fettle, whilst the tyres were changed as a precaution, for the run to Cannes was going to be very hard on them.

That night the rally hotel in Chamonix was a miniature Tower of Babel, with crews recounting their experiences in six languages. Good stories were rife, and I particularly liked the one about the small Italian boys who urged a rally car to go faster, only to turn as white as sheets and fall backwards over a wall when the car's tail slid viciously as the driver responded too enthusiastically to their urgings. Marcus capped this by recounting how he had come

into an Italian village to be cheered by the villagers on sighting his Rally Service plate, but booed on exit because he didn't drift the bend and was only doing about 70 m.p.h. The Italians like drivers to go fast!

From what we could learn over a Dubonnet, the Austin-Healeys didn't seem to be doing too badly, and Bill and I retired fairly satisfied for eleven hours' solid sleep.

LEADING OUR CLASS

The official results issued on the following morning showed that the team was doing better than we had thought. Of the 66 crews which had started from Marseilles, 49 had reached Chamonix, of whom 23 were unpenalised; of these latter only 15 had managed to keep within the test percentage. Included amongst these were the Austin-Healeys, which were 1, 2 and 3 in their class, whilst the girls were second to Oreiller/Masoero in the G.T. category. As far as the team awards were concerned only the Healeys and the Citroëns were unpenalised, whilst Alfa, Jaguar, Porsche, Volvo and Triumph no longer had full teams.

It is perhaps superfluous to add that our girls were firmly in command of the Ladies' Section, in which Anne Hall (accident) and Annie Soisbault (wheel off) had retired.

I have done every 'Alpine' since 1947 but cannot remember a harder run-in than the 1960 one. We started in brilliant sunshine to tackle the twisty 4000-foot cols around the Lake of Annecy, and at dawn were up in the high Alps around Briançon. The 8000-foot Galibier was particularly tricky, as the upper hairpins glittered with ice, and we saw from marks on the rocks that more than one driver had 'lost' it. Throughout that gruelling night we had passed cars whose rally was run, either from accident or mechanical failure, but the Austin-Healeys rumbled tirelessly on. Then, on the 7300-foot Allos, trouble hit us. On the way up we passed Rupert Jones standing dejectedly by his Mini-Minor, which had obviously come off second-best in an argument with a rock. Worse still, at the control at the foot we saw what we had been subconsciously expecting for some time—the Morley's car having difficulty in getting away. Bill and I ran up to hear that they only had top gear left. Fortunately they were over the steepest passes, but they had 200 miles to go and the Quatre Chemins still to come. Giving them a shove off, we took up station astern to make sure that

CONTINUED ON PAGE 7

A Very Hot Healey

THE energies of the majority of speed-shop proprietors are directed towards extracting high b.h.p. figures from small displacement engines, with the idea of turning Britain's small saloons into "Q" cars capable of vanquishing their larger brothers. Just occasionally a tuner will attempt to extract even more horse-power from an engine which is already extremely powerful in standard form. Such a man is Ken Rudd, well known for his activities with the A.C. Ace, who in more recent times has turned his attention to tuning the Austin Healey 3000 at his garage in Worthing High Street.

The power unit of the latest Healey is the six-cylinder B.M.C. "C" series engine, which in its Healey form delivered from the factory gives 124 b.h.p. (net). This provides the 3000 with a top speed of around 112 m.p.h. and pretty exciting acceleration to match, bearing in mind the humble parentage of the engine. But when Ken Rudd has finished with the car it is transformed into a really fast machine with a top speed approaching 125 m.p.h. and quite staggering acceleration.

Only three major engine modifications are made, the whole lot costing a modest £86 (well, modest to anyone who can afford £1,168 for the car in standard form). For a start, the cylinder head is machined to give a compression ratio of 9.7 : 1, the ports and combustion chambers are machined and polished, and the valve seats are modified. All this costs £25 complete with new gaskets. A high-lift camshaft can be obtained for £25 and for a further £36 one can have a triple carburetter manifold and a third S.U. carburetter complete with linkages, which helps the Austin engine to breathe very deeply indeed.

It is, however, no secret that the ride and cornering characteristics of the big Healey are not the best in the world, and with this engine conversion it is virtually essential to incorporate the suspension modifications offered by Ken Rudd, which include stiffer dampers and springs for the front and rear suspension at a cost of £37. A brake servo is also recommended at £19 10s.

We were recently able to borrow a demonstration car from Ken Rudd for an extended test to see for ourselves just how good the performance was. Our first impression on taking over the car in London traffic was that we were in for a tough time, as the needle of the water-temperature gauge was already on 190°F. and the cockpit

POWER HOUSE.— *Ken Rudd's modifications include the fitting of a third carburetter while several other important changes are hidden from view. This unit can be tuned to give 185 b.h.p.*

was pretty hot. However, trickling out of the City in the rush hour we found that this was a very docile monster which would burble along in top gear at 20 m.p.h. if necessary with the temperature needle never going above 190°F. Despite liberal usage of asbestos around the bulkhead and cooling slots in the body sides, the interior became rather hot and the Smiths heater will probably never be called into use.

Out on the open road (or what's left of it) the Healey began to show its true character. The acceleration was quite prodigious, allowing queues of "mimsers" to be passed in a flash and an indicated 100 m.p.h. to be seen on quite short stretches of straight road. The gearbox has rather a slow change which if hurried produces audible protest from the gears. The lever has been slightly lengthened and combined with a general loosening up after 8,000 miles the gearbox on the test car was somewhat more pleasant to use than those on new cars we have tried. The accelerator has also been modified so that the inch or so of free play which becomes so annoying on the standard product is not now apparent.

Quite high average speeds can be made on cross-country journeys merely by using the impressive acceleration and top speed. On a journey to Silverstone the speedometer needle went off the clock along the new Missenden By-Pass, and since the figures finish at 120 m.p.h. this can be considered as quite impressive! It must be mentioned that the brakes are quite capable of coping with this speed, the combination of front discs and rear drums bringing the car to rest with no sign of fade or grab. The hood should also be praised as there was no sign of flap at speeds which would have torn the hoods from many other cars.

The ride offered by this modified Healey is very firm and on bad roads the occupants are thrown about a good deal, but corners can be taken at surprisingly high speeds in spite of a good deal of pitching. Michelin "X" tyres of 6.40–15 in. size are fitted, which no doubt help to accentuate the firm ride, but on the other hand they offer excellent grip in the corners, especially when the driver imprudently depresses the accelerator pedal a little too far and the car tries to fling itself off the road. On full lock the tyres tend to foul the bodywork.

When taking performance figures the red line of the rev.-counter, set at 5,200 r.p.m., was not passed but even so the following impressive figures were taken : 0-30 m.p.h., 2.9 sec.; 0-50 m.p.h., 6 sec.; 0-60 m.p.h., 9.6 sec.; 0-80 m.p.h., 14.9 sec.; and 0-100 m.p.h., 21.8 sec.; and, in fact, a best-one-way 0-100 m.p.h. on a slight down gradient came out at 20.6 sec. No attempt was made to check maximum speed as the stretch of road the tests were carried out on was a little too short for comfort, but Ken Rudd claims 130 m.p.h., and a true 125 m.p.h. certainly looks to be quite feasible. Thus it can be seen that the Ruddspeed conversion enables the Healey to compete with other much more powerful but heavier cars such as the XK150, and only some very exotic and expensive machines have markedly superior acceleration figures. Petrol consumption varied between 16 and 19 m.p.g. according to conditions.

In its modified form the Austin Healey 3000 shows little refinement compared with say a Porsche or Jaguar, and it is undeniably a "man's car" as defined by vintage-car enthusiasts. The steering is fairly heavy, the suspension is definitely stiff, the exhaust note is on the throaty side—although not of the type to attract the attention of the law if used properly, and the gearbox needs a strong left arm, but on the basis of excitement per m.p.h. per £1 this car is undoubtedly tops.—M. L. T.

Deutschland-Rallye

The story **by Tony Ambrose** of a team effort in the International German Rally. Ecurie Safety Fast took a class one-two-three and two class seconds

THE 2nd International Deutschland Rally, held from 29 September to 1 October, gave the B.M.C. works team an opportunity to underline the list of successes recently scored in the Liège-Rome-Liège Rally. Our team entries (the only ones from Britain) consisted of Pat Moss/Ann Wisdom, David Seigle-Morris/Stuart Turner and Donald Morley/Barry Hercock, all in Austin-Healey '3000's, and Peter Riley and myself in an M.G.A. 1600. John Sprinzel was also competing, together with his sister Norma, in the Austin-Healey Sprite with which he and John Patten finished third overall in the Liège-Rome-Liège. The only other British-made car entered was the 2.6-litre Austin-Healey of Metzker and von Schulmann from Dusseldorf.

The start was at Freiburg in south-western Germany at 6 a.m. on an uninviting morning with steady rain and low cloud, providing little encouragement for the crews to leave their warm beds in the excellent Colombi Hotel, but as the rain eased the crews' enthusiasm gained strength. While the cavalcade made its way in a well-ordered procession to the foot of the Freiburg-Schauinsland hill-climb, we were able to take stock of the opposition in the three classes with which we were concerned. The big Austin-Healeys were very impressive, their twin side exhausts heralding their arrival at the foot of the hill.

STIFF OPPOSITION

Number 1 in the rally and the only other car in their class was the Mahle/Ott works Mercedes 300SL; what the class lacked in quantity was more than compensated by the quality of the entries. As expected, Mahle achieved fastest time of the rally in the first climb with a time of 9 min. 01.8 sec., followed by David Seigle-Morris with

9 min. 13.9 sec. Donald Morley did well to climb in 9 min. 32 sec. with an engine which was firing on only five cylinders, and Pat Moss's climb in 9 min. 40.6 sec. showed that the Austin-Healeys might well be a force to be reckoned with on hills where the local knowledge of the Germans was not so great.

In the class for Grand Touring cars from 1301–2000 c.c., the M.G. had for opposition a formidable array; no less than nine Porsches in various states of tune. In the Freiburg climb the M.G. was not particularly impressive, achieving eighth fastest time in 10 min. 11.8 sec. compared with the fastest Porsche Carrera's 9 min. 35.6 sec. John Sprinzel, whose Sprite was competing against a diversity of cars such as two Conrero-tuned Alfa Romeos and a D.B., climbed in 10 min. 36.4 sec. to take third place in his class.

After the climb the rally route quickly left German soil, crossing the Rhine just south of Strasbourg and passing into a complexity of narrow lanes in the Jura. This type of route suited the British crews, whose experienced navigators demonstrated to their less able Continental counterparts that 'a map is a map in any language', and a rather self-satisfied B.M.C. team arrived at Pontarlier having made light of the tricky route, while members of the Mercedes and Citröen works teams were seen to take several wrong turnings.

CROSSING THE ALPS

The rally continued at a leisurely 50 k.p.h. average, the scheduled speed for the entire route, heading south for Annecy where a half-hour stop was allowed, during which the sun came out and revealed the beauties of early autumn in Haute Savoie in their full splendour. As dusk fell the cars approached the control at St. Etienne

en-Devulay which was the start of the first potentially difficult section. This was of 140 kilometres, embracing the Col du Glandon, Col de Croix de Fer, Col de Telegraphe and Col du Galibier, with the final control at the Col de Lauteret. The first two cols, in typical Alpine Rally terrain, are known to British competitors as 'Hellfire Loop', but on dry roads a 50 k.p.h. average was well within the capabilities of our contingent. Rumours of snow and ice on the upper reaches of the Galibier (8,300 ft.) were not without foundation, we found, but most crews had sufficient time in hand to treat the icy roads with respect and still avoid penalties.

The rest of the night was spent in some fairly hectic motoring taking in such famed Cols as the Izoard, Cayolle, Allos and Noyer. It was on the Cayolle that electrical troubles beset two of our cars, the Seigle-Morris/Turner Austin-Healey and our M.G., and in each case as headlights began to fail the cars tagged on to the most convenient competitor in order to get a 'tow'.

HEALEY SANDWICH

David Seigle-Morris was able to choose Pat Moss's similar car, but Peter Riley and I had to make do with the Porsche Super 90 of Heyse/Schuler. At the control at Annot, just before the Col d'Allos, it was necessary for us to leave before the Porsche, and, in the light of the last glimmer from its battery, the M.G. was hurled up the slopes in pursuit of the Austin-Healeys. Owing to an error in the distance quoted on the route card for this section, it was obvious that a true average of about 54 k.p.h. was needed to avoid penalty. By half-distance, however, we had caught the Austin-Healeys, and the rest of the journey to the summit was achieved by sandwiching

David Seigle-Morris and Stuart Turner move up for a close look, as the Morley twins try to overtake a low-flying cow on a twisty section of the route

Photos by Stuart Turner

the two blind mice between the two far-seeing Healeys.

The run down to the control on the far side of the pass was taken in leisurely fashion, as by this time the entire team was well ahead of schedule. Unfortunately for us, the results of this section, on which about half the entry was late, were not taken into consideration in calculating the final results due to the error in the distance.

Dawn once more brought heavy rain and low cloud. At one point, where the route had been diverted due to a landslide, we had to cross a raging torrent flowing over a recently bull-dozed dirt track. By the time John Sprinzel's Sprite reached this the flow of water had increased, and, as the Sprite was negotiating the river (passing a Citröen which had stalled its engine) it was lifted clear of the road by the current and only rescued by the manhandling of generous fellow-competitors. It was here, also, that the German-entered Austin-Healey was retired with a damaged sump.

By mid-morning on the second day the cars had reached Mont Ventoux for the second speed hill-climb. Unfortunately only the lower eight kilometres were free from cloud, and many performances were spoilt by minor excursions from the road. The first of these was made by Mahle/Ott (300SL Mercedes), whose excursion into the shale allowed the Morley/Hercock Austin-Healey to take first place with a climb of 16 min. 5 sec.—six seconds faster than the Mercedes. Seigle-Morris climbed in 16 min. 15.4 sec., and Pat Moss in 17 min. 0.4 sec. after going a short distance up a wrong fork in the cloud. Our M.G. achieved 18 min. 12.2 sec., which was fourth fastest in the class.

A short section on narrow roads taking in a difficult new pass, the Col. de Pennes,

which will surely be used again by other organisers, brought competitors to the foot of the Col de Rousset for the third timed climb. The three Austin-Healeys and the Mercedes were remarkably consistent in their performance here, less than 1 per cent. separating the fastest, Mahle/Ott, from the slowest.

FASTEST IN THE CLASS

As soon as the cars reached the northern slopes the light rain which had been falling steadily turned to a torrential downpour, causing the mountainsides to ooze brown liquid mud which flowed across the road in waves of slime. There was considerable speculation on whether the fourth speed test on the St. Jean 'circuit' would be held in such conditions, but fortunately the course for this special stage was sheltered from the full force of the storm. This stage was a very severe test of a driver's ability

to handle his car under appalling weather conditions and it is pleasing to note that the Austin-Healeys were all faster than the Mercedes by more than 10 per cent. And our trusty M.G., I'm glad to say, also put up a pretty remarkable performance, for we beat the fastest of the Porsches by 45 sec.

The competitors then made their way across country on minor roads to Char-bonnières, just west of Lyon. Navigation was tricky and not helped by floods and fog. Again many of the Continentals showed their fear of navigational sections by choosing to use main roads, risking fear of elimination for missing a secret control; they were either very lucky or extremely well-informed, as no check was established. However, on this section the Nyffeler/ Lambart Porsche made a navigational error, losing six minutes and allowing our M.G. to climb to second place in the class. After a three-hour rest at Charbonnières, competitors were routed across country via St. Claude and Pontarlier and then were made to follow, in the opposite direction, the route from the Rhine used on the outward journey.

Arrival at the attractive spa of Baden-Baden revealed success yet again for *Ecurie Safety Fast*. The Austin-Healey '3000's of Seigle-Morris/Turner, Morley/ Hercock and Pat Moss/Ann Wisdom took the first three places in their class in that order. With the M.G., Peter Riley and I retained second place in the 2-litre class, to the embarrassment of a whole bevy of Porsche drivers, and the Sprinzels' Sprite was also second in its class (which included cars of up to 1300 c.c.), underlining very firmly its recent third place in the Liège-Rome-Liège.

The three Austin-Healeys in procession through a German village, with the population out to watch – or at least the junior element !

Our test car was by no means new. In this photograph it is climbing the Gavia pass in the 1959 Liège-Rome-Liège Rally wearing extra lights but no bumpers.

Policeman's

Getting the Measure of a Works Austin-Healey Rally Car

WATCHING the works Austin-Healeys motoring spectacularly fast on the soaking Brands Hatch circuit at the end of the R.A.C. Rally aroused our curiosity about the development that has made these three-litre machines into such formidable G.T. cars during the past two rally seasons. Mentioning only a few highlights, the Pat Moss/Ann Wisdom team followed up their 2nd place in the 1960 Alpine with an outright win in the Liège-Rome-Liège; in both events the Healeys took the team prize as they did in the recent R.A.C. Rally in which the Morley brothers finished 3rd and the Riley/Ambrose crew 11th.

On the whole, successful competition people are a disillusioned lot, given more to sorrow over the failings of their motorcars than to recognition of any virtues, and it was rather impressive, therefore, to find amongst the team members a genuine respect and admiration for the cars, a feeling that their performance was a match for any G.T. car competing in rallies and their durability much greater than most.

The season having finished, most of the cars had been sold, but we were fortunate to be able to borrow the one with which John Gott (now Chief Constable of Northamptonshire) and Rupert Jones finished 10th in the Liège-Rome-Liège. This car, with a long history of events in 1959 as well as in 1960, was being rebuilt for sale to John Gott, and some of the special rally fittings had been removed, including the usual row of auxiliary lamps. An ordinary boot lid was fitted instead of the special one which allows two spare wheels to be carried for certain events, and a plain bonnet replaced the one with large louvres in the top. The latter proved rather a disappointment anyway, as the openings turned out to be in a high-pressure region and, instead of the hot under-bonnet air emerging through them, the flow was in the opposite direction. As on the ordinary production car, bonnet, boot lid and wings are all made of steel, and the fairly small remaining area of the "top deck" of the body is aluminium. The weighbridge showed that SMO 746 was half a hundredweight heavier than the standard car we road tested last year (*The Motor*, July 13, 1960) so that the competition cars do not gain their performance by extensive and expensive lightening.

The outside of the Healey reveals little that is non-standard. The twin exhaust system ends in front of the nearside wheel to avoid the loss of ground clearance inevitable when pipes have to pass below the rear axle, the wire wheels have 60 spokes instead of 48 and reveal Girling disc brakes all round, and there is an air intake on the scuttle, together with an opening ventilator in the roof.

The Competition Department makes a point of using the maximum possible number of standard parts (not necessarily from the same B.M.C. model) to reduce costs and to simplify the spares position, and the modified engines have standard but carefully balanced crankshafts, connecting rods and pistons. A special (B.M.C.) camshaft operates ordinary valve gear with stronger springs and the 6-port cylinder head is gas-flowed, reshaped and polished, leaving the compression ratio unchanged at 9 to 1. Three 2 in. S.U. carburetters on long inlet pipes replace the ordinary 1¾ in. pair. The engine drives through a 10-in. single-dry-plate Borg and Beck clutch with strong springs to a special B.M.C. gearbox with very close ratio straight-cut gears, and the standard Laycock overdrive is wired to work on 2nd, 3rd and top. At the flywheel the engine is claimed to give 180 b.h.p. at 5,200 r.p.m., but we were also shown some figures taken at the back wheels on a chassis dynamometer. For reasons connected with cooling problems and the power consumption

The navigator has his own switches, one of which is for the flexible map reading light clipped out of the way behind the screen. He also has a selection of grab handles and a personal horn button, operated by the left toe, which is not shown in the photographs.

A lap-strap for the driver and harness for the navigator supplements the built-in shaping of the luxurious seats. A headlamp flasher switch projects near the left-hand rim of the wheel, the overdrive switch can be flicked by the fingers of the right hand, and the rev-counter has special red-light illumination.

elight

The quick filler cap, roof ventilator, reversing light and short exhaust system are special features visible in a picture which conveys some sense of the car's urgent function.

of tyres on rollers, these dynamometers usually seem to give rather pessimistic results, but even so, figures of 142 b.h.p. at 4,000 r.p.m. and 145 at 5,500 are indicated. In passing it is amusing to note that our technique for quick but unobtrusive passage through towns was to use the gearbox freely but keep the revs right down in the 1,500 to 2,500 r.p.m. band. The dynamometer figures show that even then 40 to 70 b.h.p. were available at the back wheels.

Suspension modifications include heavier coil springs at the front, with standard dampers re-valved to increase the damping by about 20%, and a stronger anti-roll bar. The rear dampers are replaced by the "click adjusting" Armstrong type DAS 10, and the normal 7-leaf semi-elliptics give way to special springs with 14 (thinner) leaves which are better able to resist the rude assault of Yugoslav roads passing very quickly underneath, whilst supporting two spare wheels and a petrol tank up to 20 gallons in capacity. Both ends of the car are raised about an inch to increase ground clearance, and the special rear springs are not advised for light loads as there is then little rebound clearance between the back axle and the underslung chassis.

(*Below*) Thick heat-insulating washers separate the big S.U. carburetters from the bifurcated inlet stubs. The neat arrangement of the very progressive throttle linkage is interesting. Note the wired-on oil and water filler caps and the spare coil.

All the cars have the same very comfortable special seats, but alterations to their mountings and to the pedal positions are necessary to accommodate say, Pat Moss on the one hand or the enormous John Gott on the other. The Healey does not lend itself to the long reach driving position now favoured in racing, but it is doubtful whether this would be appropriate to very long rallies. An exaggerated arms'-length steering position becomes rather tiring long before the sun has set for the third time, and the 99% concentrated effort of the race circuit is only necessary for parts of a long road event. One of the team thought that the Alpine Rally probably demanded the greatest percentage of really hard driving, and estimated the proportion of such motoring as about one-third of the total. In most events, darkness, rain, snow, fog or dust in various combinations will create conditions in which it is a great advantage to sit fairly close to the screen; not only does visibility through the glass improve but the greater angular spread of vision subtended by the width of the screen wiper arcs helps in negotiating hairpin corners.

As soon as one drives this car away it becomes apparent that the feel is entirely different from that of the ordinary Healey 3000. The touring character of the latter has entirely vanished in favour of the hard, taut feeling of the sports-racing car. Although one knows at once that this is an impressive car, it is not one with which the conductor establishes an immediate *rapport*. The reasons for this are by no means clear, and certainly after a few hundred miles it leaves the driver very thoroughly and completely at home and with a firmly established liking and respect for the car; it is tremendous fun to drive in a way which has almost vanished with the passing of the bigger sports-racing cars of the post-war decade. The exhaust, which has a deep bathplug gurgle at tickover, develops the most purposeful hard and hollow ring as soon as the revs start to rise, almost drowning the crescendo howl of straight-cut gears. A clutch which is immensely positive, not unduly heavy and yet needs only the token movements of a pre-war Austin 7, a gearbox with very close ratios, powerful synchromesh and short, light movements and a carefully arranged progressive throttle linkage all combine to provide the most enjoyable gear-change we have encountered on a large-engined car and one which we used far more than necessary just for the fun of it.

In fact, the engine is very flexible and the car can be driven happily through London traffic using mostly overdrive top or direct top gear in which it will accelerate smoothly and rapidly from under 10 m.p.h., but excellent torque at low r.p.m. is succeeded by even better torque which comes in half way up the speed range. The rev. limit is 5,500 r.p.m., with permission to use a momentary 6,000 on occasions, but during our performance tests we

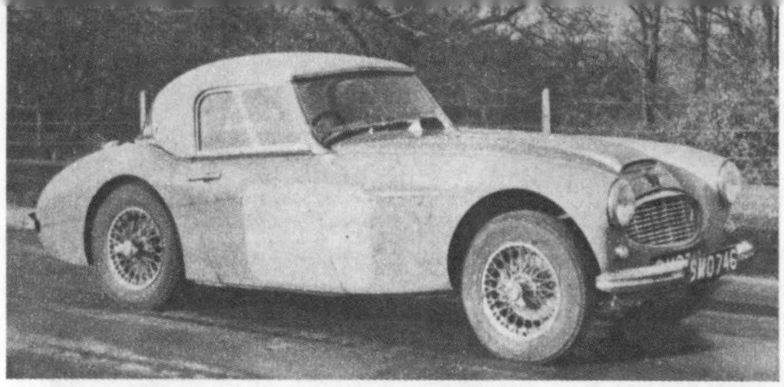

Just in front of the windscreen is a fresh air intake which can deliver a really stiff breeze to the interior. Modern bonnets enable bonnet straps to be worn shorter than was customary in the past.

Policeman's Delight

exceeded by only a small margin the lower figure, above which the engine sounds less happy. Conditions were far from ideal for the acceleration runs, with a wet track on which take-off from rest was both difficult and slow. In these circumstances a standing ¼ mile (with full test load) in 16.7 sec. with 100 m.p.h. appearing after 23.9 sec. is a remarkable performance but one which the car could better considerably on a dry surface using one of the lower axle ratios fitted for some rallies. These figures were registered without using overdrive at all, overdrive top being selected at just over 100 m.p.h.; a full throttle change at peak revs into overdrive second gear would have improved the ¼ mile time, but gives the unit a very limited life.

At this time of the year it is most difficult to get reliable maximum speed figures for such a fast car in this country, and one attempt was abandoned when it was found that a sliding Perspex side window departed on a quickly diverging course at a speed in excess of 115 m.p.h. This speed was reached after accelerating for only about ⅞ mile from rest, and from the way in which it was still rising it seems likely that the terminal velocity must be in the region of 125 m.p.h. (about 5,700 r.p.m.), but suitable conditions to confirm this never arose again. From the competition point of view this is significant only in the Monza speed test of the Alpine Rally; generally the range up to 100 m.p.h. or less is the important one, although on the Acropolis very high averages are called for on the straight but undulating roads through the foothills of the mountains where 100-110 m.p.h. may be held for some time.

It is, however, in the handling and the ride that the general feel differs most markedly from that of the touring version. The steering is remarkably light for a 22½ cwt. car wearing Dunlop Duraband tyres, and there is no very obvious reason why this should be so. It has the benefit of skilled assembly, careful maintenance and frequent greasing, but the steering box is the standard one made by Cam Gears, the castor angle is not reduced and the general geometry is altered only as a by-product of the suspension raising. At first we ran the tyres at standard Duraband pressures (23 lb. front and 26 lb. rear) but later, on advice from B.M.C. Competition Department, we raised them to 30 and 35 respectively with improvement to directional stability, but for straight running at very high speeds on bumpy roads the Healey is not as good as some more softly sprung vehicles.

The ride is definitely hard and, thinking of the appalling surfaces of some of the more obscure mountain passes that have to be taken against the clock, we were rather surprised until we reflected that a hard spring which never bottoms is probably less destructive to the car than a better insulator which occasionally crashes to the limits of its travel; the crews are obviously very durable. On English main roads this ride is far from unpleasant. Except for a bonnet lid which floated in its recess, it failed to provoke any shakes or rattles from the structure. The whole car feels immensely solid and in one rigid piece and sits down at speed with a steadiness that inspires the greatest confidence.

Having encountered nearly all weather conditions during our test (but mostly bad) we would summarize the silent and almost completely roll-free cornering as being outstanding in the dry, good on wet surfaces and indifferent on ice, a gradation very common with sports cars which seldom feel as controllable when the coefficient of friction is really low as some family saloons do. Driving near the limit of adhesion in wet weather calls for some experience of the car, as the braced-tread tyres characteristically fail to indicate the proximity of the approaching stall and the car continues to feel "on rails" until the moment the back wheels break away; rather confusing is the occasional loss of steering resistance which feels like front-end breakaway but is, in fact, caused by the drop in self-aligning torque which is experienced prematurely with this type of tyre. The Girling brakes which are boosted by a Dewandre Mot-A-Vac servo unit, seem to be very good indeed on all kinds of surface, and simultaneous operation of brake and throttle is possible but not easy.

It was a considerable surprise to find that heaters are never fitted to the team Healeys, but engine and exhaust heat kept the interior tolerably warm in December and January. Even with all the vents closed the car keeps reasonably free of mist when travelling quickly, and the driver has the assistance of an electrical de-mister on his side of the screen. In summer events, for which the Healeys are mostly used, the problem is to keep the occupants below melting point; various bits of asbestos insulation are to be seen on the engine side of the bulkhead, a raised intake just ahead of the windscreen discharges air in controllable quantities through ducts on to the feet and legs and there is a small opening vent in the roof.

After more than 1,500 miles of very varied motoring, at an overall fuel consumption of 19 m.p.g., we handed the car back to competitions manager Marcus Chambers with real regret. Most of the really fast cars that pass through our hands are relatively large and luxurious touring machines. The rare combination of tremendous performance with real sports car compactness and agility is something to remember. C.H.B.

THE AUSTIN-HEALEY 3000 RALLY TEAM CAR

TEST DATA

World copyright reserved; no unauthorized reproduction in whole or in part.

CONDITIONS: *Weather: Cold and wet with light wind. (Temperature 35°-36° F., Barometer 29.0-29.3 in. Hg.). Surface: Wet tarmacadam. Fuel: Premium pump petrol (96 Octane Rating by Research Method).*

INSTRUMENTS

Speedometer at 30 m.p.h.	1½% fast
Speedometer at 60 m.p.h.	1½% fast
Speedometer at 90 m.p.h.	3¼% fast
Speedometer at 110 m.p.h.	5% fast
Distance recorder	1½% fast

WEIGHT

Kerb weight (unladen, but with oil, water and fuel for approx. 50 miles)	22½ cwt.
Front/rear distribution of kerb weight	50/50
Weight laden as tested	26¼ cwt.

MAXIMUM SPEEDS

Speed in gears (at 5,500 r.p.m.)

Max. speed in overdrive top	See text
Max. speed in direct top gear	99 m.p.h.
Max. speed in overdrive 3rd gear ...	101 m.p.h.
Max. speed in direct 3rd gear	83 m.p.h.
Max. speed in direct 2nd gear ...	57 m.p.h.
Max. speed in 1st gear	41 m.p.h.

FUEL CONSUMPTION

(Overdrive top gear).

30½ m.p.g. at constant 30 m.p.h. on level.
29 m.p.g. at constant 40 m.p.h. on level.
28 m.p.g. at constant 50 m.p.h. on level.
25½ m.p.g. at constant 60 m.p.h. on level.
23½ m.p.g. at constant 70 m.p.h. on level.
22 m.p.g. at constant 80 m.p.h. on level.
19½ m.p.g. at constant 90 m.p.h. on level.
17½ m.p.g. at constant 100 m.p.h. on level.

(Direct top gear).

26½ m.p.g. at constant 30 m.p.h. on level.
26 m.p.g. at constant 40 m.p.h. on level.
24½ m.p.g. at constant 50 m.p.h. on level.
22½ m.p.g. at constant 60 m.p.h. on level.
21 m.p.g. at constant 70 m.p.h. on level.
19 m.p.g. at constant 80 m.p.h. on level.

Overall Fuel Consumption for 1,519 miles, 79.9 gallons, equals 19.0 m.p.g. (14.9 litres/100 km.).

Touring Fuel Consumption (m.p.g. at steady speed midway between 30 m.p.h. and maximum, less 5% allowance for acceleration). 21.3 (approx.)

Fuel tank capacity (maker's figure) ... 15 gallons

ACCELERATION TIMES from standstill

0-30 m.p.h.	4.2 sec.
0-40 m.p.h.	5.7 sec.
0-50 m.p.h.	7.6 sec.
0-60 m.p.h.	10.2 sec.
0-70 m.p.h.	13.0 sec.
0-80 m.p.h.	16.0 sec.
0-90 m.p.h.	19.8 sec.
0-100 m.p.h.	23.9 sec.
0-110 m.p.h.	31.9 sec.
Standing quarter mile	16.7 sec.

ACCELERATION TIMES on Upper Ratios

	Overdrive top gear	Direct top gear	3rd gear
10-30 m.p.h. ...	—	6.0 sec.	5.2 sec.
20-40 m.p.h. ...	7.4 sec.	6.0 sec.	5.2 sec.
30-50 m.p.h. ...	7.8 sec.	5.8 sec.	5.0 sec.
40-60 m.p.h. ...	8.5 sec.	6.1 sec.	5.3 sec.
50-70 m.p.h. ...	8.6 sec.	6.2 sec.	5.5 sec.
60-80 m.p.h. ...	8.1 sec.	6.1 sec.	5.8 sec.
70-90 m.p.h. ...	8.5 sec.	7.0 sec.	—
80-100 m.p.h. ...	9.6 sec.	7.9 sec.	—
90-110 m.p.h. ...	13.7 sec.	—	—

HILL CLIMBING at sustained steady speeds

Max. gradient on o/d top gear 1 in 7.8 (Tapley 285 lb./ton)
Max. gradient on direct top gear 1 in 5.9 (Tapley 375 lb./ton)
Max. gradient on 3rd gear 1 in 4.8 (Tapley 460 lb./ton)
Max. gradient on 2nd gear 1 in 3.3 (Tapley 650 lb./ton)

SPECIFICATION

Engine

Cylinders	6
Bore	83.36 mm.
Stroke	88.9 mm.
Cubic capacity	2,912 c.c.
Piston area	47.1 sq. in.
Valves	Pushrod o.h.v.
Compression ratio	9/1
Carburetter	3 S.U. type H8
Fuel pump	S.U. electric
Ignition timing control ...	Centrifugal
Oil filter	Tecalemit full-flow
Max. power (gross)	180 b.h.p.
at	5,200 r.p.m.
Piston speed at max. b.h.p. ...	3,030 ft./min.

Transmission

Clutch	10 in. Borg & Beck s.d.p.
Top gear (s/m) ...	4.10 (Overdrive, 3.47)
3rd gear (s/m) ...	4.90 (Overdrive, 4.02)
2nd gear (s/m) ...	7.06 (Overdrive, 5.80)
1st gear	9.90
Overdrive	Laycock-de Normanville
Propeller shaft ...	Hardy-Spicer open
Final drive	Hypoid
Top gear m.p.h. at 1,000 r.p.m. ...	18.0 (Overdrive, 21.9)
Top gear m.p.h. at 1,000 ft./min. piston speed	30.8 (Overdrive, 37.5)

Chassis

Brakes	Girling disc with Dewandre Mot-A-Vac servo
Brake diameters	11¼ in.

Suspension:
Front: Independent by coil springs, wishbones and anti-roll bar.
Rear: Rigid axle with semi-elliptic leaf springs, panhard rod.

Shock Absorbers:

Front:	Armstrong lever type
Rear: ...	Armstrong lever type DAS 10 (adjustable)
Steering gear	Cam and peg
Tyres ...	Dunlop Duraband 6.5 × 16

GET INTO AN
AUSTIN HEALEY
AND SEE WHAT
YOU GET
OUT OF IT!

THERE'S no one way to describe the Austin Healeys. There couldn't be. For the Austin Healeys are so many brilliant things at once. They are powerful, vigorous cars. Briskly, they take you in and out of corners. Swiftly, surely they surge out ahead on the long, open road. Yet high sustained speeds are only one result of their exceptional power. For the Austin Healeys are lithe and agile too. They slip through traffic with impudent ease: park themselves neatly in the tiniest vacant lot. These are the Austin Healeys — real sportsmen's cars.

Austin Healey 3000 Luxurious 2- or occasional 4-seater sports car. Robust 6-cylinder, 2912 ccs engine. Top speed over 100 mph. Disc brakes fitted to match its performance.
Austin Healey Sprite Energetic 2-seater sports car. Fast yet docile. An economist on petrol.

And yours for a price that's more than reasonable. £445 plus £186.10.10 P.T.
See the Austin Healeys at your nearest Austin distributor's showroom. Look over them. Look into them. And ask for a free trial run.

THE AUSTIN MOTOR COMPANY LIMITED · LONGBRIDGE · BIRMINGHAM

By Appointment to
Her Majesty The Queen
Motor Car Manufacturers
The Austin Motor
Company Limited

Backed by
BMC 12-month
warranty
and BMC
service

**AUSTIN LOOKS
YEARS AHEAD**

The Cambodian crest.

A HEALEY

RIDE IN AUSTRALIA'S ONLY

AUSTIN-HEALEY 3000,

WITH HARDTOP COMFORT AS WELL

Badge on left of grille is in Cambodian colors.

CANBERRA is the ideal city for motoring enthusiasts with the flock of exclusive cars on display there — all owned by members of Diplomatic Corps and usually sporting left-hand drive. On a recent visit to the Albury International meeting we dropped off at the Cambodian Embassy, in Vancouver Street, Canberra, where the secretary (Mr Doeuskoma Poc) is the owner of Australia's first Austin Healey 3000, with a hardtop adding to trimness and comfort.

Being a Sydneysider I did not know the existence of a 3000 in our land, so I asked the Austin agents, Larke Hoskins, through their publicity man Ron Gill,

Distinguishing word "3000" under the writing "Austin Healey".

WITH EXTRA STING

when the first of the handful could be expected. I was told the 3000's were being brought out to order only, but the Cambodian Ambassador Mr Poc had one already. I dispatched a letter to Mr Poc requesting a test of his flyer and eagerly awaited results.

A week later I visited Sydney's luxury Chevron-Hilton Hotel to farewell BMC team manager Arthur Grogan and his team on the pre-release run to Perth and back in the Morris 850. Outside the hotel I sighted a newcomer to Sydney streets — a cream hardtop sports car, with the undoubted lines of a Healey. Then I saw the number plates, DC999, and realised my quarry was in Sydney, so that I might not have to make the trip to Canberra afterall.

Next morning I found the owner, Mr Doeuskoma Poc, nephew of the Cambodian Ambassador (Mr. Thieun Poc). Mr Doeuskoma Poc was in Sydney while his wife was in hospital. Between visiting hours and business appointments he found it hard to talk motoring, but he was most helpful. How-

ever, the car had only 3000 miles on the speedo and needed another 2000 before he considered it should be driven at top speed.

But we arranged to take some color shots for Sports Car World cover before Mr Poc departed for Canberra on the Sunday morning. The morning came up with the skies opened up and continual rain. Still I took a shot of the Healey during a shower. But it was too

S.C.W. FULL ROAD TEST

dark and not up to the standards of our SCW covers. I had to wait another month for the 3000 to be fully run in.

Mr Poc rang just prior to the Albury International meeting, so that I was able to drop in at Canberra en route to the NSW-Victoria border. Unfortunately, racing petrol was not available in

Canberra and we were unable to get the best out of this potent machine.

While waiting for Mr Poc at the Embassy I learnt a little about the country of Cambodia. One of the smallest Asian countries still strictly neutral in the "cold" war. There are four Cambodian families in Australia—three at the Embassy and another in Adelaide. Yet this tiny independence is very happy to have its team of diplomats in Australia just for the sake of good relations. After 80 years under French rule, Cambodia now has been independent for eight years.

Soon after, the cream Healey, with hardtop giving it an exclusive look for Australia, swung through the Embassy gates and I was invited to take the controls. Body work is the same as in the previous 100-Six model.

The left-hand drive was a novelty to me and I took extreme care for the first few miles as we swung towards a deserted road just outside of Canberra where we could carry out our speed runs in safety.

It looks the same Healey as old, but the hardtop adds distinction.

I was particularly careful to give way to the left, a very strict rule in Canberra, despite the fact we carried the DC numberplates and their immunity from traffic conditions. As we wound through the picturesque streets Mr Poc told me his ambition was to own an Aston Martin. But he could not afford one, even with the free-of-tax price to members of the Diplomatic Corps. Next best, in his opinion, was the Healey. He had raced previously in France and was a friend of Maurice Trintignant. His ambition was to race the Healey at Warwick Farm. I arranged for Australian Automobile Racing Club secretary Mr Geoff Sykes to send him an entry form on my return to Sydney.

The roof, made of fibreglass, had padding underneath to guard against bumps on a bad road. It rattled slightly at high speeds, but so slight that I would not have noticed it if Mr Poc had not pointed it out.

The left-hand drive proved no problem, in fact I felt it had advantages as you could go right to the edge of the road with safety, and would be especially good on narrow roads. But it would have its problems. On one occasion Mr Poc turned the car round and placed it on the right-hand side of the road, probably remembering his days in Paris and Washington.

The rev counter was ideally placed and could be seen through one side of the steering wheel, with the speedo through the other. Revolutions were red lined at 5200, which we decided would be the limit for our tests, though it went up to 6000 rpm for anyone who wanted to thrash such a machine.

With a compression ratio of 9.03 to 1, the 3000 reaches its maximum power of 124 bhp net (or 130 gross) at 4600 rpm and maximum torque of 167 lb/ft at 2700 rpm.

With this compression ratio there was knocking at top speed, which would be eliminated by the use of a racing fuel such as Shell 100 with ICA. Fuel experts also calculated this fuel should raise top speed by about six miles per hour, that is at Canberra, where the height above sea level cuts down speed nearly two mph, despite the boost of the lesser air resistance. This probably accounts for the excellent rolling resistance figures recorded by the 3000.

Our best speed in one direction was a true 109 mph with an average both ways of 107. This was well ahead of the Healey 100-Six which averaged 98.9 in fourth and 104.2 in overdrive when tested by SPORTS CAR WORLD in June, 1957. But even then we felt the

3000 could have done better with a longer run up as the speedo needle was still climbing when we had to ease down due to road conditions. Mr Poc has done 110 with his wife and son Eric (aged eight), while tests in England regularly reach 115 mph.

Well fitted cockpit with tachometer and speedo seen through the wheel.

Upward view of the lights and grille.

Acceleration of the 3000 was well ahead of the 100-Six times, while slightly slower than overseas tests using racing fuel. The speedo was really accurate, being two miles out at 30 mph, one at 40 and 50, then right on the dot for the higher speeds.

The gear lever, placed a little over towards the passenger's side perhaps as the Healeys are made in England generally with right-hand drive, took a little getting used to. As a result acceleration times (even by Mr Poc) were slow early until he had the real feel of the car. There was no synchromesh on first gear. Our changes were generally made when the 3000 reached the 4600 rpm mark, or its maximum power.

Braking with all anchors out was really good and shaded some of the fine sports cars we have tested in the past. Using our Bronder Brake Graph, it took only 15 ft 7 in to stop the 3000 from 20 mph, which rates excellent. However, Mr Poc felt the Healey would be made safer still by the fitting of disc brakes on all four wheels, not just on the front as in the standard version.

Opening the bonnet one is struck by the two SU carburettors which are fed by an SU pump. Though sporting a big motor for an engine compartment of its size the 3000 is still fairly accessible. Boot space is somewhat restricted, but what sports car isn't? As well as the spare wheel it has to carry side covers and has tucked away to one side the usual Healey safety switch to turn off your petrol when parked.

Inside the twin bucket seats are most spacious, but room behind is most occasional, only being big enough for the carriage of adults on extremely short trips, or for children. The 3000 boasts big pockets in each of the widely arced doors, as well as a parcel tray under the passenger's side of the well padded dashboard. Other controls are for choke, push starter and trafficators. Oil and water gauges also are set before the driver.

As extras Mr Poc had fitted a IMV imported radio and a cigarette lighter. Selling at £2300 (inc. tax) for a canvas top model the 3000 is £140 dearer than the 100-Six model, putting it even further into the luxury class.

A real man's car that goes as expected by the Healeys, the 3000 won last year's Liege-Rome-Liege Rally, when it was driven by two women — Pat Moss and Ann Wisdom. But who would deny that his pair can drive as well as any two men.

The Healey 3000 celebrates its

Heart of the Healey 3000, and the boot with safety petrol device and spare wheel.

second birthday this month, so that it is strange that more of this potent vehicle have not found their way to our shores. Bearing the type name BN7, it is hard to pick from its predecessors without being close enough to read the inscription on the radiator grille or on the boot.

Finally just a few comparisons between the old and the new Healeys. The 3000 marked the first appearance of the BMC C type engine of 2912 cc, which later was used in the full range of six-cylinder cars offered by this manufacturer. Capacity formerly was 2639 cc. The change over increased net power output from 117 bhp to 124, using a compression ratio of 9.03 to 1.

Rear axle ratio on the 3000 is 3.545 to 1, which gives a road speed of 20.9 mph for every 1000 rpm. Overdrive is available at extra cost, but it was not installed on Mr Poc's car. #

A potent machine with twin exhausts ready to roar into action.

The Healey 100-Six, predecessor to the 3000, and (just announced in England) the 3000 Mark II.

AUSTIN HEALEY

PERFORMANCE

TOP SPEED:
Two-way average .... 107 mph
Fastest one way .... 109 mph

ACCELERATION:
(Test limit, 4600 rpm)
Through gears:
0-30 mph .... 3.5 sec
0-40 mph .... 5.3 sec
0-50 mph .... 8.0 sec
0-60 mph .... 10.9 sec
0-70 mph .... 14.2 sec
0-80 mph .... 19.2 sec
0-90 mph .... 27.5 sec
0-100 mph .... 31.1 sec

MAXIMUM SPEEDS IN GEARS (Calculated):
(at 5200 rpm)
I .... 37.6 mph
II .... 52.7 mph
III .... 81.1 mph
IV .... 108.6 mph

SPEEDOMETER ERROR:
30 mph actual — indicated 32 mph.
40 mph actual — indicated 41 mph.
50 mph actual — indicated 51 mph.
60 mph actual — indicated 60 mph.
70 mph actual — indicated 70 mph.
80 mph actual — indicated 80 mph.

TAPLEY DATA:
Maximum pull in gears:
I .... 550 lb ton at 25 mph
II .... 520 lb/ton at 40 mph
III .... 370 lb/ton at 60 mph
IV .... 290 lb/ton at 65 mph

ROLLING RESISTANCE:
90 mph .... 100 lb/ton
80 mph .... 58 lb/ton
70 mph .... 49 lb/ton
60 mph .... 30 lb/ton
50 mph .... 25 lb/ton

BRAKING:
Stop from 20 mph: 15 ft 7 in (excellent).
FADE:
Nil.

CALCULATED DATA:
Weight as tested (2 men) 23½ cwt.
Max bhp, 124 at 4600 rpm (130 gross)
Max torque, 167 lb/ft at 2700 rpm
Lb/hp (nett) 21.2
Mph/1000 rpm top gear, 20.9.
Mph at 2500 ft/min piston speed top gear, 89.2.
Cub cm/lb ft torque 17.4
BHP/litre 42.5
BHP/ton as tested 105.5
Piston speed at max bhp 2995

SPECIFICATIONS

PRICE:

£2300 (inc tax), with canvas hood.

ENGINE:

Type .... 6 Cylinders, water cooled
Valves .... pushrod overhead
Capacity .... 2912 cc
Bore and Stroke .... 83.34 x 88.9 mm
Piston area .... 50.7 sq in
Compression ratio .... 9.03 to 1
Carburettors: Two SU (type HD6).
Fuel Pump: SU (Type LCS)
Spark Plugs: Champion N5.
Oil Filter: Tecalemit or Purolator full flow.

CHASSIS:

Wheelbase .... 7ft 7¾ in
Track, front 4ft 0¾in
       rear .... 4 ft 2in
Suspension, front .... Coil and wishbone independent
       Rear .... Half-Elliptic
Shock absorbers .... Armstrong piston type
Brakes: Type .... Girling Hydraulic
       Operation: Disc front .... (11¼ in diameter);
       Drum rear .... (11 in x 2¼ in)
Steering: Cam and peg.

TRANSMISSION:

Clutch .... 10 in Borg and Beck.

GEAR RATIOS:

I 10.209
II 7.302
III 4.743
IV 3.545
Synchromesh on 2, 3, 4.

GENERAL:

Length overall .... 13 ft 1½ in
Width .... 5 ft 0 in
Test weather: Fine, dry.

All test runs made on dry, bitumen-bound gravel road
with driver and one passenger aboard.

Austin-Healey **3000** *Mark II*

Vertical slats of the Healey Mk. II grille are reminiscent of earlier models, although the shape of the opening is not the same. This re-styling clearly distinguishes the three-carburettor from the two-carburettor cars

A T the same time as their announcement of the Austin-Healey Sprite II, British Motor Corporation also introduce modifications to the well-established Austin-Healey 3000 model, affecting both its performance and apearance. By the addition of an extra carburettor to the 2·9-litre engine, maximum output has been increased by 8 b.h.p. Styling changes to the radiator grille distinguish this model from the two carburettor version. At the same time servo-assisted braking is to be offered as an optional extra.

For some time, competition Healey 3000s have been using three carburettors, so their adoption for the production model is not unexpected. The three now fitted are 1½in. HS4 S.U.s, replacing the two 1¾in. HS6s of the earlier model. To suit the different characteristics of these three carburettors and the redesigned inlet manifold, a new camshaft giving higher lift to the inlet valves and a longer dwell to the exhaust valves has been adopted. Stronger outer valve springs and a timing chain damper steady pad look after the increased loads involved. The result of these modifications is an increase in maximum b.h.p. from 124 net at 4,600 r.p.m. to 132 b.h.p. net at 4,750 r.p.m. Maximum torque remains at 167 lb ft but the engine speed at which it is attained rises from 2,700 to 3,000 r.p.m. The compression ratio remains at 9 to 1.

When redesigning the induction manifold and throttle linkage, the opportunity was taken of improving the choke control. This is still cable operated, but the main control cable now runs to a central distribution unit mounted on top of the manifold. A simple lever arrangement there operates three separate cables to the carburettor choke levers. The effort required to use the choke is now reduced.

A 10in. diameter single plate Borg and Beck clutch was introduced at the same time as the 2·9-litre engine and no change to this unit has been necessary to cope with the extra power of the three-carburettor engine. Gear ratios and rear axle ratios remain unaltered.

For those who find the brake operation rather heavy, a Girling servo-assisted braking system will be offered as an optional extra at a later date. The vacuum cylinder fits neatly into the recess between the right-hand frame member and the bonnet side, forward of the scuttle. As this system requires new brake pipes, different brake pads and rear brake linings, it will normally be a factory fitting, installed before the car leaves the works.

Apart from the change from horizontal to vertical grille slats to distinguish this car from the two-carburettor version, there is a redesigned bonnet motif incorporating the Mark II designation. As with the new Sprite, safety strap attachments are a standard fitting and modifications to the frame, side floor panels, wheel arches and centre tunnel have been made to provide secure anchorages for these. The price is unchanged.

This view of the Mk. II engine compartment shows the new carburettor arrangement and the distribution unit for the choke control, which is mounted on the carburettor balance pipe

BRIEF SPECIFICATION

Engine: No. of cylinders, 6 in line; Bore and stroke 83·3 x 88·9 mm (3·28 x 3·5in); Displacement 2,912 c.c. (177·7 cu in.); Valve position and operation, pushrods and rockers; Compression ratio 9·0 to 1; Max. b.h.p. (net) 132 at 4,750 r.p.m.; Max. b.m.e.p. 142 p.s.i. at 3,000 r.p.m.; Max. torque 167 lb ft at 3,000 r.p.m.; Carburettors, three S.U. type HS4; Fuel pump, S.U. electric type LCS; Tank capacity, 12 Imperial gallons (55 litres); Sump capacity 12·75 pints (7·25 litres); Cooling system, pump, fan and thermostat; Battery 12 volt, 57 amp hr.

The NEW AUSTIN-HEALEY
3000 Mark II!

Still more power for this rally-winning 3-litre sports car! Now with three carburetters, the engine output goes up from 124 to 132 b.h.p.

New frontal treatment (above) gives the Austin-Healey '3000' Mark II an even bolder look, while under the bonnet (below) three S.U. carburetters help it to pack a bigger punch than ever

ALREADY an outstandingly successful, high-performance sports car, the Austin-Healey '3000' now appears in still more powerful form, as the '3000' Mark II. The experience gained in rugged Continental rallies now goes into this luxury roadster to give still more effortless power for overtaking, hill-climbing and high-speed highway cruising.

Externally, the change is apparent in the new, bolder front grille and the distinctive bonnet motif. In the cockpit there are now built-in fittings for equipping your car with the added security and comfort of seat belts.

But under the bonnet there are now three S.U. carburetters instead of two. New manifolding, special valve springs and a redesigned camshaft combine to give a power output of no less than 132 b.h.p., compared to 124 b.h.p. of the earlier model—and this increase, believe it or not, is accompanied by an appreciable *reduction* in fuel consumption!

Three carburetters have for some time been part of the specification of the specially-prepared versions of the Austin-Healey '3000' which have been available to carefully selected private owners for competition use, and of course this configuration has also contributed to the remarkable run of successes by the works team cars in Continental rallying. In 18 months of competition, these cars won their class nine times in International events, including the impressive outright victory in the Liège-Rome-Liège Rally last year, driven by Pat Moss and Ann Wisdom.

The three-carburetter Austin-Healey '3000' Mark II for the time being available only for export.

The Motor Road Test No. 26/61

Make: Austin-Healey — Type: 3000 Mark II 4-seater (with overdrive and hardtop)

Makers: The Austin Motor Co., Ltd., Longbridge, Birmingham

Test Data

World copyright reserved; no unauthorized reproduction in whole or in part.

CONDITIONS. *Weather: Mild and damp, calm for maximum speed trials with wind rising to 10-15 m.p.h. later. (Temperature 54°-58°F. Barometer 28.8-29.0 in. Hg.) Surface: Damp concrete and tarred macadam (dry for braking tests). Fuel: Premium grade pump petrol (approx. 97 Research Method Octane Rating).*

INSTRUMENTS

Speedometer at 30 m.p.h.	accurate
Speedometer at 60 m.p.h.	4% fast
Speedometer at 90 m.p.h	4% fast
Distance recorder	2% slow

WEIGHT

Kerb weight (unladen, but with oil, coolant and fuel for approx. 50 miles)	22¾ cwt.
Front/rear distribution of kerb weight	48½/51½
Weight laden as tested	26½ cwt.

MAXIMUM SPEEDS

Flying Mile

Mean of four opposite runs	112.9 m.p.h.
Best one-way time equals	113.6 m.p.h.

"Maximile" Speed. (Timed quarter mile after one mile accelerating from rest.)

Mean of four opposite runs	107.8 m.p.h.
Best one-way time equals	108.4 m.p.h.

Speed in gears (at 5,200 r.p.m.)

Max. speed in direct top gear	97 m.p.h.
Max. speed in overdrive 3rd gear	90 m.p.h.
Max. speed in direct 3rd gear	74 m.p.h.
Max. speed in 2nd gear	47 m.p.h.
Max. speed in 1st gear	33 m.p.h.

FUEL CONSUMPTION

(Overdrive top gear)

34 m.p.g. at constant 30 m.p.h. on level.
33 m.p.g. at constant 40 m.p.h. on level.
30 m.p.g. at constant 50 m.p.h. on level.
28 m.p.g. at constant 60 m.p.h. on level.
25 m.p.g. at constant 70 m.p.h. on level.
22½ m.p.g. at constant 80 m.p.h. on level.
20 m.p.g. at constant 90 m.p.h. on level.
16 m.p.g. at constant 100 m.p.h. on level

(Direct top gear)

31½ m.p.g. at constant 30 m.p.h. on level.
28 m.p.g. at constant 40 m.p.h. on level.
25½ m.p.g. at constant 50 m.p.h. on level.
23½ m.p.g. at constant 60 m.p.h. on level.
22 m.p.g. at constant 70 m.p.h. on level
19½ m.p.g. at constant 80 m.p.h. on level
17 m.p.g. at constant 90 m.p.h. on level

STEERING

Turning circle between kerbs

Left	32½ feet
Right	32¼ feet
Turns of steering wheel from lock to lock	3¼

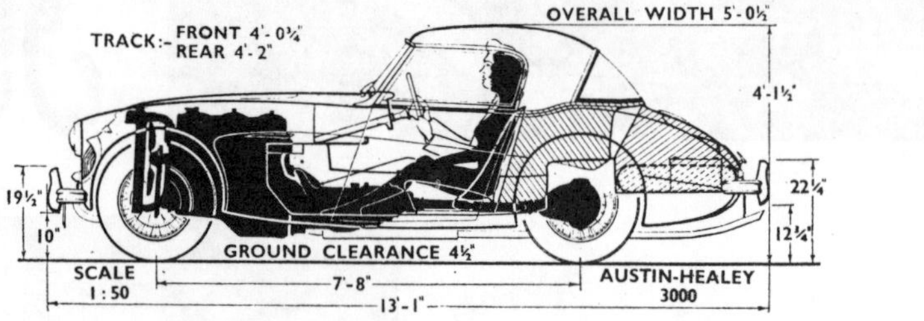
TRACK:- FRONT 4'-0¾"
REAR 4'-2"
OVERALL WIDTH 5'-0½"
4'-1½"
19½"
10"
22¼"
12¾"
GROUND CLEARANCE 4½"
SCALE
1:50
7'-8"
13'-1"
AUSTIN-HEALEY
3000

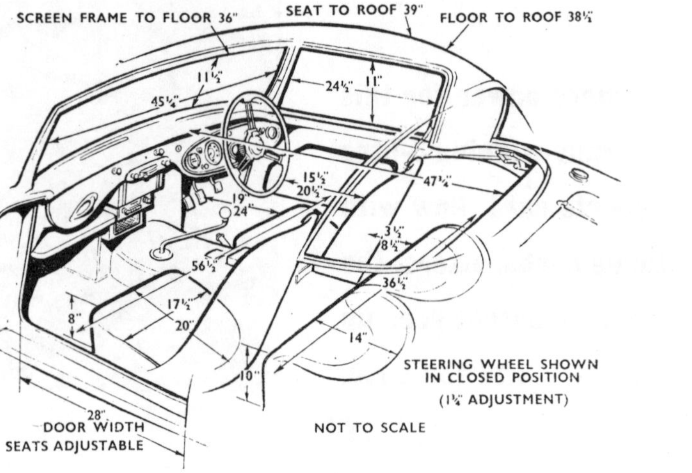
SCREEN FRAME TO FLOOR 36"
SEAT TO ROOF 39"
FLOOR TO ROOF 38½"
11½"
24½"
11"
45¼"
15½"
20½"
19"
24"
47¼"
3½"
8½"
56½"
36½"
17½"
8"
20"
14"
10"
28"
DOOR WIDTH
SEATS ADJUSTABLE
STEERING WHEEL SHOWN IN CLOSED POSITION
(1¼" ADJUSTMENT)
NOT TO SCALE

Overall Fuel Consumption for 3,767 miles, 181.3 gallons, equals 20.8 m.p.g. (13.6 litres/100 km.)

Touring Fuel Consumption (m.p.g. at steady speed midway between 30 m.p.h. and maximum, less 5% allowance for acceleration) 23.5 m.p.g.
Fuel tank capacity (makers' figure) 12 gallons

ACCELERATION TIMES from standstill

0-30 m.p.h.	3.8 sec.
0-40 m.p.h.	5.8 sec.
0-50 m.p.h.	8.3 sec.
0-60 m.p.h.	10.9 sec.
0-70 m.p.h.	14.3 sec.
0-80 m.p.h.	19.2 sec.
0-90 m.p.h.	25.9 sec.
0-100 m.p.h.	36.4 sec.
Standing quarter mile	18.3 sec.

ACCELERATION TIMES on Upper Ratios

	Overdrive top gear	Direct top gear	Direct 3rd gear
10-30 m.p.h.	8.8 sec.	6.8 sec.	4.9 sec.
20-40 m.p.h.	9.2 sec.	7.0 sec.	5.3 sec.
30-50 m.p.h.	9.8 sec.	7.2 sec.	5.5 sec.
40-60 m.p.h.	10.5 sec.	7.4 sec.	5.7 sec.
50-70 m.p.h.	11.2 sec.	7.9 sec.	6.3 sec.
60-80 m.p.h.	11.8 sec.	8.9 sec.	—
70-90 m.p.h.	13.4 sec.	10.9 sec.	—
80-100 m.p.h.	18.8 sec.	16.7 sec.	—

BRAKES from 30 m.p.h.

1.00 g retardation (equivalent to 30 ft. stopping distance) with 120 lb. pedal pressure.
0.95 g retardation (equivalent to 31¾ ft. stopping distance) with 100 lb. pedal pressure.
0.71 g retardation (equivalent to 42½ ft. stopping distance) with 75 lb. pedal pressure.
0.47 g retardation (equivalent to 64 ft. stopping distance) with 50 lb. pedal pressure.
0.22 g retardation (equivalent to 137 ft. stopping distance) with 25 lb. pedal pressure.

HILL CLIMBING at sustained steady speeds.

Max. gradient on overdrive top	1 in 8.7	(Tapley 255 lb./ton)
Max. gradient on direct top	1 in 6.9	(Tapley 320 lb./ton)
Max. gradient on overdrive 3rd	1 in 6.5	(Tapley 340 lb./ton)
Max. gradient on direct 3rd	1 in 5.1	(Tapley 430 lb./ton)
Max. gradient on 2nd gear	1 in 3.3	(Tapley 645 lb./ton)

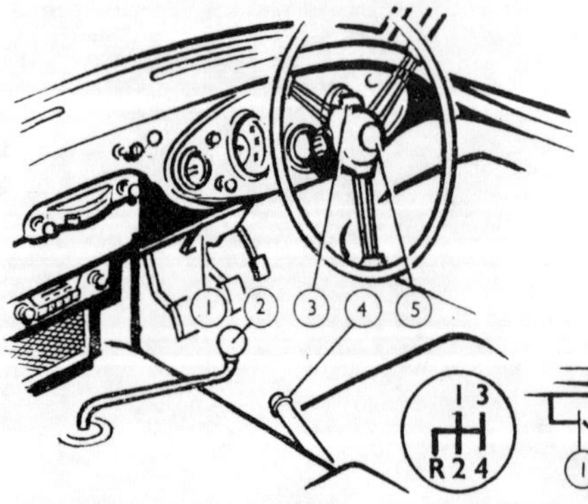
1
2
3
4
5
1 3
R 2 4

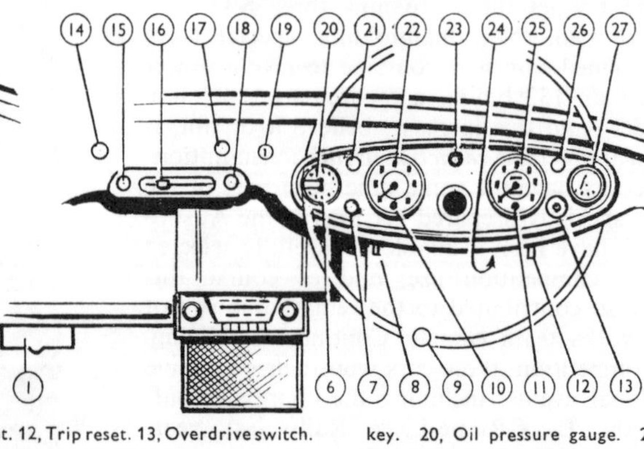
14 15 16 17 18 19 20 21 22 23 24 25 26 27
1
6 7 8 9 10 11 12 13

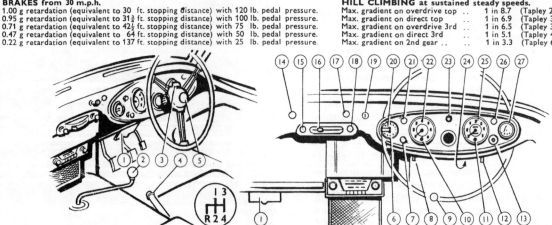

1, Heater air outlet shutters. 2, Gear lever. 3, Direction indicator control. 4, Handbrake. 5, Horn button. 6, Water temperature gauge. 7, Wipers switch. 8, Panel light switch. 9, Dip switch. 10, Dynamo charge warning light. 11, High beam warning light. 12, Trip reset. 13, Overdrive switch. 14, Screen washer. 15, Cold air control. 16, Heater temperature control and fan switch. 17, Choke. 18, Heater air-intake control. 19, Ignition key. 20, Oil pressure gauge. 21, Starter. 22, Rev. counter. 23, Direction indicator warning light. 24, Bonnet release. 25, Speedometer. 26, Light switch. 27, Fuel gauge.

The Austin-Healey 3000 Mark II

(with overdrive)

Velvet-gloved High Performance from the Latest Triple-carburetter 4-seater

POWER in ample quantities over a wide range of engine speeds makes the big Austin-Healey a quick and effortless mountaineering car, although ground clearance is limited for rough surfaces such as this one on the Great St. Bernard Pass.

EXTENDING our test of the Austin-Healey 3000 to something more than 4,000 miles, and sampling this triple-carburetter Mark II version of the British Motor Corporation's fastest model in France, Italy and Switzerland as well as in Britain, we found ourselves with quite extraordinarily mixed reactions. One might say that 85% of what we felt was keen enthusiasm for this car; it is capable of well over 110 m.p.h. on level road, has acceleration and braking to match its top speed, is quite pleasantly controllable, and delights both driver and passenger by providing a really comfortable ride in two excellent seats. The remaining 15% of our reaction was dismay that a company which has big resources and has been developing this series of Austin-Healeys for eight years is still delivering cars with two familiar and quite serious, but demonstrably curable, shortcomings in respect of ground clearance and heat in the cockpit.

From the fact that differences between a Mark II Austin-Healey and its immediate predecessors centre around a third carburetter and a high-lift camshaft, one might be forgiven for expecting this version to put all the emphasis on high performance. In actual fact, whilst an ability to reach 100 m.p.h. from rest in 36.4 sec. and less than ¾-mile of road testifies to the reality of its performance, smooth running and easy riding are the characteristics which really distinguish this model from other fast cars. Its primary appeal may be sporting, as appearances suggest, but the comfort and driving ease which accompany a delightful power to accelerate clear of obstructive traffic could make this a better "executive's car" than are many more cumbrous saloons.

Built as low to the ground as it is, the Austin-Healey 3000 has almost complete natural immunity from body roll on cor-

ners, and is able to ride on comfortably flexible springs. Although the suspension is slightly firmer than on most modern saloons, excellent matching of the front and rear springs gives a delightfully flat ride at all times; even with the extra-high tyre pressures advised for very fast driving, the car is very comfortable on British roads and not unduly lively over the fast but rough roads of northern France. Greater curvature of the backrest might save the driver from a tendency to rest one shoulder against the body side when cornering fast, but the seats are comfortable even when judged from the passenger's side during fast progress along secondary roads. The doors extend reasonably far forward and down to floor level, making this a tolerably easy car to enter or leave in spite of its low roof.

With all its emphasis on riding comfort, this is, nevertheless, an easy car to swing along winding roads, its Dunlop RS5 tyres having excellent adhesion on most sorts of

THREE carburetters with individual air filters make an impressive looking array, and with a new camshaft they put extra emphasis on power in the upper-middle range of r.p.m.

In Brief

Price (including overdrive, wire wheels and hardtop as tested), £960 17s. 6d. plus purchase tax £401 9s. 10d., equals £1,362 7s. 4d.

Price without extras (including purchase tax), £1,175 10s. 10d.

Capacity	2,912 c.c.
Unladen kerb weight	22¾ cwt.
Acceleration:	
20-40 m.p.h. in top gear	7.0 sec.
0-50 m.p.h. through gears	8.3 sec.
Maximum direct top gear gradient	1 in 6.9
Maximum speed	112.9 m.p.h.
"Maximile" speed	107.8 m.p.h.
Touring fuel consumption	23.5 m.p.g.

Gearing: 18.6 m.p.h. in top gear at 1,000 r.p.m. (overdrive, 22.6 m.p.h.); 31.8 m.p.h. at 1,000 ft./min. piston speed (overdrive, 38.8 m.p.h.).

The Austin-Healey 3000 Mk. II

OCCASIONAL rear seats add to the usefulness of this Austin-Healey in its four-seater form, can accommodate children under cover or will carry adults when the car is open. Cockpit details include an effective pull-up handbrake and an oddly-shaped but sturdy central gear lever.

road surface, and the car slides only gradually when pushed towards the limit. Although the steering is not quite quick enough in its gearing or free enough from lost motion to satisfy the most fastidious sporting tastes, the light control with some feel but very little kick-back pleases a majority of drivers.

At times, the controls seem disappointingly clumsy to use, as all three pedals have a rather long travel and are arranged so that toe-and-heel operation of brake and accelerator is impossible; the gear lever curves oddly from the left side of a broad gearbox cover, and the overdrive switch is irritatingly farther to one side of the steering wheel rim than it could have been on a less stylized facia panel. Gear ratio spacings which are not ideal (1st and 2nd are surprisingly similar ratios) matter little with such a flexibly powerful engine, and occasional complaints of a poor gearchange are usually traceable to incomplete declutching, the long pedal travel being rather awkward from a straight-leg driving position. Most initial complaints concerning the controls are soon forgotten, this

being an untiring car in which to drive 500 miles when the weather is reasonably cool.

Should the weather be even moderately hot, some cockpit surfaces become fairly warm (despite a substantial amount of asbestos sheeting, visible only when the car is raised on a hoist), and a most unwelcome volume of hot (but not smelly) air from the engine blows into the body through concealed bonnet hinges, around the doors or past the corners of the facia panel. Using our test model to follow and report the French Alpine Rally, which was won by a factory-entered Austin-Healey 3000 fitted with neat-looking additional hot-air outlets alongside the engine and additional air inlets and outlets for the cockpit, we wondered very much why production cars could not be similarly equipped: our test car's engine did not overheat, but its passengers (who had retained the removable hard-top as an anti-theft protection for their photographic equipment) certainly did.

A contrast with the team cars was also very evident in respect of ground clearance, and whilst a great increase could not be

obtained without sacrificing some of the spring travel which lets production models ride so comfortably, it would not be difficult to eliminate vulnerable projections below the flat underside of this model's sturdy chassis. The low-set exhaust pipes have already been arranged and mounted so that frequent use of them as toboggan runners does no harm, as a moderately well laden car will ground them occasionally even on main road undulations, and very frequently on bad roads; but during our test mileage the electrical wiring to all the rear lights was severed and there were visible signs of abrasion on the clutch operating hydraulic pipe, the main petrol pipe and the steel sump of the engine.

Wide Speed Range

Triple carburetters in place of the former two have brought a useful improvement in power over the upper-middle range of engine speeds, giving enhanced acceleration through-the-gears and from 70 m.p.h. in top. Lower in the engine r.p.m. range, a twin-carburetter car which we tested a year ago showed even better acceleration than this Mark II model although it was very much harsher in feel. As the triple carburetters reduce accessibility under the bonnet, give very poor throttle response during the first mile after a start from cold and have little overall effect on petrol consumption, one can reasonably suggest that other rally-developed features should have been applied to production cars in advance of this one.

Regardless of delicate comparisons with the preceding model however, this car really does accelerate quickly, anywhere in its speed range. The overdrive top gear in

NEAT lines of the removable hardtop, secured by four clamps and leaving the folded hood frame in position, are shown here. Centre-lock wire wheels are an optional extra.

which it was timed at a two-way mean speed of 112.9 m.p.h. also gave acceleration from 10 to 30 m.p.h. in only 8.8 sec., demonstrating the torque which this 3-litre 6-cylinder engine develops right down to the bottom of the speed range. In traffic on de-restricted roads, second gear provides really ferocious acceleration up to nearly 50 m.p.h. before the red mark on the rev counter dial is reached, or third gear will swing the speed from 20 m.p.h. up to 70 m.p.h. in under 14½ sec. before the driver need consider changing up into either overdrive third or direct top. Such quick acceleration over a wide range of speeds allows a driver to get clear away from awkward groups of traffic at times when with less performance it might be unsafe to overtake.

Oddly, and not as a matter of any practical importance, this Mark II Austin-Healey was slower by 2 m.p.h. than the far-less-refined example which we drove in 1960. On a hot, dry day in Italy measured kilometres were timed at a mean speed of 112.7 m.p.h., and on a cool day in Britain with the road damp, measured miles were timed at a mean speed of 112.9 m.p.h., with the engine turning over at about 5,000 r.p.m. which is rather short of the suggested r.p.m. limit. On an autostrada or motorway, cruising at 80, 90 or 100 m.p.h. does not seem to be hard driving although above 75-80 m.p.h. there is rather a lot of wind noise. Equally, one potters quietly through speed limits in overdrive top gear; exhaust noise from the mechanically quiet engine is never conspicuous for long because when the exhaust does become fairly loud, the Austin-Healey is a rapidly disappearing object. The strange gobbling sounds which the three carburetters emit during acceleration at some speeds and throttle openings neither tire nor offend.

Comfortable as a two seater, this car can only be called a four-seater when neither the hardtop (secured by 2 clamps and 2 screw attachments) nor hood are in use, although two small children can ride in the back under cover, and it is not impossible for one adult to coil himself into the rear compartment. This model has less luggage space in the rear locker than the two-seater in which the spare wheel and battery are mounted farther forward, but two week-end bags can be stowed under lock and key. Despite a fabric cover to the battery, over-filling of this component can lead to luggage being damaged by acid.

LOCKABLE accommodation for luggage will take two week-end bags, which in the four-seat model must fit alongside the battery and above the spare wheel: an alternative two-seat version has more room in its luggage locker.

Disc Brakes

Although our 4,000-mile test showed up certain assembly details which an owner would have had rectified under guarantee (tightening numerous nuts to eliminate rattles or thuds from sidescreens, bonnet, rear axle U-bolts and other points) no breakages whatever occurred, and once going well this model has a reputation for sturdiness. Oil consumption in brisk touring was around 3,000 m.p.g., although frequent use of maximum engine r.p.m. could treble this rate of consumption. The brakes, of self-adjusting disc pattern at the front, and with drums which do not quickly go out of adjustment at the rear, gave excellent power without ever fading, and on a good surface they could swing a brake meter to the end of its scale before any trace of rear wheel locking occurred. Brake pedal pressures, in the absence of any servo, were slightly higher than is nowadays normal, and when warm the front brakes sometimes squealed very loudly indeed.

We have felt it necessary to criticize some aspects of this Austin-Healey quite strongly, and we know many owners of slightly earlier models are equally critical about the same faults of cockpit overheating and underside vulnerability which could and should be cured. We also know that despite these complaints many an Austin-Healey is changed only for a later model of the same car, because owners would rather put up with the faults than forgo the unique combination of comfort and high performance which this car offers at a very reasonable price. Despite its shortcomings, many other people (whether graduating from a smaller car, or seeking a faster and more entertaining alternative to a luxury saloon) will find that this model ranks as their "best buy."

Specification

Engine
- Cylinders ... 6
- Bore ... 83.34 mm.
- Stroke ... 88.9 mm.
- Cubic capacity ... 2,912 c.c.
- Piston area ... 50.7 sq. in.
- Valves ... Overhead (pushrods)
- Compression ratio ... 9/1
- Carburetter ... 3 inclined S.U. type HS.4
- Fuel pump S.U. electrical, rear mounted
- Ignition timing control ... Centrifugal and vacuum
- Oil filter Full-flow (Tecalemit or Purolator)
- Max. power (net) ... 132 b.h.p.
- at ... 4,750 r.p.m.
- Piston speed at max. b.h.p. 2,770 ft./min.

Transmission
- Clutch ... Borg & Beck 10 in. s.d.p.
- Top gear (s/m) ... 3.909 (overdrive, 3.205)
- 3rd gear (s/m) ... 5.12 (overdrive, 4.20)
- 2nd gear (s/m) ... 8.02
- 1st gear ... 11.45
- Reverse ... 14.78
- Overdrive ... Laycock-de Normanville
- Propeller shaft ... Hardy Spicer single-piece open
- Final drive ... 11/43 spiral bevel (without overdrive, 11/39)
- Top gear m.p.h. at 1,000 r.p.m. 18.6 (overdrive, 22.6)
- Top gear m.p.h. at 1,000 ft./min. piston speed ... 31.8 (overdrive, 38.8)

Chassis
- Brakes: Girling hydraulic, drum type at rear and self-adjusting disc type at front.
- Brake diameters:
  - Front discs ... 11¼ in. dia.
  - Rear drums ... 11 in. dia. by 2¼ in. wide
- Friction areas: 112 sq. in. of lining area working on 383 sq. in. of rubbed area.
- Suspension:
  - Front: Independent by coil springs, transverse wishbones and anti-roll torsion bar.
  - Rear: Rigid axle, semi-elliptic leaf springs and Panhard rod.
- Shock absorbers: Girling lever-arm hydraulic (front units form upper wishbone pivots).
- Steering gear ... Cam and peg
- Tyres 5.90—15 Dunlop Road Speed, tubed

Coachwork and Equipment

- Starting handle ... None
- Battery mounting ... In rear locker
- Jack ... Rachet screw type
- Jacking points Under front spring base plates and under rear spring leaves
- Standard tool kit: Jack and handle, copper-head hammer, sparking plug spanner and tommy bar.
- Exterior lights: 2 headlamps, 2 sidelamps, 2 stop/tail/flasher lamps, rear number plate lamp.
- Number of electrical fuses ... 2
- Direction indicators: Self-cancelling flashers combined with side and stop lamps.
- Windscreen wipers ... Electrical twin-blade, self-parking
- Windscreen washers Trico hand-pump type
- Sun visors ... None
- Instruments: Speedometer with total and decimal trip distance recorders, rev. counter, fuel contents gauge, oil pressure gauge, water thermometer.
- Warning lights: Dynamo charge, headlamp main beam, turn indicators.
- Locks:
  - With ignition key Ignition switch and luggage locker
  - With other keys ... None
- Glove lockers ... None
- Map pockets Two wide compartments in doors
- Parcel shelves One below left half of facia
- Ashtrays ... One on gearbox cover
- Cigar lighters ... None
- Interior lights ... None
- Interior heater: Fresh-air heater and screen de-mister as optional extra.
- Car radio Optional extra H.M.V. Radiomobile
- Extras available: Wire wheels, overdrive, hardtop, heater, radio.
- Upholstery material: Hide facings, leathercloth on non-wearing surfaces.
- Floor covering ... Pile carpet
- Exterior colours standardized: 5 single colours and 5 duotone combinations.
- Alternative body styles ... 2-seater

Maintenance

- Sump ... 11¼ pints, S.A.E. 30 above freezing
- Gearbox 5 pints plus 1¼ pints in overdrive, S.A.E. 30
- Rear axle ... 3 pints, S.A.E. 90 hypoid oil
- Steering gear lubricant ... S.A.E. 90 gear oil
- Cooling system capacity 19 pints (2 drain taps)
- Chassis lubrication ... By oil gun every 1,000 miles to 17 points
- Ignition timing ... 12° before t.d.c. static
- Contact-breaker gap ... 0.014-0.016 in.
- Sparking plug type: Champion N3 (fast driving) or N5 (town use), 14 mm. long reach
- Sparking plug gap ... 0.025 in.
- Carburetter jet needles ... Type DJ
- Valve timing: Inlet opens 5° before t.d.c. and closes 45° after b.d.c.; exhaust opens 51° before b.d.c. and closes 21° after t.d.c.
- Tappet clearances (hot):
  - Inlet and exhaust ... 0.012 in.
- Front wheel toe-in ... $\frac{1}{16}$-$\frac{1}{8}$ in.
- Camber angle ... 1°
- Castor angle ... 2°
- Steering swivel pin inclination ... 6½°
- Tyre pressures:
  - Front ... 20 lb.
  - Rear 23-26 lb. according to load (increase front and rear pressures by 6-8 lb. for sustained high-speed driving).
- Brake fluid Girling, or to S.A.E. spec. 70R1
- Battery type and capacity 12-volt, 50 amp. hr.
- Miscellaneous: Top up carburetter dashpots with S.A.E. 20 engine oil.

for the new

Austin Healey

3000 Mk II

Laycock De Normanville overdrive, available on the latest, most powerful version yet of the Austin Healey 3000, adds enormously to the pleasures of owning and driving this highly-successful sports car.

Consider the advantages that this rally-proved overdrive offers: extra high top and third ratios for effortless high-speed cruising at low engine revs, less driver fatigue, less engine noise and wear, much lower petrol consumption. All this at the flick of a switch . . . no declutching, no lever-fiddling, no pause or loss of acceleration.

And remember, only Laycock De Normanville Overdrive has these 3 unique advantages: power-sustained changes, up or down; engine braking in all gears; full driver control of transmission ratio at all times.

These are the reasons why experienced motorists insist on Laycock De Normanville Overdrive, now available as optional equipment on 35 British cars.

A MUST FOR MOTORWAYS

LAYCOCK
DE NORMANVILLE
OVERDRIVE

- *Higher cruising speed at lower r.p.m.* • *Full driver control* • *More m.p.g.*
- *Reduced engine wear and maintenance*
- *Less driver fatigue*

LAYCOCK ENGINEERING LIMITED · MILLHOUSES · SHEFFIELD, 8

AUTOMOTIVE DIVISION OF BIRFIELD INDUSTRIES LIMITED

Member of the

Birfield Group

EIGHT MORE HORSES FOR THE HEALEY

A face lift and three carburettors give a boost to this popular marque.

THE 1961 version of the Austin Healey 3000, the Mark II, has a revised front grille with vertical bars, instead of horizontal. It has an improved engine with three carburettors, raising power to 132 bhp, an increase of eight horsepower over the former twin unit.

Modifications include a new camshaft, stronger outer valve springs an improved tuning chain damper and a new air cleaner. The frame, side floor panels, wheel arches and centre tunnel have been modified to provide built-in anchorages for safety harness, which is offered as an optional extra.

There also is a new heat shield for the silencer.

The brakes, with Girling discs at the front, are unchanged. However, servo assistance is available as an optional.

The Mk. II is available as a two-seater or as an occasional four-seater tourer.

A fibreglass hardtop and wire-spoked wheels are available as optional extras while the car is fitted with a theft-proof switch in the boot.　　　　#

Austin-Healey

Three carbs mean added power, and
suspension changes give this
'62 model even better handling

by Bob Russo

INITIAL THE NAME Austin-Healey and you come up with something like "AH," which, except for a few misgivings, describes our reaction to BMC's new "3000" roadster. This is not simply a rash reaction, either, but a solid opinion gained during a cross-country, six-state driving test that even included a run over the fabulous world speed record course at Bonneville and a trip up Pikes Peak.

Since its birth in 1953, the Austin-Healey has scored heavily with sports car buffs in this country, due mostly to its perky performance on road racing courses and its deep-throated roar of performance on the street. Its basic design has always made it readily adaptable for racing and fun. With a few exceptions, it has captured the hearts of sportsmen and enthusiasts alike.

The new "3000" for 1962, which BMC bills as the successor to the 100-

Six, is not too noticeably different from the '61 model. Except for slight grille modifications, in fact, it is difficult to distinguish the '62 from the '60. Under the hood, however, there is a marked difference — one of great improvement insofar as performance is concerned.

Officially designated the Austin-Healey 3000 Mark II, the '62 houses a stepped-up six-banger equipped with triple SU carburetors, a new camshaft and stronger valve springs. Horsepower has been increased from 124 hp (put out by the previous, twin-carburetor version) to 132 hp, which is especially noticeable at the top end.

Going along with the horsepower increase is improved handling — a marked improvement at that. Suspension remains nearly the same, with independent wishbones and coil springs in front and leaf springs, solid axle and panhard rod at the rear. But the sagging,

almost unstable feeling experienc[ed] with the previous model has been [re-] placed by a solid, more secure feeli[ng] under hard cornering. The harder [we] pushed it, in fact, the better the [car] felt, especially in the winding Rock[ies] that were part of our extensive t[est] route. A stronger stabilizer bar and [a] slight change in shocking are the reas[on.]

Domestic car exponents and ev[en] some sports car buffs will argue that [the] Austin-Healey is definitely not a cro[ss] country car. Limited luggage space, [the] roar of the engine and exhaust, the la[ck] of ventilation in the cockpit are [the] points of contention. We found some [of] this to be true. Traveling any gr[eat] distance is a problem where luggage [is] concerned, and cockpit ventilation [is] poor. Still, we had no problem fitti[ng] in suitcases and even a picnic lun[ch] and for the most part the journey w[as] a real ball. *continu[ed]*

Healey's cornering ability is improved this year through minor chassis changes. Its mild tendency to rock and roll has been completely eliminated.

3000 Road Test

SSO PUT THE CAR THROUGH ITS PACES IN MANY PLACES — INCLUDING PIKES PEAK AND HERE ON BONNEVILLE'S WELL-KNOWN SALT FLATS.

Jump seats are too small to reasonably carry adults, but they're fine for luggage and hauling small items.

Telescopic steering wheel may be adjusted while car is in motion, gives driver a variety of stances on long journeys.

Austin-Healey 3000

Although limited in space, the Healey is surprisingly comfortable for two adults. True bucket seats with individual long-track adjustments accommodate long or short legs and provide needed support and comfort for long periods of travel. Adding to this, an adjustable steering column is easily set to nearly any desired driving position, which may be changed while traveling to help ease strain after many hours behind the wheel.

While our test car was what is designated as "an occasional four-seater tourer," with two jump seats in the rear, use of these extra seats by anyone but a pygmy is highly impractical. These seats do come in handy for stowing luggage or other cargo that has to be taken on an extensive trip. Or they can be used on a short trip to the grocery store, since trunk space is very limited. Spare tire and battery take up most of the room.

As mentioned, cockpit ventilation is inadequate and was a particular prob-

lem in desert country. The Mark II is equipped with a heater/ventilating system that draws air through ducts on either side of the engine, but there simply was not enough volume — and what there was, wasn't distributed to the right places. Even in cool weather, the driver is bothered with lack of heat dissipation on his throttle foot. Ventilating doors in each fender would be a great improvement.

Fully convertible with a soft top that folds behind the rear jump seats, the '62 Healey may be purchased with a fiberglass hardtop although it is our opinion that this detracts slightly from the out-and-out sports car look and feel. Portions of our cross-country hop were made with the top folded, but long periods under a broiling sun didn't always make this a practical way to travel. For short trips and in-city driving, though, the open air comfort is hard to beat on hot days.

Removable, plexiglass side curtains (which stow in the trunk when not in use) are necessary under extremely cold conditions, but are hardly worth the effort of installing on brisk days. Turning up the heater and wearing a good windbreaker works almost as well.

Two features, in addition to fine han-

dling, are particularly impressive with the Mark II. One is braking, with Girling hydraulic discs in front and drums in the rear; and the other is an electrically controlled overdrive unit. Both of these items add greatly to the safety, comfort and economy of one's trip.

Braking with the Girlings was devoid of any sudden swerves and, most of all without fade of any kind. We paid particular note to this, avoiding the downshift in many cases in order to give the brakes full emphasis. In panic-stop test at 60 mph, the car came to a halt in less than 130 feet.

The overdrive unit, which helped bring our mileage figure to 26 mpg on the open highway, is electrically operated through a toggle switch on the instrument panel. Flip it up and the transmission shifts into a higher gear. Flip it down and the gearbox shifts back to top. In heavy traffic or for passing, this simple device saves time and effort. Rear axle ratio is 3.91 with overdrive and 3.54 for conventional. Transmission is a standard four-speed with synchromesh in all but first gear. Control is by a floor-mounted, short stick.

One other outstanding feature of the '62 Austin-Healey is an "immobilization" device situated in the trunk. This consists of a knob which, when turned, cuts off the power supply from the battery. Once the power is turned off and the trunk is locked, the car may be left without fear of theft, a major consideration since the doors themselves cannot be locked.

It's been eight years now since the Austin-Healey went on the market, and the tastes of motorists have changed a great deal. But there can be little doubt that, when it comes to a pure sports car aimed directly at the sportsman/enthusiast, the Healey has nestled into a permanent niche of popularity that shows no sign of abating. BMC has taken great pains to preserve this popularity without drastic changes from its original design — and, if the Mark II is any yardstick, their efforts have been successful.

Major engine change is the new three-carburetor set-up which contributes to engine's 132 hp. Formerly the ohv Six had 124 horses. Other changes include different cam and valve springs.

Top is a one-man operation, stores out of sight behind the jump seats. Hard top is extra.

AUSTIN-HEALEY 3000
2-4-passenger roadster

Options on car tested: Overdrive, wire wheels
Odometer reading at start of test: 1578 miles
Recommended engine red line: 5000 rpm

PERFORMANCE

ACCELERATION (2 aboard)

0-30 mph	4.1 secs.
0-45 mph	7.7
0-60 mph	12.2

Standing start ¼-mile 19.7 secs. and 74 mph

Speeds in gears @ 4800 rpm

1st	27 mph	3rd	63 mph
2nd	41 mph		

Speedometer Error on Test Car

Car's speedometer reading	30	45	50	60	70	80
Weston electric speedometer	30	45	50	60	70	80

Miles per hour per 1000 rpm in top gear (actual meter reading) ....23 mph
(Overdrive 20.9 mph)

Stopping Distances — from 30 mph, 39 ft.; from 60 mph, 127 ft.

SPECIFICATIONS FROM MANUFACTURER

Engine
Ohv, in-line Six
Bore: 3.282 ins. Stroke: 3.5 ins.
Displacement: 177.7 cubic inches
Compression ratio: 9:1
Horsepower: 132 @ 4750 rpm
Ignition: 12-volt battery/coil

Gearbox
Manual 4-speed, floor stick

Driveshaft
Open

Differential
Ring gear and pinion
Standard ratio 3.54:1
Overdrive ratio 3.91:1

Suspension
Front: Independent with wishbones, coil springs,
hydraulic shocks,
anti-roll bar

Rear: Semi-elliptic leaf springs,
hydraulic shocks,
panhard rod

Wheels and Tires
Standard 15-in. steel discs —
optional wire knock-offs
5.90 x 15 Dunlop tires

Brakes
Girling hydraulics
Front: 11¼-in. discs
Rear: 11-in. drums

Body and Frame
Box-section frame; aluminum and
steel body
Wheelbase 92 ins.
Track, front 48.75 ins.,
rear 50.0 ins.
Overall length 157 ins.
Dry weight 2390 lbs.

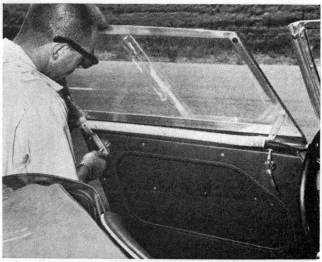

Side curtains are plexiglass with aluminum frames. They have wing nuts which hold them fast. Door compartment is for maps.

(Above) Trunk is cramped, will carry little more than a small suitcase. Switch shuts off battery and makes car theft-proof.

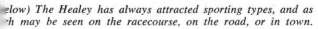

below) The Healey has always attracted sporting types, and as such may be seen on the racecourse, on the road, or in town.

ROAD TEST/22-61

The new Mk. II has much more to offer than simply a face-lift

ALONG WITH THE OTHER BMC CAR LINES, the Mark II tag has been placed on the latest 3-liter Healey and — as their press release states — "It can be readily distinguished by its slightly modified radiator grille which now has vertical slats." But it hasn't been all play and no work for their styling department; there are other, more subtle changes.

The real difference lies beneath the hood, however, where output has been upped from 124 bhp to 132 by the addition of (among other things) a third SU carburetor. This is a successful improvement since it increases performance and mileage without decreasing any other factors. Example: the throttle can be dumped wide open at any speed without the usual gasping associated with full-potential carburetion. Starting is almost instantaneous and idling exceptionally smooth. Our acceleration times didn't quite equal those claimed by the factory, but were still fast enough to be impressive *and* convincing that the Mk II is a powerful machine.

Ride and comfort in the new Healey are optimum, without sacrifice in roadability. The slightly-rubbery-but-still-firm feel that we identified with previous models remains, but it's even softer, yet just as controllable. The increased production of the four-seater with its two molded-in back seats behind the regular seats will be a blessing to Healey fanciers with families, providing their offspring are small in stature. The additional cut-away makes the entire cockpit feel a lot roomier, as well. Positioning of controls remain about the same, however, and we have our share of gripes with these. Even with column adjustment tight against the dash, a fairly short driver still finds the big steering wheel

tangling with his nose if he has the seat adjusted far enough forward to reach the pedals. This positioning had, in the past, been somewhat of a British trademark, but many other cars, including some made by BMC have a more realistic distance between face and steering wheel. Magnifying the discomfort for short folk is the fact that the wheel is mounted high to lift it away from the driver's legs. The gearshift lever is no improvement either, with its long, flexing shaft making positive shifts a matter of chance. Instrumentation is good, as are hand controls. These remain unchanged from previous models. Seat belt attachment points are now standard equipment on all Healeys.

Stopping power of the Mk II is excellent. High-speed braking required some pedal pressure, but the stop was extremely rapid and stable. So was the second, and the third. On the fourth, however, one of the big, 11¼-inch disc brakes started to chatter and it was 15 minutes before an ear-splitting squeak disappeared. This was likely a peculiarity individual to the test car and possibly was caused by some external factor such as dirt or grease on the pads. When the squeak disappeared it stayed gone even under some later rough use. No trouble with the drum brakes on the rear, though.

While quite a bit of play was present in the engine and driveline mounting during hard initial acceleration, the clutch, etc., were able to cope with the torque and moved the big car off the line very positively. A new camshaft and stronger valve springs are other improvements incorporated in the Mk II engine along with the triple, 1¾-inch

PHOTOS: RANDY HOLT

Austin-Healey Mk. II

Interior of the "4-seater" is impressive looking, but roomy for two. As Randy demonstrates, left, the rear seats are strictly for kiddies. New look in the engine compartment includes triple SU's.

Below, Healey's lines have always had a neat, tailored appearance and streamlining is efficient for its velocity. Car is heavy, but balanced and rugged.

Trunk space is minimal, with both spare and battery there. Also, this is the only place to store side windows and top. The space behind the front seats remains the only other storage area of any size that can accommodate luggage or large objects.

Disconnect switch, hidden in trunk is a good safety and anti-theft device. It intersects ground cable from the battery and, turned off, shuts down the complete electrical system, is then locked in the trunk. Are you watching, car-snatchers?

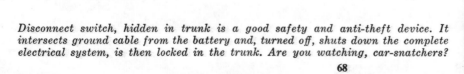

AUSTIN-HEALEY MK II

carburetors, and they undoubtedly contributed to the strong acceleration we were able to get from the very new test unit. The Healey engine as it comes off the regular production line is not a high twister, being red-lined still at 5200 rpm. In fact most Healeys, except those prepared with competition with the optional cam, will definitely sign off before 5500 revs are reached. The performance comes from sheer brute torque. This is the most noticeable aspect of the big six-holer; it comes on low on the rpm scale, so low in fact that second gear can be used for starts with some regularity if the clutch and throttle are properly coordinated.

Handling remains as good as ever, with typical initial understeer. It is an easy car to drift, with excellent adhesion on most surfaces. The Dunlop RS5 tires do a very creditable job of sticking, with minimal noise. Gone forever is the old tendency of fast, chattering rear end breakaway. The Healey is definitely a car that must be powered through a corner — or rather out of it and the remarkable torque output makes this a relatively simple operation. The best technique in hard driving as in competition with the Healey is to use the very excellent brakes going into the turns, motoring through and then climbing back on the throttle as soon as the car is lined up for the exit — but please, not too early. Too much, too soon especially in too low a gear, can result in some pretty spectacular spinning, generally toward the inside, in which case it's best to concentrate on where the car is going to end up rather to make any wild attempts to pull off a complete save. So low is the Healey's center of gravity that it usually takes something in the nature of a derrick or a wheel-ripping curb or ditch to turn one over. These things don't happen on the road unless the driver is indulging in some pretty goofy foolishness but they can happen on the race track.

There are certain small detail changes in the new Mk II that are worthy of comment. One is the top. Healey tops, especially four-seater tops, in the past have been something to make strong men weep in angry frustration. On earlier four-seaters the top frame was hinged to the car and the front bow had no connection with the rest of the frame. It still doesn't but the frame is not attached to the top fabric either. The frame is removable now and separate from the top itself a-la Sprite. The top is an envelope that fits over the frame, snapping at the rear and fastening, still with that tricky bow, at the windshield. Putting it up and down is still time consuming but no longer an exercise in finger-breaking.

Another detail is in the overdrive. Normally the Laycock unit is instantaneous when the switch is flipped — it's either in or out just like that. Injudicious use of this switch has in the past resulted in damaged overdrives. Not so with the new Healey. Now the switch acts almost as a pre-selector. To go into overdrive from direct the switch is flipped up and the throttle backed off slightly. It'll go in without backing off but there's short time lag that makes it silly not to adjust engine speed to the upward change. In going out of overdrive the switch is flipped down and the throttle kicked. In this case it won't go out until the throttle is depressed to pick up the slack and take the shock out of the driveline. Very likely this little change will save a few OD repair bills due to damage from sloppy downshifts out of overdrive into direct.

All in all the new Mark II is fit continuation of a line that has been successively and successfully improved since it was introduced. With all its muscle and good handling qualities the latest Austin Healey is probably the most car for a given amount of money, taken in terms of amount of car received per dollar spent, that can be bought today. &

TEST DATA

VEHICLE	Austin-Healey	MODEL	MK II
PRICE (as tested)	$3639.00 POE L.A., inbound	OPTIONS	Adj. steering $15

ENGINE:

Type	6 cylinder, in-line, 4 cycle, water-cooled
Head	Removable, cast-iron
Valves	Ohv, pushrod/rocker actuated
Max. bhp	132 @ 4750 rpms
Max. torque	n.a.
Bore	3.281 in. 83.34 mm.
Stroke	3.5 in. 88.9 mm.
Displacement	177.7 cu. in. 2912 cc.
Compression Ratio	9.1 to 1
Induction System	3 SU 1¾" HD6
Exhaust System	Cast manifold into double muffler
Electrical System	12V Lucas, single distrib.

CLUTCH:	Borg-Beck single	DIFFERENTIAL:	Salsbury
Diameter:	10½ in.	Ratio:	3.9 to 1.
Actuation:	hydraulic disc	Drive Axles (type)	Live, enclosed, semi-floating

TRANSMISSION:	4 speed, synchro top 3 — Laycock de Normanville OD	STEERING: Turns Lock to Lock	3¼
		Turn Circle:	35.7 ft.

Ratios: 1st	2.94 to 1	BRAKES:	Drum rear, 2¼" width
2nd	2.058 to 1	Disc front	2" pad width
3rd	1.32 to 1	Drum or Disc Diameter.	11.25 &
4th	1.0 to 1		11.0 in.
3rd O.D.	1.075 to 1	Swept Area	302.16 sq. in.
4th O.D.	.822 to 1		

CHASSIS:

Frame:	Box section, conventional
Body:	Steel, semi-unit
Front Suspension:	Unequal control arms, arm shock, coil springs
Rear Suspension:	Live, leaf springs, arm shock
Tire Size & Type:	5.90 x 15 Dunlop RS5

WEIGHTS AND MEASURES

Wheelbase:	91.7 in.	Ground Clearance	4.6 in.
Front Track:	48¾ in.	Curb Weight	2465 lbs.
Rear Track:	50 in.	Test Weight	2765 lbs.
Overall Height	46 in.	Crankcase	7½ qts.
Overall Width	60 in.	Cooling System	12½ qts.
Overall Length	157½ in.	Gas Tank	14.4 gals.

PERFORMANCE:

0-30	3.5 sec.	0-70	15.0 sec.
0-40	5.9 sec.	0-80	20.3 sec.
0-50	8.6 sec.	0-90	26.6 sec.
0-60	11.9 sec.	0-100	— sec.

Standing ¼ mile 16.3 sec. @ 72 mph			Top Speed (av. two-way run) 112 mph		
Speed Error	30	40	50	60 70 80 90
Actual	31	41	50	60 70 79 89

Fuel Consumption Test:	19 mpg	RPM Red-line	5200 rpm
Average	25 mpg	Speed Ranges in gears:	
Recommended Shift Points:		1st	0 to 32 mph
Max. 1st	32 mph	2nd	15 to 47 mph
Max. 2nd	47 mph	3rd	35 to 79 mph 3rd. O.D. 88
Max. 3rd	79 mph	4th .43 to top mph 4th. O.D. 50-top	

Brake Test:	.78 Average % G, over 8 stops.
	Squeal encountered on 6th stop.

REFERENCE FACTORS:

Bhp per cubic inch	0.745
Lbs. per bhp	18.7
Piston Speed @ Peak rpm	2771 ft./min.
Swept brake area per lb.	0.1225 Sq. In.

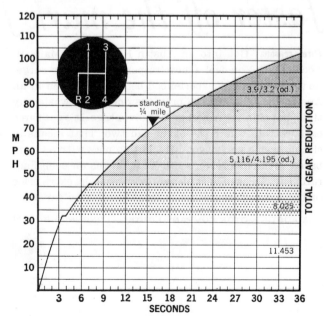

AUSTIN HEALEY 3000
MARK II

faster off the mark for three good reason

Three reasons: Get into an Austin Healey 3000 Mark II. Accelerate. You feel a new response. A joyous surge-forward you never experienced before—not even in an Austin Healey 3000. The previous one didn't waste any time, but this one has an unfair advantage. It's got three carburettors where the other had two. That means in simple terms you've got 130 b.h.p. to play with as compared with the previous 124. That means an even finer rally car. An even finer pleasure car. And the extra price of the extra carburettor is frankly nil: the car costs £824 plus £378.18.1 Purchase Tax and Surcharge.

More points: The Mark II is not only an even faster ca it's also an even safer car. It's still got disc brakes o the front of course, but as an optional extra the brakin can now be servo-assisted. And inside the car are all th necessary fittings for seat belts.

Still more points: New camshaft. New air cleaner. New hea shield for silencer. New grille and air-intake slats.

GET INTO AN AUSTIN AND OUT OF THE ORDINARY

THE AUSTIN MOTOR COMPANY LIMITED · LONGBRIDGE · BIRMINGHAM · Personal Exports Division: 41/46 Piccadilly · London · V

**By Appointment to
Her Majesty The Queen
Motor Car Manufacturers
The Austin Motor
Company Limited**

Backed by BMC 12-month
warranty and BMC service

*Detail modifications—including radiator grille and the air intake on the bonnet top—h*ɔ*ve been made, but the basic outline of the "big" Healey remains much the same as when it was introduced in 1952. In certain ways, the Healey preserves earlier British sports car traditions*

AUSTIN-HEALEY 3000

No. 1852

WHEN the Healey 100 made its début at the Earls Court Show of 1952, fitted with the four-cylinder 2·6-litre engine used in the Austin A.90 Atlantic coupé, it was clear that the car was destined for a successful competition career. However, one doubts whether anyone foresaw its becoming, eight years later, one of the most successful rally cars in the world, winning outright the tough Liège-Rome-Liège and Alpine rallies. Except for detail changes, the clean, attractive lines of the car have remained very much the same. Mechanically, the changes have centred largely around the power unit, the Austin-Healey 100 becoming the Austin-Healey 100-Six in 1957, when the four-cylinder engine was replaced by a six of similar capacity.

Three years later it became the Austin-Healey 3000, when the capacity was increased to 2,912 c.c., and this year the Mark 2 was introduced. Apart from a restyled radiator grille, the latest car is fitted with three 1½-in. HS4 S.U. carburettors in place of the two 1¾-in. HS6s of the previous model, together with a redesigned inlet manifold and a new camshaft giving higher lift to the inlet valves and a longer dwell to the exhausts. All this has brought the production car allegedly into line with the specification of the successful competition cars used by the B.M.C. Competitions Department. Thus, through the years, the engine output has increased from the 90 b.h.p. of the Healey 100 to the 132 b.h.p. of the Mark 2 Austin-Healey 3000, with the weight increasing from 1,960lb to 2,526. The b.h.p. per ton figure, therefore, has been increased only from 102 to 117.

First impressions of the car are that it is comfortable, has plenty of leg room, is moderately well appointed, and

Central pull-up handbrake, all-black finish, near-vertical steering wheel, and full instrumentation—this is very much a "competition" cockpit

The engine compartment is packed, yet everything that matters—carburettors, hydraulic reservoirs, distributor and radiator cap—are readily accessible. The screenwash bottle is mounted inside the cockpit

Austin-Healey 3000 . . .

is immensely strong and rigid. Also, it has a pleasant, long-legged feeling of being able to lollop along all day at a cruising speed of 90 m.p.h. or more with very little effort.

The cockpit is very well arranged and is finished throughout in black leather, or leather-cloth where wear is light. The driving seat on the car tested was hard and seemed to have inadequate upholstery; this, together with one or two other points, suggested that the 10,000 miles indicated in the speedometer window had been fairly strenuous ones. For a tall person the forward visibility is excellent; but, with the seat so compressed, a shorter driver had his view interrupted by the top of the large steering wheel. The instruments are comprehensive and well set out, while all the "driving" controls are within comfortable reach. Instrument lighting is good, without being so bright as to worry one, though there is no rheostat control. The screen pillars are slim and the extremities of both front wings are seen easily, so that placing the car in heavy traffic is no problem.

The hard-top was draught- and water-proof, making the interior of the car snug and warm. This is an optional extra, costing £60, the conventional soft hood being standard equipment; with either in position, the occasional rear seat(s) can be used only for short runs, headroom being decidedly cramped. Rigid, aluminium-framed transparent plastic sidescreens are fitted, the rearmost panels of which slide forwards. There is no method of locking the driving compartment, and no lockable glove locker, so that valuables should not be left in the car. By turning off the battery master-switch in the boot, and locking the boot lid, the car can be made secure against a thief in a hurry.

Large pockets are provided in the doors, and there is a parcels shelf above the foot-well on the passenger's side. This would be much more useful if it did not house the screenwash bottle, for which there is no room in the very full engine compartment. The heating-demisting system is most efficient, as is the fresh-air cooling system, and one

is no longer worried by the high cockpit temperatures found in earlier models of this car. The range of seat adjustment for both passenger and driver is considerable, and desirable if the rear seats are to be used. However, if one sets the driving seat to achieve a "straight-armed" position, the pedals become out of reach, despite the provision of an adjustment in steering column length of around 3in. The situation is not improved by the unusually long travel in the clutch pedal and gear lever. Adding to the impression that the particular car tested had seen a very active life was the fact that the synchromesh was practically non-existent, particularly on top gear.

The hand-brake is of the pull-up type, conveniently placed between the front seats. When the car is travelling forward it is extremely efficient, and will apply the rear drum brakes with sufficient force to lock the rear wheels; it will also hold the car from running forwards on a 1-in-3 test hill. Surprisingly, however, it will not prevent the car from running backwards on the 1-in-4 test gradient.

Cold Starting

With use of the choke, the engine starts quickly and easily from cold, though it reaches its working temperature somewhat slowly. It does not appreciate a diet of premium-grade fuel, on which it pinks and tends to run-on after being switched off. With the compression ratio of 9·0 to 1 this is scarcely surprising, and both faults were eliminated by using super-premium fuel. It is extremely smooth and flexible, and has plenty of torque at low speeds. It will pull the car away in top gear without hesitation or snatch from the surprisingly low speed of 8 m.p.h., so that it is able to trickle through traffic happily in third gear. It is reasonably quiet and unobtrusive up to 3,000 r.p.m., but above this speed there are some intake roar and roughness.

The clutch is light in operation, and very smooth in take-up; there was no prolonged slip when the standing-start figures were taken, nor when full-throttle changes were made, and it had no trouble in moving the car off quickly and cleanly on a 1-in-3 test gradient. The Laycock-de Normanville overdrive, which is available as an optional extra and was fitted on the test car, works on top and third gears. It is invaluable in keeping the engine speed down, and thus saving petrol; and it helps one to avoid the critical engine speed of 3,000 r.p.m. at which there is a noticeable resonance in the exhaust system. The transmission as a whole is very quiet, and there are no vibration periods throughout the speed range.

In general "feel" the car inspires great confidence, being undoubtedly very safe indeed and entirely without whims or idiosyncrasies. It has excellent directional stability, and will hurry along at 100 m.p.h. or more "hands off," without any desire to wander off-line. It has a slight—and de-

Very much an "occasional four-seater," the Healey offers limited space for rear passengers; headroom beneath the hard-top is cramped

The rear bumper wraps round to give good protection. Ground clearance is limited below the exhaust pipe where it runs beneath the rear cross member. The hard-top is optional

sirable—understeering characteristic; and, except when speeds are so high that the engine has run out of power, it is always possible to help the tail round by means of the throttle. If the rear wheels do begin to slide—which they will do fairly easily at the manufacturers' recommended high-speed tyre pressures of 26 p.s.i. front and 29 rear—the response to opposite lock is immediate, the car quickly straightening up. So "right" does the handling feel that one gets the impression that it would be difficult even for an inexperienced driver to get into any serious trouble. The steering is light though one would prefer slightly higher

Luggage space, if the rear seats are to be used for passengers, is strictly of the "toothbrush-and-pyjamas" variety, though when the car is used as a two-seater—as it normally would be on long runs—there is plenty of space behind the front seats

gearing than its present 3¼ turns from lock to lock. Self-centring action is pleasantly strong.

Second gear is too low, maximum speeds in the gears being 34, 48, 77, and 106 m.p.h.—and 98 in overdrive third. The gear-change is precise, and smooth in operation. In taking the standing-start acceleration figures it was difficult to avoid wheelspin on the initial take-off, even on a dry road, and in the wet one had to be decidedly gentle with the throttle.

Although surprisingly soft, the suspension is sufficiently damped to avoid much roll when the car is cornering fast, and ride comfort is excellent. Not only does it iron out the normal, main road long-frequency irregularities completely, but it rides well over the shorter bumps, such as

potholes. Very little road noise is transmitted to the interior of the car. On a rough, pavé-type surface, however, the occupants are bounced about to some extent at slow speeds, though the ride levels off as the speed is increased; on such surfaces there is reasonably little outward patter of the wheels on cornering. On the washboard test surface, the whole body structure of the car was amazingly stable, confirming the impression that it is very rigidly built. Coupled with the safe handling characteristics of the Healey, the first-class ride makes it a very restful car for long-distance travel.

Reliable Brakes

From start to finish the brakes inspired great trust, giving plenty of "feel," always pulling the car up in a straight line, and never showing signs of fade, even after repeated stops from high speeds. The car has always been sound in this particular aspect; of the drum brakes fitted to the car tested in 1953 it was said that they were "entirely suitable," and the same was said of the rear drums and front discs of the car tested last year—equipment which the Mark 2 also uses. A brake servo was not fitted to the car tested, though this is available as an optional extra, and pedal pressures were therefore somewhat high, as shown by the meter readings. Due to the angle of the pedal, however, or the relative positions of the seat and brake pedal, one never appeared to be pressing particularly hard; it seems that the use of a servo is scarcely justified, even if the car is to be driven exclusively by a woman.

There are several points about the car which, though in keeping with its honest-to-goodness, no-frills character, seem somewhat out of place in a £1,200 car in 1961. There are, for example, no automatic supports for the bonnet or boot lid when they are open; instead one has to reach for their props and fit them into the slots provided. The doors are stiff to open, due to the use of friction-damper-type devices to stop them from swinging shut; and wheel-changing involves the use of an old-fashioned screw-up jack and the business of groping underneath the car for a suitable jacking point. The forepart of the hardtop is sensibly padded, to protect the occupants' heads—yet, proud of the padding, protrude potentially dangerous sharp clips which secure the roof to the windscreen. If the Austin-Healey were an out-and-out competition car one would readily forgive a lack of concessions to creature comforts, but it is essentially a fast sports-tourer, at least in its production form.

Luggage accommodation is rather meagre, the spare wheel and battery occupying most of the boot. For long-distance touring, however, when carrying space is at a premium, the car must in any case be regarded as no more than a two-seater, and the compartment behind the front seats will take a substantial amount of baggage. The fuel tank capacity is 12 gallons, giving the car a range between fill-up stops of about 200 miles. The lighting equipment is in keeping with the performance, the headlamps giving a powerful enough beam almost for the daytime cruising speeds to be maintained. They are foot-dipped by a switch alongside the clutch, where the left foot normally rests. This space, in fact. is larger than it needs to be—and the pedals could with advantage have greater separation; it would be difficult to drive the car wearing wide shoes.

Though there are a few points of criticism, the Mark 2 Austin-Healey is a good quality, strongly built sporting car with great charm and an amazing aptitude for hard work. It has a lively performance in standard trim, a performance to which the figures achieved by this far from new car scarcely do justice; almost all of them are appreciably down on those recorded by its predecessor, road-tested last year. The general quality of finish, and attention to detail is first class, except for those points mentioned. That it is capable of giving a much enhanced performance—for those who seek it—is shown by its remarkable run of successes in International rallies.

AUSTIN-HEALEY 3000

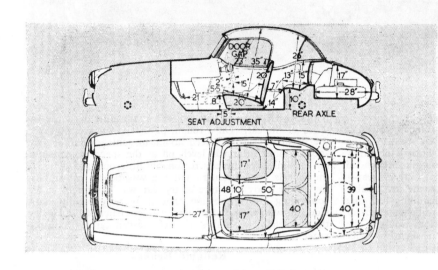

Scale ⅛in. to 1ft. Driving seat in central position. Cushions uncompressed.

———————— DATA ————————

PRICE (basic), with four-seater body, £829.
British purchase tax, £381 3s 11d.
Total (in Great Britain), £1,210 3s 11d.
Extras (inc. p.t.):   Radio, £35.   Heater, £22 12s 1d. Overdrive, £69 7s 3d. Hardtop, £87 10s. Wire wheels, £36 9s 2d.

ENGINE: Capacity, 2,912 c.c. (177·7 cu. in.)
Number of cylinders, 6.
Bore and stroke, 83·36 × 89·0mm (3·28 × 3·5in.).
Valve gear, overhead, pushrods and rockers.
Compression ratio, 9·0 to 1.
B.h.p. (net), 130 at 4,750 r.p.m. (b.h.p. per ton laden 100·7).
Torque (net), 167 lb. ft at 3,000 r.p.m.
M.p.h. per 1,000 r.p.m. in top gear, 20·9; in overdrive, 23·1.

WEIGHT (with 5 gal fuel): 22·8 cwt (2,555 lb).
Weight distribution (per cent): F, 48·8; R, 51·2.
Laden as tested, 25·8 cwt (2,891 lb).
Lb per c.c. (laden), 0·9.

BRAKES: Type, Girling, disc front, drum rear, hydraulic.
Disc diameter: 11·25in.
Drum dimensions: 11in. diameter; 2·25in. wide.
Swept area: F, 228 sq. in.; R, 155·5 sq. in. (297 sq. in. per ton laden).

TYRES: 5·90—15in. Dunlop RS5.
Pressures (p.s.i.): F, 20; R, 23 (normal); F, 26; R, 29 (fast driving).

TANK CAPACITY: 12 Imperial gallons.
Oil sump, 12 pints.
Cooling system, 20 pints (plus 1 pint if heater fitted).

DIMENSIONS: Wheelbase, 7ft 8in.
Track: F, 4ft 0·75in.; R, 4ft 2in.
Length (overall), 13ft 1·5in.
Width, 5ft 0·5in.
Height, 4ft 6in.
Ground clearance, 4·5in.

ELECTRICAL SYSTEM: 12-volt; 50 ampère-hour battery.
Headlamps, 50–40 watt bulbs.

SUSPENSION: Front, wishbones and coil springs, anti-roll bar.
Rear, live axle, half-elliptic springs and Panhard rod.

———————— PERFORMANCE ————————

ACCELERATION TIMES (mean):
Speed range, Gear Ratios, and Time in Sec.

m.p.h.	3·21* to 1	3·91 to 1	4·2* to 1	5·12 to 1	8·05 to 1	11·26 to 1
10– 30	—	—	—	7·0	4·1	3·5
20– 40	11·0	8·6	7·9	6·2	4·0	—
30– 50	11·3	8·3	8·1	6·2	—	—
40– 60	11·2	7·8	7·9	6·3	—	—
50– 70	13·1	8·9	8·8	7·6	—	—
60– 80	13·6	10·0	9·7	—	—	—
70– 90	15·0	13·2	13·9	—	—	—
80–100	18·5	17·5	—	—	—	—

* Overdrive

From rest through gears to:

30 m.p.h.	..	3·7 sec.	
40	,,	..	6·2 ,,
50	,,	..	9·3 ,,
60	,,	..	11·5 ,,
70	,,	..	15·6 ,,
80	,,	..	22·0 ,,
90	,,	..	30·0 ,,
100	,,	..	36·9 ,,

Standing quarter mile 18·8 sec.

MAXIMUM SPEEDS ON GEARS:

Gear			m.p.h.	k.p.h.
O.D. Top	(mean)		112·5	181·1
	(best)		115·0	185·1
Top	..	..	106	170
O.D. 3rd	..	..	98	158
3rd	..	..	81	130
2nd	..	..	50	80
1st	..	..	37	60

TRACTIVE EFFORT (by Tapley meter):

			Pull (lb per ton)	Equivalent gradient
O.D.	..	..	260	1 in 8·6
Top	..	..	340	1 in 6·5
O.D. Third	..		355	1 in 6·4
Third	..	..	445	1 in 5·0
Second	..	..	670	1 in 3·2

BRAKES (at 30 m.p.h. in neutral):

Pedal load in lb	Retardation	Equiv. stopping distance in ft
50	0·31g	97
75	0·47g	64
100	0·72g	42
125	0·84g	36
130	0·94g	32·1

FUEL CONSUMPTION (at constant speeds):

		Direct Top	O.D. Top
30 m.p.h.		30·5 m.p.g.	31·3 m.p.g.
40	,,	27·2 ,,	30·0 ,,
50	,,	25·1 ,,	28·0 ,,
60	,,	23·3 ,,	26·0 ,,
70	,,	21·2 ,,	24·2 ,,
80	,,	19·1 ,,	23·3 ,,
90	,,	15·0 ,,	18·0 ,,
100	,,	11·0 ,,	15·1 ,,

Overall fuel consumption for 1,223 miles, 17·7 m.p.g. (16·0 litres per 100 km.).
Approximate normal range 13–20 m.p.g. (21·7—14·1 litres per 100 km.).
Fuel: Super premium grades.

TEST CONDITIONS : Weather: Damp surface.
0–5 m.p.h. wind.
Air temperature, 55 deg. F.
Model described in *The Autocar* of 2 June, 1961.

STEERING: Turning circle:
Between kerbs: L, 34ft 4in.; R, 35ft 4in.
Between walls: L, 35ft 4in.; R, 36ft 4in.
Turns of steering wheel from lock to lock, 3·25.

SPEEDOMETER CORRECTION: m.p.h.

Car speedometer:	..		10	20	30	40	50	60	70	80	90	100	110	120
True speed: ..	..	..	9	19	28	37	47	57	66	75	84	94	106	115

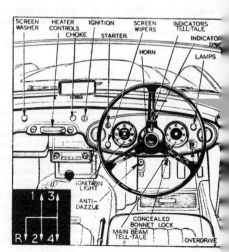

Austin-Healey 3000 sports convertible

With the accent on comfort

STEADILY developed over the past 10 years—and with an extremely successful team of rally cars always pointing the way ahead—the big Austin-Healey has been further improved for the coming season. This time, the accent is mainly on added comfort and weather protection, although changes have also been made to the engine and chassis.

The new model, which is known as the Austin-Healey 3000 Sports Convertible, is an occasional four-seater and replaces both the two-seater and occasional four-seater Mark II models.

Both the body shape and the seating accommodation are virtually identical to the Mark II occasional four-seater, but its rounded screen and all-weather equipment are entirely new. Frameless winding door windows, with hinged ventilating panels on their leading edges replace the former sliding side screens. The winders are conveniently placed below the interior door handles and, despite the need to accommodate drop windows within the doors, map pockets have been retained.

The sloping rear edges of the windows give a wide field of side vision from the front seats. Rearward vision is also good, through a large, flexible backlight attached to the hood by fasteners so that it can be dropped into the hood-well for increased ventilation in hot weather.

The head design makes one-man operation very simple. The

Top: The curved and sloping screen, hood and frameless winding side windows distinguish the new model. *Below:* The hood is simple to stow or erect, and this can be done from inside the car.

drill for lowering it consists of pulling the rear squab forward slightly, undoing a pair of toggle fasteners securing the backlight and folding the latter into the hood-well, releasing the two toggle fasteners attaching the hood to the screen and then swinging the hood back into its well by a handle on the top rail. No tricky folding is needed and the whole job can be done from inside the car in a minute or so. The driver need alight only if he decides to button the hood envelope in place. The appearance with the hood down is not quite so "concours" as some, but the design is far more practical than most for those who like to take advantage of fine weather.

With the hood closed there is generous headroom and neat appearance. The driver's head does not come immediately below a hood iron and soft, circular-section rubber seals suggest freedom from draughts and water leaks. But despite the comparative security of the interior there are no door locks, the only lockable space being the boot.

Two adjustable bucket seats are provided as before, but better foot room has been achieved by re-designing the gearbox tunnel to give comfortable pedal spacing with plenty of room for the driver's left foot to the side of the clutch pedal. The tunnel is of glass fibre which gives better insulation from both heat and noise. It is not, strictly, a 1963 innovation, having been introduced during production earlier this year to go with a new central, remote-control gear change, more conventional and positive than that previously used because the gearbox has been turned through 90° to bring the selectors to the top instead of at one side. As before, Laycock-de Normanville overdrive

At a glance . . .

ENGINE.—6 cyl., 83.36 mm. x 89 mm., 2,912 c.c.; o.h.v. (push rods); two S.U. HS6 carburetters; max. power, approx. 130 b.h.p. net at 4,750 r.p.m.; max. torque, 167 lb. ft. at 3,000 r.p.m.

TRANSMISSION.—10-in. s.d.p. clutch; 4-speed gearbox with synchromesh on 2-3-4. Ratios (normal): 3.545, 4.640, 7.278, 10.39; rev., 13.41. Ratios (with opt. Laycock-de Normanville overdrive): 3.91 (O/D 3.215), 5.118 (O/D 4.207), 8.027, 11.46; rev., 14.78. Road speed in top gear at 1,000 r.p.m., 20.9 m.p.h. (with O/D: direct, 18.94 m.p.h.; O/D, 23.1 m.p.h.).

RUNNING GEAR.—Girling hydraulic brakes, disc front/drum rear (vacuum servo optional extra); coil and wishbone i.f.s.; semi-elliptic rear springs; anti-roll bar front and rear; cam-and-peg steering; 5.90-15 Dunlop Road Speed tyres.

DIMENSIONS.—Length, 13 ft. 1½ in.; width, 5 ft. 0½ in.; turning circle, 35 ft.; weight, 21½ cwt.

PRICES.—Basic, £865 (total with P.T., £1,190 7s. 9d.). Extras (including P.T.): overdrive, £64 9s. 1d.; wire wheels, £34 7s. 6d.; tonneau cover, £13 15s.

Austin-Healey 3000

Continued

Back to twin carburetters, mainly for the benefit of U.S. dealers who had difficulty in synchronizing three of them. Power and torque are unaffected by the change.

controlled by a switch on the facia board is an optional extra.

The reversion to two carburetters, instead of the three adopted for the Mark II model, is an interesting engine change. This has been done largely because U.S. dealers have complained of the complexity of three and the difficulty of synchronization. Imperfectly tuned, three instruments gave less satisfactory results than two larger, more easily synchronized carburetters. The 1¾-in. S.U. carburetters are of the latest HS6 type; and the new camshaft which was largely responsible for an increase in power on the Mark II is retained in the latest engine. In addition the increased under-bonnet space given by the two carburetters permits better heat insulation (by means of both washers and an asbestos-lined metal shield). As a result, b.h.p. and torque figures are said to be unaltered despite a simplified specification.

The only other significant chassis change concerns the front suspension, the coil springs having been stiffened considerably in the light of competition experience. The spring rate at the wheel is now 115 lb./in. compared with the former 96 lb./in. and damper settings have been modified to suit. The effect is to transfer some roll load from the rear to the front, with a general improvement in cornering and a reduced tendency to rear-end breakaway. A short run on one of the new models suggested that the improvement has not been achieved at the expense of the ride.

One further innovation is the availability, as an optional extra, of a Girling vacuum servo which greatly reduces the pedal effort for the disc-front drum-rear brakes.

A short straight gear lever, padded transmission tunnel, and the hood envelope are points to note in this picture. The rear seats are strictly occasional but useful for luggage.

CONTINUED FROM PAGE 40

they finished. The torque of that Austin engine was staggering, for it pulled the car uphill past tourists who must have thought they were standing still. Don Morley drove superbly, for despite the handicap he lost no time at all up to the start of the Quatre Chemins.

TWENTY SECONDS TO SPARE

Bill and I regard this as the tightest section we have done in more than sixty Continental rallies. It was only 21 miles long and ran over no pass higher than 4000 feet, but the longest straight was only about 100 yards and the road was only occasionally wide enough for two cars. The route ran through a gorge where the air shimmered with the heat, which had melted the tar on the bends, so that each was taken in a slide as a private calculated risk. I gave the Austin-Healey all it could take and it responded magnificently except towards the end when the terrific under-bonnet temperature caused a slight miss at peak revs. We passed the Ferrari, Gerry

Burgess's Ford and Coltelloni's Citroën; each overtaking cost us valuable seconds, although the drivers did their best to give us free passage. However, at the top of the Col de Bleine, with four kilometres to go, we had 20 seconds in hand. The section seemed to be in the bag, but, as so often happens, it didn't turn out that way! Coming downhill very fast, I didn't realise until too late that there was loose gravel on the far side of one corner. The resultant slide wasn't caught quite quickly enough and we ended broadside across the road. Even with the knowledge that one may be collected at high velocity by another competitor, it takes a long time to straighten up on a 15-foot road with a 13-foot car, and flat-out driving for the rest of the section couldn't prevent us from being 23 seconds late.

Our Coupe des Alpes was gone, but what of the team? Pat came through with a thumbs-up; the girls had done it by 9 seconds! Then came the Morleys with a broad grin, which well they might have.

On top gear only they had lost but 4 minutes—a staggering drive when the best Ford performance, with all five gears, was 3 minutes late!

And so, in team order, the Austin-Healeys drove quietly into the finish. Their successes are possibly the best ever obtained by a works team in the 'Alpine'. We finished 1, 2 and 3 in our class, won every team and class prize open to us, and Pat and Ann were only beaten in General Classification by a fine car, magnificently driven, which, however, probably cost more than all our team put together! To round it off, the Gold/Hughes Mini-Minor won its class—in which, indeed, it was the only survivor.

Finally, we provided the information which the 'boffins' wanted for their stress calculations. But, for me, the 1960 'Alpine' will always be the supreme example of a justified calculated risk which came off for the team but not for the individual—and the former is more important than the latter!

The **AUSTIN HEALEY** 3000

goes convertible ►

By Appointment to
Her Majesty The Queen
Motor Car Manufacturers
The Austin Motor
Company Limited

BMC
THE BRITISH MOTOR
CORPORATION

Backed by BMC 12-month
warranty and BMC service

Now the brilliant Austin Healey 3000 is a slicker, more practical 2/4 seater, with a quick-folding convertible top that stows away neatly round the top of the new back seat. We call it the Sports Convertible—and a dream of a sports car it is:—130 b.h.p.; disc front brakes (optionally servo assisted); twin carburettors. All give you—performance plus safety, plus luxurious styling. ☐ The Austin Healey 3000 was outright winner of the Alpine Rally in both 1961 and 1962. The Sports Convertible costs £1045.15.4 (£865 plus £180.15.4 purchase tax). At a price like that, it's a match for any sports car in the world. See it and drive it—at your Austin Dealer's showroom.

THE AUSTIN HEALEY 3000 SPORTS CONVERTIBLE

AUSTIN-HEALEY 3000
Sports Convertible

IN keeping with the current trend in sports car body design, the British Motor Corporation announce the Austin-Healey 3000 Sports Convertible as a replacement for the well-established 3000 Mark II model. Retaining the same body lines as that model it offers greatly enhanced weather protection. As a result of minor engine changes, the low speed behaviour of the car has been brought into line with its new role without, however, detracting appreciably from its top end performance. An internal re-arrangement of the gearbox has reduced the effective dimensions of that unit, resulting in slightly more toeboard space.

A new windscreen with a stout, chromium-plated frame is the main apparent change to the appearance of the car. The line of the screen bottom rail is continued along the top of the doors by the use of a stainless steel moulding—a trick which raises the waist line. Plated quarter-vent frames are functional as well as adding to the area of bright metal work; they have channels in their rear edge for the new curved side window glasses, which are frameless and wind down flush with the tops of the doors. Conventional window lifts are employed, with the handles set well forward on the doors, clear of the occupants' knees.

Internally, little is altered except that trim pads with map pockets replace the door compartments of the earlier model. There is also slight loss of width across the rear compartment because of the wider boxes required to house the more complex hood frame. The main trim change is in the upholstery material itself, which is a new porous, leather-grained plastic. This covering retains its flexibility in a wide range of temperature conditions. The upholstery is in a choice of colours to contrast with the main body paint.

Folded, the hood does not drop below the main body level but makes a neat line along the rear deck and should help to reduce back swirl of wind at speed. Although it is necessary to get out of the car to stow the hood neatly, it can be lowered from the driving seat by un-fastening two over-centre clasps which hold it to the screen rail, and pushing it back with one hand. The hood frame is sturdy without being complicated and the covering, in stout black plastic, is suffi-ciently flexible to pull tight without wrinkles.

While enthusiasts may not approve of the reversion to two 1·75in. HS6 S.U. carburettors on basically the old inlet manifold, maximum power is reduced by only 1 b.h.p. With this change goes an improved torque curve which is now substantially flat between 2,800 r.p.m. and 3,700 r.p.m., a figure of 158lb./ft. (equal to a net b.m.e.p. of 135 p.s.i.) being

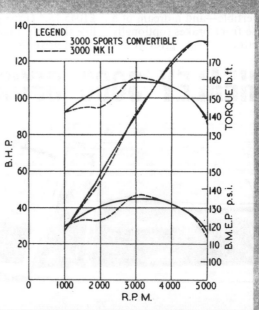

LEGEND
— 3000 SPORTS CONVERTIBLE
--- 3000 MK II

Left : Induction layout, using two 1·75in. HS6 S.U. carburettors in place of three 1·5in. instru-ments. It gives better accessibility for tuning, and two units are more easily synchronized

Comparative performance curves of the new and old engines, torque has been improved without signifi-cant top-end power loss

Left: Furled, the hood stands proud above the rear deck and forms a windbreak. The hood cover is standard equipment. Right: Introduction of wind-down windows has meant that the large door lockers of previous 3000 models have been lost in accommodating the window winding mechanism. However, map pockets are retained on both doors

Above: A useful feature in hot climates is the ability to roll down the rear window and obtain a flow of cool air through the car. The flexible clear plastic light is attached internally with press studs. Right: Suitable for one-man operation, the new hood is sturdy and neat. The heavy sponge rubber window seals can be seen along the edge of the frame

maintained within this range. Moreover, greater flexibility at very low speeds is claimed, and it was certainly possible to drive an early production model at less than 10 m.p.h. in top gear. Among the detail changes is a camshaft with slightly reduced dwell.

An engineering change, which considerably reduces the complication of the remote gear-change mechanism, has been a redesign of the gearbox casting to bring the selector mechanism to the top of the box. Previously this was at the side, a relic from the time when the gearbox was common to a B.M.C. model with steering column change. Apart from bringing the gear lever to the centreline of the car, the gear casing is narrower, permitting an increase of 0·75in. in toeboard width. A further improvement in this vicinity is that the transmission cover material has been changed to glass-fibre reinforced plastic, resulting in reduced heat transfer into the driving compartment.

To improve handling, the front roll stiffness has been increased by the incorporation of stiffer front springs and harder damper settings.

The incorporation of so many minor changes has had a marked influence on the character of the car. A brief run in an early production model confirmed that

the level of refinement is noticeably higher because of greatly improved flexibility and increased quietness, and very little bite has been lost. The impression of refinement is owed partly to extra attention to soundproofing generally and in particular to the sound damping of the new door trim pads and side window glasses. At the moment production is concentrated on cars for the export market; however home buyers should not have too long to wait. As a result of these improvements, the basic price has increased by £36, or £49 10s with tax.

PRICES	Basic £	U.K. List £ s d
Austin-Healey 3000 Sports Convertible..	865	1,190 7 9
Extras :		
Wire-spoke wheels		34 7 6
Radio		33 0 0
Heater		21 6 3
Servo brakes		13 15 0
Tonneau cover		13 15 0
Overdrive		64 9 1

BOOK REVIEWED

More Wild Drivers, by Red Daniels. Published by The Scorpion Press, 11 Rofant Road, Northwood, Middlesex. Price, 7s 6d.

With terrifying insight and accuracy, the author caricatures, in line and in words, the mental make-up of the multitude of driver types (and their cars) that one meets around the roads today. From cover to cover, the book is a riot, as was its predecessor, *Drivers Wild*, published last November. Mostly, it will make you

split your sides with laughter; but it will also shake you from time to time, when the author unearths some undesirable traits in your own character as a motorist. All our secrets are laid bare—and one sincerely hopes that the police, appreciating his potential value in their field, do not enlist his services as lecturer to trainee "speed cops." Perhaps they won't, however, for they too have not escaped his pen. P.G.

AUSTIN HEALEY '3000'

goes conver

A quick action disappearing hood, wind-up windows and wrap-around windscreen add saloon

THE world's most successful sports car in international rallying, the Austin-Healey '3000', now makes its appearance in a new form as an occasional four-seater sports convertible with wrap-round windscreen, wind-up glass side windows, and quick-action folding hood.

This popular sports car thus develops what is truly a dual personality. The big six-cylinder 2912 c.c. engine, with its power output of 136 b.h.p. (gross) at 4,750 r.p.m., gives the outstanding performance which Austin-Healey owners have come to expect, and this can be enjoyed at its best in open form with the hood and side windows lowered. In a matter of seconds the hood can be raised to transform the Sports Convertible into a snug, all-weather car for high-speed motoring in comfort. Open or closed, the Austin-Healey '3000' will out-perform most other sports cars on the road, yet the flexibility of the six-cylinder engine makes the car just as suitable for low-speed pottering if desired.

All the best features of the well-proved chassis specification have been retained in the new model. The power unit is largely

---

SPECIFICATION...

Engine: Six-cylinder 2912 c.c. (83.36×89 mm.) with four-bearing crankshaft and overhead valves operated by pushrods. Full-flow oil filter with renewable element. Centrifugal water pump with four-blade fan (six-blade fan available overseas). Ignition by coil and 12-volt battery; distributor with combined centrifugal and vacuum advance control. KE965 steel exhaust valves. Twin exhaust system. Twin semi-downdraught S.U. HS6 carburetters and S.U. electric fuel pump. Power output, 130 b.h.p. net (136 gross) at 4,750 r.p.m. Max. torque, 167 lb. ft. at 3,000 r.p.m. Compression ratio, 9.03 to 1.

Transmission: Single dry-plate clutch to four-speed synchromesh gearbox with short central gear-lever mounted on transmission tunnel. Open propeller shaft with needle-roller universal joints. Hypoid final drive, ratio 3.545 to 1 (3.91 to 1 with overdrive). Gearbox ratios: reverse, 3.72; first 2.88; second, 2.06; third, 1.31; overdrive third, 1.077; top, 1.0; overdrive top, 0.822 to 1.

Suspension: Independent front by coil spring and wishbone, with anti-roll bar. Non-independent rear by semi-elliptic leaf springs, with anti-sway bar. Hydraulic lever-type shock absorbers, front and rear.

Steering: Cam and peg, ratio 14 to 1. Spring-spoke steering wheel, 17 in. dia.

Wheels and brakes: Ventilated steel disc wheels with 590×15 in. Dunlop Road Speed tyres (wire-spoke wheels obtainable if preferred). Girling brakes: 11¼ in. disc type on front; 11×2¼ in. drum type on rear.

Bodywork: Occasional four-seater, two-door convertible with wind-down glass side windows and hinged ventilators. Forward-hinged doors with locking handles. Fixed wrap-round windscreen with stainless steel frame. Vinyl-treated fabric hood anchored to top of windscreen by two quick-release catches; folds completely behind rear seats when lowered. Lockable luggage compartment. Paint finish in single or dual colours.

Instruments: Grouped on driver's side of facia. Trip speedometer, tachometer, fuel gauge, combined water temperature and oil pressure gauge.

Leading dimensions: Wheelbase, 7 ft. 8 in. Track, 4 ft. 0¾ in. (front); 4 ft. 2 in. (rear). Length, 13 ft. 1½ in. Height (hood up), 4 ft. 2 in. Width, 5 ft. 0½ in. Turning circle, 35 ft. Ground clearance, 4½ in. Unladen weight, approx. 2393 lb.

Price: £865 basic (£1190 7s. 9d. with Purchase Tax in U.K.).

ble

rt to an outstanding sports car

unchanged, but the enthusiast will welcome the new close-ratio gearbox with higher first, second and reverse gears—and especially the new short gear-lever mounted

continued overleaf

The Austin-Healey '3000' Sports Convertible, Model BJ7

With hood furled neatly, the new convertible version of the Austin-Healey '3000' is as exhilarating an open-air car as its predecessor, while the new windscreen gives even better visibility; the new side windows can be instantly raised or lowered and in conjunction with the swivelling quarter vents can provide complete control of cockpit ventilation

centrally on the transmission tunnel, giving a crisper and more positive gear-change than the previous type. High gearing (3.545 to 1 in top) gives the 'long-legged' gait which is so untiring for long journeys, and as before the Austin-Healey '3000' is obtainable with Laycock de Normanville overdrive on third and top gears, engaged at will by flicking a switch on the facia. Normal top gear gives 20.9 m.p.h. per 1,000 r.p.m. On overdrive models, a 3.91 to 1 final drive ratio provides 19 m.p.h. per 1,000 r.p.m. in normal top, rising to 23 m.p.h. per 1,000 r.p.m. when the overdrive is engaged.

The acceleration is outstanding, 30 m.p.h.

being reached from a standing start in 3.7 seconds, 60 m.p.h. in 10.9 seconds, and 90 m.p.h. in 26 seconds. Mean maximum speed is 116 m.p.h., yet the Austin-Healey '3000' has returned 34 m.p.g. at a constant 40 m.p.h. in overdrive top. Normal fuel consumption under fast driving conditions averages 20 to 25 m.p.g. To this performance is added the safety of disc front brakes and Dunlop Road Speed tyres, while sturdy seat belt anchorages are built into the car during manufacture.

Although basically similar to its predecessor, the new bodywork gives improved aerodynamics and the lines are subtly sleeker. The wrap-around windscreen gives

better visibility, and the wind-down side windows are combined with hinged ventilators to provide complete control over cockpit ventilation. The hood design is particularly ingenious, the frame being counterbalanced by concealed springs so that it can be raised or lowered in a moment, whether the side windows are up or down. In the lowered position, the hood folds behind the occasional rear seats, where it is concealed by a neatly-fitting cover. When raised, it is quickly attached to the windscreen frame by two quick-release catches.

A special feature of this hood is the new rear light, which is made of flexible plastic material and attached to the hood by fasteners. It can be quickly unfastened and lowered out of sight behind the seats, leaving the hood raised. In hot countries this provides the best possible form of ventilation for an open car.

With its new side windows, the Austin-Healey '3000' has now been provided with locks on both doors, that on the driver's side being operated by the ignition key from outside the car. As there is also a battery master switch located inside the lockable luggage boot, the Sports Convertible can safely be left unattended.

The price of the Austin-Healey '3000' Sports Convertible is £865, plus £325 7s. 9d. purchase tax in the U.K. Optional extras include radio, heater, overdrive, wire-spoked wheels, tonneau cover and servo-assisted brakes.

The wind-up side windows retract into the doors, but there is still a useful pocket for maps. Also in the cockpit view above is shown the remote control gear lever and the curved windscreen. On the right is seen the quickly detachable rear window incorporated in the new hood, giving the ideal hot weather combination of shade and through-ventilation

Austin-Healey 3000 MK. II SPORTS CONVERTIBLE 2,912 c.c.

BETWEEN the range of small four-cylinder-engined sports cars in the up-to-100 m.p.h. class and the true tiger cars, capable of travelling nearly half as fast again, is a select group of individualistic sports cars of which the cheapest is the Austin-Healey 3000. Over the years it has developed in power considerably from the form in which it was originally introduced as the 100 in 1952, but the recent modifications are the first real move to increase the refinement and convenience of the car as a whole, widening its appeal.

For simplification and ease of maintenance there has also been a reduction in the number of carburettors, from three to two, and this has been made without any apparent loss of peak engine performance. Instead, the Healey in its latest form proved considerably quicker throughout the performance range than the three-carburettor version which we tested at the end of last year. The twin-carburettor car saved 6sec in acceleration from rest to 100 m.p.h., which took just over half a minute, while its excellent time of 17·8sec for a standing start quarter-mile is a second less than the figure obtained with the previous model.

In terms of maximum speed, the latest car again proved faster by returning a best figure of 120 m.p.h., with a mean for a two-way run at 117 m.p.h., in overdrive top gear. At this top end of the performance range, the driver is certainly well aware of the rate of progress, and, while the car is still perfectly stable, the front begins to feel "light" at the steering, and there is a tremendous roar of noise from wind, engine and exhaust. Wind noise is sufficiently loud from about 80 m.p.h. onwards to discourage conversation.

Overdrive is an optional extra, operating on third and top gears, and is priced at some £64 including purchase tax. When this component is specified, the car is supplied with a 3·91 to 1 axle in place of the 3·55 unit. This is a pity in some respects, as it converts overdrive from a geared-up cruising ratio to an essential top gear. When the car had

to be used for some miles during the test with overdrive out of action as a result of an internal fault, it felt decidedly under-geared, and maximum speed was limited by engine revs. In overdrive top, the Austin-Healey runs at 25·4 m.p.h. per 1,000 r.p.m., compared with 23·1 m.p.h. in top with the all-direct drive version. If the standard 3·55 axle were retained, overdrive would give 28·1 m.p.h. per 1,000 r.p.m. and easy 100 m.p.h. cruising at only 3,570 r.p.m., which would seem more appropriate.

These comments need to be amplified by emphasizing the commendable smoothness and evenness of torque of the six-cylinder three-litre engine, which beg for high gearing; but there is advantage for the driver who does not like to bother with gear changing. The car may be taken away from rest in second gear, and will pull smoothly from 10 m.p.h. in third, which is pleasant and convenient even if out of character for a sports car. Above 30 m.p.h. one may make perfectly good progress using simply top gear and the overdrive switch, which may suit the habits and temperament of some less sporting owners. There is little difference in overall ratio between overdrive third and direct top gears, and when accelerating hard through the gears it is quickest to engage overdrive while remaining in third gear, at about 75 m.p.h., and then change straight to

PRICES				
2-door convertible	..	..	..	£865
Purchase tax	..		..	£325 7s 9d
		Total (in G.B.)		£1,190 7s 9d
Extras (including tax)				
Overdrive	.. ..			£64 9s 1d
Heater	.. ..			£21 6s 3d
Wire wheels	.. ..			£34 7s 6d
Brake servo	.. ..			£13 15s 0d
Radio	.. ..			£33 0s 0d
Tonneau cover	.. ..			£13 15s 0d

Leather is used for the wearing surfaces of the seats. The remainder, and the door and facia trim, are in p.v.c. A tiny ashtray is built into the transmission tunnel, part of which is padded

Austin-Healey 3000 Mk. II . . .

overdrive top gear after 90 m.p.h. An inhibitor switch prevents operation of the overdrive solenoid with the throttle closed.

Engine smoothness continues through the range up to the limit of just over 5,000 r.p.m. The unit is also quite quiet up to about 3,000 r.p.m., but begins to sound busy at the higher crankshaft speeds. A distinct induction hiss is audible from the carburettor air intakes in normal driving, even at a steady throttle opening, and there is a resonant boom from the exhaust around 2,500-3,000 r.p.m. The engine is an instant starter from cold, but considerable use of the choke is necessary for the first few minutes of running, and the power unit is slow to warm up, misfiring and hesitating if the choke is returned too early. A low-temperature thermostat was fitted in the cooling system of the test car, with the result that the engine was generally running below the ideal temperature. In traffic, however, with much ticking over, the coolant became decidedly hot but never actually boiled.

A new gear change with straight lever and remote control linkage replaces the cranked, direct-acting lever of earlier models. It is an accurate, sturdy gear change, which proves quite satisfying to use, and fast changes may be made. Yet the synchromesh on top gear is largely in-

B.M.C.'s big three-litre engine, now with twin carburettors, fills the under-bonnet space, but essential service points are accessible

effective—a fault which was observed with the previous model—and the change from third to top has to be made slowly or with double-declutching if the gears are not to crash. There is no synchromesh on bottom gear.

Light pedal pressure operates the clutch, for which there is considerable pedal travel. The clutch is fully adequate for the engine torque available, and coupled to the fairly low bottom gear it enabled a very easy restart to be made on the 1-in-3 test hill. Some clutch judder with the test car occurred occasionally but may, perhaps, be blamed on the severe use which this demonstrator has endured. There was also a tendency to axle hop when the standing-start performance figures were being measured.

This model is the only sports car manufactured by B.M.C. which does not have rack-and-pinion steering, and although the control is fairly heavy and high-geared it does not have quite the degree of accuracy desirable for the very considerable performance potential. Slight movement of the wheel may be made when travelling straight without influencing the car's course; but the directional stability is really excellent, and little steering correction is necessary to hold the car to a straight line even in severe side winds.

Appreciable understeer is balanced by a ready tendency for the rear wheels to lose adhesion on a rough or slippery surface; at high cornering speeds the Healey still remains properly controllable and is delightfully quick to respond to steering correction.

Tauter than before, the suspension gives a decidedly harsh and bumpy passage even on fairly smooth town surfaces. There is some flattening out of the ride above 60 m.p.h., and the tautness and resistance to roll undoubtedly pay dividends in the predictable and responsive handling characteristics at high speed, though on rough roads it is evident that the wheels make a poor job of following the surface contours. The car is certainly designed for rapid travel on good roads, but increased tyre pressures recommended for maximum performance naturally amplify the hardness of the ride.

Girling disc front and drum rear brakes are retained, and the test car was fitted with a vacuum servo, priced at £13 15s extra including tax. This relieved much of the effort of applying the brakes, which set a standard of excellence leaving little room for improvement; and it is highly commendable that a load of 100lb on the brake pedal at 30 m.p.h. resulted in the theoretical maximum efficiency of 1 g, which could be repeated for demonstration again and again without any need to cool the brakes. Firmer pressure on the pedal simply resulted in rear wheel locking,

Chromed door fillets with winding windows and a true convertible hood make the car more practical for changeable climates, while the familiar Austin-Healey outline is retained. Winking indicator lights are still shared with the side and tail lamps; the rear reflectors are separate

but without any loss of control or serious reduction in braking effort.

A chromium-plated lever between the driving seat and the propeller shaft tunnel operates the handbrake. It has to be pulled through a considerable arc of travel, but provides tremendous leverage. The figure of 0·4g recorded is the maximum achieved before the handbrake locked the rear wheels, which occurred readily on a dry road, while a perfectly normal application was sufficient to hold the car securely on 1 in 3.

Great strides have been made, compared with the previous model, to improve the weather protection, and it may be said straight away that the operation of the p.v.c. hood of the new Cabriolet is delightfully simple. The flexible rear window is attached by two over-centre catches at the top which, when released, allow it to lie flat in the well formed behind the backrests of the occasional seats. This is normally done before lowering the hood, but it is quite pleasant to drive the car with the rear window open.

With the rear window lowered one simply releases the two over-centre windscreen catches—each of which has a simple threaded adjustment for tensioning—and then pushes the screen rail back. This normally involves getting out, though a passenger can do the job from inside with

The spare wheel and battery occupy the lion's share of the luggage locker. A prop holds the boot lid open. Below, right: The rear window may be lowered, as here

the car travelling very slowly. A neat hood cover is provided, and stowed in the luggage locker when not in use, to attach to press studs over the lowered hood. It can be fastened without a struggle or the need to pull it tremendously tight. When open the Healey is particularly enjoyable to drive, and the fixed quarter-lights and winding windows allow the occupants to enjoy the maximum of fresh air in really hot weather, or to have little more than a cheering back draught at restricted speeds with the side windows wound up.

There remain some points which call for further attention. For example, there is too much rattling of the hood mechanism and supports over any but the smoothest surfaces. On the test car the side windows were extremely stiff to wind up or down, and although the frameless glass butts against a thick rubber surround attached to the hood a strong draught entered from the trailing edge on each side above about 40 m.p.h. The doors are held in any position by adjustable friction stops which accordingly make them rather stiff to open; with the side windows down care is needed when entering the car to avoid the sharp edge of the quarter-light frame.

Apart from replacement of the roomy door pockets of the previous model by map pockets (on account of the space taken by the window mechanism) there are few changes to the interior, and some old criticisms still apply. The pedals are sited too close together for most drivers, and the steering-wheel is too big and too high, so that its upper rim interferes with forward vision of short-in-the-body drivers.

About two inches of telescopic steering-wheel adjustment are available when the locking hand-wheel is slackened. The bucket seats are somewhat thinly padded, but give good lateral support for cornering. The backrests tilt forward to give access to the rear compartment, which will accommodate two small children or one adult (sitting

Austin-Healey 3000 Mk. II...

slightly sideways) without too much complaint on short trips during a rail strike.

A parcels tray with shallow lip is fitted beneath the facia on the left, but a locking cubby-hole would be more welcome, especially as there are still no locks on the doors, even though the car is now essentially a convertible. For one of our test staff this inexcusable omission was highlighted when some of his property was, in fact, stolen from the car. The only locked compartment is the luggage boot, which is so filled by the spare wheel and battery that there is space for little more than a small portmanteau. An anti-theft precaution is to turn off the battery master switch, provided the parking lights are not required, and then to lock the boot lid.

Instruments, in addition to the speedometer—which has a trip mileometer—and the rev counter, include gauges for oil pressure, water temperature and fuel level. The tank is fairly flat in shape, and the fuel gauge is greatly influenced by the attitude of the car, and by acceleration and braking, so at best its indications are only a vague guide to the state of the tank.

Hard driving, such as the Healey invites and obviously enjoys, formed the majority of the test mileage, with the result that fuel consumption was decidedly heavy—only just over 17 m.p.g. for more than 2,000 miles. This distance included a fast drive from London to Scotland and back,

and a number of high-speed runs on M1. Owners may expect consumption in the region of 18 m.p.g., the most favourable figure of 24 m.p.g. being obtained only in very subdued driving, never exceeding 60 m.p.h. As the fuel tank holds only 12 gallons, stops for petrol have to be made inconveniently often on a long journey, and usually will be less than 200 miles apart.

Different material is now used for the insulation of the bulkhead, but considerable engine heat still comes back to the passenger compartment in warm weather. A fresh air heater is available, and was fitted to the test car. It is difficult to adjust so as to admit small quantities of warmed air, but has tremendous capacity for keeping the car snug in winter, perhaps even with the hood down on fine days.

Normal Lucas 700 headlamps are fitted, which restrict the amount of performance which may be used at night owing to their limited penetration and unduly short throw when dipped. No fewer than 17 grease points require attention every 1,000 miles. Only five pints of oil were consumed in 2,264 hard miles.

While there are many relatively minor points open to criticism on this car, there are other much more significant and less tangible factors which are decidedly creditable. They resulted in the Austin-Healey 3000 always being in demand while in our care, especially for long journeys. The more one drives it, the easier it becomes to understand the long and successful competition career of the type, especially in those gruelling continental rallies fought for days on end.

Specification

Scale: 0·3in. to 1ft.

Cushions uncompressed.

ENGINE

Cylinders	...	6
Bore	...	83·34mm (3·28in.)
Stroke	...	88·90mm (3·50in.)
Displacement	...	2,912 c.c. (177·7 cu. in.)
Valve gear	...	Overhead, pushrods and rockers
Compression ratio		9·0-to-1
Carburettor	...	Twin S.U. H56 semi-downdraught
Fuel pump	...	S.U. electric
Oil filter	...	Tecalemit full flow, replaceable element
Max. power	...	130 b.h.p. (net) at 4,750 r.p.m.
Max. torque	...	167 lb. ft. at 3,000 r.p.m.

TRANSMISSION

Clutch	...	Single dry plate, Borg and Beck, 10in. dia.
Gearbox	...	Four speed, synchromesh on 2nd, 3rd and top, central floor change
Overall ratios	...	OD Top 3·21, Top 3·91, OD 3rd, 4·20, 3rd 5·12, 2nd 8·02, 1st 11·45, Reverse 14·78
Final drive	...	Hypoid bevel, 3·91 to 1

CHASSIS

Construction	...	Steel and aluminium body welded to boxed, cruciform frame

SUSPENSION

Front	...	Independent, wishbones and coil springs, Armstrong lever arm dampers and anti-roll bar arm
Rear	...	Semi-elliptic leaf springs, Armstrong lever arm dampers and anti-roll bar arm
Steering	...	Cam Gears, cam and peg. Wheel dia., 17in.

BRAKES

Type	...	Girling, hydraulic, disc front, drum rear; vacuum servo.
Dimensions	...	F. 11·25in. dia. discs; R. 11in. dia., drums, 2·25in. wide shoes
Swept area	...	F. 228 sq. in.; R. 155·5 sq. in. Total: 383·5 sq. in. (296 sq. in. per ton laden)

WHEELS

Type	...	Pressed steel disc, 5 studs
Tyres	...	5·90-15in. Dunlop RS5

EQUIPMENT

Battery	...	12-volt 50-amp .hr.
Headlamps	...	Lucas 36-48 watt
Reversing lamp	...	None
Electric fuses	...	2
Screen wipers	...	Single speed, self parking
Screen washer	...	Standard, manual plunger
Interior heater	...	Extra, Smith's fresh air, with electric booster
Safety belts	...	Extra, anchorages provided
Interior trim	...	Hide on wearing surfaces
Floor covering	...	Carpet
Starting handle	...	No provision
Jack	...	Screw type
Jacking points	...	4, on suspension
Other bodies	...	None

MAINTENANCE

Fuel tank	...	12 Imp. gallons (no reserve)
Cooling system	...	20 pints (including heater)
Engine sump	...	12 pints. Change oil every 3,000 miles; Change filter element every 6,000 miles
Gearbox and overdrive	...	5·3 pints SAE30. Change oil every 6,000 miles
Final drive	...	3 pints SAE90. Change oil every 6,000 miles
Grease	...	17 points every 1,000 miles
Tyre pressures	...	F. 20; R. 23 p.s.i. (normal driving) F. 25; R. 28 p.s.i. (fast driving); F. 20; R. 26 p.s.i. (full load)

OVERALL LENGTH 13' 1·5"
OVERALL WIDTH 5'
OVERALL HEIGHT 4' 0·75"
GROUND CLEARANCE 4·5"
WHEELBASE 7' 7·75"
FRONT TRACK 4' 0·75"
REAR TRACK 4' 2"

Make · AUSTIN-HEALEY Type · 3000 Mk. II Sports Convertible

Manufacturers : Austin Motor Co. Ltd., Longbridge, Birmingham

Test Conditions

Weather ... Heavily overcast with 5-10 m.p.h. wind
Temperature .... 60 deg. F. (16 deg. C.).
Barometer 29·2 in. Hg.
Dry surfaces for standing start acceleration and braking tests.

Weight

Kerb weight (with oil, water and half-full fuel tank)
22·9cwt (2,562lb-1,162kg)
Front-rear distribution, per cent F, 49; R, 51.
Laden as tested ...... 25·9cwt (2,898lb-1,309kg).

Turning Circles

Between kerbs .... L, 36ft 5in.; R, 34ft 3in.
Between walls .... L, 37ft 7in.; R, 35ft 5in.
Turns of steering wheel lock to lock 3

Performance Data

Overdrive top gear m.p.h. per 1,000 r.p.m.... 25·4
Top gear m.p.h. per 1,000 r.p.m. .... 20·9
Mean piston speed at max. power ... 2,775ft/min.
Engine revs. at mean max. speed ...... 4,500 r.p.m.
B.h.p. per ton laden .... 102·6

FUEL AND OIL CONSUMPTION

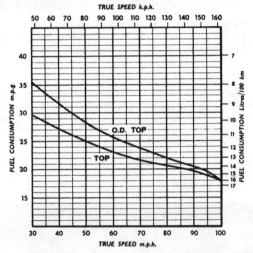

FUEL...........................Premium Grade
(97 octane RM)

Test Distance........................ 2,264 miles

Overall Consumption .... 17·1 m.p.g.
(16·6 litres/100 km.)

Normal Range.................... 16-24 m.p.g.
(17·7—11·8 litres/100 km.)

OIL: S.A.E. 30 ... Consumption: 3,600 m.p.g.

HILL CLIMBING AT STEADY SPEEDS

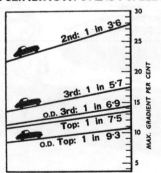

GEAR	O.D. Top	Top	O.D. 3rd	3rd	2nd
Tapley Reading (lb per ton)	240	295	320	385	600
	1 in 9·3	1 in 7·5	1 in 6·9	1 in 5·7	1 in 3·6
Speed range (m.p.h.)	59-64	53-58	52-57	50-55	38-43

MAXIMUM SPEEDS AND ACCELERATION (mean) TIMES

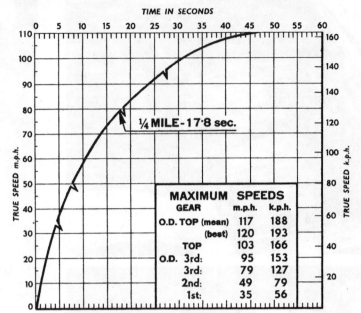

¼ MILE - 17·8 sec.

MAXIMUM	SPEEDS	
GEAR	m.p.h.	k.p.h.
O.D. TOP (mean)	117	188
(best)	120	193
TOP	103	166
O.D. 3rd:	95	153
3rd:	79	127
2nd:	49	79
1st:	35	56

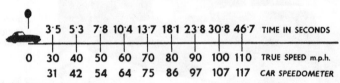

	3·5	5·3	7·8	10·4	13·7	18·1	23·8	30·8	46·7	TIME IN SECONDS
0	30	40	50	60	70	80	90	100	110	TRUE SPEED m.p.h.
	31	42	54	64	75	86	97	107	117	CAR SPEEDOMETER

Speed range and time in seconds

m.p.h.	O.D. Top	Top	O.D. 3rd	3rd	2nd	1st
10— 30	—	—	—	5·9	3·9	2·9
20— 40	—	7·3	7·4	5·6	3·7	—
30— 50	9·2	8·1	7·5	5·2	—	—
40— 60	10·3	7·3	6·6	5·3	—	—
50— 70	9·1	7·1	7·2	5·7	—	—
60— 80	10·2	8·0	7·8	—	—	—
70— 90	11·8	9·5	10·2	—	—	—
80—100	17·1	12·7	—	—	—	—
90—110	25·1	—	—	—	—	—

BRAKES

(from 30 m.p.h. in neutral)	Pedal Load	Retardation	Equiv. distance
	25lb	0·20g	150ft
	50lb	0·55g	55ft
	75lb	0·85g	36ft
	100lb	1·0g	30·2ft
Handbrake		0·40g	75ft

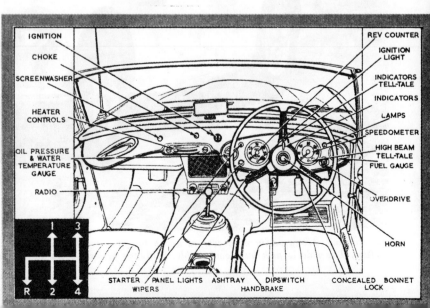

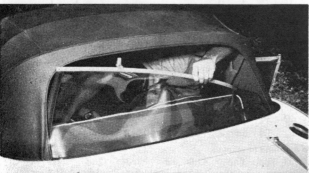

The interior, above left, is basically unchanged. The ne~ door design does not interfere with available space. Top ~ covered by this snap-on boot in its folded-down positio~

Above is the biggest change in the '63 Healey; the roll-u~ windows. Glass is nicely tapered. Note the long pocket ~ the door bottom, redesigned hardware, new latch mechanis~

At left, the wide rear window fastens in place with two cli~ and has a metal frame at top. The transparent material is ~ a heavy gauge, yet very flexible and more scratch-resistan~

As solid and strong as its predecessors and a lot more weathertight, the BJ7 smoothly negotiates a corner on broken roa~ surface. The ride is firm but comfortable. Stiffened by new bows and framing, the top is tight and rattle-free at all time~

THE PAST TWO OR THREE YEARS have seen little change in the stalwart Austin-Healey. Though not hurting from a sales-volume standpoint, dealers have made the almost singular request for roll-up windows. The factory was apparently in accord with these suggestions, as the biggest change over the previous models incorporated in the '63 is — you guessed it — roll up windows! It is a welcome change, too, as we feel the day of the side-curtain is long since past and only excusable on economy-type roadsters at the bottom of the price scale. The Healey has been, since its inception, a quality sports car and should have incorporated the windows with the first 3-liter model.

Our test car was a 2-plus-2 similar to the '62 model we analyzed in the October 1961 issue of SCG; a *family* sports car, if there is such a thing. But the small, neatly-molded seats built over the rear-axle hump do an admirable job of holding the youngsters, and it was the first time in quite a while that this writer could pile wife and two pre-teen boys in comfortably for an extended cruise in sporty-type equipment. What also made it interesting was the comparison of acceleration figures. The new model has one less carburetor and this has made such a tremendous improvement in low-end response that its times are noticeably better throughout the entire range, with practically no sacrifice in top speed, and an improvement in gas mileage to boot. This is a classic example disproving the common theory that, if two carburetors work well, three will work even better! The '63 Healey idles smoothly, starts eagerly, is hard to stall, and the usual "spit-back" tendency has been almost entirely eliminated in cold-starts.

Installing windows naturally dictated some door modifications and this has been accomplished neatly, without noticeable loss of interior room. The upholstery is nicely styled and durably fastened, includes a long-but-shallow pocket in

ROAD TEST/35-62

AUSTIN HEALEY BJ7 3-liter

If you're looking for a "family sports car," the 1963 Austin Healey is hard to beat indeed!

PHOTOS: RANDY HOLT

AUSTIN-HEALEY BJ7

the bottom. All the hardware, including the latch mechanism, is new and modern. The inside door handle is easy to operate but the window crank, by necessity, is a bit too near the seat cushion and best operated with the door open. There is nothing noteworthy about the narrow vent window except that it appears durable. On our test unit, rushed through inspection, there were slight rattles with the window rolled all the way down. It is probable that this could be eliminated by tightening or realigning the felt channels. The convertible top is *much* improved, with a latched-in, semi-framed rear window and the molding incorporated for the sidewindows. Relatively simple to fold down, the top does not sink into the rear boot, but lays above it and only looks neat when the snap-on cover is in place. This is probably not the case with the regular two-seater, but we've been unable to see one as yet.

No changes in suspension or steering were mentioned by the factory, so we concluded that the front end of our test car had less than standard caster settings. Steering was very light in comparsion with the normal Healey "feel" and we found this very pleasing. There was a sacrifice in high-speed stability, however, as the car had a tendency to wander around a bit above 70 mph, unlike the usual Healey steadiness at speeds well in excess of this.

With the up-dating of the Sprite in 1962, the remodeled MG in 1963, it's highly probable that this is the last year for the now-classic Healey body style. There's also a V-6 engine kicking around BMC, though we don't know what size it is or will be. Meanwhile, they have a solid, well-developed product in the 1963 Healey, with the weatherproofing and low-end performance bringing it a lot nearer perfection.

— *Jerry Titus*

How 'bout that; less for more money! Engine is equipped with one less carburetor than previous but is a lot more responsive in all aspects; starting, idling, and acceleration.

VEHICLE ....AH 3000 BJ7   MODEL ....Convertible
PRICE (as tested) ....$3730   OPTIONS ....Radio $50

ENGINE:

Type: ....6-cylinder, in-line, 4-cycle, water-cooled
Head: ....Cast-iron, removable
Valves: ....OHV, pushrod/rocker actuated
Max. bhp ....136 @ 4750 rpm
Max. Torque ....167 lbs. ft. @ 3000 rpm
Bore ....3.281 in. 83.34 mm.
Stroke ....3.5 in. 88.9 mm.
Displacement ....177.7 cu. in 2912 cc.
Compression Ratio ....9.0 to 1
Induction System: ....2 SU type HS6 carburetors
Exhaust System: ....Cast manifold into dual pipes and mufflers (tandem)
Electrical System: ....12V Lucas distributor ign.

CLUTCH: Borg & Beck, single disc, dry
Diameter: ....10.5 in.
Actuation: ....Hydraulic
TRANSMISSION: ......4-speed, top 3
synchronized
Ratios: 1st ....2.879 to 1
2nd ....2.06 to 1
3rd ....1.304 to 1
4th ....1.0 to 1
O.D. 0.822

DIFFERENTIAL:
Ratio: ....3.9 to 1
Drive Axles (type): ....enclosed, semi-floating
STEERING:
Turns Lock to Lock: 3.25
Turn Circle: ....35.7 ft.
BRAKES:
Drum/rear Disc/front
Diameter ....11.25 in.
Swept Area ....302.16 sq. in.

CHASSIS:

Frame: ....Box section conventional
Body: ....Steel semi-unit
Front Suspension: ....Unequal A's, arm shocks, coil springs, anti-sway bar
Rear Suspension: ....Live, leaf springs, arm shocks
Tire Size and Type: ....5.90 x 15 Dunlop

WEIGHTS AND MEASURES:

Wheelbase: ....91.7 in.   Ground Clearance ....4.6 in.
Front Track: ....48.75 in.   Curb Weight ....2490 lbs.
Rear Track: ....50.0 in.   Test Weight ....2783 lbs.
Overall Height ....46 in.   Crankcase ....7.5 qts.
Overall Width ....60 in.   Cooling System ....12.5 qts.
Overall Length ....157.5 in.   Gas Tank ....14.4 gals.

PERFORMANCE:

0-30	3.1 sec.	0-80		17.5 sec.
0-40	5.5 sec.	0-90		22.5 sec.
0-50	7.7 sec.	0-100		28.4 sec.
0-60	10.0 sec.	Standing ¼ mile 15.9 sec. @ 77 mph		
0-70	13.8 sec.	Top Speed (av. two-way run) 110 mph		

Speed Error	'30	40	50	60	79	80	90
Actual	30	40	50	59	69	79	89

Fuel Consumption: Average: ....26 mpg
Test: ....21 mpg

Speed Ranges in gears:
1st .... 0 to 32 mph   3rd ....35 to 79 mph
2nd ....15 to 47 mph   4th ....43 to top mph

Brake Test: 74 Average % G, over 10 stops. Fade encountered on 9th stop.

REFERENCE FACTORS:

Bhp per Cubic Inch 0.77
Lbs. per bhp 18.3
Piston Speed @ Peak rpm ....2771 ft./min.
Swept Brake area per Lb. ....0.121 Sq. In.

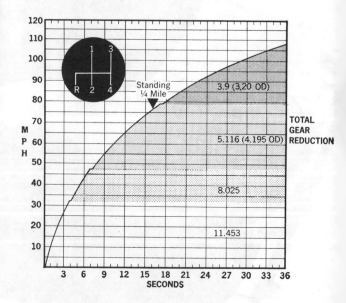

CAR and DRIVER
ROAD TEST
Austin Healey 3000

A long hood covers the powerful six-cylinder engine, which is set well back in the chassis. The forward slope provides a good view from behind steering wheel.

Aerodynamic Edwardian with roll-up windows

Capping a three-year period which has seen BMC score a series of truly dramatic engineering and marketing breakthroughs with cars like the Mini-Minor, the MG/Morris 1100, and the MGB, the new Austin-Healey is a bit of an anachronism. It really doesn't seem to be in keeping with the newly won BMC reputation for brilliantly executed dream-cars-come-true. It's marvelous fun to drive, it makes a great whomping six-cylinder noise, and it has all the qualities one traditionally associates with wind-in-the-face sports cars. But somehow these qualities, of themselves, aren't enough to keep us from being a trifle disappointed with the over-all result.

When first introduced at the London Motor Show of 1952, the Austin-Healey was an overnight sensation. This creation, inspired by Donald Healey and designed by B. Bildy and G. Coker, has withstood the test of time, and the body lines remain basically the same, although the car has undergone numerous mechanical changes through the years. British Motor Corporation ceased to enter it in sports-car races when the six-cylinder engine replaced the old Austin 16-based four, but it is now a contender for international rally honors.

With a hard-to-beat combination of great structural strength and booming performance, the Austin-Healey has been a consistent top finisher in the hands of drivers like Pat Moss and David Seigle-Morris. The sight and sound of Pat Moss howling over an Alpine pass in hairy-looking Healey, sans bumpers and loaded with lights, is a never-to-be-forgotten thrill. In more than one rally the straight-line performance of the Healey has given it the edge over many more sophisticated, more expensive automobiles.

Repeated efforts to up-date the car have been successful in that its appeal has been broadened and sales have continued at a high level. But looking at the 1963

version one sees much evidence of a 10-year-old design. This is particularly true of the suspension, which provides a harder ride than many lighter and later sports cars. The main attraction of the Austin-Healey 3000 lies in its powerful and untemperamental engine—a sports version of the BMC C-type unit that powers the Austin A-110, the Wolseley 6/110 and the Vanden Plas Three-Liter. The latest Austin-Healey version has two carburetors instead of the three that have been standard equipment for three years—BMC has managed to cut manufacturing costs and simplify maintenance without

Wind-up windows and a central gear lever set the interior of the new model apart from earlier Austin-Healey versions.

AUSTIN-HEALEY 3000

accepting any reduction in performance. The big and heavy engine develops maximum torque at 3,000 rpm and begs for high gearing. A good compromise has been found by using a 3.91-to-one rear axle ratio and fitting a Laycock-de Normanville overdrive unit on the transmission. In this manner, normal top gear gives brisk acceleration while overdrive top provides economical and relatively silent high-speed cruising. The engine is quiet up to about 3,000 rpm; after that noise seems to increase in direct proportion to rpm.

A new centrally located gear lever has replaced the cranked direct-working side lever of previous models, but the remote-control linkage is no quicker than the offset mechanism, and during warm-up requires much more muscle than the old linkage. As on so many BMC models, the main complaint in the transmission department remains the absence of synchromesh on bottom gear. The gate itself is the same as before, and reverse engagement is excellent. You positively cannot get reverse by mistake, yet when you want it a sharp sideways tap on the lever brings it over the catch so easily as to make parking almost a pleasure.

In many ways the fun of driving a Healey is directly traceable to this transmission and its Laycock de Normanville overdrive. Running fast in third and fourth, using the overdrive switch like another shift lever, can be pure joy. The shift lever's action is stiff but accurate, and declutching to switch the overdrive in and out, though quite unnecessary, results in crisp, fast shifts that are a delight to the ear and the seat of the pants. The ponderous nature of all the controls is a factor which lends a kind of appealing massive masculinity to the car. Again, this is traditional, harking back to those days when sports cars were meat for men only and the ladies rode reluctantly if at all or, better yet,

stood timidly and admiringly by the side of the road.

On older Austin-Healeys, competition-minded customers often installed special higher-rate springs to improve high-speed cornering. New standard springs on the 1963 model are an approximation to those, and steering characteristics are improved throughout the speed range. As before the Healey understeers mildly up to the point where the rear lets go, but directional stability is better. Stiffer springs have done nothing to eliminate road shocks reaching the steering wheel, and bumps on a corner can affect the car's stability to an uncomfortable degree.

Body roll is as absent as ever on the 3000. There are no complications about seeing your line through a turn since you sit in exactly the same vertical position regardless of how many times you may have to alter your direction. This is an inherent quality of the Austin-Healey which probably has served to endear it to more

An engine produced in large volume in its single-carburetor form provides a highly reliable power plant for a sports car

---

AUSTIN-HEALEY 3000

Price as tested: $3,535 POE N.Y.
Importer: Hambro Automotive Corporation
27 West 57th Street,
New York 19, N.Y.

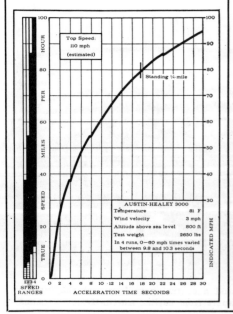

Temperature	81 F
Wind velocity	3 mph
Altitude above sea level	800 ft
Test weight	2650 lbs
In 4 runs, 0—60 mph times varied between 9.8 and 10.3 seconds	

Top Speed: 110 mph (estimated)

Standing ¼-mile

ENGINE:

Displacement	177.7 cu in, 2,912 cc
Dimensions	6 cyl, 3.28-in bore, 3.50-in stroke
Valve gear:	Pushrod-operated overhead valves
Compression ratio	9.03 to one
Power (SAE)	136 bhp @ 4,750 rpm
Torque	167 lb-ft @ 3,000 rpm
Usable range of engine speeds	650-6,000 rpm
Carburetion: Twin semi-downdraft SU HS-6 carburetors	
Fuel recommended	Premium
Mileage	14-22 mpg
Range on 14.2-gallon tank	200-315 miles

CHASSIS:

Wheelbase	92 in
Track	F 49 in, R 50 in
Length	157.5 in
Ground clearance	4.5 in
Suspension: F: Ind., wishbones and coil springs, anti-roll bar. R: Rigid axle, semi-elliptic leaf springs, anti-roll bar.	
Steering	Cam and peg
Turns, lock to lock	3
Turning circle diameter between curbs	35 ft
Tire size	5.90 x 15
Pressures recommended	F 26, R 28 psi
Brakes, Girling 11¾-in disc front, 11-in drums rear, 192 sq in swept area	
Curb weight (full tank)	2,465 lbs
Percentage on the driving wheels	52

DRIVE TRAIN:

Clutch....................10-in single dry plate

Gear	Synchro	Ratio	Step	Over-all	Mph per 1000 rpm
Rev	No	3.78		14.80	−5.01
1st	No	2.93	43%	11.46	6.47
2nd	Yes	2.05	49%	8.03	9.24
3rd	Yes	1.31	21%	5.12	14.47
3rd OD	Yes	1.08	8%	4.23	17.65
4th	Yes	1.00	22%	3.91	18.94
4th OD	Yes	0.82		3.21	23.10
Final drive ratio					3.91 to one

uggage space is not the Healey's strong suit. However, the ccasional rear seats can be easily pressed into service.

One of the car's happiest features is its good-looking, tight-fitting top. It goes up or down with truly minimal effort.

rivers than has any other one of its good qualities.

As for habitability, there are new improvements. We ll remember the great step forward initiated in 1957, vhen the top could be put up or down by one man alone. Tow he can complete this operation without getting out f the driver's seat. And instead of side curtains the car ow has roll-up windows. These refinements, coupled vith the Healey's two occasional rear seats, make genine sports-car driving acceptable to a new class of cusomer. The extra seats are, of course, just as occasional s those in a Porsche 356-B or a Volvo P-1800, and on a ong trip should be considered just storage space.

We have always had difficulty in trying to drive traight-armed in an Austin-Healey. The short seat ravel makes it almost impossible even in the 1963

model, and the muscular force required to turn the wheel makes it inadvisable anyway. The large-diameter steering wheel provides good leverage for taking sharp turns, however, and the steering ratio is high enough to enable women to drive it enthusiastically.

Whether the car, as a two-seater, provides any enjoyment that, for instance, the MGB does not give, is questionable. With a top speed perhaps 10 mph higher, and taking about one second less over the standing quarter-mile, the Austin-Healey is so closely matched to the MGB in performance as to make you wonder about the monetary value of two occasional seats.

Servo brakes are optional at extra cost, but we found that the Girling system, with discs front and drums rear, required pedal pressures so normal that power assistance seemed quite superfluous. Stopping distances were minimal, and no fade could be provoked.

As for maintenance, the car has not stayed with the times. There are 17 grease points that require attention every 1,000 miles. The fuel tank holds only 14.2 gallons, which gives a range below average for any type of car.

We drove a couple of cars in the course of this test. They were identical, differing only in color. Our impressions of the Healey are drawn from several hundred miles of all kinds of driving on all kinds of surfaces. We found the car to be a nearly perfect expression of the pre-war two-seater brought up to date. It has the same kind of go-to-hell rakishness we all loved in the TCs and Healey Silverstones, but it tempers these characteristics with wind-up windows and creature comfort that those semi-classics never knew. As we've pointed out, it's strong and reliable. We just wish that it had a more modern chassis and suspension system to match its up-to-date mates in the BMC model line-up.

Though its basic design is a decade old, the Healey will still find an eager audience with the more traditionally minded enthusiast. It is a true sporting machine in the sense that it looks fine, sounds fierce, and goes fast. If it rides hard and crosses cracks in the road with a loud thump, so what? We can remember when unyielding suspension and continual tightening of all the nuts and bolts on the automobile were status symbols to be treasured by any true aficionado. **C/D**

oll-up windows and vent panes! Creature comfort and connience come to the traditional sports car, English style.

THE Motor

MAKE: *Austin-Healey* *TYPE:* 3000

MAKERS: *Austin Motor Company Ltd., Longbridge, Birmingham*

ROAD TEST • No. 14/63

TEST DATA:

CONDITIONS: *Weather: Mild, dry, 10 m.p.h. wind. (Temperature 42°-46°F., Barometer 29.1-29.2 in. Hg.) Surface: Damp tarmacadam and concrete. Fuel: Premium grade pump petrol (98 Octane by Research Method.)*

MAXIMUM SPEEDS

Flying Mile

Mean of four opposite runs	116·0 m.p.h.
Best one-way time equals	119·1 m.p.h.

"Maximile" Speed: (Timed quarter mile after one mile accelerating from rest)

Mean of opposite runs	112·3 m.p.h.
Best one-way time equals	114·1 m.p.h.

Speed in gears (at 5,200 r.p.m.)

Max. speed in direct top	97 m.p.h.
Max. speed in overdrive third ..	90 m.p.h.
Max. speed in direct third	74 m.p.h.
Max. speed in second	47 m.p.h.
Max. speed in first	33 m.p.h.

ACCELERATION TIMES From standstill

0-30 m.p.h.	3·2 sec.
0-40 m.p.h.	5·1 sec.
0-50 m.p.h.	7·2 sec.
0-60 m.p.h.	10·3 sec.
0-70 m.p.h.	12·9 sec.
0-80 m.p.h.	16·7 sec.
0-90 m.p.h.	21·3 sec.
0-100 m.p.h.	29·4 sec.
0-110 m.p.h.	45·3 sec.
Standing quarter mile	17·3 sec.

ACCELERATION TIMES on upper ratios

	Overdrive Top gear	Direct Top gear	Overdrive 3rd gear	Direct 3rd gear
10-30 m.p.h.	9·6 sec.	7·5 sec.	6·9 sec.	5·5 sec.
20-40 m.p.h.	9·6 sec.	7·2 sec.	6.9 sec.	5·2 sec.
30-50 m.p.h.	9·9 sec.	7·2 sec.	6·8 sec.	5·1 sec.
40-60 m.p.h.	10·0 sec.	7·4 sec.	6·6 sec.	5·1 sec.
50-70 m.p.h.	11·1 sec.	7·8 sec.	7·2 sec.	5·9 sec.
60-80 m.p.h.	11·2 sec.	8·2 sec.	8·0 sec.	—
70-90 m.p.h.	12·1 sec.	9·1 sec.	8·8 sec.	—
80-100 m.p.h.	14·9 sec.	—	—	—
90-110 m.p.h.	24·8 sec.	—	—	—

FUEL CONSUMPTION

Overall Fuel Consumption for 1,184 miles, 66·8 gallons, equals 17·8 m.p.g. (15·82 litres/100 km.)

Touring Fuel Consumption (m.p.g. at steady speed midway between 30 m.p.h. and maximum, less 5% allowance for acceleration) 22·66 m.p.g.

Fuel tank capacity (maker's figure) 12 gallons

Direct top gear

29¼ m.p.g. ..	at constant	30 m.p.h. on level
28 m.p.g. ..	at constant	40 m.p.h. on level
25¼ m.p.g. ..	at constant	50 m.p.h. on level
23 m.p.g. ..	at constant	60 m.p.h. on level
22 m.p.g. ..	at constant	70 m.p.h. on level
20½ m.p.g. ..	at constant	80 m.p.h. on level
18¾ m.p.g. ..	at constant	90 m.p.h. on level

Overdrive top gear

37 m.p.g. ..	at constant	30 m.p.h. on level
31¼ m.p.g. ..	at constant	40 m.p.h. on level
28¼ m.p.g. ..	at constant	50 m.p.h. on level
26 m.p.g. ..	at constant	60 m.p.h. on level
24¾ m.p.g. ..	at constant	70 m.p.h. on level
21¾ m.p.g. ..	at constant	80 m.p.h. on level
20¾ m.p.g. ..	at constant	90 m.p.h. on level
18½ m.p.g. ..	at constant	100 m.p.h. on level

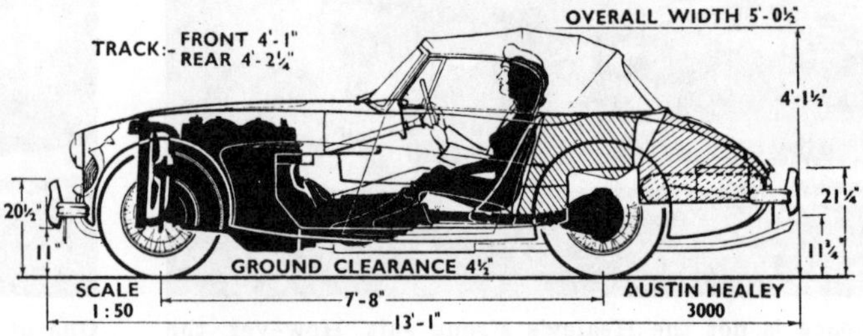

OVERALL WIDTH 5'-0½"
TRACK:- FRONT 4'-1"
REAR 4'-2¼"
4'-1½"
20½"
21¼"
11"
11¼"
GROUND CLEARANCE 4½"
SCALE
1:50
7'-8"
13'-1"
AUSTIN HEALEY
3000

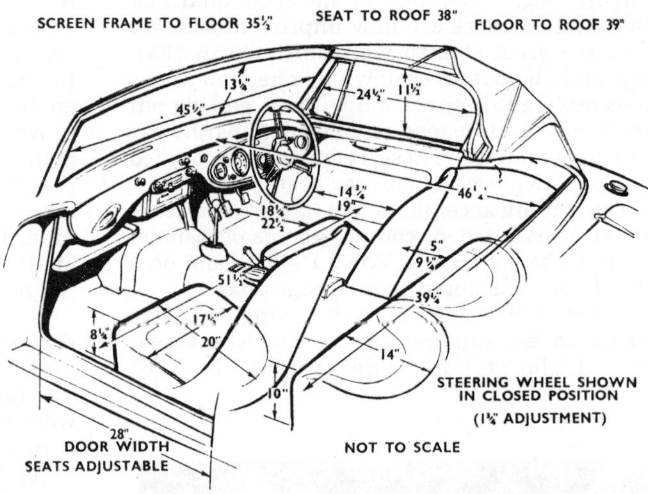

SCREEN FRAME TO FLOOR 35½"
SEAT TO ROOF 38"
FLOOR TO ROOF 39"
13¾"
45¼"
24½"
11½"
14¾"
19"
18¼"
22½"
46¼"
5"
9¼"
39¼"
51½"
17¼"
20"
8¼"
14"
10"
28"
DOOR WIDTH
SEATS ADJUSTABLE
STEERING WHEEL SHOWN
IN CLOSED POSITION
(1¼" ADJUSTMENT)
NOT TO SCALE

HILL CLIMBING

Max. gradient climbable at steady speed.

Overdrive top gear	1 in 9·2 (Tapley 240 lb./ton)
Direct top gear	1 in 6·5 (Tapley 340 lb./ton)
Overdrive third gear	1 in 6·1 (Tapley 365 lb./ton)
Direct third gear	1 in 4·8 (Tapley 455 lb./ton)
Second gear ..	1 in 2·9 (Tapley 680 lb./ton)

BRAKES

Deceleration and equivalent stopping distance from 30 m.p.h.

1·0 g with 85 lb. pedal pressure ..	(30 ft.)
0·99 g with 80 lb. pedal pressure ..	(30¼ ft.)
0·87 g with 75 lb. pedal pressure ..	(34½ ft.)
0·51 g with 50 lb. pedal pressure ..	(59 ft.)
0·27 g with 25 lb. pedal pressure ..	(110½ ft.)

STEERING

Turning circle between kerbs:

Left	32½ft.
Right	32¼ ft.
Turns of steering wheel from lock to lock	3⅓

INSTRUMENTS

Speedometer at 30 m.p.h.	1½% fast
Speedometer at 60 m.p.h.	2½% fast
Speedometer at 90 m.p.h.	3¼% fast
Distance recorder	3% fast

WEIGHT

Kerb weight (unladen but with oil coolant and fuel for approximately 50 miles) .. 21¾ cwt.

Front/rear distribution of kerb weight 52/48

Weight laden as tested .. .. .. 25½ cwt.

Specification

Engine

Cylinders	6
Bore	83·36 mm.
Stroke	89 mm.
Cubic capacity	2,912 c.c.
Piston Area	50·7 sq. in.
Valves	Overhead (pushrod)
Compression ratio	9/1
Carburetter	2, S.U. type H.S.6
Fuel pump	S.U. electric
Ignition timing control ..	Centrifugal and vacuum
Oil filter	Tecalemit full flow
Maximum power (net)	130 b.h.p.
at	4,750 r.p.m.
Maximum torque (net)	167 lb. ft. at 3,000 r.p.m.
Piston speed at maximum b.h.p.	2,770 ft./min.

Transmission

Clutch, Borg and Beck, 10 in. s.d.p.

Top gear (s/m) ..	3·909 (Overdrive, 3·205)
3rd gear (s/m) ..	5·116 (Overdrive, 4·195)
2nd gear (s/m)	8·025
1st gear	11·453
Reverse	14·776
Overdrive ..	.. Laycock-de Normanville
Propeller shaft	Hardy Spicer, one-piece, open
Final drive	Hypoid bevel
Top gear m.p.h. at 1,000 r.p.m. ..	18·6 (Overdrive, 22·6)
Top gear m.p.h. at 1,000 ft./min. piston speed	31·8 (Overdrive, 38·8)

Chassis

Brakes: Girling hydraulic, disc front, drum rear

Brake dimensions: Front discs: 11¼ in. dia. Rear drums: 11 in. dia.

Friction areas: 112 sq. in. of lining working on 383 sq. in. rubbed area of discs and drums

Suspension:

Front: Independent by coil springs, transverse wishbones and anti-roll torsion bar

Rear: Rigid axle, semi-elliptic leaf springs, and Panhard rod

Shock absorbers:

Front } Rear } Armstrong lever hydraulic

Steering gear: Cam gears, cam and peg

Tyres: 5·90—15 tubed Dunlop Road Speed

AUSTIN-HEALEY 3000

SOME enthusiasts feel that the modern, refined, open two-seater is insufficiently masculine to qualify as a sports car. There are, however, some manufacturers who have not yet started making velvety, all-independent sporting machines with a sort of unobtrusive high performance. B.M.C. turn out the Austin-Healey 3000 which, despite a number of up-to-date attractions is a strong-willed survivor of a more hairy-chested era. It has a big, six-cylinder engine which revs lazily in a sturdy chassis and gives lots of smooth power and an exciting performance. Cornering is good without much body roll, the steering is light, and the brakes with the optional servo are first-class. The new hood is easy to fold away, although it does not stow completely out of sight, and the winding windows and more deeply curved screen are useful concessions to comfort. It is a pity the concessions do not extend to an improvement in driving comfort, but the old problem of cockpit overheating seems to have been alleviated, although the persistent Austin-Healey

shortcoming of restricted ground clearance remains. This is surprising as seasons pass with further rally successes by the works Austin-Healeys whose spectacular wins have demanded better clearance than the standard machine. One wonders why the rather obvious modifications necessary to give something more than a niggardly 4½ inches have not been made. Of the masculinity of the Austin-Healey 3000 there is no doubt; whether taming 130-odd horsepower is actually *liked* or not depends on the driver possessing the necessary skill and a certain amount of stoutheartedness. Certainly, on a performance/price basis, the car has few equals.

How it goes

THE "big Healey" makes a splendid noise. It *can* be driven quietly and in fact it is better to allow only moderate throttle openings and low engine speeds in towns or late at night. But the noise is by no means purely for effect because

The Austin-Healey's big straight six-cylinder engine takes up much of the available underbonnet space. There are two safety catches on the front-opening lid which is held open by a rod on the left.

In Brief

Price (including overdrive and servo brakes as tested) £925 plus purchase tax £193 5s. 4d. equals £1,118 5s. 4d.

Capacity	2,912 c.c.
Unladen kerb weight	21¾ cwt.

Acceleration:

20-40 m.p.h. in top gear	7.2 sec.
0-50 m.p.h. through gears	7.2 sec.
Maximum top gear gradient	1 in 6.5
Maximum speed	116.0 m.p.h.
Overall fuel consumption	17.8 m.p.g.
Touring fuel consumption	20.8 m.p.g.

Gearing: 18.6 m.p.h. in top gear at 1,000 r.p.m. (overdrive 22.6 m.p.h.)

the performance, right up to the maximum speed not very far short of 120 m.p.h. is rousing. Tuning and service problems have caused a reversion from three to two carburetters, but since a high-lift camshaft produced most of the last power increase, the loss of one of the 1¾ in. S.U.'s has only meant a decrease of 2 b.h.p. The performance seems a little flat under about 2,300 r.p.m. but thereafter the torque can really be felt right up to a red mark on the tachometer at 5,200. With such a deep note from the dual exhaust the engine doesn't sound as if it is working hard, and in fact it can easily be over-revved quite substantially. Cold starting is somewhat problematical with a reluctance to fire evenly on part choke and a determination to stall on no choke at all. This lasts for only a short time, however, a little over half a mile in traffic usually being sufficient to reach running temperature. Prolonged halts in traffic one mild, wet afternoon caused the engine temperature to rise to around 200°F., indicating that overheating might become something of a problem in a hot climate.

The clutch pedal has an unusually long travel, making it necessary to sit close to the steering wheel in order to operate the clutch properly. The full 6½ inches of movement have to be used up for every gear change, otherwise movement of the lever is difficult. The 10-inch diameter clutch takes up the drive smoothly and standing start acceleration tests showed that the most brutal methods were usually the best. There was very little slip when letting it in abruptly at 3,800 r.p.m., although the back axle dithered momentarily and there was a little wheelspin in first. Over-enthusiasm left black lines several feet long on dry concrete.

The gear change is distinctly heavy, and even when the clutch was being used properly, it was notchy and rather sticky. The lever no longer projects from the passenger's side of the tunnel, the gearbox having been turned through 90 degrees to bring the selectors to the top and provide a short, more sporting lever. The synchromesh, which is on the upper three gears, is very powerful, however, and fast changes require a firm push. Overdrive works on third and top and engages smoothly enough on an open throttle but downward changes on the overrun are made with a jerk; when making them it is preferable to blip the throttle. First and second gear ratios are very close; so are third and top. For the best results it is necessary to use second right up to peak r.p.m. or the gap between it and third becomes noticeable. Overdrive third is of little practical value because it is so close to direct top; it is only useful as a more easily selected gear. There is a little whine from first gear, but otherwise the transmission seems quite quiet.

A little body roll

THE Austin-Healey can be cornered very quickly on its RS5's and on fairly smooth surfaces the ride is outstandingly good for a firmly sprung sports car. On rough roads with closely spaced bumps, however, the rigid back axle becomes rather unruly and there is a good deal of scuttle shake. The effect is worsened by side windows which rattle in their guides, making this an uncomfortable car to drive over indifferent roads. Again one is surprised in view of the

AUSTIN-HEALEY 3000

Right: The cover for the furled hood is neat and easily fitted. In this picture the driver's seat is not at its rearmost adjustment, leaving some space between it and the rear "seat." The ashtray on the transmission hump has a neat cover to prevent the contents being blown out when the car is open.

Above: The spare wheel takes up a good deal of the boot which is the car's only lockable compartment. The master switch is on the right, aft of the battery.

Right: The floor of the Healey is fully carpeted and the facia has a padded roll along the top with a matt finish the same colour as the upholstery. There are slim map pockets in the doors. Switch on bottom right of the facia controls the overdrive and the ignition and starter are separate. The handbrake is not of the fly-off type.

Left: Open or closed, the Healey's broad-shouldered good looks are still elegant and only slightly "dated". Back-draught in the cockpit with the side windows up was quite moderate.

Upright driving position

A HIGH scuttle and steering wheel, the long travel of the clutch pedal, and the small, straight-backed seat heighten the Austin-Healey's "vintage" feel. Even quite tall drivers have to sit close to the wheel in order to press the clutch out far enough. The seat has a flat cushion and a curved backrest which is too short and upright, and it would be better if the whole seat were tilted backwards slightly to give a better reach to the pedals and a more long-arm driving position. The optional adjustable steering column would appear to give a driving position either for people with unusually long legs and short arms or a taste for sitting very close to the wheel indeed. The transmission tunnel (which is now made of glass fibre for better sound and heat insulation) takes up a good deal of space but there is plenty of room left for long legs. Clutch and brake pedals are rather close together with plenty of space for the left foot to rest, and "heel-and-toeing" is possible, if not very easy.

The two rear seats are meant for small children. Their shape makes them poor luggage carriers, as suitcases and boxes slide off them; some customers would probably be happier if they were optional, as this is now the only model of Healey 3000.

In the middle of a useful parcels shelf under the facia is the screen washer reservoir. It is not very accessible and has its control on the passenger's side. Not calibrated with the thoroughness sports car owners like (the speedometer reads in 10 m.p.h. divisions and the fuel gauge wriggles violently with the movement of petrol in the tank) the instruments are easy to see and comprehensive. An indicator switch in the middle of the steering wheel strikes one as rather old-fashioned, and a headlamps flasher would be welcomed.

Luggage space is restricted by the spare wheel in the boot and also the battery, which leave only enough capacity for a couple of small suitcases or some soft bags. There is a master switch which isolates the whole electrical system and the car can thus be left immobile with a locked boot lid, although there are no door locks. Engine accessibility is not very good, the space being quite narrow and crowded; replenishing with oil and water is comparatively simple and the dipstick is quite easy to get at. During the 1,184 miles of our test, almost all of which encompassed hard driving, the car used 5 pints of oil.

The hard driving also accounts for the quite heavy fuel consumption of 17.8 m.p.g.; on one run, however, at an average speed of 50 m.p.h., cruising mostly on fairly winding secondary roads in overdrive top at around 65 m.p.h. and avoiding wide throttle openings, 33 m.p.g. was recorded.

The big Healey is a good sports car. It is excellent value for money, fun, even exciting to drive, and provided one learns to accept the scuttle shake, low ground clearance and some of the other rather dated features that go with the car, it would be easy to live with. It is fast, safe, and has an appealing, "long-legged" character which suits the good riding qualities and makes it pleasant as a long-distance car.

rally record of the works Austin-Healeys. There is some body roll on corners and an initial understeer but the driver can confidently pile on power to hold a chosen line. The steering is very light and although perhaps a little insensitive to small movements of the steering wheel, it is accurate and pleasant to use. The brakes also inspire a great deal of confidence, although on a long descent without the engine supplying the vacuum servo mechanism, it became obvious how necessary the servo is. The pedal pressure needed to produce locking of the wheels from 40 m.p.h. without it was very high.

Stability at speed is excellent and there is every encouragement for cruising on motorways at near maximum except for the very high noise level. The exhaust note has already been mentioned, and above 90 m.p.h. wind noise makes conversation difficult; above 110 it becomes impossible except by shouting. The new hood is very rigid, however, and does not flap at any speed of which the car is capable, although near maximum gaps let in a draught at the tops of the side windows. It is particularly easy to dismantle and erect the hood; there are only two over-centre catches on the top windscreen rail and it folds away quite smoothly and easily, and can be managed comfortably by one person. A cover is provided for it in the closed position, and this fits neatly but the hood does not disappear flush with the body. During prolonged, very heavy rain taken at up to 110 m.p.h. there were no leaks or draughts except round the opening rear window in the hood. This seems rather casually fitted; although it may be nice to have an openable back window, one hardly expects gaps between the Vybak sheet and the hood cloth. Visibility forward is good, although the screen pillars and quarter lights are approaching saloon car standards of thickness and there are large blind areas in the rear quarters. The side windows fit neatly against rigid hood frames but they were stiff to wind.

Coachwork and Equipment

Starting handle .. .. None	
Battery mounting .. .. .. In rear boot	
Jack .. .. Screw type	
Jacking points .. Front spring base plates, rear spring leaves	
Standard tool kit: Jack, plug spanner, tommy bar, wheel nut hammer.	
Exterior lights: 2 headlamps, 2 sidelamps/flashers, 2 stop/tail flashers, 1 number plate light.	
Number of electrical fuses 2	
Direction indicators Self-cancelling flashers	
Windscreen wipers .. Single-speed, electric, self-parking	

Windscreen washers Manual, standard equipment
Sun visors .. .. None
Instruments: Speedometer with total and decimal trip distance recorders, rev. counter, fuel gauge, combined water temperature and oil pressure gauge.
Warning lights: Main beam, dynamo charge, flashers.
Locks: With ignition key, ignition and boot No other keys.
Glove lockers .. .. None
Map pockets .. .. 1 in each door
Parcel shelves .. .. .. 1 under facia

Ashtrays .. .. 1 on transmission tunnel
Cigar lighters .. .. None
Interior lights .. .. None
Interior heater .. Fresh air type; optional extra
Car radio: Optional extra through B.M.C. Service
Extras available: Fresh air heater; servo-assisted brakes; wire wheels; overdrive; adjustable steering column; tonneau cover.
Upholstery material .. .. .. Hide
Floor covering .. .. Carpet
Exterior colours standardized .. 6 single-tone, 5 duo-tone
Alternative body styles .. .. .. None

Maintenance

Sump .. .. .. 12 pints, S.A.E. 30	
Gearbox (including overdrive) 5½ pints, S.A.E. 30	
Rear axle .. .. .. 3 pints, S.A.E. 90	
Steering gear lubricant .. .. S.A.E. 90	
Cooling system capacity .. 20 pints (2 drain taps)	
Chassis lubrication: By grease gun every 3,000 miles to 15 points.	
Ignition timing .. .. .. 6° b.t.d.c. static	
Contact breaker gap .. .. .014-.016 in.	

Sparking plug type .. .. .. Champion N5
Champion N3 (high speeds)
Sparking plug gap .. .. .024 in.
Valve timing: Inlet opens 5° b.t.d.c. and closes 45° a.b.d.c. Exhaust opens 40° b.b.d.c. and closes 10° a.t.d.c.
Tappet clearances (hot) .. .. Inlet .012 in.
Exhaust .012 in.
Front wheel toe-in .. .. 1/16 in. to 1/8 in.

Camber angle .. .. 1°
Castor angle .. .. 2°
Steering swivel pin inclination .. .. 6½°
Tyre pressures:
Front 20 lb.⎫ Increase by 5 lb.
Rear 25 lb.⎭ for fast driving
Brake fluid .. .. Girling
Battery type and capacity .. .. Lucas 12-volt, 50 amp.-hr.

BEFORE I took delivery of the Austin-Healey 3000 various comments had led me to believe that this model was unpredictable in its handling, not particularly attractive and extremely thirsty. Perhaps this increased my pleasure when after only brief acquaintance I had already become quite fond of the big Healey, and found it to be a most pleasing and comfortable car.

The re-styled radiator grille and the wrap-round screen gives the Mark 2 a much more expensive look. In every way the car has been improved upon and is now very much the modern G.T. car. The wind-up windows with opening quarter lights exclude all draughts as they actually home into a channel in the hood supports. The wrap-round screen gives excellent forward and angled vision, the pillar blind spots being much reduced. The seats are more or less the same as on earlier models, giving good support to the back, but lacking lateral assistance in favour of ease of entrance. The steering wheel, which is adjustable, allows for a relaxed style of driving but does not quite permit the now popular straight arm position unless, of course, you have exceptionally long legs and short arms!

There is ample room for moderately sized luggage behind the seats in the "plus two" compartment—a space designed for children and legless dwarfs. The boot, which houses the battery and spare wheel, is rather inadequate for all but the smallest luggage.

The facia is well laid out with the rev. counter and speedometer directly in front of the driver. The oil pressure, water temperature and fuel gauges flank these major instruments. All these instruments are easily visible, the steering wheel causing little or no restricted vision.

The controls are much improved—especially the gear lever which now is placed conveniently to hand. The Abingdon people have done away with the old, long, cranked lever in favour of a remote control, which brings the lever into the optimum position. The accelerator pedal is not as close to the brake as

the AUSTIN-HEALEY 3000 Mark 2

it might be and, in order to heel-toe, it is important to have an extremely flexible ankle. A simple modification, however, would overcome this irritating but small point.

The engine is still the well-tried 3-litre which has seen a good deal of development since its introduction in 1959 and now produces 130 b.h.p. The gearbox has improved synchromesh, but the ratios remain as before with overdrive fitted to third and top. The overdrive is controlled by a conveniently placed panel switch.

Braking is provided by Girling 11¼ in. discs on the front with 11 in. drums on the rear. These are actuated through a single master cylinder and are servo assisted. The hand-brake, which is positioned alongside the propshaft tunnel, is on the driver's side.

One of the most pleasant features of this car is that long journeys can be accomplished with remarkably little driver fatigue. This is mainly due to the excellent torque characteristics of the big 3-litre engine, which enables the car to be driven with a minimum amount of gear changing. The car will happily toddle along at 30 m.p.h. in top and still accelerate away without complaint from either engine or transmission. The clutch takes up smoothly at all times and no slip was detected even under adverse conditions. The only criticism that can be made is the heavy clutch pedal pressure. The gearbox is extremely robust and, although greatly improved, the synchromesh is unable to cope with some unsynchronized gear changes by the driver. This feature makes heel-toe vital if advantage is to be taken of engine braking. Changing down does not necessitate double de-clutch as such but, unless one is prepared to wait, these down changes must be accompanied by enough revs. to synchronize the change. The brakes appear fade-free in normal road use and never gave the writer any disconcerting moments. After several really hard applications, if anything their efficiency was improved. At no time was there any tendency for the brakes to pull or grab.

With overdrive engaged, open road can be covered at well over the 100 mark without any apparent effort. It must be stated here, however, that the controllability of the car, which is excellent up to 110 m.p.h., when approaching its maximum is not so good, and between 110 and 120 road surfaces and side winds have adverse effects on the handling.

The performance of the car is such as to make it the fastest production car available at its price today. Maximum speed is 118.5 m.p.h. with the best one-way time of 120 exactly (7.5 secs. over the flying quarter mile). The 0 to 60 time is now 9.8 secs., whilst 30 m.p.h. is reached in 3.2 secs. and 50 m.p.h.

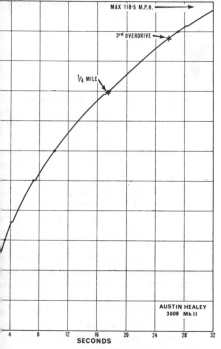

MAX 118·5 M.P.H.

3rd OVERDRIVE

¼ MILE

AUSTIN HEALEY
3000 Mk II

SECONDS

ACCELERATION GRAPH

SPECIFICATION AND PERFORMANCE DATA

Car Tested: Austin-Healey 3000 Mark 2 occasional four-seater. Price £1,064 including P.T. Extras on test car: overdrive, heater, wire wheels, radio.

Engine: Six cylinders, 83.36 mm. x 88.9 mm. (2,912 c.c.). Pushrod operated overhead valves. 9.03 to 1 compression ratio. 130 b.h.p. at 4,750 r.p.m. Twin HS6 semi-downdraught SU carburetters. Lucas coil and distributor.

Transmission: Single dry plate Borg and Beck 10 ins. clutch. Four-speed gearbox with synchromesh on upper three ratios with remote gear lever. Laycock-de Normanville overdrive. Open Hardy Spicer propeller shaft. Hypoid rear axle.

Chassis: Box section pressed steel frame. Independent front suspension by wishbones and coil springs with anti-roll torsion bar. Cam and peg steering gear, 14 to 1 ratio. Rigid rear axle on semi-elliptic springs with anti-sway bar. Hydraulic lever type shock absorbers. Girling hydraulic brakes, 11¼ ins. discs front, 11 ins. drums rear. Knock-on 4J wire wheels fitted 5.90 x 15 ins. tyres.

Equipment: 12 volt lighting and starting. Speedometer, rev. counter, oil pressure, water temperature and fuel gauges. Windscreen washer. Flashing indicators. Extra: heater and radio.

Dimensions: Wheelbase, 7 ft. 8 ins. Track (front), 4 ft. 0¾ in.; (rear), 4 ft. 2 ins. Overall length, 13 ft. 1½ ins. Width, 5 ft. 0½ in. Turning circle, 35 ft. Weight, 1 ton, 1 cwt.

Performance: Maximum speed, 118.5 m.p.h. Best one way speed, 120 m.p.h. Speeds in gears: direct top, 102 m.p.h.; overdrive 3rd, 98 m.p.h.; 3rd, 79 m.p.h.; 2nd, 50 m.p.h.; 1st, 36 m.p.h. Standing quarter-mile, 17.5 secs. Acceleration: 0-30 m.p.h., 3.2 secs.; 0-50 m.p.h., 7.3 secs.; 0-60 m.p.h., 9.5 secs.; 0.80 m.p.h., 17.8 secs.; 0-100 m.p.h., 27.2 secs.

Fuel Consumption: 15-18 m.p.g.

scuttle shake had no apparent effect on the handling of the car—it was just annoying. This appears to be a characteristic of this model.

Fuel consumption was not bad at all and figures of 15 m.p.g. and 20 m.p.g. were recorded under different conditions, the overall consumption working out at a fraction over 17 m.p.g. Despite the large capacity sump, oil consumption was negligible.

The general impression gained of this car is that it is a first-class all-rounder. It is comfortable, relatively quiet and can be driven slowly with as much enjoyment as it can be driven quickly. For the man who wants a big car with plenty of power, the Austin-Healey 3000 Mark 2 fills the bill admirably.

takes 7.3 secs. The most impressive figure, however, is the 0-80, which is 17.8 secs.—this gives a very useful turn of acceleration. The 100, which tends to be an everyday feature of this car, takes just over 27 secs. These figures show a big improvement over the earlier 3000.

Whilst taking these figures, the following speeds in gears were used: first, 36 m.p.h.; second, 50 m.p.h. (into the red); third, 80 m.p.h. (into the red); third overdrive, 95 m.p.h.; fourth, 102 m.p.h. If speed proved the essence, for road use speeds of 30 m.p.h., 45 m.p.h., 70 m.p.h., 90 m.p.h. and 100 m.p.h. were more than adequate, for there was no advantage in going into the red.

The type of gear change employed made an appreciable difference to the performance figures and when one waited for the synchromesh the acceleration figures generally suffered by a second or so.

The much maligned handling of the 3000 proved, in fact, to be quite tolerable. Corners could be taken in grand style and the rear end had to be pushed out with a twitch of the wheel, but only needed the smallest fraction of opposite lock to bring it to order. The suspension gave a pleasant ride without the harsh characteristics normally found in a sports car. In the wet, a certain amount of discretion was needed but no more than any other car with three litres to propel it. The steering was perhaps a little heavy and the slightest bit remote, but it afforded excellent straight-line running manners. The castor return action was heavy but not aggressively so.

A criticism which must be made is the scuttle shake which sets in under certain conditions—namely, under power and fast cornering. Initially, I had attributed this shake to kick-back and judder on the steering but, on investigation, it proved to be caused by the lack of rigidity in the scuttle. It must be stated that this

AUSTIN-HEALEY
3000 MARK 2

THE AUSTIN HEALEY 3000—the "big Healey"—has held a high place in the affection of keen drivers for a long time: since the introduction of the original model it has enjoyed a reputation as a rugged, enduring sort of high performance sports car.

The latest in the long line of Austin-Healeys retains that impression of rugged strength, but, with it, has acquired rather more comfort than is possessed by some other cars of similar performance. With a maximum speed in overdrive top gear of comfortably over 120 m.p.h., it is an extremely fast car by any standards: the suspension gives a firm ride, and driver and passenger alike are conscious of sitting very close to the ground. Thick carpets, wind-up windows and "convertible top", as opposed to a hood, give the occupants a feeling of well-being which seems foreign to such a car.

The engine in this machine is the six-cylinder B.M.C. 3-litre unit of 2,912 c.c. with, in the Mark 2 Healey, a compression ratio of 9 to 1 and a power output of 136 b.h.p. at 4,750 r.p.m. This is mated to a four-speed and reverse gearbox with overdrive on 3rd and top

gears, and synchromesh on the upper three ratios. Suspension is entirely conventional, being independent, with coil springs at the front, and using semi-elliptic leaf springs at the rear.

The engine is extremely smooth, and the car can be driven in a really gentlemanly manner. Idling is smooth and reliable, and the considerable punch of 136 b.h.p. is delivered smoothly, with a steady "flow" of power throughout the engine speed range. It is an extremely flexible unit, and the car will potter along at 20 m.p.h. in top gear: only depression of the loud pedal and the flick of the overdrive switch is then necessary for brisk acceleration right up to 120 m.p.h. to be provided.

The gearbox now has its ratios selected by means of a centrally-mounted lever of traditional type and usual mounting, rather than the floor-mounted fitting used in earlier models. The lever is now comfortably placed, and falls easily into the hand, but the gearbox itself is spoiled by rather weak synchromesh: additionally, second gear is rather too low, and leaves a wide gap between 2nd and 3rd speeds. Overdrive was, on the test car, rather reluctant to

engage on 3rd gear, but was entirel satisfactory on top. The clutch is ligh and the pedals are suitably arranged fo "heel-and-toe" gear changing.

As we have said above, the suspensio provided a ride which is firm to th point of harshness, and over roug surfaces the car hops about con siderably. The ground clearance i rather too slight for fast motoring o any but first-class roads: the exhaus pipes scraped the ground on severa occasions during the test, even a modest speeds, in country lanes whic other cars have found far from rough On the credit side, however, the drive retains a delightful feeling of being a one with the car, and from the per formance standpoint the ride smooth out at high speed.

On this model, designated the "Sport Convertible", considerable trouble ha been taken to provide occasional seat in the rear which are of real value a passenger accommodation. This en deavour has met with success, but i has meant that the driving position is little cramped, even for a driver o average height and build. Althoug sufficient seat adjustment is availabl to make the legs comfortable, on remains rather too close to the whee All the controls are handily placed however, and can be reached withou contortions. The lateral suppor afforded by the seats could be muc improved.

The instruments are placed in a nacell immediately in front of the driver

A rev.-counter reading to 6,000 r.p.m., and "red-lined" at 5,200 r.p.m., is matched by a speedometer reading to 120 m.p.h. It is distinctly unusual to find a car which is endowed with a maximum speed in excess of that to which the speedometer will read! Flanking these two large dials are a combined oil pressure/water temperature gauge, and a fuel contents gauge; warning lights are provided for headlamp main beams and ignition charge, as well as for the flashing direction indicators which are controlled, in delightfully "vintage" style, by a switch mounted on the steering wheel boss. There is, unfortunately, no provision made for flashing the headlights, which must be physically turned on by a "pull and twist" switch. The handbrake, which is not of "fly-off"

type, is fitted between the driver's seat and the transmission tunnel, where it is occasionally inaccessible.

The whole of the interior is thickly carpeted, and the occasional rear seats are properly upholstered, with ample leg-room for two children. Visibility with the top erected is not as good as it might be: one sits very low down in the car, and forward vision is impeded noticeably by the rather high bonnet line, the parked screenwipers, and by the upper part of the steering wheel rim. An absence of transparent quarter panels in the hood seriously impedes rearward vision.

The test car was a hard-worked example, and had covered some 19,000 miles when it came into our hands. Thus it was not surprising to find several rattles and squeaks. The doors,

however, closed well, and the car was waterproof in wet weather.

The brakes are the popular disc and drum combination, with $11\frac{1}{4}$ in. discs on the front wheels and 11 in. drums at the back. No servo is fitted as standard, although one is available as an option: without it, however, firm, powerful and progressive braking is provided for only light pedal pressure. The car's roadholding, despite an unfortunate reputation which it seems to have acquired for no very apparent reason, is in fact excellent. Directional stability at very high speed needs careful attention, but in other respects this big, powerful car can be driven hard with relative ease. It is, in fact, at its best on long, fast sweeping curves, when all four wheels will slide gently and controllably. Full use of the acceleration from rest promotes a good deal of axle tramp and wheel spin, while emerging quickly from tight corners also tends to get things moving at the back. Wheelspin in the wet is, understandably, readily provoked.

The acceleration itself is outstanding: its mean time of 16.75 seconds for the standing quarter-mile, together with a time from rest to 60 m.p.h. of well under ten seconds presents a picture of a very powerful car indeed: these figures could be improved considerably if the axle tramp at take-off could be eliminated. Acceleration from a standstill to 100 m.p.h. takes only 23.5 seconds— a time lapse at the end of which several medium-sized family cars are sometimes hard put to it to be travelling at 60 m.p.h.! Three figure speeds can be encompassed in each of the three upper ratios—overdrive third, direct and overdrive top gears. Once under way, easy 100 m.p.h. cruising speeds can be adopted at only 4,000 r.p.m. in overdrive top, leaving well over 1,000 revs. in hand and leaving the car completely easy: a machine with a very long stride, this. Travelling at 118 m.p.h.—4,500 r.p.m. in overdrive top—covers the ground with great celerity, but prolonged use of this sort of speed caused the oil pressure to start dropping, suggesting that for the man who likes to travel really fast an oil-cooler would be a worthwhile investment.

At high speed there is some scuttle shake on rough surfaces: patches of the M1 which have yet to recover fully from last winter's frosts induced this condition quite readily. Further, it is extremely warm in the driving compartment with the hood raised, and the opening quarter lights do little to alleviate this. The demister system is efficient, the lights powerful: a great improvement would be effected by the use of two-speed windscreen wipers.

SPECIFICATION AND PERFORMANCE DATA

Austin-Healey 3000 Mark 2 Sports Convertible. Price: £865, plus £180 15s. 4d. P.T.=£1,045 15s. 4d.

Engine: Six-cylinder, 83.36 × 89 mm. (2,912 c.c.). Compression ratio 9 : 1, 136 b.h.p. at 4,750 r.p.m. Twin SU HS6 carburettors; push rod operated overhead valves.

Transmission: Four-speed and reverse gearbox with synchromesh on upper three forward ratios and overdrive on 3rd and 4th. Central floor-mounted control. Single dry-plate clutch.

Suspension: Front, independent with wishbones, coil springs and stabilising bar. Rear, semi-elliptic leaf springs and anti-sway bar. Tyres: 5.90 × 15.

Brakes: Front, $11\frac{1}{4}$ in. discs; rear, 11 in. drums.

Equipment: 12-volt lighting and starting. Self-parking windscreen wipers. Windscreen washers. Speedometer, rev.-counter, oil pressure, fuel contents and water temperature gauges. Flashing direction indicators. Heating, demisting and ventilating equipment. Overdrive. Radio. Knock-on wire wheels.

Dimensions: Overall length 13 ft. $1\frac{1}{2}$ in.; overall width 5 ft. $0\frac{1}{2}$ in.; overall height 4 ft. 2 in. Ground clearance $4\frac{1}{2}$ in. Turning circle 35 ft. Weight 2,375 lb.

Performance: Maximum speed 122.1 m.p.h. (mean), 124.2 m.p.h. (best). Speeds in gears: 1st, 38 m.p.h.; 2nd, 55 m.p.h.; 3rd, 82.5 m.p.h.; overdrive 3rd, 101 m.p.h.; 4th, 110 m.p.h. Acceleration; 0–30 m.p.h., 3.4 sec.; 0–40, 4.0 sec.; 0–50, 6.0 sec.; 0–60, 9.1 sec.; 0–70, 12.9 sec.; 0–80, 15.4 sec.; 0–90, 20.2 sec.; 0–100, 23.5 sec. Standing quarter-mile: 16.75 sec. Fuel consumption: 17–19 m.p.g.

THIS IS THE AUSTIN HEALEY 3000 that didn't win at Sebring. Four makes finished ahead of our No. 33. They cost $2,000 to $8,000 more. Not quite the highest accelerating machine in the world, the Healey will do an honest 120 mph, and 53 Sebring entrants will attest to the fact that you can't beat it by trying to wear it down.

THIS IS THE AUSTIN HEALEY 3000 that could be yours. Some people think it's almost ugly. We feel it is a rather handsome motor car: lean and clean ... and somewhat mean. All the creature comforts, too—roll up windows, room for a couple of children in back and a true "one-hand" convertible top. All this and 2,380 lbs. of enduring pride.

English as "tea and crumpets", the revamped Austin Healey 3000 Mk2A has picked up a few Americanisms.

By CHRIS BECK

AUSTIN HEALEY'S REDOUBTABLE BULLDOG

SIDEWAYS, ever sideways. This was the result of too much clog, too much lock into too much corner in the famous 100 series Austin Healeys that were familiar on Australian roads in the middle and late 1950s.

But the latest piece of big sports car machinery to come from this famed Longbridge lineage, the Austin Healey 3000 Mk 2A, a direct descendant of the 100 series, has had its suspension reworked, and so tamed this inherent lateral slippage to a point which now makes it almost conventional.

The older type Healeys were interesting, challenging cars to drive, and really needed to be driven; in every sense of the word. They were popular cars in this country until the early sixties, when suddenly, for some unknown reason, the demand for these highly desirable cars dwindled to a trickle. Now if you want one you virtually have to import it.

Recently a Sydney firm of sports car dealers, P. and R. Williams Pty Ltd, anticipated an upswing in the sales of big sports cars and made a speculative gamble by importing two of the latest Healeys, to feel out the market.

One car was a completely standard unit fitted with wire wheels, while the other had an overdrive as an optional extra. Not having driven a "big" Healey for some time and because SCW

Not a good-looking car by any means, the latest Healey retains the basic body lines of its predecessors.

had not had a story on the latest model, I hot-footed it down to the dealers. A few well-placed words to the company's sales manager and everything was set for a road impressions run in the more expensive, overdrive, model of the two cars.

Next day I called to pick up the car and the last thing I heard as I drove away from the showroom was a hoarse salesman's voice pleading: "Don't take it above 3500 rpm in the gears." It was not necessary to exceed this limit, and I did not, but acceleration was still neck-snappingly good. Above 1700 rpm acceleration in all gears seemed so constant that one felt that the torque curve must be plateau-like. Delivering a lusty 130 bhp net at 4750 rpm the six cylinder 2.9 litre BMC C-series engine has a maximum torque output of 167 ft/lb at 3000 rpm. Compression ratio is high by Australian standards at 9.03 to 1 and the engine "pinked" low in the rev range and tended to run-on a little.

One of the main changes in this model from the Mk 2 is that the latter's three 1.5 in SU carburettors are replaced by two 1.75 in units, which will make the engine tuner's job easier. This really was the only major engine modification undertaken on the latest models.

When working, the noises of the four bearing motor — the thresh of the rocker and valve gear, the hiss of the carburettors and the throaty throb of the exhaust — mingle to produce a blood-stirring automotive symphony.

Ideally spaced ratios make the remote shift gearbox a delight to use and fairly fast shifts can be executed with precision. Only the stiffness of the new car seemed to hinder what would have otherwise been extremely rapid changes. Downward shifts, from fourth to third gear only, present a few problems as the gate seems to stop it falling into position — even double de-clutching does not help.

Sitting atop the seven inch chromium plated gear-lever is a patterned plastic ball - knob. Operating on third and top gears only, the Laycock de Normanville overdrive is excellent for the driver with a conscience and a heavy foot, and with its use the car would be easy to cruise around the 100 mph mark all day long — if the roads permitted — without harming the engine.

Clutch operation is by a single 10 inch dry plate unit which left little to be desired. The pedal needed to be depressed to different depths as take up varied right throughout the rev range.

Eleven inch disc brakes on the front and un-finned cast 11 inch drums on the rear take care of the car's stopping needs and effectively hauled it down from 80 mph (or 3500 rpm in top/overdrive), the highest speed attained during our run. A brake pedal sponginess, sometimes associated with discs, could be felt and the travel seemed a little more than in similar cars fitted with

this form of braking; then again, of course, the system may have only needed adjusting.

Handling, as we said earlier, is a great improvement on earlier model Healeys and although it is a little tricky when cornering near the limit, it does not spring any surprises. It becomes easily predictable with familiarity. But I couldn't help feeling that if you overstepped the mark through a corner and lost the car, there would be very little you could do to rectify the matter.

Like most English sports cars limit handling is the familiar initial understeer/final oversteer combination which can be quite tricky because the car is well on the way before you realise it. Judiciously used, the car's excess power can push it through a corner in many different ways and in varying attitudes — tail out or more lock. Once you have learned knack, power becomes a dominating factor in hard cornering and the sideways technique produces a rather queer sensation in such a large and heavy sports car.

Styling, to put it bluntly, would never win a designer's award and probably is not intended to. It is incongruous, bulbous and out of date by about seven years. Still the American and English sports car buying public must love the rugged, typically "John Bull" lines. Perhaps one of the primary reasons for the cars enduring success is that it has not undergone a major

An unfamiliar insignia to Australians. This rear badge is often the only thing seen of the car by competitors in European rallies.

body change since the introduction of the original 100 series. Minor changes have been made over the years — different grills, a new bonnet with a small air intake has been fitted and many other unobtrusive details — but the basic form remains.

Maybe Americans do not like wrestling with hood ribs and soft tops in sudden rainstorms. This is the impression I gained after trying BMCs latest innovation for the 3000 — an American-type pull-up and clip convertible hood. When not in use it folds neatly and is stowed behind the two small rear passenger seats. Really suitable only for children, these seats could only be used to carry an average sized adult short distances.

For better weather-proofing, wind-up windows with quarter-lights replace those terrible unslidable, sliding side curtains on earlier models. Window winders, door handles and pulls are all chromed cast metal.

The dash panel is straightforward. There is a Smiths 120 mph speedometer on the right of the adjustable steering column, with on the left a 6000 rpm tachometer, redlined at 5250. Both were markedly free of flutter. To the right of the speedometer is a quarter-scale electric fuel gauge which tells one the contents of the 12 gallon petrol tank. On the left of the tachometer is a combined oil pressure and water temperature gauge. A spring spoked, 12 in diameter, plastic rimmed steering wheel is situated just short of

the straight-arms position and the blinker light mechanism and the horn button are housed in the boss. Even by altering both the seat and the steering column I could not find a comfortable straight arms driving position. In the Healey tradition pedals are offset and pressures are fairly firm. The well-designed bucket seats provide excellent lateral support and are adjustable so that even a six-footer would have ample leg room.

In circuit racing the car would be completely outclassed, but that it is fast and tough is evident from its magnificent performances in high speed European rallies. On special stages and timed hill climbs it consistently whips all opposition, but this year the cars have been troubled by Ford Falcon Sprints fitted with a 4.2-litre V8 motor. As a fast, able-to-take-it car, it is hard to see why the popularity of the Austin Healey 3000 Mk 2A has diminished to such an extent in Australia.

Since we drove the Austin Healey 3000 Mk 2A — to once again enunciate its full and correct title — it has been purchased by well-known Sydney architect Andrew Findlay. At last reports he was learning to master that lateral slip and is as pleased as punch with the silver-blue and white car which is as British as tea and muffins or cricket on the village common on Saturday afternoons. It is the type of car I would like to own if I had a Georgian manor house, a stable of polo ponies and a dozen tweed jackets with leather elbow inserts. #

Although the interior is quite roomy, entry and exit is difficult.

Austin-Healey 3000 Mk. III

PRICES	Basic	Total (inc. P.T.)		
	£	£	s	d
Austin-Healey 300. Mk. III Sports Convertible	915	1,106	3	9
Extras (including P.T.)				
Overdrive		£60	8	4
Wire wheels		£30	4	2
Fresh-air heater		£18	14	7
Adjustable steering column		£2	8	4
Tonneau cover		£12	1	4
Leather upholstery		Price not available		

A YEAR and a half ago the Austin-Healey 3000 became a sports convertible with added comfort and refinement as its main features. To-day B.M.C. go further along these lines by announcing the Mark III version with a more luxurious interior, better exhaust silencing and a 12 per cent increase in power. To cope with the extra performance, servo brakes are standard equipment. Externally the car is unchanged, but the price in Britain has been increased from £1,046 to £1,106.

The most obvious difference in the interior of the car is the facia design, now changed from the functional lay-out of earlier models to a symmetrical arrangement of wooden panels with a central console merging with the transmission tunnel. In front of the driver, on the walnut-veneered panel, are the speedometer and an electronic rev counter, visible through the spring-spoked steering wheel, and also the petrol gauge, water thermometer and choke control. On the passenger side is a glove box with a lockable lid.

Ignition and other switches are on a small strip on the console with the heater controls above them. Below the switch panel is a standard radio aperture and the speaker grille, blanked off when a radio is not fitted. Lower edges of the facia are finished with a plated bead, and the console is covered in black leather-cloth.

The same arrangement of separate bucket seats at the front and miniature bucket seats for children in the back is retained. But the appearance of the trim is improved by fluting the centre panels of the seats with a new embossed Ambla two-way stretch leathercloth, giving the appearance of hand-tooled leather. Real leather upholstery is available at extra cost.

Suitcases and large objects carried on the back seats of earlier 3000s balanced precariously on the uneven platform provided by the half-seats. Now those owners who normally travel two up will appreciate the new design of the rear seat backrest, which is made to double out forwards to form a large, flat, carpet-covered platform over the rear seats. Two sturdy bolts underneath its forward edge hold it firmly in place. A further addition is a small companion-box built into the armrest between the front seats.

Two engine modifications have increased power output from 136 b.h.p. (gross) at 4,750 r.p.m. to 154 b.h.p gross (148 b.h.p. net) at 5,250 r.p.m. One is a camshaft with longer dwell, which besides providing better cylinder filling has the advantage of giving the tappets an easier time. Secondly, the two 1·75in. HS6 S.U. carburettors fitted to the Mark II Healey have been replaced by a pair of larger HD8 2in. instruments. While the main gain in power has been at the top end of the speed range, it will be seen from the power curve that torque, which determines the accelerative ability, is much

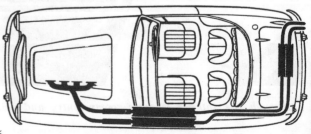

Layout of the new dual exhaust system

Below: New facia with walnut panels and centre console.

Right: Only external engine change is the substitution of larger S.U. carburettors

improved above 1,700 r.p.m. or 35 m.p.h. in top gear.

A short drive in a Mark III showed that the reduced exhaust noise increased the impression of power. In fact, the new dual exhaust system, made necessary by impending restrictions in the U.S.A. which could well be extended to this country, absorbs no more power than the old system. The gross power output figure was achieved with the new exhaust system fitted on the test bed but without fan and dynamo. Dual cast-iron manifolds are used and flexible down pipes lead the gases to a pair of straight-through silencers mounted amidships outside the left chassis side member. The dual tail pipes then follow the line of the side member and turn across beneath the tail of the car, where

the gases pass through dual expansion boxes.

A further improvement, which gives lighter clutch operation, is the adoption of a 9.5in. Borg and Beck diaphragm spring clutch. This modification was actually introduced some time ago to bring the Austin-Healey 3000 into line with other B.M.C. cars fitted with the C-series engine.

These changes confirm the Austin-Healey 3000 Mark III as a comfortable, high-speed touring car which will hold its own with most things on the road. The ruggedness of this model is a by-word—it is the only British model ever to have won the destructive Liège-Rome-Liège Rally—and its lines have a quality which should appeal to a buyer who likes to keep a car for several years.

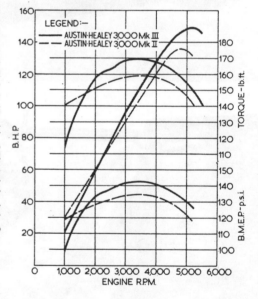

Gross performance curves for the new engine compared with the old

Specification

ENGINE (front-mounted, water-cooled)

No. of cylinders	...	Six in-line
Bore	...	83.4mm (3.28in.)
Stroke	...	89mm (3.5in.)
Displacement	...	2,912 c.c. (178 cu. in.)
Valve operation	...	Overhead, pushrods and rockers
Compression ratio	...	9.0 to 1
Max. b.h.p. (net)	...	148 at 5,250 r.p.m.
Max b.m.e.p. (net)	...	140.2 p.s.i. at 3,500 r.p.m.
Max torque (net)	...	165.2 at 3,500 r.p.m.
Carburettors	...	Twin S.U. HD8
Fuel pump	...	S.U. electric
Tank capacity	...	12 Imp. gallons (54.5 litres)
Sump capacity	...	12.75 pints (10 litres)
Oil filter	...	Tecalemit or Purolator full-flow
Cooling system	...	Centrifugal pump, fan and thermostat, pressurized to 7 p.s.i.
Battery	...	12 volt, 57 amp. hr.

TRANSMISSION

Clutch	...	Borg and Beck diaphragm spring single dry plate, 9.5in. dia.
Gearbox	...	Four-speed, synchromesh on 2nd, 3rd and top; central floor change. Optional Laycock de Normanville overdrive

Overall gear ratios		Standard	Overdrive
OD Top		—	3.14
	Top	3.55	3.91
OD 3rd		—	5.12
	3rd	4.11	4.74
	2nd	7.73	8.05
	1st	10.21	11.26
	Rev	13.13	14.54
Final drive	...	Hypoid bevel 3.55 (3.91 with OD)	

CHASSIS

Brakes	...	Girling hydraulic, vacuum servo-assisted. Front discs, 11.25in. dia.; rear drums, 11in. dia.; 2.25in. wide shoes
Suspension: front		Independent, coil springs and wishbones, anti-roll bar
Suspension: rear		Live axle, half-elliptic leaf springs, Panhard rod
Dampers	...	Armstrong lever arm type
Wheels	...	Ventilated steel disc, 4in. wide rims
Tyre size	...	5.90–15in.
Steering	...	Cam and peg
Steering wheel	...	Three-spoke, 17in. diameter
Turns, lock to lock		3

DIMENSIONS

Wheelbase	...	7ft 8in. (234cm)
Track: front	...	4ft 0.75in. (124cm)
Track: rear	...	4ft 2in. (127 cm)
Overall length	...	13ft 1.5in. (400cm)
Overall width	...	5ft 0in. (152cm)
Overall height (unladen)		4ft 2in. (127cm)
Ground clearance (laden)		4.6in. (12cm)
Turning circle	...	35ft 7in. (10.8m)
Kerb weight	...	23cwt (2,548lb—1,145kg)

PERFORMANCE DATA

Top gear m.p.h. per 1,000 r.p.m. 20.72 (23.01 OD)
Torque lb. ft. per cu. in. engine capacity.........0.93
Brake surface swept by linings......... 383.5 sq. in.
Weight distribution: F, 49.3 per cent, R, 50.7 per cent.

Austin Healey 3000 mark III

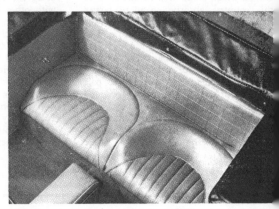

The cockpit is lavishly furnished now.
The central console incorporates minor controls,
radio installation, gearchange, ashtray and padded
glove-box, while the backrest of the 'jump-seat'
double-folds down to provide a carpeted luggage platform

... she looks the same, but under the skin there's still more power, still more luxury

YET another new and improved version of the rally-proved Austin-Healey 3000 was announced on 28 February. This is to be known as the Austin-Healey 3000 Sports Convertible Mark III and apart from a substantial increase in power output, the cockpit layout and trim has been completely redesigned to make this mile-eater even more luxurious than before.

The six-cylinder, 2,912 cc, C-Series engine now develops a full 150 b.h.p. (gross) at 5,250 r.p.m. compared with 136 b.h.p. at 4,750 r.p.m. previously, raising the maximum speed to around 125 m.p.h. with a corresponding boost in acceleration. Early production models have been timed to go from 0-80 m.p.h. in 15.5 seconds, yet smoothness and flexibility have not been impaired and fuel consumption figures are, if anything, slightly better than before. The power increase stems from the use of a new camshaft and the fitting of

twin HD8 S.U. carburetters, with 2 in. chokes, in place of the 1¾ in. S.Us. fitted to the Mark II. To provide comparable stopping power, the brakes (disc front, drum rear) are now equipped with vacuum servo assistance as standard, instead of as an optional extra.

In addition, a completely new silencing system has been developed, which actually contributes to the increase in power, but cuts the level of exhaust noise considerably, making the car much less tiring to travel in on a long journey. Several countries have (or are about to have) legislation governing vehicle noise and the new exhaust system meets all anticipated requirements.

The main feature of the interior trim is an entirely new fascia panel in polished wood veneers, with a central console, leathercloth covered, carrying switches and the optional radio installation. The console sweeps down between the seats and incorporates the

remote-control gear lever, a lidded ash-tray and a glove-box, the padded lid of which forms an arm rest. On the passenger's side there is a large lockable glove compartment while in front of the driver is a 140 m.p.h. speedometer and an electric tachometer, with clear white figures on black dials, in addition to fuel, water temperature and oil pressure gauges. The ignition key now also operates the starter instead of a separate button being needed.

The bucket seats are luxuriously upholstered in 'Ambla' vinyl material with a smart new punched pattern on the centre panels, while the backrest of the occasional rear seat double-folds forwards to provide a flat and sturdy luggage platform. Leather upholstery is available as an optional extra.

The price in Great Britain is £915, plus purchase tax of £191 3s. 9d. total, £1,106 3s. 9d.

Power output has been raised to 150 bhp by means that include the fitting of larger carburetters. The handsome new facia panel is finished in wood veneers, with black-faced instruments in front of the driver and a glove locker on the other side

more power, more comfort, less noise

Polished wood and four silencers for the Austin-Healey 3000

LEATHER coats and gauntlet gloves went out long ago for sports-car drivers. To be with it, the modern fun-motor has to feather-bed its driver and fan his passenger with gentle breezes from the heater; and all at a ton plus.

The new with-version of the Austin-Healey 3000 is known as the Mk. III and looks just like the Mk. II from the outside. They've even used the same picture for the cover of the latest catalogue; but the inside of the catalogue, like the inside of the car, reveals some notable changes; and the same goes for the technical bit at the end.

Power has gone up from 132 b.h.p. net to 149 b.h.p. net (with a little more torque as well), the noise level has come down with the aid of four cunningly contrived silencers, and light-footed braking no longer costs more because a vacuum servo is now standard. Inside the car, the former severely practical cockpit has been transformed into an equally practical driving compartment, with a central console to carry the switches, plus some polished woodwork on each side to house the instruments and a useful glove locker as well, adding a traditional touch of English luxury for the benefit of the 91.5 per cent of buyers who live overseas.

And the cost at home? £50 more on the price without tax, giving a basic figure of £915 and a total with British purchase tax of £1,106 3s. 9d.

Engine size and compression ratio are unchanged; the 13 per cent improvement in output comes from better breathing. Two HD8 S.U. carburetters with a choke diameter of 2 inches take the place of the former HS6 type with 1¾-in. chokes, and a new camshaft gives a total opening period of 252° for both inlets and exhausts compared with the previous 240°. The actual timing (with the previous figures in brackets) is: inlet opens 16° (10°) b.t.d.c.; inlet closes 56° (50°) a.b.d.c.; exhaust opens 51° (45°) b.b.d.c.; exhaust closes 21° (15°) a.t.d.c. Valve lift has been increased from 0.332 in. to 0.354 in.

Unlike many changes of this kind which boost the top-end performance at the expense of torque lower down, the new camshaft gives a useful improvement throughout the normal usable speed range; as the accompanying power curves of the Mk. II and Mk. III engines show, it is only below approximately 1,700 r.p.m. that there is any loss of torque.

Coinciding with these changes, much work has been put into reducing exhaust noise without loss of power. The latest system has been evolved in the light of West German and other European restrictions on exhaust noise which are likely to be followed by similar regulations in this country.

The new system has two pipes and four silencers—no easy matter to accommodate on a low-built sports car. The twin down-pipes

from the manifold go to a pair of silencers tucked away side by side below the driving compartment and then to a second pair of separate silencers housed across the car beneath the tail. Ground clearance remains at 4½ inches as before.

The only other mechanical change concerns the brakes, in which the vacuum servo, previously an extra, is standard.

There are lots of changes inside the convertible body. The 3000 is in fashion with a console connecting the transmission tunnel with its new facia board, to house the principal switches, heater controls and optional radio. The main instruments—speedometer, rev counter (now electrically operated), fuel gauge and combined thermometer and oil gauge—are still in front of the driver, now in a polished wood facia panel; a matching panel on the passenger's side holds a lockable glove box.

The console goes back between the seats and includes an ashtray and a neat combined arm rest and companion box with a magnetic catch. Other interior refinements include an improved type of vinyl upholstery material known as Ambla (leather is an optional extra) and a rearrangement of the rear squab so that it can be folded forward to form a luggage platform measuring 19¼ in. by 36½ in. when the occasional seats are not required.

A road test of the new model will be published shortly. The Mk. II clocked a mean speed of 116 m.p.h. and reached 100 m.p.h. from rest in 29.4 sec. The Mk. III should do even better—and with more "hush".

Bigger S.U. carburetters and better breathing help to increase power from 132 to 149 b.h.p. The 3-litre C-series engine remains fundamentally unchanged. Comparative figures are shown in the graph (far right).

A Pressing Getaway . . .

● *Snap impressions showed several big improvements. The getaway seemed to press the squab more firmly in one's back than ever, and although there was no opportunity for proper tests in a mere 20-mile run, 120 m.p.h. came up on the clock remarkably quickly. The new silencers have subdued the exhaust system to a point at which the occupants are no longer conscious of an exhaust note when the car is closed, but this, in turn has emphasized the fact that this is far from a silent car mechanically; a few extra pounds (sterling and avoirdupois) of sound-deadening materials might have been a good thing to add to the new specification for full measure.*

Bodywise, the modifications seemed all to the good. Altogether the best "Big Healey" yet.

Room for the kids. Rear seats fold forward to give flat luggage platform.

Bowing to the overseas buyers who want traditional British styling, the new Healey has a polished wood facia, central console and neat circular dials set in front of the driver.

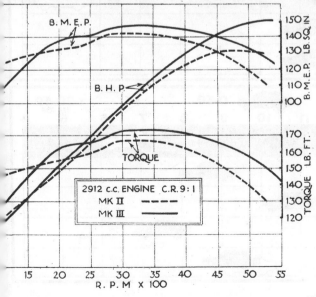

IN BRIEF

ENGINE.—6 cyl., 83.36 mm. × 89 mm., 2,912 c.c.; o.h.v. (push rods); two S.U. HD8 carburetters; max. power, 149 b.h.p. net at 5,250 r.p.m.; max. torque, 173 lb. ft. at 3,000 r.p.m.

TRANSMISSION.—10-in. diaphragm-type, s.d.p. clutch; 4-speed gearbox with synchromesh on 2-3-4. Ratios (normal): 3.545, 4.644, 7.730 and 10.209; rev. 13.187. Ratios (with opt. Laycock-de Normanville overdrive): 3.909 (O/D 3.213), 5.120 (O/D 4.210), 8.052 and 11.257; rev. 14.541. Road speed in top gear at 1,000 r.p.m. 20.9 m.p.h. (with O/D: direct, 18.94 m.p.h.; O/D, 23.1 m.p.h.).

RUNNING GEAR.—Girling hydraulic brakes, disc-front/drum-rear with vacuum servo; coil and wishbone i.f.s. with anti-roll bar; semi-elliptic rear springs and Panhard rod; cam-and-peg steering; 5.90-15 Dunlop Road Speed tyres.

DIMENSIONS.—Length, 13 ft. 1½ in.; width, 5 ft. 0½ in.; turning circle, 35 ft.; weight 21¼ cwt. approx.

Number 13
MOTOR TESTED
1301 MILES

" . . . a unique blend of vintage sports and modern GT . . . great fun to drive".

PRICES
(including overdrive, wire wheels, heater as tested) £1,005 10s. plus purchase tax equals £1,223 10s. 1d.
Price without extras
(including p.t.) £1,106 3s. 6d.

AUSTIN - HEALEY
3000 Mk III

How they run . . .

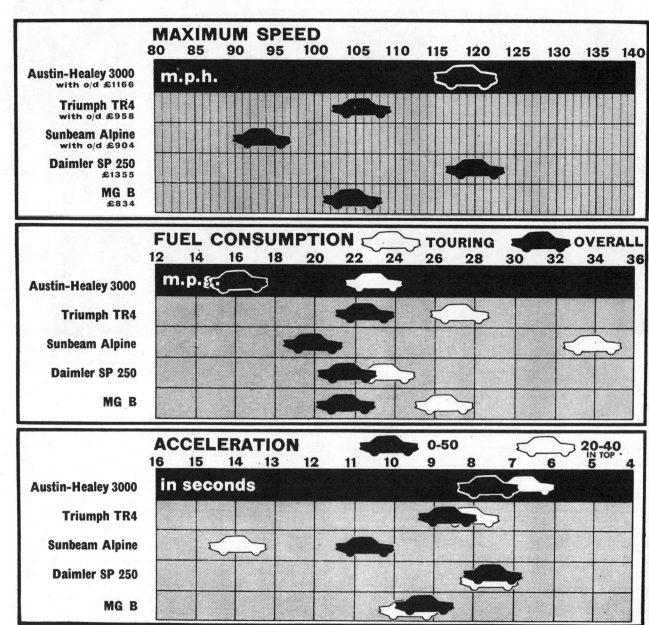

MAXIMUM SPEED

m.p.h.

	80	85	90	95	100	105	110	115	120	125	130	135	140
Austin-Healey 3000 with o/d £1166													
Triumph TR4 with o/d £958													
Sunbeam Alpine with o/d £904													
Daimler SP 250 £1355													
MG B £834													

FUEL CONSUMPTION   TOURING   OVERALL

m.p.g.

	12	14	16	18	20	22	24	26	28	30	32	34	36
Austin-Healey 3000													
Triumph TR4													
Sunbeam Alpine													
Daimler SP 250													
MG B													

ACCELERATION   0-50   20-40 IN TOP

in seconds

	16	15	14	13	12	11	10	9	8	7	6	5	4
Austin-Healey 3000													
Triumph TR4													
Sunbeam Alpine													
Daimler SP 250													
MG B													

gets in the way. Even the passenger's grab handle has been replaced by a glove box. Gone too is the lovable bark. Two exhaust pipes and four silencers have subdued the noise to a pleasant grumble that is drowned at high speeds by the whirl of fan, intakes and wind.

Yet this is no cissy sports car. A top speed of 122.5 m.p.h. is fast by any standards and quite exceptional for £1,200. Moreover, it will accelerate to 120 m.p.h. in little more than a mile in satisfying surges that whip it across country at high average speeds. Handling and steering are by no means outstanding by modern standards but better than first acquaintance (and many old hands) would suggest and the car satisfies the sporting tradition by being great fun to drive even if it takes time and know-how to make firm friends.

In a nutshell, you now go much faster in greater (but by no means sumptuous) comfort on no more petrol—a fair return for long-term development.

MAKES and models come and go while the Big Healey still gathers momentum. With a production run reaching back 12 years to 1952, the car must surely be approaching the end of an unusually long and successful line that has bred international competition winners, earned a lot of dollars and, above all, provided relatively inexpensive high performance for enthusiasts throughout the world. In its latest form the combination of speed, refinement and character is still outstanding value.

In several easy stages, the Healey has matured over the years: it gained two more cylinders from the rationalized B.M.C. C-series engine, another gear, an extra 352 c.c., much more power and torque, better handling and brakes, more refinement and room, and various face lifts, until it reached the unique blend of vintage sports and modern GT in the Mk. III 3000 announced a month ago.

A little of the original Healey 100 still remains: the classic looks; firm ride; only marginal ground clearance; the vintage driving position and a take-off that few cars can equal regardless of price. In other respects it has mellowed with age reflecting the changing tastes of its ardent supporters—or perhaps a new, more sophisticated generation of sports car drivers. Popular demand has turned the original stark cockpit into a snug and fashionable office with polished wood on the facia and a dividing console down the middle that looks good but

Performance and Economy

THIS is the fastest production Austin-Healey yet made. Larger carburetters, a new camshaft and a more efficient (and quieter) exhaust system have raised the power of the 6-cylinder, 3-litre engine from 131 to 150 b.h.p. with a useful increase in torque above 1,700 r.p.m. Compared with the Mk. II car tested in April, 1963, it has gained nearly 7 m.p.h. in top speed (122·5 m.p.h.), knocked 6 secs. off the time needed to reach 100 m.p.h. (23.7 sec.) and pulls even better at low and moderate engine speeds. Sports cars do not usually attract lazy drivers but anyone who tires of changing gear can set it in top or third and motor smoothly on from 10 m.p.h. through traffic.

Surprisingly, this impressive performance has been achieved on less fuel, nearly all the steady-speed consumption figures showing a slight improvement. Only at very low r.p.m. when the big lazy engine is working below maximum efficiency is there a slight drop. High-speed motorway cruising is utterly relaxed if rather noisy, 4,000 r.p.m. corresponding to about 100 m.p.h. in overdrive top, so it is possible to amble along in the hundreds without any fear of overstressing the engine. Only when the tachometer needle approaches the red sector starting at 5,500 r.p.m. (the recommended rev. limit) do you begin to wince at the howl from beneath the bonnet, but there is seldom any need to use such high revs.

continued on next page

Flowing vintage lines and as fast as it looks: the latest Mk III will accelerate from a standstill to 100 m.p.h. and stop again in 29 seconds.

Performance figures

Conditions: Weather: Cold, calm and dry. (Temperature 40°F, Barometer 29.85 in. Hg.) Surface: Tarmacadam and concrete. Fuel: Super Premium (101 octane)

MAXIMUM SPEEDS

Mean of 4 runs (o/d top)	..	122.5 m.p.h.
Best one way ¼-mile ..		123.5
Direct top gear at 5,500 r.p.m.	..	114.0
O/d 3rd gear ..	..	104.0
3rd gear ..	..	85.0
2nd gear ..	..	52.0
1st gear ..	..	42.0

"Maximile" Speed: (Timed quarter mile after 1 mile accelerating from rest)

Mean	..	..	..	117.8
Best	..	..	..	120.0

ACCELERATION TIMES

0-30 m.p.h.	..	..	..	3.6 sec.
0-40	..	..	..	..	4.8
0-50	..	..	..	..	6.9
0-60	..	..	..	..	9.8
0-70	..	..	..	..	12.1
0-80	..	..	..	..	14.8
0-90	..	..	..	..	18.2
0-100	..	..	..	..	23.7
0-110	..	..	..	..	34.1
Standing quarter mile		..		17.0

		O/d Top sec.	Top sec.	O/d 3rd sec.	3rd sec.
m.p.h.					
20-40	..	9.0	6.0	5.5	4.3
30-50	..	10.5	6.8	6.4	5.1

AUSTIN - HEALEY
3000 MkIII

Twin pipes and a massive exhaust system look impressive but subdue the noise to a low growl. There is very little ground clearance beneath the silencers.

The spare wheel, held down by a rod and strap, steals a lot of boot room but there is enough space left for small cases or flexible bags. The two left-hand boxes fit behind the seats.

Our test car was an easy starter, although it would occasionally spit back through the twin 2-in. S.U. carburetters with a jerk if the choke was pushed home too soon after a cold start. There was pinking on premium grade petrol and the engine often ran on even if the throttle was blipped before switching off. Plenty of revs and clutch slip are needed to start on a 1 in 3 hill with the rather high first gear, and as an indication of the massive torque, 2nd will cope with a 1 in 4.

By absolute standards, the Healey is quite an expensive car to run, its overall fuel consumption of 17.7 m.p.g. representing a cost of £13 10s. per thousand miles on petrol at 4s. 9d. a gallon. During the first part of our test, it recorded an all-time high in oil consumption—about 45 miles to the pint. This was later rectified by B.M.C. who fitted new piston rings after the original ones were found to be excessively scuffed—possibly the result of incomplete running in.

Servicing demands are quite heavy too by modern greaseless standards, 13 points needing attention every 3,000 miles.

Transmission

AN unusually smooth-acting Laycock overdrive working on third and top gears gives six forward speeds to play with. Choice of ratios is never so critical when there is ample torque throughout the rev range, and five of the six are quite acceptable. The exception is second, which is so close to first that it is hard to detect any change of note when accelerating hard. The first three gears' maxima are about 42, 52 and 85

m.p.h. at 5,250 r.p.m.—mid-way through the tachometer's yellow warning sector. Something nearer 62 m.p.h. for second would seem to be a better gap filler. Overdrive third, 10 m.p.h. slower than direct top, is used more as an instant high town gear than an extra ratio when shifting through the box although we used all six gears when taking performance figures. Powerful but obstructive synchromesh works on the top three ratios, leaving accurate double-declutching to find first: most people settled for second instead—a point in favour of its low gearing. Unlike some sports cars on which the clutch is either in or out, the Healey's has a long travel and the gentle bite and smoothness of a touring car. What little whine there is from the gearbox and axle is soon drowned by other more aggressive noises.

Steering and handling

GIVEN sufficient practice and not a little nerve, it is possible to corner the Healey very fast indeed, but it is not the sort of car that you drive on the limit first time out. The steering

The narrow bonnet opening is crammed full of engine—a tuned version of the 2,912 c.c. C-series developing 150 b.h.p. Key to numbers: 1 brake reservoir, 2 coil, 3 distributor, 4 dip stick, 5 oil filler cap, 6 carburetters, 7 windscreen washer reservoir.

40-60	..	..	9.0	6.8	6.1	5.2
50-70	..	..	9.4	6.7	6.5	4.9
60-80	..	..	11.0	7.9	7.1	5.7
70-90	..	..	11.2	7.6	7.9	—
80-100	..	..	13.2	8.6	8.8	—
90-110	..	..	16.7	—	—	—
100-120	..	..	—	—	—	—

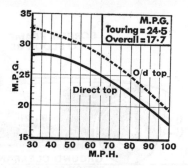

M.P.G.
Touring = 24·5
Overall = 17·7

O/d top
Direct top

HILL CLIMBING

At steady speed			lb/ton
O/d top	..	1 in 12.1	(Tapley 235)
Top	..	1 in 7.0	(Tapley 317)
O/d 3rd ..		1 in 6.5	(Tapley 340)
3rd	..	1 in 5.4	(Tapley 412)
2nd	..	1 in 3.4	(Tapley 650)

FUEL CONSUMPTION

Total test distance	..	.. 1,301 miles
17.7 m.p.g.		15.9 litres/100 km.

BRAKES

Pedal pressure, deceleration and equivalent
stopping distance from 30 m.p.h.

lb.	g	ft.
25	35	86
50	65	46
75	90	33½
100	92	32½
Handbrake	35	86

STEERING

Turning circle between kerbs:					ft.
Left ..	..	..	..	..	32
Right ..	..	..	..	..	32
Turns of steering wheel from lock					
to lock	..	..	..	..	3¼

SPEEDOMETER

30 m.p.h.	..	..	..	1½% slow
60	..	..	..	1½% slow
90	..	..	..	2% fast
Distance recorder	..	..	3½% slow

WEIGHT

			cwt.
Kerb weight (unladen with fuel for			
approximately 50 miles)	..	..	23
Front/rear distribution	..	..	48/52
Weight laden as tested	..	..	26½

is averagely light and not particularly positive by sports car standards except when cornering quickly, when a delicate touch is needed on both the throttle and steering wheel, either of which can be used to direct the car. In this respect it is far removed from the typical understeering family saloon which remains stodgily stable with big sweeps of the wheel. This is not Healey technique and would soon land anyone who tried it in trouble. With a light throttle the steering is practically neutral but under power it reverts to oversteer and, in the extreme, a power slide although the vicious breakaway of earlier cars appears to have been cured: even in the wet, an impressive amount of torque can be turned on out of a sharp bend without sliding the tail. As a safety factor, lifting the throttle mid-way through a corner makes the front tuck in after a pause—like a front-wheel drive car in slow motion—by amounts depending on the speed and radius of the corner when indelicate opposite lock prevents the car from going sideways and tyre-scrub soon slows it down.

Firm suspension, which tends to twitch the car off course on roughish roads, emphasizes the need to concentrate quite hard to hold the right line when driving quickly. At lower speeds it just goes where it is aimed.

The old trouble of poor ground clearance is still there; you have to pick a careful path along rough tracks, and the right speed over hump-back bridges to avoid scraping the exhaust pipes. Even backing off a pavement ramp can make them touch the ground.

Big brakes (11¼ in. discs at the front, drums rear) need lots of push and a vacuum servo has now been standardized to take the he-man effort out of stopping. Most of the time the brakes felt powerful and reassuring but a front wheel locked before the best recorded stop of ·92g. The same locking brake probably accounted for the mild veering after being soaked by heavy rain, and twitching even in the dry when stopping from high speeds: we felt this was a peculiarity of our test car and not typical of the model. The handbrake would almost certainly have held on a 1 in 3 hill if another notch had been found by adjustment. It coped easily with 1 in 4.

Comfort and control

LIKE most good sports cars, the Healey has firm springing (independent coil and wishbone at the front and a leaf-sprung rear axle) that only feels unduly harsh over rough roads: sports car drivers will not complain. Two absurd failings mar the seats and driving position: the poor rearward adjustment which, despite a telescopic steering column, prevents drivers of any size from getting very far

continued on next page

The excellent hood can be erected without getting out, and it stows neatly in its own well.

New to the Mark III car are a wood veneer facia and central console with a small box.

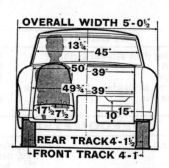

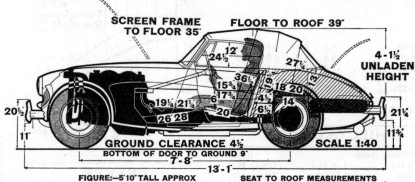

OVERALL WIDTH 5′-0½″

REAR TRACK 4′-1½″
FRONT TRACK 4′-1″

SCREEN FRAME TO FLOOR 35″ FLOOR TO ROOF 39″

4-1½
UNLADEN HEIGHT

GROUND CLEARANCE 4½″
BOTTOM OF DOOR TO GROUND 9″
7-8
13-1
SCALE 1:40

FIGURE:—5′10″ TALL APPROX

SEAT TO ROOF MEASUREMENTS TAKEN WITH SEATS COMPRESSED

AUSTIN - HEALEY
3000 Mk III

from the wheel if they want to; and the upright squab that compels a right-angled, elbows-out posture that most people did not like much although they soon got accustomed to it. A few extra shillings spent on longer runners and an adjustable squab angle would make far more people fit in greater comfort.

The combination of negligible body roll and good side support keeps you firmly in place when cornering hard: anyone in the back is so firmly wedged that no side-support is needed. On long journeys, the rear seats—little more than an upholstered ledge—are strictly for small children (a good excuse to retain a sports car *and* a growing family) and they are just tolerable for adults on short hops. Alternatively, the rear seat can be folded forward to form a useful luggage platform, supplementing a boot which is already half filled with spare wheel.

The low seating and large transmission hump/console have made the short gear lever rather high and it must be worked with the elbow raised and cranked. You soon get used to the position. The pedals are fairly comfortable but not very well placed for heel and toeing: many saloons are much better.

An easily erected and well fitting hood, wind-up windows and a heater make the Healey quickly adaptable to all weathers. Heavy rain revealed a small leak in the sealing which dripped cold water onto the gear lever. Otherwise, the inside is attractive and snug, air seepage rather than draughts giving the modest output of the heater plenty to fight on a cold day, but there is certainly never any need for the overcoats and gauntlets that were once essential sports-car wear. For such a low car, visibility is quite good, only the rear quarters of the hood making any objectionable blind spots. A large rear-view mirror on top of the scuttle gives a good view through a big plastic window and the lights are powerful if not outstanding.

There is no audible flapping of the taut hood but the noise rises with revs and speed until normal conversation ceases at about 75 m.p.h. and shouting is useless above 100 m.p.h. The optional radio would only be audible during fairly gentle driving, when a loud carburetter intake hiss can be heard above the woffle of the exhaust. Sound damping on the bulkhead would help to reduce this and other mechanical noises.

Fittings and Furniture

ALTHOUGH the new facia layout with its polished wood, neat dials and symmetrical switch gear looks neat and tidy, most drivers preferred the less stylish but more practical layout of the Mk. II car. The overdrive switch, for instance, which could formerly be flicked with a right-hand finger without lifting it from the wheel, is now grouped with four other toggle switches in the centre where it is easy to confuse with the wipers. On the other hand, it is now more logically placed near the gear lever.

Smallish dials for the almost accurate speedometer and rev counter are neatly calibrated but not angled towards the driver, making the top of the scales invisible. Well-fitted carpet covers the floor and vinyl cloth the seats, sides and the new central console which houses a radio and a small container for oddments. Its padded lid forms an armrest which got in the way of gearchanging so much that it was left permanently open. Any other luggage can be thrown behind the seats or, if small enough, locked in the passenger's cubby hole on the facia. Unlike the boot, the doors (stiff but self-supporting when open) cannot be locked, but the car can be immobilized by turning an electric master switch in the boot. There is no interior light; even worse, no headlamp flasher.

The B.M.C. safety belts are comfortable to wear and easy to adjust but only the anchorage points are standard fittings.

MAKE Austin-Healey • TYPE 3000 Mk III • MAKERS Austin Motor Co. Ltd., Longbridge, Birmingham.

ENGINE
Cylinders	..	6
Bore and stroke	..	83·36 mm. × 89 mm.
Cubic capacity	..	2,912 c.c.
Valves	..	O.h.v.
Compression ratio	..	9·03 : 1
Carburetter(s)	..	Twin S.U. HD8
Fuel pump	..	S.U. electric
Oil filter	..	Tecalemit or Purolator full flow
Max. power (gross)		150 b.h.p. at 5,250 r.p.m.
Max. torque (gross)		173 lb. ft. at 3,000 r.p.m.

TRANSMISSION
Clutch	..	Borg and Beck 9½ in. single dry plate
Top gear (s/m)	..	3·545 (overdrive, 2·91)
3rd gear (s/m)	..	4·629 (overdrive, 3·81)
2nd gear (s/m)	..	7·341
1st gear	..	9·348
Reverse	..	12·021
Overdrive	..	Laycock-de Normanville electrically operated
Final drive	..	Hypoid bevel
M.p.h. at 1,000 r.p.m. in:—		
O/d. top gear	..	25·0
Top gear	..	20·5
O/d. 3rd gear	..	19·1

3rd gear	..	15·7
2nd gear	..	9·9
1st gear	..	6·05

MAINTENANCE
Sump	..	12¼ pints S.A.E. 30
Gearbox with overdrive	..	6¼ pints S.A.E. 30
Rear axle	..	3 pints S.A.E. 30
Steering gear	..	S.A.E. 90
Cooling system	..	18 pints (2 drain taps)
Chassis lubrication		Every 3,000 miles to 13 points
Ignition timing	..	10° B.T.D.C.
Contact breaker gap	..	0·014–0·016 in.
Sparking plug type		Champion UN12Y
Sparking plug gap		0·024–0·026 in.
Tappet clearances (cold)	..	Inlet 0·012 in., exhaust 0·012 in.
Front wheel toe-in		$\frac{1}{16}$–$\frac{1}{8}$ in.
Castor angle	..	2°
Tyre pressures	..	20 lb. front, 25 lb. rear (fast driving, 25 lb. front, 30 lb. rear)

CHASSIS
Construction	..	Separate ladder frame

BRAKES
Type	..	Girling hydraulic, disc front, drum rear
Dimensions	..	11¼ in. front, 11 in. rear
Total friction area		112 sq. in. of lining working on 383 sq. in. rubbed area of discs and drums

SUSPENSION AND STEERING
Front	..	Independent coil and wishbone and an anti-roll bar.
Rear	..	Live rear axle located by Panhard rod and semi-elliptic leaf springs
Shock absorbers	..	Lever Armstrong
Steering gear	..	Cam and peg, ratio 15 to 1.
Tyres	..	Dunlop Road Speed 5·90–15

COACHWORK AND EQUIPMENT
Starting handle	..	Yes
Jack	..	Screw thread
Jacking points	..	4: beneath springs
Battery	..	Offside in boot
Number of electrical fuses	..	2
Indicators	..	Flashers, self cancelling
Screen wipers	..	Lucas electric DR3/A
Screen washers	..	Push button Tudor
Sun visors	..	None
Locks:		
With ignition key		Starter, boot and facia glove box
Interior heater	..	Smith fresh air (optional)
Extras	..	Heater, overdrive, wire spoke wheels, tonneau cover, leather seats, luggage carrier, whitewall tyres, etc.
Upholstery	..	Ambla vinyl
Floor covering	..	Fitted carpet
Alternative body types	..	None

Austin Healey changes up!

DXP 606

All the way up to a faster, more comfortable, new 3000 <u>Mark III</u>!

As sports cars go, the Austin Healey 3000 Mark II went faster (117 mph) than any other sports car in its price range. Faster, in fact, than many cars priced £500 or £600 more.

Now Austin Healey have taken the 3000 yet another step forward—to <u>Mark III</u>.

Brake horsepower is up from 136 to 150. And top speed now soars to a breathtaking 125 mph!

Other under-the-bonnet developments include twin carburettors, changed to deliver the extra power. Gear ratios modified to accommodate it. And an effortless new braking system, power assisted to cope with the improved performance.

Behind the wheel, too, you see a vastly different 3000. A sumptuous looking walnut fascia stretches all the way across the cockpit. The main controls are grouped together in a central console which descends to a transmission tunnel faced in leather.

There's a new lock-up glove compartment. A new gadget box within easy reach of the driver. And the rear seat folds down to become a convenient platform for luggage.

The price, including £191.3.9 purchase tax, is £1,106.3.9. (Electrically operated Laycock overdrive is extra.) Which makes the new Austin Healey 3000 Mark III the fastest sports car you can own for less than £1,500!

By Appointment to
Her Majesty The Queen
Motor Car Manufacturers
The Austin Motor
Company Limited

you <u>invest</u> in an **AUSTIN**

Austi

300

The Healey's face-lifting over a decade has amounted to little, but weather protection at high speed is much improved

THE Austin-Healey 3000 is not a pretty sports car for pretty girls to drive, unless they stay within earshot of Knightsbridge or else possess the qualities that James Bond admires. In its Mark III form the car retains all the ruggedness that has made it a favourite among sportsmen during the past 11 years, but with the additional comfort of wind-up side windows. Servo assistance is now standard equipment for the braking system, and a pair of bigger HD8 SU carburettors combine with a new camshaft to raise the maximum power output to 150 bhp, resulting in spectacular performance up to 100 mph (in less than 23 seconds) and a maximum speed of 121 mph.

In all essentials the Healey is now a drop-head and not a roadster, but its sporting instincts are scarcely muted

This latest model is still a driver's car, feeling almost vintage so far as suspension and chassis design is concerned and demanding more concentration on control than is usual with the current run of high-performance models. Confidence thus comes with familiarity, and the potential of the Healey is clearly shown in the impressive list of competition successes in many different types of event.

Comfort and convenience

Seating is one of the very good features of the Healey, the two front seats being well padded and nicely shaped to support the body under hard cornering conditions. The upholstery, leather on our test car but normally 'Ambla' vinyl material, is punched on the centre panels to allow air to circulate, preventing too much body warmth on a hot day. The driving seat extends well back to allow straight-leg driving, but the steering wheel is still set near the body despite telescopic adjustment of the column.

There are two small, shaped seats in the back suitable for young children, and an adult could be inserted into this area for a short distance although with very little headroom if the hood is raised. When the seats are not being used the back folds flat to make a useful amount of room available for luggage; this is necessary for continental touring, for the big spoked spare wheel and the battery take up most of the usable space in the boot, leaving room for one small suitcase or a couple of hold-alls. There is no provision for locking the car, so valuables have to be locked in the fascia cubby hole or in the boot.

The fold-away hood merits high praise for ease of operation, erection taking but a few moments if there is a sudden downpour of rain. When stowed away the hood fits into a well and lies well down in the body-line, a cover being supplied to make a tidy job. The rear window zips into place and has to be three parts removed before the hood is stowed, so as to avoid damaging or distorting the clear plastic, and it is essential to re-secure the window before fastening the hood in its raised position, otherwise its tautness defeats the exercise. Two simple fasteners which batten the hood can be fixed by one person without assistance.

The rear window is usefully large and the mirror takes good advantage of the view, but when the hood is lowered

Healey
Mark III

A revised dashboard is neat and sensibly laid out, while the old spring-spoke steering wheel holds its own against new-fangled rigid wood-rimmers

the mirror is set too low and would be better suspended from the top rail or else on a vertical bar. The boot, which slopes rather sharply, is difficult to gauge for length when the car is reversed, but otherwise the all-round visibility is extremely good.

Under-bonnet accessibility is good, the bonnet aperture appearing narrow by modern standards but still offering good working space. Reversion to twin carburettors in the place of three has greatly simplified the process of tuning without sacrificing any power.

The Mark III version of the Healey is no more comfortable on the road than its predecessors, yet the many devotees who are loyal to the marque find sufficient compensation for this in the abundance of power which takes the car so far ahead of its price-rivals. The electric petrol pump in the boot clicks loudly enough to annoy new acquaintances; the carburettor intakes hiss louder than ever, and the scuttle shakes badly enough to make the instruments illegible on bad roads. At more than 70 mph wind noise concerts to drown all these aggravations, while at 100 mph conversation becomes quite impossible and thought nearly so. Ride comfort is poor except on roads of motorway standard. The short semi-elliptic rear springs transmit the feel of the road to the driver by the shortest route through his and the car's seat, preceded by advance warning through the steering wheel.

Fittings and controls

Although exterior appearance of the Mark III is unchanged, the interior contains some improvements which suggest luxury to people who owned earlier models. Wood capping runs the width of the fascia panel, and a central console which is covered with leathercloth carries switches and the optional radio set. The console sweeps down astride the transmission tunnel, and the remote-control gear lever no longer needs to be raked, falling readily to hand. A box mounted rather far back between the seats is upholstered to serve as an armrest, the top flipping open to house maps and oddments. The handbrake is mounted on the right-hand side of the tunnel and is badly placed for easy operation.

Instruments are well grouped in front of the driver, and the combined water temperature and oil pressure gauge is

appreciated for the ease with which the two functions can be checked during a split-second glance. Less happy is the petrol gauge which swings from full to empty and back during acceleration and braking, rendering the instrument practically useless.

Optional overdrive is operated by a switch on the fascia, and if a little less handy than is usual its operation soon became a natural movement. Foot controls are well placed, although the pedals are rather too close together for some drivers. Heel-and-toe gearchanges are soon mastered.

Surprisingly for such a fast car, there is no headlight flasher and the headlight switch is far away to the left,

Tight-as-a-glove buckets are supplemented in the rear by two indentations more commode-like than commodious

Few will remember it now, but the Austin Healey grille owes its abiding shape to the kite-like shape of early Riley-engined Healeys

causing the driver to rely on the powerful horn for early warning.

The jacking system is a suspect feature of this car. A puncture in the nearside rear tyre reduced ground clearance so drastically that we could find no way to place the jack under the axle spring (the recommended position) or any other reasonably solid piece of bodywork. Jacking the rear chassis cross member was possible, but did not lift the wheel from the ground. Garage assistance had to be sought eventually and we concluded a puncture was not a prospect we would relish for a wet night.

Performance
Docile as a lamb in traffic (the Healey *can* potter at 25 mph in overdrive top), full depression of the throttle

The shapely rounded tail leaves little room for a boot, but who cares in a car meant for fun?

transforms the car into a spirited beast on the open road. Clutch action is long and smooth, the throttle being equally progressive. Thus bad starts cannot be excused, and full performance is available only when the accelerator is pushed right to the floor.

It is a compliment to say that the Healey's bite is now worse than its bark, for the new exhaust system has reduced this source of noise to insignificant proportions. Instead, the driver is aware of the fan noise and a little gear whine—mainly in indirect ratios—vying with an acceptable level of mechanical chatter. Cockpit insulation is almost non-existent, and the driver gets full reward for his enthusiasm. Maximum power take-offs produce a little wheelspin, and a quick change into second gear suggests a nice, close-ratio gearbox. In fact second is really too low, taking the car from 42 mph in first gear to 52 mph before a change into third is necessary; the car badly needs a higher second gear, or else an overdrive ratio to bridge the gap up to third.

Care has to be taken not to stray from the tachometer's amber section—from 5,000 to 5,500 rpm—into the red in lower ratios, but in third overdrive the car runs easily up to 100 mph. Nifty manipulation of the gear lever and overdrive switch can, if need be, select direct top which rushes the car up to 117 mph, although for normal purposes overdrive top is the correct gear at more than 100 mph. At the ton the car is ambling along at 4,000 rpm and the natural cruising speed is in the region of 110 mph. When this speed is sustained on motorways the water temperature and oil pressure remain constant at satisfactory levels.

The gearlever moves easily through a fairly small gate, the powerful synchromesh completely overcoming any possible grating noises although introducing a certain amount of notchiness which slows the movement just a little.

Despite the introduction of a servo, the brakes require firm, but not really heavy pressure. Girling $11\frac{1}{4}$ in discs at the front are matched by 11 in drums at the rear, the system being entirely reassuring even on wet roads and virtually immune from fade in punishing conditions.

The six-cylinder engine is unlikely to work very hard unless the driver is normally in a considerable hurry, so petrol consumption figures should normally work out better than the 16 mpg obtained from our test car.

Handling
The scuttle vibration previously referred to is symptomatic of a degree of flexibility in the chassis which may well contribute to the Healey being an uncertain performer so far as handling is concerned. Greater familiarity is no doubt an asset, but even so the car is easily deflected from its course by bumps and undulations in the road, so that control requires a high degree of concentration at higher speeds.

Yet the car is undoubtedly rapid round corners, always displaying a degree of oversteer which can be used to advantage. The majority of manufacturers instill understeer into their cars, at least at lower speeds, in the interests of accurate control and good straight-line running, but competent drivers soon find themselves at home with the Healey's characteristics. On wet roads a fair amount of discretion is called for, more restraint being needed in slow corners than in the fast ones, but in the dry the accelerator can be used to set the car up nicely for a corner and help it through on a good line. Cam and peg steering is em-

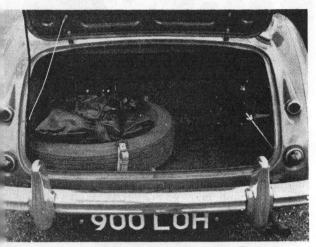

*falsely spacious air is lent to the boot in our picture. The spare
wheel was on the car, so we substituted a tyre to show positioning*

...loyed, and this system gives accurate control with reason-
...ble lightness, although some road shock reaches the
...eering wheel on particularly bumpy roads.

The Austin-Healey is not likely to be first choice for the
...ajority of drivers, even the sporting ones, but anyone
...ho strikes up a good friendship with it and is prepared
... accept one or two basic faults is sure to be well satisfied
...ith his choice.

*...e faithful six-cylinder engine still crowds the underbonnet
...ace menacingly, still performs remarkably*

SPECIFICATION

ENGINE:
Six cylinders; bore 83.36 mm (3.25 in), stroke 89 mm (3.52 in).
Cubic capacity 2,912 cc. Compression ratio 9.03:1. Maximum bhp
(gross) 150 at 5,250 rpm. Maximum torque 173 lb ft at 3,000 rpm;
Twin SU HD8 carburettors. Overhead valves. SU electric fuel pump.
Fuel tank capacity 10 gallons. Water capacity 18 pints. Sump capacity
12.75 pints. 12v battery of 57 amp/hr capacity.

TRANSMISSION:
Borg and Beck 9½ in dia. single dry plate clutch. Four-speed gearbox
with synchromesh on 2nd, 3rd and top, and optional overdrive on
3rd and top. Overall gear ratios: 1st, 9.348. 2nd, 7.341. 3rd, 4.629.
Top, 3.545. Gearing, 20.5 mph per 1000 rpm in direct top; 25.0 mph
per 1000 rpm in overdrive top. Rear axle ratio 3.54 or 3.91 with
overdrive.

CHASSIS:
Suspension: front, independent coil and wishbone and anti-roll bar.
Lever Armstrong shock absorbers: rear, live rear axle located by
Panhard rod and semi-elliptic leaf springs. Armstrong shock
absorbers. Girling hydraulic brakes, disc front, drum rear. Cam and
peg steering. 15 in disc wheels with wire spoke option. Dunlop
Road Speed tyres, size 5.90-15.

DIMENSIONS:

	ft	in
Wheelbase	7	8
Track, front	4	1
Track, rear	4	1½
Overall length	13	1
Overall width	5	0½
Overall height	4	1½
Ground clearance		4½
Turning circle	32	
Kerb weight	23 cwt	

PERFORMANCE:

mph	sec
0-30	3.9
0-40	5.8
0-50	7.7
0-60	10.9
0-70	13.2
0-80	16.8
0-90	19.0
0-100	22.8

Maximum speed in gears:

1st	42 mph
2nd	52 mph
3rd	87 mph
Overdrive 3rd	103 mph
4th	117 mph
Overdrive 4th	121 mph

Fuel consumption: 16 mpg

PRICE:
£1,106 basic
£1,223 with extras as tested

AUSTIN-HEALEY
3000 MARK 3

Although based on a design that is some years old, the Austin-Healey 3000 has recently acquired extra engine power and is still a most potent force in rallies. It is a tough, rugged car, with the reputation of being nearly unbreakable. Now that it has winding windows and a really good hood, it can be regarded as a practical coupé rather than a "hairy" sports car, yet it is still primarily for the he-man.

The basis of the big Healey is a steel box-section frame which is carried close to the ground, passing beneath the back axle to which it is attached by semi-elliptic springs and a Panhard rod. In front there are wishbones and helical springs with a hefty anti-roll torsion bar. A cam and peg steering gear is fitted. Girling hydraulic brakes are used, servo assisted, with discs in front and drums behind. Knock-on wire wheels and overdrive, two worthwhile extras, were installed on the test car.

The six-cylinder engine, with cast-iron block and cylinder head, has push-rod operated overhead valves and a four-bearing crankshaft. Steel-backed copper-lead bearings are used and the solid-skirt pistons have flat tops and a tin-plated finish. Twin S.U. downdraught carburetters, type HD8, permit sufficient breathing for 150 b.h.p. to be developed at 5,250 r.p.m.

The body is really a two-seater, though there are two extra seat pans without leg room. These may be covered to provide useful luggage space, the boot in the tail being largely occupied by the spare wheel. The hood is easy to raise and lower, the windscreen being curiously shallow by modern standards. However, the view all round is quite satisfactory. A raised section above the propeller shaft tunnel may be struck by the left elbow on occasion, but the gear lever is better placed than in the past. The adjustable steering column is a

excellent feature that should be found on many more cars.

When I first drove the Austin-Healey, the hood was raised and London traffic had to be negotiated. I was not impressed, for I thought that a six-cylinder engine might idle more smoothly and it seemed noisy when revved on the gears. In the open country with the hood down, however, it was a different story. The big machine had a wonderfully long stride and could put the miles behind it in a most effortless manner. In open form the tendency of the hood to magnify mechanical noises had gone, though the power unit still tended to be rather rough as maximum revolutions were approached. The large engine fills the bonnet and one is therefore conscious of its song.

The Mark 3 is much more stable than previous big Healeys, but at first one feels an occasional "wiggle" at speed which one later learns to ignore. The steering does not at first inspire confidence, but, again, it turns out to be much more accurate than appeared to be the case. The brakes are powerful, and though they smelt hot after a circuit test there was no fading.

The gears are easier to change with the new position of the lever. Third is a very useful ratio, which can be extended still further by the use of the overdrive. There is a large gap between third and second speeds, though first is quite high and curiously close to second. With the considerable torque of the big engine the gap is, in fact, not particularly noticeable.

A maximum speed of 118.4 m.p.h. was recorded on overdrive. It is possible that 120 m.p.h. could be exceeded on the direct drive, but as the timed runs would have entailed driving for several miles with the rev-counter needle on or near the red mark, I resisted the temptation. Obviously, 120 m.p.h. could be exceeded on overdrive with a favourable wind or gradient.

A cruising speed of 110 m.p.h. can be held with ease, though fuel economy may dictate a slightly lower speed. There is something most satisfying about the high-speed cruising, and a short burst on the direct drive can bring the car back into its stride when checked.

On Brands Hatch, the Austin-Healey cornered remarkably well. It "hung on," refusing to break away easily, and would take full throttle coming out of the corners without tending to run wide. I did not inflate the tyres especially for this exercise, as of course one would if one were doing it seriously, but it was obvious that the behaviour of the rear end was unusually good. Harder tyres would also increase the maximum speed. The car is too heavy to flick through a corner like a single-seater, but considered as the substantial sports convertible that it is the handling must be regarded as most satisfactory.

If the car is at its best with the hood folded away, it is also very cosy with the top up, and it is pleasant to be able to erect it quickly when the evening becomes chilly. Naturally, the sound of the engine is then more prominent, but this only becomes insistent during hard acceleration through the gears. The general impression is that the big machine is enjoying its work, which is very different from a poor little engine that seems to be in distress.

It took me several days before I could find reverse gear—a matter of using both hands! However, it was easy once I had got the knack, but I am informed that the test car was not up to standard in this respect.

Towards the end of my "ownership" the overdrive went out of action, but this may have been something trivial, such as a fuse.

The Austin-Healey 3000 is a car for long journeys. It will go anywhere, and fast, too, without wilting under the worst conditions. There are smoother and quieter town carriages, but for the man who likes to feel a big engine gobbling up the miles, this is an attractive buy.

ACCELERATION GRAPH

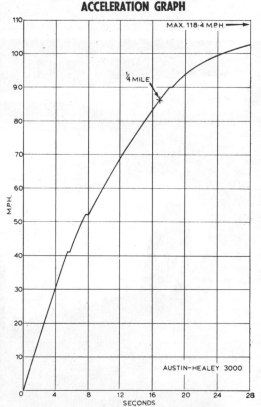

MAX. 118·4 M.P.H.

¼ MILE

M.P.H.

SECONDS

AUSTIN-HEALEY 3000

SPECIFICATION AND PERFORMANCE DATA

Car Tested: Austin-Healey 3000 Mk. 3 Sports Convertible. Price, with fresh air heater, wire-spoked wheels, overdrive, and adjustable steering column, £1,217 19s. 2d. including P.T.

Engine: Six-cylinders 83.36 mm. x 89 mm. (2,912 c.c.). Compression ratio 9.03 to 1. 150 b.h.p. at 5,250 r.p.m. Twin S.U. carburetters. Lucas coil and distributor.

Transmission: Diaphragm type clutch. Four-speed gearbox, with central lever and synchromesh on upper three-speeds, plus Laycock-de Normanville overdrive. Ratios 3.205 (overdrive top), 3.909 4.195 (overdrive third), 5.116, 8.025, and 11.453 to 1. Open propeller shaft. Hypoid rear axle.

Chassis: Box-section frame, underslung at rear. Independent front suspension by wishbones, helical springs, and anti-roll torsion bar. Cam and peg steering gear with adjustable column. Rear axle on semi-elliptic springs with Panhard rod. Lever-type hydraulic dampers all round. Girling hydraulic brakes with servo assistance, 11¼ ins. discs in front, 11 ins. x 2¼ ins. drums at rear. 5.90 x 15 ins. Dunlop Road Speed tyres.

Equipment: 12-volt lighting and starting. Speedometer. Rev. counter. Fuel, water temperature, and oil pressure gauges. Heating and demisting. Flashing direction indicators.

Dimensions: Wheelbase, 7 ft. 8 ins.; Track (front), 4 ft. 0¾ in.; (rear), 4 ft. 2 in.; Overall length, 13 ft. 1½ ins.; Width, 5 ft. 0½ in.; Weight, 1 ton 1¼ cwt.

Performance: Maximum speed (overdrive), 118.4 m.p.h. Speeds in gears: Direct top, 118 m.p.h.; Overdrive third, 109 m.p.h.; third, 90 m.p.h.; second, 52 m.p.h. Standing quarter-mile, 16.8 secs. Acceleration: 0-30 m.p.h., 4 secs.; 0-50 m.p.h., 7.2 secs.; 0-60 m.p.h., 9.9 secs.; 0-80 m.p.h., 15 secs.; 0-100 m.p.h., 24.3 secs.

Fuel Consumption: 17 to 19 m.p.g.

Austin-Healey 3000 Mk. III CONVERTIBLE 2,912 c.c.

SUN-CAPPED Dolomites and the distant roar and squeal of one of the works rally cars scrambling its way up the Gavia pass—this perhaps is the image that some people have of the big Austin-Healey at work. But there is a world of difference between those frequent winners, the former Spartan works rally cars, and the over-the-counter product of today—the 3000 Mk. III

For as long as many of us care to remember there has been a big Healey in the price lists. The car has been through several variations of engine size, but now, like an ageing but still beautiful dowager, repeated face lifts can no longer wholly hide the ravages of time and progress.

For many years a change in the model of the Healey has been marked with either the subtraction or addition of a carburettor; however, the Mk. III continues with two S.U. carburettors for the Series C 2,912 c.c. engine, with diameter increased by 0·25in. to 2in. With the new carburettors and a camshaft of improved design the power output of the engine has been raised from 137 b.h.p. at 4,750 r.p.m. to 148 b.h.p. at 5,250 r.p.m. Although this comparatively unsophisticated six-cylinder engine must now be very near the end of its development, it seems to have gained in flexibility and is virtually free from any temperament.

Provided full use is made of the choke, starting from cold is good. The engine takes a long time to warm through and

spits back through the carburettors if pushed at all hard before it is warm. The all-too-frequent trouble of running-on still persists and could only be prevented by opening the throttles wide as the ignition was switched off.

Although the big Healey has never been a noisy car in standard form, the latest design of exhaust system, with two silencers on the left side of the car and a further two set transversely under the boot floor, cuts the noise down to almost saloon car level at anything but near-peak engine

PRICES	£	s	d
Sports Convertible	915	0	0
Purchase tax	191	3	9
Total (in G.B.)	1,106	3	9
Extras (including P.T.)			
Overdrive	60	8	4
Wire wheels	30	4	2
Fresh air heater	18	14	7
Telescopic steering column	2	8	4
Seat belts (each)	5	5	0

How the Austin-Healey 3000 Mk. III compares:

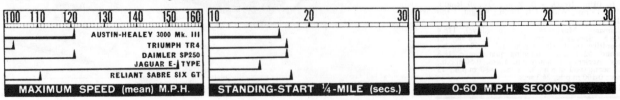

MAXIMUM SPEED (mean) M.P.H. STANDING-START ¼-MILE (secs.) 0-60 M.P.H. SECONDS

AUSTIN-HEALEY 3000 Mk. III
TRIUMPH TR4
DAIMLER SP250
JAGUAR E-TYPE
RELIANT SABRE SIX GT

Make • AUSTIN-HEALEY   Type • 3000 Mk. III (2,912 c.c.)
(Front engine, rear-wheel drive)

Manufacturers : Austin Motor Co. Ltd., Longbridge, Birmingham

Test Conditions
Weather ... Dry and sunny with 0-5 m.p.h. wind
Temperature .... 9 deg. C. (48 deg. F.)
Barometer .... 29·6in. Hg.
Dry concrete and tarmac surfaces.

Weight
Kerb weight (with oil, water and half-full fuel tank)
      23·5 cwt (2,604lb-1,180kg)
Front-rear distribution, per cent F, 52; R, 48
Laden as tested ......26·5 cwt (2,940lb-1,333kg)

Turning Circles
Between kerbs ...... L, 35ft 0in.; R, 34ft 10in.
Between walls ...... L, 36ft 3in.; R, 35ft 10in.
Turns of steering wheel lock to lock 3

FUEL AND OIL CONSUMPTION

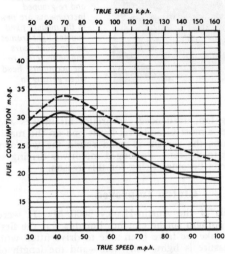

FUEL ....Super premium grade
(101 octane RM)

Test Distance .... 1,583 miles
Overall Consumption ...... 20·3 m.p.g.
(13·9 litres/100 km.)
Estimated Consumption (DIN) 24·9 m.p.g.
(11·4 litres/100 km.)
OIL: SAE 10W30 ... Consumption 1,600 m.p.g.

HILL CLIMBING AT STEADY SPEEDS

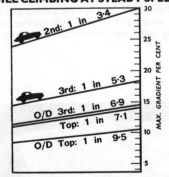

GEAR	O.D. Top	Top	O.D. 3rd	3rd	2nd
PULL (lb per ton)	235	310	340	410	635

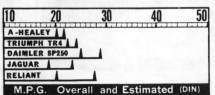

M.P.G. Overall and Estimated (DIN)

A-HEALEY
TRIUMPH TR4
DAIMLER SP250
JAGUAR
RELIANT

MAXIMUM SPEEDS AND ACCELERATION TIMES

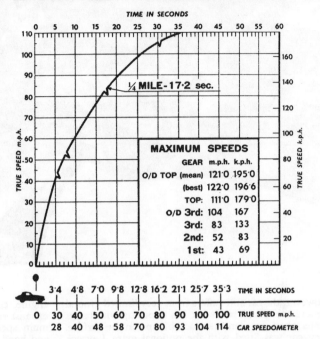

¼ MILE - 17·2 sec.

MAXIMUM SPEEDS		
GEAR	m.p.h.	k.p.h.
O/D TOP (mean)	121·0	195·0
(best)	122·0	196·6
TOP:	111·0	179·0
O/D 3rd:	104	167
3rd:	83	133
2nd:	52	83
1st:	43	69

TIME IN SECONDS	3·4	4·8	7·0	9·8	12·8	16·2	21·1	25·7	35·3	
TRUE SPEED m.p.h.	0	30	40	50	60	70	80	90	100	100
CAR SPEEDOMETER		28	40	48	58	70	80	93	104	114

Speed range, gear ratios and time in seconds

m.p.h.	O.D. Top (3·14)	Top (3·91)	O. Third (4·74)	Third (5·12)	Second (8·05)	First (11·26)
10—30	—	—	—	6·1	4·2	3·0
20—40	—	7·5	6·6	4·1	3·2	2·8
30—50	9·3	6·8	6·3	5·4	3·4	—
40—60	8·7	6·9	6·8	4·9	—	—
50—70	10·7	7·9	7·3	5·5	—	—
60—80	12·1	8·1	7·8	6·4	—	—
70—90	13·6	9·0	8·2	—	—	—
80—100	15·7	9·9	9·0	—	—	—
90—110	18·2	14·2	—	—	—	—

BRAKES	Pedal load	Retardation	Equiv. distance
(from 30 m.p.h. in neutral)	25lb	0·23g	131ft
	50lb	0·72g	42ft
	75lb	0·81g	37ft
	100lb	0·92g	32·8ft
	Handbrake	0·37g	81ft

CLUTCH   Pedal load and travel—40lb and 6in.

A central console, wood-trimmed facia and re-grouped instruments are new to the model; fixed quarter-light frames on the front doors can be too close to the occupants' head when getting in

revs. However, the car still suffers from very limited ground clearance and over rough roads one has to put up with bangs and thumps when the silencers touch bumps on the surface.

The test car was fitted with the optional extra Laycock de Normanville overdrive, working on third and top gears. With overdrive, a lower back axle ratio is used—3·91 in place of the normal 3·55 to 1 ratio. While this does make the car extremely flexible in the upper ratios at low engine revs, it tends to emphasize the large gap between second and third gears, with their respective maximum speeds of 52 and 83 m.p.h. Overdrive third gear produced a maximum of 104 m.p.h., direct top 111 m.p.h. and overdrive top gave a mean maximum speed of 121 m.p.h. Overdrive, operated by a switch on the facia, engages very smoothly indeed; to return to direct drive the engine has to be pulling before an inhibitor switch will release the overdrive. This prevents jolts in the transmission.

In practice, very high averages can be maintained on main roads by using just direct and overdrive top gears, the car wafting along at around the 90 mark with no more than 4,000 r.p.m. on the rev counter.

The big Healey's take-off from standstill is impressive. Without tyre squeal or wheel-spin, it reached 30 m.p.h. in 3·4 40 in 4·8, 60 in 9·8 and 100 in 25·7sec. At maximum revs—5,250 r.p.m. in this case—the combined noise of engine, cooling fan, unsilenced carburettor air intakes and exhaust reaches almost Grand Prix levels and on the maximum speed runs the scream of wind round the windows and hood adds to the din. Prolonged motorway driving at very high speeds becomes tiring for this reason.

Clutch Improved

Later models of the Austin-Healey 3000 Mk. II were fitted with diaphragm spring clutches but this was the first model of the make we have been able to drive fitted with one. The pressure is light—only 40lb—and the length of travel and smoothness of engagement are more like those of a touring car than a 120 m.p.h. sports car. Effective, rather heavy synchromesh makes gear-changing a bit slow on the upper three ratios and it is almost impossible to get into first gear while on the move without crunching. The position of the gear lever is such that one has to use a cranked elbow action to make changes, but this soon becomes quite a natural movement.

The years of competition and development have certainly improved the car's handling. For normal motoring, the car has slight understeer, but when time is short, the right foot can turn this into an accurately controllable power oversteer. When cornering hard the driver has to beware of

Left: The back of the rear seat folds forward to make a good luggage platform—which is needed as the boot (right) is much taken up by spare wheel, battery and hood covers

The unmistakable lines of the big Healey still suggest potency. The small upper rear "lamps" are reflectors

bumps in the road, which can throw the car off course with unexpected force. In the wet, an unwary jab on the accelerator can bring the tail of the car skating round and a good deal of caution has to be used on corners.

We were unable to test the car's handling on our special *pavé* track for fear of wiping off the exhaust system, but on a rough side road, the short suspension movements and firm damping make the car twitch about unless the driver concentrates on holding direction. The steering itself is heavy at low speeds, but once the car gets on to the open road it becomes a good deal lighter. At near-maximum speed, the car controls very well and holds a straight course.

Although a vacuum servo is standard equipment on the Mk. III models—it was an extra on the previous model— the brakes still feel heavy, but they are very powerful. Heavy braking from high speeds is accompanied by slight weaving; this never builds up to anything near dangerous proportions, but is nevertheless disconcerting. The pull-up handbrake, located between the driving seat and transmission tunnel held the car easily on a 1-in-3 hill, from where take-off was of the "rocket" variety, with spinning wheels.

Driving Position

In its appointments the Austin-Healey 3000 Mk. III is now more of a touring car than a sports car. The new panel design and the trim are attractive, almost luxurious. In these days of straight-arm steering, the driver of the big Healey has to get used to the old Vintage bent arm position again, with the huge 17in. diameter steering wheel only a matter of inches from his chest. On the test car the telescopic steering column (an extra) was fitted. If it had put the wheel 3in *nearer* the facia it would have been more help. The pedals are small and set close together. If space and layout allowed the pedal group to be brought back three inches and the seat moved back a similar distance, the driving position would be far more comfortable. The seats are rather small and hard, with cushions that "set" after a few miles. At the end of a long drive you are glad to have a good stretch to restore the circulation.

The "traditional" British love of wood has extended to this Healey and the dashboard has walnut veneer on its two outer panels. The centre of the facia now extends downwards to form a central console with the deep transmission tunnel. There are spaces in this console for a radio and loudspeaker.

A comprehensive set of instruments is grouped behind the steering wheel and comprises a speedometer, with total and trip mileage recorders, rev counter, combined oil pressure and water temperature gauge and fuel gauge. While driving, this last instrument swings freely between full and empty as soon as the tank contents have dropped to about three-quarters full. In the centre of the facia are four identical switches in pairs on each side of the ignition-starter switch; they control driving and panel lamps, and screenwipers and overdrive. A differently shaped toggle for the O.D. switch would make it more easily identifiable; at

Not a spare inch is wasted under the bonnet; the lid still has to be propped open with a stay

night it is easy to flick the wrong switch and start the single speed wipers working instead of selecting overdrive. A single quadrant control adjusts the temperature of the heater, distribution of flow between the car and windscreen being adjusted by two flaps set high under the back of the dashboard.

There is a large lockable cubby in the facia and a non-locking glove box on the transmission tunnel, with a padded top to form an armrest for driver or passenger. Two small seats for children are fitted in the back, and an adult, sitting sideways, could be packed in for short trips. The backrest of this seat folds forward and is held by two substantial bolts to form a large luggage platform, with a lip on the leading edge to prevent suitcases sliding forward. This platform is really valuable because the boot is mainly occupied by the spare wheel and battery and can hold only one small grip and some odds and ends. Now that winding windows are fitted and a hardtop is offered, B.M.C. ought to provide locks for the doors. They do provide a battery master switch in the boot which cuts off all current—including the side lamps for parking at night. A prop rod has to be slotted into a catch to hold the boot open.

In these days of international conformity over direction indicators, the big Healey still uses the side and tail lamps as indicators and at night they can be confusing to following traffic if one is braking and indicating at the same time. Twin horns with an impressive volume are fitted.

The well-fitting hood was rain-tight and did not flap at high speeds; it is held down on to the screen rail by two over-centre clips with ominously sharp projections. The convertible type hood can be folded back easily and in a matter of seconds, and a hood cover is provided. Fresh-air ventilation can be greatly increased in warm weather by un-zipping the whole of the back window and folding it down. In summer, the car still suffers from too much heat coming through from the engine and to help overcome this a cold air vent is fitted under the dash—on the left-hand side.

This car is much faster than the Mk. II version, and is more economical, averaging 20·3 m.p.g. overall. Commuting and a series of fast, short runs, where maximum revs were frequently being used, dropped the consumption to 18·7 m.p.g.; on everyday motoring, the fuel consumption is around the 22 m.p.g. mark. The 12-gallon fuel tank filled easily, without any blow back. During the 1,583 miles of testing eight pints of oil were used, but the car had been fitted with new piston rings shortly before it was handed over for test and probably they were still bedding-in.

Under the bonnet, the husky six-cylinder engine fills every inch of available space, with wires and cables running everywhere. The screenwasher bottle, which used to be inside the passenger cockpit, has now been moved under the bonnet. The lid is held shut by two safety catches and is held open with a stay.

Despite some dated features, the big Healey is still terrific fun to drive. Tractable, capable of an immense amount of hard work with reasonable economy, it will still have its devotees long after production has ceased.

Specification: Austin-Healey 3000 Mk. III Convertible

PERFORMANCE DATA

Overdrive top gear m.p.h. per 1,000 r.p.m. ...	23·0
Top gear m.p.h. per 1,000 r.p.m.	18·9
Mean piston speed at max. power	3,035ft/min.
Engine revs. at mean max. speed	5,260 r.p.m.
B.h.p. per ton laden	111·2

▼ *Scale: 0.3in. to 1ft. Cushions uncompressed.*

ENGINE

Cylinders ...	6-in-line
Bore ...	83·4mm (3·28in.)
Stroke ...	88·9mm (3·50in.)
Displacement ...	2,912 c.c. (178 cu. in.)
Valve gear ...	Overhead, pushrods and rockers
Compression ratio	9·0-to-1
Carburettors ...	2 S.U. HD8
Fuel pump ...	S.U. electric
Oil filter ...	Full flow, renewable element
Max. power ...	148 b.h.p. (net) at 5,250 r.p.m.
Max. torque ...	165·2 lb. ft. at 3,500 r.p.m.

TRANSMISSION

Clutch ...	Borg and Beck diaphragm spring, 9·5in. dia.
Gearbox ...	Four speed, synchromesh on 2nd, 3rd and Top; central control
Overall ratios ...	O.D. Top 0·82, Top 1·00; O.D. Third 1·08, Third 1·31, Second 2·06; First 2·88; Reverse 3·72
Final drive ...	Hypoid bevel, 3·91

CHASSIS

Construction ...	Boxed cruciform chassis, with steel and aluminium body

SUSPENSION

Front ...	Independent, coil springs and wishbones, lever arm dampers, anti-roll bar
Rear ...	Live axle, half elliptic leaf springs, Panhard rod, lever arm dampers
Steering ...	Cam and peg
Wheel dia. ...	17in.

BRAKES

Type ...	Girling hydraulic, disc front drum rear, vacuum servo
Dimensions ...	F, 11·25in. dia. R, 11·0in. dia., 2·25in. wide shoes
Swept area ...	F, 228 sq. in.; R, 155·5 sq. in. Total: 383·5 sq. in. (286 sq. in. per ton laden)

WHEELS

Type ...	Pressed steel disc standard, wire-spoked, centre-lock extra, 4·5in. wide rim
Tyres ...	5·90—15in. Dunlop RS5 with tubes

EQUIPMENT

Battery ...	12-volt 57-amp. hr.
Headlamps ...	36-48 watt
Reversing lamp ...	None
Electric fuses ...	2
Screen wipers ...	2, single speed, self parking
Screen washer ...	Standard, manual plunger
Interior heater ...	Extra, fresh air, electric booster
Safety belts ...	Extra, anchorages provided
Interior trim ...	Ambla leathercloth
Floor covering ...	Carpet
Starting handle ...	No provision
Jack ...	Screw type
Jacking points ...	4, on suspension
Other bodies ...	None

MAINTENANCE

Fuel tank ...	12 Imp. gallons (no reserve)
Cooling system ...	20 pints (including heater)
Engine sump ...	12·75 pints SAE 10W30. Change oil every 3,000 miles; change filter element every 6,000 miles
Gearbox and overdrive ...	7 pints SAE 30. Change oil every 6,000 miles
Final drive ...	3 pints SAE 90EP. Change oil every 6,000 miles
Grease ...	11 points every 3,000 miles
Tyre pressures ...	F, 20; R, 25 p.s.i. (normal driving). F, 25; R, 30 p.s.i. (fast driving)

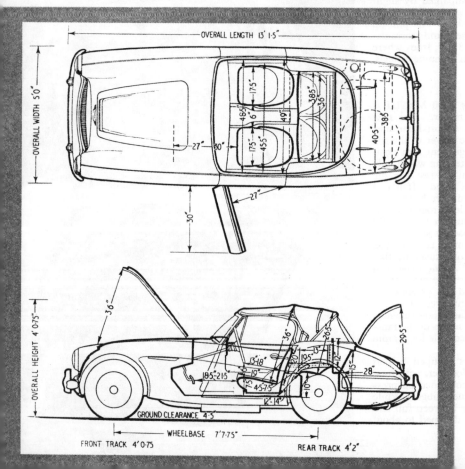

OVERALL LENGTH 13' 1·5"
OVERALL WIDTH 5·0"
OVERALL HEIGHT 4' 0·75"
GROUND CLEARANCE 4·5"
WHEELBASE 7'7·75"
FRONT TRACK 4'0·75
REAR TRACK 4'2"

AUSTIN-HEALEY 3000 MK III

The latest model has an additional 11 bhp, a bit of tarting up and still retains that classic cowl shake

TEN YEARS AGO, the Austin-Healey 100 was first intro-duced to the American market. The man behind it was Donald Healey, who had previously built a limited quantity of very advanced and successful sports cars using Riley engines. The demise of the Riley and the many problems confronting the small manufacturer caused Healey to seek an easier way of making a living, so he sold the Austin company on the idea of using production Austin parts to build a sports car aimed specifically at the American market. The result was the Austin-Healey 100, which has been gradually updated during the ensuing years to become the Austin-Healey 3000 Mk III Sports Convertible.

In its original form, the Healey was a conventional low-priced sports car, which offered the fast and responsive rag-top-and-flapping-side-curtains type of driving demanded by the enthusiast of the day. Its 4-cyl engine was lusty and reliable, its 3-speed and overdrive transmission was a novelty and, even if the car did have some extremely annoying faults, at least it provided enjoyable and exciting driving at a time when the Detroit product was nothing short of ghastly.

In its 1964 form, the Healey is a much more refined car although it retains many of the characteristics of the original version, both desirable and undesirable. The major changes consist of a general tarting up of the interior, which now has walnut veneer on the instrument panel and much more luxuri-ous finish and detailing throughout. The top is good by sports car standards because it can be erected from inside the car, and it is secured by two over-center clamps on the windshield pillars. The windows are of the wind-up variety so that the car

is well weatherproofed for the winter, at least in some climates.

BMC discarded the 4-cyl engine in 1956, substituting its rugged Six in the Healey, and this power unit has undergone a number of changes over the years so that it is now rated at 148 bhp. This is an increase of 11 bhp over the MK II version of the car, and the extra power is obtained from a different camshaft and the use of two 2-in. HD-8-SU carburetors. These carburetors require a lot of choke when starting from cold, and even then there is a tendency to spit back if too much throttle is used during the long warm-up period the engine seems to demand.

Another relatively insignificant but worthwhile improvement

AUSTIN-HEALEY 3000
AT A GLANCE...

Price as tested	$3828
Engine	6 cyl, ohv, 2912 cc, 148 bhp
Curb weight, lb	2650
Top speed, mph	116
Acceleration, 0–60 mph, sec	9.8
Passing test, 50–70 mph, sec	5.7
Average fuel consumption, mpg	19

AUSTIN-HEALEY 3000 MK III

concerns the rear suspension. Here the chassis frame has been curved to allow for additional axle movement, and springs of a lower rate are used. In order to control the movement of the axle more positively, it is now located by twin radius arms, and the results of these modifications are a better ride, improved handling and increased ground clearance.

Despite improvements to the rear suspension, the ride and handling of the Healey are still in the classic sports car tradition of the early '50s, before people like Chapman and Cooper had got in on the act. The ride is firm and there is some chassis flexing evident from the authentic cowl shake which occurs on any but the smoothest surfaces. In common with the rigidly sprung cars of the time, the road-holding of the Healey is quite good on smooth surfaces, but a fast turn on a poor surface may produce surprises, because the rear end has a tendency to jump and skip over bumps.

Under normal conditions, the Healey has slight understeer, but plenty of throttle opening in a corner will change this to oversteer, and the tail can be hung out a long way with delicate throttle control. However, one should select the road surface rather carefully before experimenting because any irregularity will throw the car off its line, and a wet surface tends to make the handling treacherous.

At low speeds the steering is comparatively heavy, but it lightens as the speed increases and the car holds its line accurately at normal cruising speeds, although there is a tendency for the rear end to twitch on rougher surfaces.

Due to the improved rear suspension and the slight rearward weight bias, one can apply a surprising amount of power when coming out of a slow turn without any tendency for the car to break away, lift its inside rear wheel, or lose traction. The Austin-Healey is no sluggard on the road, but one has to work hard and use some skill and experience to extract the maximum from it.

Although the car has an adjustable steering column, it is difficult for tall drivers to accommodate themselves comfortably, as a glance at the Driver Comfort Rating on the data panel will show. Apart from the driver and passenger seats, there is accommodation for two children behind, or, alternatively, one adult can be carried for short trips. This space can also be used to supplement the limited trunk space, which is almost entirely filled by the spare wheel and the battery. The controls are a mixture of ancient and modern. The transmission, in particular, needs updating because 1st is unsynchron-

SCALE: 10" DIVISIONS

PRICE

List price.................$3699
Price as tested...........$3828

ENGINE

No. cylinders & type....6 cyl, ohv
Bore x stroke, in.......3.28 x 3.50
Displacement cc............2912
  Equivalent cu in.........177.7
Compression ratio..........9:1
Bph @ rpm..........148 @ 5250
  Equivalent mph............123
Torque @ rpm, lb-ft..165 @ 3500
  Equivalent mph.............82
Carburetors, no. & make....2 SU
  No. barrels & dia........1–2 in
Type fuel required......premium

DRIVE TRAIN

Clutch type.single plate, diaphragm
  Diameter, in.............9.5
Gear ratios: o'drive (0.82)...3.21:1
  4th (1.00)..............3.91:1
  3rd (1.31)..............5.12:1
  2nd (2.06)..............8.05:1
  1st (2.88)..............11.3:1
Synchromesh...........on top 3
Differential type.....hypoid bevel
  Ratio..................3.91:1
  Optional ratio.........3.55:1

CHASSIS & SUSPENSION

Frame type...separate ladder type
Brake type.............disc/drum
  Swept area, sq in........383
Tire size....Dunlop RS-5 5.90 x 15
Steering type.......cam & lever
  Overall ratio............15:1
  Turns, lock to lock........3.0
  Turning circle, ft.........36.0
Front suspension: independent with
  A-arms, lever shocks, coil springs.
Rear suspension: live axle with
  semi-elliptic springs, lever
  shocks, Panhard rod.

ACCOMMODATION

Normal capacity, persons.......2
Occasional capacity............3
Seat width, front, in......2 x 17.5
  Rear...................2 x 16
Head room, front/rear....35.5/28.0
Seat back adjustment, deg...none
Entrance height, in........44
Step-over height............14.5
Door width, front..........26.5
Driver comfort rating:
  For driver 69-in. tall........85
  For driver 72-in..........65
  For driver 75-in. tall.......45
  (85/100, good; 70/85, fair;
    under 70, poor)

GENERAL

Curb weight, lb............2650
Test weight................3020
Weight distribution (with
  driver), front/rear, %....47/53
Wheelbase, in..............92.0
Track, front/rear........48.7/50.0
Overall length, in........157.0
  Width.................60.0
  Height................50.0
Frontal area, sq ft........16.7
Ground clearance, in........4.5
Overhang, front/rear.......25/41
Departure angle (no load), deg..14
Usable trunk space, cu ft...,..2.3
Fuel tank capacity, gal.......14.4

INSTRUMENTATION

Instruments: fuel, oil pressure,
water temperature, 140 mph
speedometer, 7000 rpm tachometer.
Warnings lights: high beam, ignition, turn signals.

MISCELLANEOUS

Body styles available: roadster as
tested.

ACCESSORIES

Included in list price: overdrive,
wire wheels, heater, windshield
washers, full instrumentation,
adjustable steering column, seat
belt anchors.
Available at extra cost: seat belts,
tonneau cover.

CALCULATED DATA

Lb/hp (test weight).........20.4
Cu ft/ton mi..............86.7
Mph/1000 rpm (overdrive)...23.3
Engine revs/mi............2560
Piston travel, ft/mi........1490
Rpm @ 2500 ft/min.......4280
  Equivalent mph..........100.3
R&T wear index............37.9

MAINTENANCE

Crankcase capacity, qt........7.5
  Change interval, mi.......3000
Oil filter type...........full flow
  Change interval, mi........6000
Chassis lube interval, mi.....3000
Tire pressure, front/rear, psi.20/25

ROAD TEST RESULTS

ACCELERATION

0–30 mph, sec...............3.6
0–40 mph....................5.1
0–50 mph....................7.0
0–60 mph....................9.8
0–70 mph...................13.0
0–80 mph...................17.1
0–100 mph..................27.4
Passing test, 50–70 mph......5.7
Standing ¼ mi...............17.4
  Speed at end, mph............82

TOP SPEEDS

Overdrive (5000), mph.......116
  4th (5500)................101
  3rd (5500).................81
  2nd (5500).................51
  1st (5500).................36

GRADE CLIMBING
(Tapley data)

Overdrive, max gradient, %.....9
  4th.....................12
  3rd.....................17
  2nd.....................27
  1st................off scale
Total drag at 60 mph, lb.......95

SPEEDOMETER ERROR

30 mph indicated.....actual 30.0
40 mph....................40.2
60 mph....................60.0
80 mph....................79.1
100 mph...................98.7

FUEL CONSUMPTION

Normal driving, mpg.......16/21
Crusing range, mi........230/302

ACCELERATION & COASTING

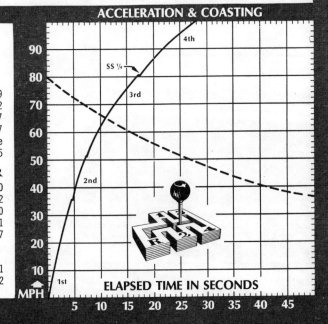

ELAPSED TIME IN SECONDS

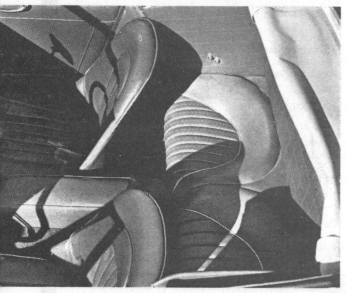

ized, noisy and difficult to select, and the synchronization of the other three gears leaves a lot to be desired. On the other hand, the shifting of the overdrive is very fast and smooth, although the positioning of the control switch makes it hard to locate in a hurry.

The overdrive operates on 3rd and high so that in effect the car has 6 speeds. Although this would seem to provide a ratio for any occasion, there is actually an excessive gap between 2nd and 3rd, which is accentuated by the fact that if the overdrive switch is in the overdrive position, the overdrive ratio will be selected automatically as soon as one shifts up from 2nd to 3rd, thereby increasing the gap.

The clutch is a great improvement over previous Healey models and, in fact, over the majority of sports car clutches. It is of the diaphragm type, and its action is light and smooth in direct contrast to the early Healey units, which were very heavy and fierce, and had an annoying habit of breaking their linkages. The car is equipped with disc brakes at the front and drums at the rear and the brakes are generally very good, although the pedal pressure required is high despite the use of a booster in the system.

One of the most noticeable features of the Healey is the unduly high noise level, which commences at about 3000 rpm and makes normal conversation impossible by 4000 rpm. It takes the form of a loud roar which is a mixture of engine, fan, transmission, carburetor, and exhaust noises, and one can't help feeling that a lot of it could be eliminated by better attention to insulation. The noise coupled with the rather uncomfortable driving position and the stiff suspension makes the car tiring to drive on a long trip. The level of exhaust noise has been reduced by the addition of a pair of supplementary mufflers located transversely at the rear of the car. However, the eternal Healey problem of low ground clearance remains, and the primary mufflers are still located beside the left frame rail where they are far too low and consequently extremely vulnerable.

The Austin-Healey is now in its 12th year, which is a long span in an age of rapid automobile development. It has served its purpose well both on road and track, and as recently as 1962 a Healey got as high as 8th place at Le Mans before piston failure put it out. However, the existing model appears to have reached the point of honorable retirement, and perhaps BMC will soon come up with a worthy successor after starting from scratch with a clean sheet of paper.

AUSTIN HEALEY

3000 SPORTS CONVERTIBLE

Sprite MARK III

IT'S SURPRISING, really, just how short a time the Austin-Healeys have been with us. So far as the big car—nowadays called the 3000—is concerned, it seems like ages, though, because apart from various body changes—a good many of them hard to find —and the step up from four to six pots, it has been winning international rallies in much the same general form for most of its life. So far as the little one, the Sprite, is concerned, this has grown up in a big way since the first frog-eyed version was spawned five or six years back.

Recently we have been covering a bit of mileage in both of them, and we thought that this time we could do a lot worse than combine the two cars in one road test. Obviously, there is no comparison between the rough, lusty "big Healey" and the Sprite unless its in the way they've both become a good deal more touring than sporting.

Let's have a look at the big 'un first. This is something of a he-man's motor-car, Pat Moss-Carlsson aside: it is heavy, rough, slightly crude, noisy, and at high speed it takes a bit of driving. In fact, it's almost vintage, really, and you might think that there is no excuse for this sort of car nowadays apart from the trifling facts that it still sells as fast as they can make it, and it is still more than capable of winning any international rally you care to mention. On the credit side—and perhaps among the reasons why it is still so popular—it is fast, exhilarating and almost unbelievably tractable. The engine, as everybody must know, is the B.M.C. "A"-series unit, bore and stroke measurements of the six cylinders of 83·4 mm x 88·9 mm measuring up to 2,912 c.c. With a compression ratio of 9 to 1 and two S.U. HD8 carburettors, maximum power is 148 b.h.p. at 5,250 r.p.m. and there is 165·2 lb. ft. of torque at 3,500 r.p.m. This may not sound a lot when compared to the 3·8-litre Jaguar's 220 b.h.p. and 240 lb. ft. of torque, but it is, believe us, sufficient. In greater detail the power unit is a pretty unrefined slab of iron—four main bearings for the crankshaft, cast-iron head, push-rod overhead valves and so forth—and, once the needle goes past 4,000, is almost terrifyingly rough in standard unbalanced tune. But of course it never has to work terribly hard, produces an adequate amount of urge and, in general, keeps the Healey galloping along at a brisk old trot in fine style. It isn't desperately thirsty, although you couldn't call 20 m.p.g. exactly economical. New owners of this sort of car would mind that, though—if you

can afford the insurance premiums you ought to be able to pour the go-juice in alright.

The engine always starts easily, takes a long time to reach full working temperature unless its a very warm day, and spits back through the carbs until it's hot enough to get going. At the other end of the journey, it will very likely want to run-on after you switch it off, especially if you've been chasing it a bit. There isn't too much mechanical noise when its going, unless you count a very noisy hiss from the carburettors, while a complicated silencing arrangement—two silencers on the nearside of the car, with two more mounted tranversely under the boot—keep the bark from the twin tail pipes down to very sociable limits.

The gearbox is abominable, without any doubt, but in practice it doesn't matter so much—we'll explain that in a minute. First let's support that libel on the gearbox. For a start, bottom gear has no synchromesh, which is anachronistic these days. Then there is second gear—we are accustomed to second speeds which are too low by comparison with third, but on the Healey it reaches ridiculous proportions. In direct third you can do ninety, but in second the absolute top whack, before everything starts to fly to pieces, is only just over fifty—and that is a mere eleven miles an hour quicker than bottom gear itself. Both third and top have overdrive, and in overdrive third you can reach 109, which is a bit more like it, while in direct top it goes a little faster—112 m.p.h., to be exact. The overdrive engages very smoothly, and is operated by a fumbly dashboard-mounted switch which can take a bit of finding, even when you're used to distinguishing between that and, say, the screen wipers switch. So that's the gearbox—now why doesn't it matter? Well, the answer is in the extraordinary flexibility of the engine. Although maximum torque is obtained quite a long way up the engine speed scale, relatively speaking, the curve is pretty flat, so that you can trickle about in overdrive top at below 20 m.p.h. if you've a mind to, and still find plenty of smooth acceleration from there on up. This low speed performance is such that in normal driving you find yourself using only third and top and their respective overdrive ratios, ignoring second altogether. Second itself is such a poorly chosen ratio that it's all too easy to obtain an acceleration that is actually poorer by using it than by ignoring it, and going straight from first to third. Other faults which are less easily ignored are the extremely heavy, stiff and awkward action of the gearlever, and the very noisy noise made by bottom gear.

Like the best vintage cars, the Healey gives you a very firm ride: unlike the best of them, it has very low ground clearance indeed, and even on main roads it is still pretty easy to scrape the silencers on the ground—to their lasting detriment, if you're unlucky. Again unlike the best vintage cars, there is a deal of scuttle shake, and the worse the surface the worse it gets. But the car does hold the road well, despite a rather evil reputation it seems to have developed, and so long as you bear in mind the fact that it is a big powerful car which, in all likelihood, is going like a bat out of hell you shouldn't come to much harm. The stiff suspension allows the wheels—all four of them at times—to dance about if the surface leaves anything to be desired, but the steering, which is precise if heavy, allows you to keep the thing going the way its pointed. Too much power under these conditions, or in the wet, will have you sideways, but that merely serves you right. The big Healey is a fire-eating monster, alright, and as such deserves to be treated with respect. In fact, it demands to be, and we have driven a lot of cars which we could truthfully call more forgiving!

With a top whack of over 120 m.p.h. the Healey, which is no lightweight at 22 cwt., deserves a big fat set of anchors, and it has all that is necessary. At the front there are 11¼ in. discs, with 11 in. drums at the back, and nowadays there is a vacuum servo which still doesn't seem to stop the pedal pressure from being pretty high. Stopping the Healey from high speed in a hurry needs a real bootful, and the car also develops an unnerving tendency to snake, even although the wheels remain unlocked, when braking hard like this. The car continues to run true, and one feels that the snake is in the suspension rather than on the road, if you follow—at all events, it never feels that it's getting out of hand, so it probably doesn't matter all that much. It's just that it frightened us!

With the passing of time the inside of the Healey has been tarted up a good deal, and nowadays you get imitation tree-wood dashboards and rather superior instruments. The speedometer is now calibrated up to 140 m.p.h., although it wasn't so long ago that the figures on the dial hadn't kept up with the performance of the car, and you could go a lot faster than the speedo said you could. The rev-counter is also smarter and more distinct than it used to be, while they give you oil pressure, water temperature and fuel gauges as well. This last item has one of those wildly-dancing needles, so that you never have any idea how much juice you've got left unless the car is stationary and level, the screen-wipers are only single-speed and the steering wheel can be adjusted to bring it nearer to you when, for most people, it would be better if you could get further away from it. The driving position is extremely vintage—you sit right on top of everything, and with two people on board it is all a bit crowded. Visibility completes the dated feel: you peer out through a little slot of a windscreen over a high bonnet, while astern solid quarters to the hood cut off vision rather more than we are used to nowadays. The seats are small and a bit on the hard side, but neither so small nor so hard as the "occasional" seats behind them, which have a folding-down squab so that you can use the space for luggage. As most of the room in the boot is taken up by the spare wheels, this is probably just as well. The boot also contains a master-switch which cuts off all the electricity, and you can turn this off, lock the boot (the only part of the car you *can* lock) and feel reasonably secure that it will be hard to pinch the car. Inevitably, however, cutting off all the electricity means that you can't even switch the lights on, so that if you take this precaution you automatically have to park without lights. Not a matter of importance if you always lock your car in the garage, of course, but then if you do that the master-switch isn't so important either!

Performance? This is what makes it all worthwhile. At just over a thousand pounds, including purchase tax, the big Healey probably offers more urge per pound sterling than nearly any other motor. Top whack, the mean of runs in opposite directions, is 121 m.p.h., and from rest it will reach 60 m.p.h. in exactly ten seconds, eighty in exactly fifteen and the ton in exactly 25. It doesn't hang about, you see: in overdrive top, 100 m.p.h. is only around 4,000 r.p.m., so that the car goes galloping along like this all day, or at least for as long as the motorway lasts. A discreet sort of understeer makes the car and the driver full of the joys of spring at those long, fast open bends, while on the sharper ones you can prod the tail round on the loud pedal provided no-one's looking. Fast getaways will obviously leave a good deal of rubber on the road if you're not careful, but you don't have to drive it like that to get places pretty rapidly.

That's the big 'un. The Sprite isn't a bit like that. The Mark 3 version, which for those who can't keep track of all these numbers of which the motor industry is so fond is the current one, is a first-class car for the sports-car apprentice, whereas to get the best out of the big Healey it's a good plan to know what you're doing. In the Sprite, you can find out what's going on without running much risk of breaking anything—not even your neck—while for those who are a bit out of the apprenticeship stage it is more than immense fun. It is lively, fast enough and handles really well, which add up to a car which anyone, novice or expert, can thoroughly enjoy living with.

The introduction of the Mark 3 meant a revised version of the 1,100 c.c. engine. Bore and stroke remain unchanged at 64·58 mm × 83·72 mm, but the cylinder head is modified, has larger inlet valves and reshaped inlet tracts, there is a higher compression ratio (8·9 to 1), a new exhaust manifold and a stouter crankshaft with main journals of two-inch diameter instead of the former 1·87 in. The power increase is in fact quite small, going up from 56 to 59 b.h.p. net at 5,750 r.p.m., with no increase in torque (62 lb. ft. at 3,250) but maximum speed has gone up to over ninety and something like four seconds is knocked off the 0-60 acceleration time. Acceleration is better throughout the range in fact, and if the Mark 3 Sprite had been available when they were making M.G.A.s they wouldn't have sold nearly so many of the latter! Such is progress.

The power starts coming in at about two-five, and from then on it's got clean, brisk acceleration all the way up to around 5,500 if you happen to have the hood down, and fully to six thousand if you are running "closed". The revs go up so easily and smoothly that you need to keep a sharp eye on the rev-counter in the lower ratios, while at the bottom end it is completely tractable—in traffic you can potter along at about fifteen hundred revs in top without fuss or judder. The power unit is mechanically quiet, with a nice sporting sort of exhaust note.

On the road, there's enough urge to make it possible to cruise at about 5,500 r.p.m., which is about 85 m.p.h., but more than a few miles of this makes the oil pressure fall quite sharply, probably due to frothing. So far as motorways are concerned they become acceptably short at a sustained 4,500 r.p.m., which is a steady seventy as near as makes no odds, and which lets the oil pressure stay where it ought to be. For shorter bursts you can, with the car "closed", get the full six thousand on any decent straight, and this represents about 92 m.p.h., which is the car's top speed in safety. During our performance testing we got a speed of 93 m.p.h. in one direction, which is "into the red" on the tachometer and therefore, presumably, not advisable.

The car's four-speed gearbox, although it hasn't got any synchromesh on bottom gear, has quite unusually well-spaced ratios. Maximum speeds in the gears are 30, 50 and 70, in first, second and third respectively, which is a lot better than you usually get. The gearlever is light, precise and has a nice short movement, and you can really put 'em through if you feel that way inclined. The clutch has a light pedal, but feels a bit soggy and fast upward changes catch it by surprise, so that it is slow to take up the drive.

Above: You have to provide your own rear end optional extra.

THE AUSTIN-HEALEY 3000

Engine: Six cylinders, 83·34 mm. × 88·9 mm.; 2,912 c.c.; compression ratio 9 to 1; pushrod-operated overhead valves; two S.U. HD8 carburettors; 148 b.h.p. at 5,250 r.p.m.

Transmission: Diaphragm-spring clutch; four-speed and reverse gearbox with synchromesh on upper three ratios; overdrive on third and top on test car; floor-mounted gear-lever.

Suspension: Front, independent with coil springs, wishbones and lever-type shock absorbers. Rear, live axle with semi-elliptic leaf springs and panhard rod. **Tyres:** 5·90 × 15.

Brakes: Front, 11¼ in. discs; rear, 11 in. drums; vacuum servo assistance.

Dimensions: Overall length, 13 ft. 1½ ins; overall width, 5 ft. 0½ in.; overall height, 4 ft. 1 in.; turning circle, 35 ft. 7 ins.; ground clearance, 4 ins.; kerb weight, 22 cwt.

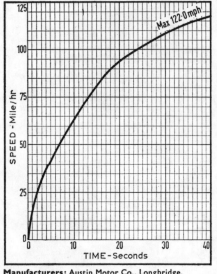

PERFORMANCE

	m.p.h.	ACCELERATION		secs.
MAXIMUM SPEED	—122·0		0– 30–	2·8
Mean of two ways	—121·0		0– 40–	5·1
			0– 50–	7·4
SPEEDS IN GEARS	First— 41		0– 60–	10·0
	Second— 52		0– 70–	12·0
	Third— 90		0– 80–	15·0
	overdrive third—109		0– 90–	17·8
	Top—112		0–100–	25·0
			0–110–	31·2
Fuel consumption	20 m.p.g.	Standing quarter-mile		—16·8

Manufacturers: Austin Motor Co., Longbridge, Birmingham.
Price: £1,045 including purchase tax.

So far as the suspension is concerned, the quarter-elliptic springs at the back which everyone made such a fuss about years ago have been replaced by semi-elliptics, to the cars' enormous benefit, while there is, of course, coil springs i.f.s. This gives a good ride, with excellent roadholding—there's a nice safe feel about the car pretty well wherever it happens to be doing, and it is extremely difficult to spin the back wheels. In the dry the handling characteristics are just about neutral, although in the wet or on loose surfaces the tail goes first. Any sort of slide is very easily held and corrected, however, and under the majority of circumstances the car goes round on rails (albeit with bags of tyre squeal) or else it slides all of a piece. The steering is light and high-geared, needing only 2¼ turns from lock to lock, and the seats are comfortable.

The whole of the driving compartment is well laid-out, even down to angling of the speedometer and rev-counter so that they can be easily and accurately read. There is plenty of room, even for the big fellows among us, all the controls are handily placed, instrumentation is complete and visibility all round is good, even with the hood up: this last item, which often presents a problem, is relatively easy to stow and erect, and when up it stays that way, without flapping or flying off even at maximum speed.

You can't expect everything on a car that only costs just over six hundred quid, of course, but the Sprite seems to have most things. You have to pay extra for a heater and a headlamp flasher, but otherwise there isn't a lot that is lacking. It's a jolly nice litttle car.

THE AUSTIN-HEALEY SPRITE

Engine: Four cylinders, 64·58 mm. × 83·72 mm.; 1,098 c.c.; pushrod-operated overhead valves; compression ratio 8·9 to 1; twin S.U. HS2 carburettors; 59 b.h.p. at 5,750 r.p.m.

Transmission: Diaphragm-spring clutch; four-speed and reverse gearbox with synchromesh on upper three ratios; floor-mounted gearlever.

Suspension: Front, independent, with coil springs and wishbones; rear, semi-elliptic leaf springs. **Tyres:** 5·20 × 13.

Brakes: Front, 8¼ in. disc; rear, 7 in. two-leading shoe drums.

Dimensions: Overall length, 11 ft. 5½ ins.; overall width, 4 ft. 5 ins.; overall height, 4 ft. 1¾ ins.; turning circle, 32 ft.; ground clearance 5 ins.; kerb weight 14 cwt.

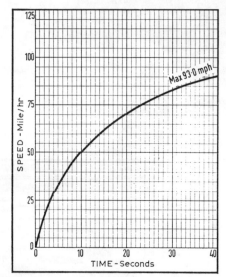

PERFORMANCE

	m.p.h.	ACCELERATION		secs.
MAXIMUM SPEED	93		0–30–	4·1
Mean of two ways	92·2		0–40–	7·0
			0–50–	9·7
SPEEDS IN GEARS	First—30		0–60–	14·4
	Second—50		0–70–	19·8
	Third—70		0–80–	32·0
Fuel consumption:	28 m.p.g.	Standing quarter-mile		—19·4

Manufacturers: Austin Motor Co., Longbridge, Birmingham.
Price: £611, including purchase tax.

From the rear the works Healey 3000 could be picked by the enormous filler top, and white circle. Tank itself carried more than 30 gallons.

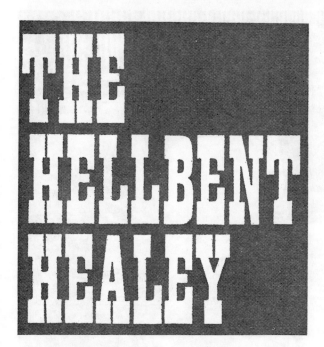

THE HELLBENT HEALEY

In which SCW columnist Eoin Young goes for the British driving test in a full house sports racer, fresh from the Targo Florio — and fails.

APART from the pair of open exhausts poking under the passenger's door, the side vents in the wings, the giant fuel filler in the middle of the boot lid, the strapped-down bonnet, and the white circle on the tail, the red Austin Healey 3000 appeared quite standard — straight from the showroom floor, as it were!

It isn't every day that scribes are allowed to borrow factory racing cars, but the Healey was 'between races' and competition manager, Stuart Turner, kindly made it available for a weekend. This was the actual car that Paul Hawkins and

SCW BRIEF ROAD TEST

Timo Makinen had been using to towel the GTO Ferraris down at the Targa Florio a few weeks earlier. Hawkins was really pressing on in the best approved hairy Aussie fashion well ahead of the red cars, but the big Healey was wearing out rubber a bit quickly at this pace and they were pitting every couple of laps for tyres. Even so, the best Healey lap for the mountain circuit was 45 min 31 sec compared with the best GTO lap at 44 min 46 sec. Two miles from the pits on the eighth lap a broken distributor arm parked the Healey on the edge of the road, and Hawkins, having diagnosed the trouble, sprinted back to the pits. Was he mad when he learned that there was a spare distributor in the boot all the time!

Counting the Hawkins footwork as well as his general hurry-along on the road, the Healey finished an undisgraced 20th in a race where just being able to finish counts for a lot.

Three Webers, an aluminium head, over-bored 40 thou, a six-branch exhaust manifold, a race camshaft 10½ to 1 compression ratio and a weight of 19½ cwt which brought it lower than the rally Healeys, made my "racer" quite a potent piece of machinery.

A broken speedo for the test made acceleration figures impossible, but BMC Competitions people quote speeds at 6000 rpm in third 71 mph, o/d third 87 mph, top 102 mph, and o/d top 125 mph.

The mods brought the engine power up to 195 bhp and turned what is a hairy and perhaps a little clumsy road car into a Ferrari-beating racer. Indoors the furnishings were definitely turned out with racing in mind. Trim was nil, and everything was matt black to cut down glare. The boot was full of petrol tank, so the spare wire wheel with its knobbly SP tyre, plus jack and tools were strapped behind the seats. The seats themselves were hip-hugging special racing jobs designed to keep the driver firmly at his place during the twisty bits.

THE HELLBENT HEALEY Continued

Instrumentation was kept to a minimum, with a combined oil pressure/water temperature gauge in the centre of the facia above a row of labelled switches for wipers, lights, windscreen washers, panel light, and the key-starter. The defunct speedometer read in kilometres while the rev counter was set at an angle to give the driver the benefit of the red sector at 6000 between the wheel spokes. The wheel was a heavily padded sprung affair of smallish diameter that felt keen after the glut of baked plastic tillers on normal production machinery. This one felt like a four wheel drift just grabbing hold of it!

The body showed signs of 'road rash' at the front where a few walls had no doubt creased its aluminium lines, and side-windows were perspex. The hardtop was securely bolted down, with rounded pieces of wood protecting occupants' heads from skull creasing on the forward bolts.

Tweaking the starter gave rise to a tremendous clattering roar from somewhere on the other side of the car. This was a real head-spinner. The gearbox was delightful to use, being smoother to slot than the standard model. The gear lever was

Cooling ducts were let into the side panel to admit more air to the engine compartment. Hardtop was securely bolted down but leaked a little.

a fist-sized lump of wood which also housed the overdrive (on third and fourth) switch.

The axle ratio had been stepped up in the interests of a longer loping stride on the open road, and also gave the intermediate gears a better burst. The shame of it all was having the speedo out of action, so no speeds could be accurately checked. We tried changing the head, but found that the standard part numbers had been scratched out and other super special ones painted in — it just didn't seem worth while going to our friendly Austin agent and trying his patience!

In gear the big Healey really started to growl, indeed on acceleration the box made as much if not more noise than the blaring exhaust.

As mentioned, the gearchange was smooth and using the two o/d ratios on the way up a fair old steady surge of pace could be wound on. A DB5 Aston Martin (definitely a 007 car) arrived in the mirror with lights flashing while I was tooling along the A3 on a semi-motorway three-lane stretch at around 80 mph. Down to third remembering that the synchromesh wasn't quite as handy on the way down, red line, switch to overdrive 111, red line, IV, red line. No Aston. Damn your eyes, James Bond.

The petrol consumption of the Healey was rather intimidating as the three Webers crowded in under the bonnet kept gulping from the tank that must have held at least 30 gallons. When I collected the car the attendant was rather embarrassed at the fact that the fuel gauge registered only ½, so we barked and bellowed round the BMC pump to top up.

Snapping open the big filler cap one could hear subterranean gurglings from deep inside. The little man turned on the pump and began one of those conversations that don't start anywhere in particular, don't go anywhere, and when you finish you can't remember what it was about. This idle reverie was broken abruptly when the bowser snapped itself off, having delivered 14 gallons — and it still wasn't full!

Chugging out into the traffic which was moving at a London traffic crawl, was rather nerve racking as I imagined fouling the plugs well

Correspondent Young opens the door to the business department. Here lurk three Webers atop an aluminium 10½ to 1 head, with six-branch exhaust and racing cam.

before home. I hadn't taken into consideration the placid truck-type qualities of the big six even in racing tune.

The best part of the weekend was the startled gapes from proud owners of other Healeys.

Once you became accustomed to the din, and mastered the art of the shouted conversation, life was easier. Top gear was quieter than the other three but the trees and walls were usually coming up fairly quick at that stage and idle chat was given over in favor of staying between the bits of grass and out of Mini boots.

Brakes were a satisfying part of the Healey performance. Four wheel discs with a servo still took a fair amount of pedal pushing but the anchors were definitely and reassuringly there.

I suppose I came to accept the Healey rather in the same way as those doggy people come to grow fond of a ginormous Alsation that barks a threatened hand amputation at anyone brave or silly enough to approach too close. My state of blissful acceptance of my growling, starkly rather indecent pet reached the stage where I decided to use it for my driving test! I had decided, as pure formality, to try (try being the operative word in this case) for my English driver's licence in addition to my perfectly valid (and un-endorsed) New Zealand licence. The English test is really rather a farce, as despite the fact that you can carry out all the test manoeuvres in an able and polished manner (let's face it: *anyone* can start on a hill, and do a three point turn in a narrow street without puncturing someone's wall) you have to do these things the *official* way. This includes ramming on the handbrake with every pause, and shuffling

Three Webers only just fitted in — must have been mechanics nightmare to tune. They swallowed fuel at a diabolical rate. BHP delivered is 195.

THE HELLBENT HEALEY

Cockpit is harshly spartan, but equipped with all necessary instruments, comfortable seats and finished in matt black to stop glare.

the wheel through your hands rather than any approach at cross-arms work. This is simply dangerous whichever way you look at it. Still, that's what the book says, and that's the way you've got to do it.

To continue: My examiner was, unfortunately, lanking around 6 ft something, and although his blank look didn't become any blanker on spotting the competition appendage of the Healey, his mood obviously didn't improve as he started to curl up into the beast, both seats of which seemed to have been designed for someone about the size of Paul Hawkins who is broad of shoulders, but not very high off the road.

All attempts at conversation were obviously going to be wasted effort, as my rather uncomfortable looking instructor delivered instructions in a sing-song up and down voice. "Now at the end of the road there is a turn to the left and I want you to turn left." Much exaggerated looking in the mirror, down changing, winkers flashing, arms waving. Full marks. "At the intersection I want you to turn right up the hill and stop in your own time at the side of the road." Repeated down changing, mirror craning, arm waving, handbrake on-off-on-off, looking every which-way, venturing bravely across the deserted intersection (failed for cutting the corner!) and then stopped on the hill with handbrake dutifully and officially on. Actually the handbrake didn't work at all, and the cranking on with each stop, and especially the hill start, was performed with great flourish while my right foot was heel-and-toeing on foot-brake and accelerator.

Continued on page 144

Spoked wheels give a glimpse of the massive four wheel discs which helped to bring the car down from 125 mph to rest in shortest possible time.

Austin-Healey 3000

Remember the gutsy old hard-
riding Healey of 10 years ago?
It hasn't changed, thank heavens

IMPORTER British Motor Corporation
    734 Grand Avenue
    Ridgefield, New Jersey

ENGINE
Type Water-cooled six-in-line, cast iron block,
    5 main bearings, pushrod-operated overhead
    valves
Bore & Stroke....................3.28 x 3.50 in.
Displacement.........................178 cu. in.
Compression ratio...................9.0 to one
Power (SAE)..............150 bhp @ 5250 rpm
Torque..................173 lbs-ft @ 3000 rpm

TRANSMISSION
4-speed manual, non-synchro first

WHEELBASE ....91.75 in.

TRACK.................F: 48.75 in. R: 48.75 in.

CURB WEIGHT................................2425 lbs.

ACCELERATION	Seconds
0-40	4.4
0-60	9.8
0-80	17.9

TOP SPEED.............................110 mph

SUSPENSION
F: Ind., unequal-length wishbones, coil springs,
    anti-sway bar
R: Rigid axle, semi-elliptic leaf springs

BRAKES 11.25-in discs front, 11-in drums rear

The British say that the Austin-Healey is "well-proved." This is certainly a fact; all the bugs have been ironed out and the buyer knows exactly what he's getting. It's also a fact that the Austin-Healey is an old car, a vestige of the older British methods of car construction.

The six cylinder engine is heavy and antiquated, putting out some 150 horse-power from 3 liters. Still, it's enough to push the 2500-pound car to 60 mph in less than 10 seconds.

The live rear axle is located by leaf springs attached to a chassis that is sadly lacking in torsional stiffness. The result is that the Austin-Healey needs smooth roads to behave itself without having the rear wheels disporting themselves like a herd of kangaroos. The handling is not quick but is virtually roll-free and the brakes (discs front, drums rear) bring the speed down swiftly and surely.

The overdrive-equipped transmission has no synchro on first, and fast up-and-down shifts can't be made without grating noises from within. The seating position is not very comfortable especially for large people, and luggage space is notably lacking although the two so-called occasional seats in the back seem to have been designed more with luggage than people in mind.

The Austin-Healey comes equipped with adjustable steering wheel, heater, windshield washers, seat belt mountings, overdrive, front disc brakes, Dunlop RS tires and wire wheels all included in the base price. This may sound like a bargain but you have to remember that the Healey's base price is close enough to more exciting merchandise such as a Lotus Elan or Alfa Giulia Sprint GT to make a prospective buyer take a longer look.

driving Abingdon's musclecar

ERIC DYMOCK describes a dramatic week-end with one of the fiercest road cars ever to come out of Abingdon—a fully modified, works rally team Austin-Healey 3000

STANDING in the middle of Salisbury Plain a year or so ago you might have heard an excited, braying noise in the distance. It would not have remained far off for long because the approaching thunder belonged to Timo Makinen's Healey 3000 and it would have burst on you out of the gathering dusk; the first car to pass in the 1965 R.A.C. Rally of Great Britain; The last time its like was ever to be seen driven 'in anger' in an international rally. This was one of the most exciting road cars in the world.

Until 1966, the big Healeys were the survivors of the sports cars that had fought out the Alpines and Lièges 10 years ago. Saloons do it now and although the other two-seaters nearly all dropped out, giving way to newer designs, the big Healey seemed to go on for ever. The new Appendix J regulations caused their retirement, at least in the tremendously powerful form they reached near the end of their career. How very nearly they went out in a

blaze of glory then, when Timo Makinen almost won the R.A.C. Rally at the end of the European Championship season! Icy roads on the very last night snatched victory away after an epic drive in which he led most of the way. Team mate Rauno Aaltonen's win was small consolation. The Healey had already been second in the R.A.C. four times and if studded tyres had not been prohibited its day would surely have come.

But studs had been banned to try and preserve the surfaces of roads and special stages, so although the book records another second place, most people will remember a stirring drive, and the car's decisive wins including two firsts in the Liège (Pat Moss and Rauno Aaltonen) and two firsts in the Alpine (the Morleys).

The Rally Healey is not much like a standard one to drive. It is faster, heavier, and much noisier. Sound-deadening material has been removed and the inside is filled with heavy

mechanical noises coming through the undamped bulkhead, and the deep boom of the exhaust resonates round inside the bare hard top. The racket at speed is like an explosion that goes on happening.

Three fat 45 DCOE Webers are shoe-horned under the narrow bonnet on the inlet side of the engine, and underneath there is a six-branch exhaust manifold which leads out under the passenger's door. The engine has an aluminium cylinder head, a high-lift camshaft, and an 11 : 1 compression ratio. There is an oil cooler and the bores are enlarged to raise the capacity from 2912 c.c. to 2982 c.c. Under-shielding protects the full length of the car and ground clearance, often criticized on Austin-Healeys, is improved from about 5 inches to $7\frac{1}{2}$ inches, by raising the suspension. Heavier springs and dampers are fitted, with close-ratio gears and a final drive of 4·3 : 1.

Inside, the wood fascia has been discarded for a simpler one in black crackle on which there is a speedometer, tachometer, a combined oil pressure and water temperature gauge, and a fuel gauge. Most of the remaining space is used by a switchgear, and there is a miniature sub-station with great banks of fuses immediately in front of the passenger's legs. Seats are improved and there are very comprehensive safety harnesses. The standard steering-wheel is replaced with a very smart Springall soft leather-rimmed one which has padded loops over the aluminium spokes for resting your thumbs on. The heater comes from a Mark I Mini and the lidded vent in the hard top from a Mini-Van. Attention to detail is obvious; there are *two* spare ignition keys screwed to the bulkhead under the bonnet. A spare fan belt is taped to the bonnet strut. There is a spare throttle spring beside the carburetters. The familiar spare-wheel-shaped bulge in the boot lid represents the space taken up by an extra wheel and a 20-gallon fuel tank. Inside the car there is a large padded roll-over cage. The wheels are 70-spoke competition pattern with Dunlop SP44 Weathermasters to grip the loose surfaces of forest roads.

The 20-gallon tank empties at an alarming rate. On rallies it will get down to 8 m.p.g., but 14½ m.p.g. on roads with a 70-m.p.h. speed limit was expensive enough. Despite a weight increase over the Mark II Healey 3000 of 2½ cwt., and over the Mark III of 1¼ cwt., the acceleration is better. The rally Healey produces 175 b.h.p. at 5,600 r.p.m. *at the wheels* and a lot more torque than the standard engine, so the increase in weight is more than

Just to prove that you don't need to be all muscle and six feet tall to handle a rally Healey, Frances Dymock drove it, too. Below is the comprehensive dash panel, all clearly labelled, even to the cigar-lighter. Over-drive switch is in the gear lever knob

compensated. The close-ratio gearbox and the altered overall gearing help acceleration, but the top speed of the car is not very much different from a good Mark III. With a lot more space than was often available, the engine would wind itself up quite smoothly to well over 120 m.p.h. in overdrive top.

As well as increasing the weight, the undershielding and extra equipment have also altered its distribution. Measured with an insignificant amount of fuel in the tank, it worked out at 51/49 front/rear compared with the standard Mark III's 48/52. Increased understeer was as noticeable as it was understandable in these conditions, especially in the wet when, on a trailing throttle, the car seriously threatened to drive off the outside of sharp bends. Road tyres instead of the special-stage knobblies would probably have improved matters; as it was, the throttle had to be used to help the car round, making driving in the rain a more exciting business than most people enjoy.

You don't really drive the Healey fast in the normal way. It has to be tamed first. It is probably the most highly developed, and the last of the conventional sports cars whose philosophy included big, slow-revving engines firm suspension, and for the driver's part, a certain amount of courage and

In its natural habitat—a rough-surfaced special stage, up in the hills. The bulge in the boot lid is necessary to accommodate the 20-gallon fuel tank and two spare wheels shod with Dunlop SP44 radial-ply Weathermasters

Abingdon's musclecar continued

muscle. On the question of courage, a drive in the rally Healey puts Timo Makinen's beyond doubt.

Not that the Healey is a very heavy car to drive. The clutch is a diaphragm-spring one, extremely light and completely untemperamental. You can use it in traffic without it snatching or getting hot. Likewise the four-wheel disc brakes with servo are light, and almost impossible to fade although they never seem to work properly until they are really hot and then they squeal a little. The pads are DS11 competition material which resists fade, and who cares if it squeaks a bit? There's so much noise already that a little extra makes no difference. The steering is also fairly light and the standard car's 32-foot turning circle is unimpaired.

By the time the gearbox had covered the R.A.C. and some subsequent, less strenuous running, the synchromesh had pretty well vanished from second and third gears although there is one similar ex-works car which has managed to retain its synchro after about 30,000 miles. On EJB 806 C however, it was essential to double-declutch changing down, and desirable when changing up, but with a little practice gear changes were crisp although the lever has to be moved with a certain amount of decision. A switch on the wooden gear lever knob operates the overdrive which engages and disengages in third and top instantly and smoothly.

Anticipating temperament in traffic proved unnecessary. Not many people would want this car for shopping, but it *will* idle at 800 r.p.m. without difficulty; it does not overheat or oil plugs in long traffic holdups. Use of oil is not excessive and although there were a few minor body rattles the rally Healey is still a road car, unlike its cardboard cousins, the stripped-bare saloon-car racers. Timo's car had carpet and comforts, although weight-saving had received attention, with alloy body panels and Perspex windows in the doors and hard top. The hard top and roll cage seemed to have the effect of stiffening-up the frame for there was virtually no scuttle shake, even on quite rough roads at speed.

A Healey like this would not find a home in *every* enthusiast's garage. The ride would put a lot of people off: the springing is so stiff you get joggled up and down even on roads other cars find smooth, and on rough 'special stages' you need the seat belts to hold you in place. But if you think the days of cars that make you gulp on fast bends, or take your breath away with noise and excitement and acceleration are gone, take one Austin-Healey 3000 Mark III, three 45 DCOE Weber carburetters, remove the padding, sound-deadening, and excess weight . . . ●

Performance figures

Acceleration through the gears: (maximum r.p.m., 6,000)

0–30 m.p.h.	2·9 sec.
0–40	5·0
0–50	6·3
0–60	8·3
0–70	10·2
0–80	12·8
0–90	15·9
0–100	19·1

Standing start ¼-mile: 15·8 sec.

Maximum speed (mean of four runs in opposite directions) : 123·3 m.p.h.

Overall fuel consumption for 250 miles: 14·4 m.p.g.

Note: With all the synchromesh operative, the acceleration figures could doubtless be improved upon. The speedometer was reasonably accurate up to 60 m.p.h., then read progressively fast until at 100 m.p.h. it was optimistic by approximately 5 per cent. Oil consumption was roughly one pint of XL 30 for every 125 miles. The weight and weight distribution quoted was certified on a public weighbridge.

HELLBENT HEALEY

Continued from page 140

The classic part came when my learned friend tapped his notebook on the dash "like this." I was to make an emergency stop "as though a child was crossing the road." It wasn't hard to judge exactly when the pad was going to alight on the dash, and my foot must have clumped the brake at the same instant. The Healey stopped in a few feet, and I glanced across to see officialdom peering through a cloud of rubber smoke.

When all the hoo-hah and kindergarten questions were over and successfully answered, I was liltingly informed, "I am sorry but you haven't passed the test. Here is a book which might help you with your next attempt." Phooey!

The Healey and I went on a few social excursions over the weekend, and while it didn't exactly charm any delicate female hearts, it certainly emptied the bars of any pubs we stopped at, and even earned a few beers while 'wottleshe-do' questions were pumped. Referring, of course, to the car.

We parted company (referring again to the Healey) on the Monday as the fuel gauge was sinking slowly to the E, and the weekend of tiger-taming was over.

Lots of fun. Thank you BMC. Sorry our speedo didn't work. Oh, and the hardtop leaks when it rains! Still, I don't suppose racing overalls are as sensitive as nylons to little things like a steady drip, drip, drip, from where the window and roof supposedly meet.

But as a proven racer and a crumpet catcher, it was ideal. Hawkins and Makinen proved it was a racer in the Targa! #

We haven't yet built a sportscar capable of flight. Meanwhile the Austin Healey 3000 offers you quite a take-off. 60 mph in 9.8 seconds.*

When motoring correspondents write about the Austin Healey 3000, they tend to let loose the adjectives. Flatterers like: Rugged. Muscular. Hairy-chested.

If you've ever driven an Austin Healey 3000 yourself, you won't quarrel with these descriptions. Ruggedness is something Austin have been working on for thirteen years, the length of time it took to arrive at the present Mark III. By now the 3000 *should* be rugged.

The muscularity is a function of the famous BMC C-series engine, tuned to give 150 bhp at 5250 rpm. This is a big, three-litre powerhouse: hence the long, sweptback rake of bonnet needed to conceal it.

The chief improvements, latterly, are details of finish. Wind-up windows, a covertible top, a more elegant cockpit. A back seat that folds forward to form a platform for extra luggage.

On the road the 3000 is a quieter car: dual exhausts reduce the noise without diminishing the power. And the disc brakes are servo-assisted to keep 120 mph plus under close rein.

Competition? The 3000 spoils for it. It's the only British sportscar ever to have won the Leige-Rome-Liege Rally, which is probably the most destructive test of them all.

It's also the only British sportscar ever to have won it twice!

*Motor, November 28, 1964.

AUSTIN

By Appointment to
Her Majesty The Queen
Motor Car Manufacturers
The Austin Motor
Company Limited

THE BRITISH MOTOR CORPORATION LTD.

Austin Healey 3000 Mk. III Sports Convertible (including £192.3.9 P.T.)—£1,107.3.9.

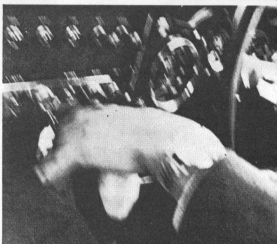

LAST OF THE LINE?

JOHN STANLEY rides shotgun on the works rally Healey

I RUN my hand along the wing. The smooth aluminium is warm from the heat of the day. White, distorted clouds chase across the familiar scarlet shell. We wait silently. He sits rugged, dignified, wearing the full battle dress of lamps and trimmings, not unlike a virile Chelsea pensioner. Indeed, the simile is well chosen for in the words of its loving owner, Peter Browning, " The age of the ralliest hairy sports car is passing, yet the incredible Healey won't die." Old soldiers never die, goes the saying, and the fortunate few who have tried to master the beast will know just why it has survived.

I have no intentions of setting before you a complex, clinical data report, linked with superior remarks comparing the thing with a Cobra or what-have-you. It would take a very insensitive enthusiast to do that. A handful of skilled, dedicated men in the BMC Competitions department have created a legend with the " Works " Healey. These cars are not activated production-line models but competition masterpieces hand built from the start. The Healey history is one of great character, the present line starting with the 100 model in 1952 and developing into the present Mark III 3000. Many great names have been associated with the marque like those of the Morleys, who chalked up two outright wins in the Alpine ; Pat Moss and Rauno Aaltonen, with respective first in the Liège, and Timo Makinen, who so nearly brought home the bacon in the '66 RAC Rally which marked the last works entry for his thoroughbred, due to the new Appendix J regulations.

The unit itself is bored out from 2912 cc to 2982 cc and is fitted with a gas-flowed aluminium head raising the compression ratio to 11.1. There is a nitrided crankshaft ; nimonic valves and a six-branch exhaust manifold linked to a modified system to improve ground clearance. A bank of triple 45DCOE Weber carburettors complete the cocktail which induces 173 bhp at the wheels ! Standard transmission is one of the weaker aspects of the basic Healey 3000 and naturally much work has gone into providing the strength and urge to cope with all those horses. The box is full of straight cut gears, which coupled with overdrive on third and top, provides six evenly spaced ratios right through the box. The overdrive switch is installed in the gear knob itself and takes effect very quickly.

The suspension is raised and toughened at the front, and at the rear, 14 leaf springs and shockers are installed. The combined effect is to raise the ground clearance from 5 in to 7½ in. Braking is a twin system with tandem master cylinders and twin servos together with DS 11 padded discs all round. The steering too, has not been missed by the improving hand of the mechanic. Standard gearing provides a full-time job when driving in anger so a smaller, leather wheel has been provided together with a lower ratio resulting in much the same handling as that of a Mini.

Drop all this powerful equipment in an aluminium body, bolt on steel guards for the sump, gearbox and 20-gallon fuel tank. Dress the eager beast with instruments, furniture and seven powerful driving lights and on paper, you have something approaching a works mount.

An interesting fact is that all the extra bits have made this lightweight-bodied machine 1¼ cwt heavier than the standard steel Mark III. In actual terms of speed, top is 135 mph with a standing quarter in some 15.5 seconds working on about eight miles to the gallon ! Ordinary road work achieves around 15 mpg and with the useful overdrive it produces a surprisingly well behaved town car getting down to a mere 800 revs without complaining. The temperature rises to 160 and just sits there. 5.6 is being used as peak revs because that's where the power is and also as there are no more gearboxes !

At last Peter arrives with some trade plates and gets into the driving seat. " We'll go somewhere private, then you squirt it about as you want," he offers, tightening his belt. I climb in. The door needs a firm pull, thank God, at least that's steel ! He turns the ignition and the unit bursts into life. The tiny cockpit fills with the lumpy sound of heavy machinery warming up. " I'm afraid this is where conversation has to end." mouths Peter, intent on the gauges. Into first gear and we arc round the forecourt to his competitions department and burble away towards the gate where the uniformed gentleman salutes. Tribute indeed. " We'll take it quietly (if ever there was a wrong word) until things warm up," shouts Peter, nosing his brooding machine through light traffic. The hard top seems a tight fit and before long the cockpit reeks with that warm, musty smell from heavy machinery, worn carpets and memories of forest thrashes. Power plant thunder apart, the constant chattering of the coachwork protesting

at the near solid suspension, is strangely reminiscent of a fine vintage Bentley I once knew.

The long road ahead flaunts itself at the Healey. Peter reflects upon the vision and in a flurry of feet and wrist movements, we drop into low gear. There is a roar quite beyond description, the long powerful bonnet lifts and takes sights on the stretching tarmac. The tail snakes, the wheel kicks, the body pitches. Peter's face is gaunt, intent. His hands twitch around the steering wheel and flash momentarily to the gears to satisfy the beast's insatiable hunger for tarmac. There's little doubt he's in control and no question of the position being assumed permanent. The Healey's heading due north by mutual agreement, any small slip and he'll go his own sweet way. Does that ring true as I watch driver and car arguing and deciding on a line round the fleeting bend. Discs whistle ; revs climb.

We straighten out and surge towards infinity. There is small point in description. Perhaps the nearest thing is that famous BBC film which shows a railway engine's view of the London–Brighton run covered in a mere three minutes. Remember the sensation of piling through the darkness of a tunnel towards the advancing daylight. Well, you're back against your seat, being thrown about by the cart-like springing and peering through the narrow screen at advancing Britain, in much the same way.

A local newspaper van appears in our path and we drop two ratios.

The big beast moves out, lifts his dignified nose and stretches out gnashing his teeth. We advance at an unpublished speed with the most incredible sound, rush the modest Mini van, air horns screaming a fanfare to this, surely the last Real sports car. A psychologist could induce endless parallels but very simply, this beast is wild. It was never intended for domesticity. To sit and experience this car's urge for long, intimate forest tracks or twisting Alpine passes, is like watching a lion pacing his zoo cage pining for the plains of central Africa.

Skilled men created this breed ; brave men fought with them ; let us hope blind men don't write its epitaph.

PERFORMANCE FIGURES
0-60 mph in 8 secs.
0-100 mph in 19 secs.
Top speed 135 mph.
Standing quarter mile 15.5 secs.
Fuel 8 mpg rally work/hard driving
15 mpg careful roadwork.

Reduce speed now! says the sign as James Ewing storms up to a roundabout in 838 ENX *Photo: Gullachsen*

Hail! *and farewell!*

It's coincidence of course, but the coming of the 70 limit and the passing of the Austin-Healey 3000 could between them mark the end of an era. At least that's how it seems to JAMES EWING, now on his third 'Big Healey'

THIS is going to be rather senti-mental. For years they've been telling me that the Big Healey is out of date. 'You're running a vintage job there, old boy,' they'd say, and when I bought my third in a line they wrote me off as bonkers.

Well that's all right with me. The Healey has always had a vintage feel about it and that's why I bought an-other. I like the ruddy things, and now that they are out of production my affection is all the greater. They are a link with the heroic days of motor-cars. The 3000 looks what I have always con-sidered a sports car should look like. And they have got better and better. My first (2838 UE) took to the road in 1960, and compared with later models, was a comparatively sedate method of transport. This still had the odd gear change coming out of the side of the

tunnel and I made some quite appalling changes at first. But we soon came to terms and I would not have parted with it had some nit in a garage not squirted brake fluid all over the bonnet. I man-aged to make a satisfactory exchange for a Mk. II (838 ENX) which, as it happens lives near by and is kept in splendid trim. This car was a snorter. It was tweaked a little and had competition rear suspension with works exhaust system. It was very fast indeed and when the rumours hardened about the end of the Healey, I thought long and painfully about the whole business. To carry on with the Mk. II or go out with flying colours with a brand new Mk. III—the last of the line.

I bought a new one. Colorado red it is and this is the best of the lot (LNX 628 E). Better torque, better balance from the new rear axle location, and vastly

better trim. And a deal more poke even than the Mk. II.

Whether there is going to be any point in really fast cars in the future remains to be seen. This may be my last, and I will have no regrets if I end my sports car career with a Healey. They have served me well and faithfully. I will never forget the feeling of exhilaration when I first sat behind that huge wheel and looked away down the long, sleek bonnet; nor the nose lifting under power, the rev.-counter swinging up, the roar of the wind and the scream of tyres. There seemed to be such a hell of a lot going on.

All my cars have been bought from and admirably maintained by that nice bunch of blokes at the Donald Healey outfit at Warwick where their know-ledge and enthusiasm has added greatly to the pleasures of Healey motoring.

So it's hail and farewell to a great sports car. The competition records and statistics are there for posterity. Soon, the Healey will be a collector's piece. But no one who has sat behind the wheel of a Big Healey will forget the enduring excitement of it all—the huge surge of power, the tumultuous exhaust, and the rest of the pack shrinking to dots in the mirror. Great days . . . .

AUSTIN-HEALEY 3000 (Mk. III)

SINCE our last article in this series, which featured the larger Austin-Healey car, many changes have taken place. Various development phases have been reached and the car has been fitted with several different carburation systems and, more recently, altered transmission. For these reasons we feel that it would serve the more useful purpose to devote this article to a specific model, rather than to attempt to cover two or more of the later series of Austin-Healey 3000 cars in this form.

Basically the car is a two-door, two-seater sports model, but this series (BJ 8) incorporates occasional seats at the rear. Also fitted on this model are winding windows and quarter lights, which distinguish its appearance from predecessors in the range. Power is provided by the familiar B.M.C. "C"-type engine, of almost exactly 3-litres swept volume capacity, overhead valves, and working at a compression ratio of 9:1.

Transmission of the drive is taken through a diaphragm spring clutch to a four-speed gearbox, with synchromesh on the upper three ratios. Overdrive is an optional. The drive is taken from the output shaft of the gearbox, or overdrive as the case may be, via a short universally jointed propeller shaft to the hypoid bevel drive gear of the three-quarter-floating rear axle, and by the half-shafts to the rear road wheels.

Braking is by an hydraulic disc/drum layout, and a servo is standard equipment on this model. Front brakes are of the calliper and disc design, rear brakes of the conventional leading and trailing shoe pattern.

Suspension is independent at the front, effected through coil springs and wishbone links. The upper links of this arrangement are formed by the arms of the double-acting hydraulic dampers. Rear suspension is by semi-elliptic leaf springs, which are damped by double-acting hydraulic shock absorbers.

Steering is by cam and peg type unit, and it should be noted that the ball joints fitted in the linkage layout on this chassis series are of the nylon seated pattern, and require no maintenance.

Identification of vehicles follows customary B.M.C. pattern, and is by car and engine numbers. The car number is to be found stamped on a plate, which is mounted on the bulkhead under the bonnet. Engine numbers are stamped on a metal plate, which is fixed to the left-hand side of the cylinder block. Other major components are numbered also, the gearbox number is stamped on the right-hand side of the gearcasing and the rear axle number is stamped on the rear of the axle tube, on the left-hand side, adjacent to the rebound rubber. It is essential that the car and engine numbers are quoted when referring to the manufacturers, or when ordering spare parts, together with any other unit numbers, which may be relevant to the inquiry.

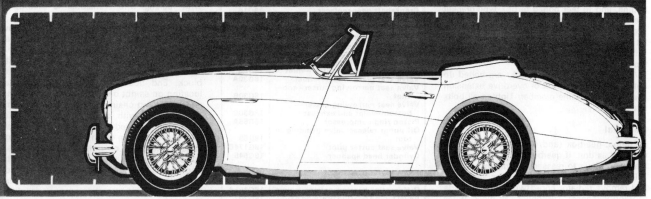

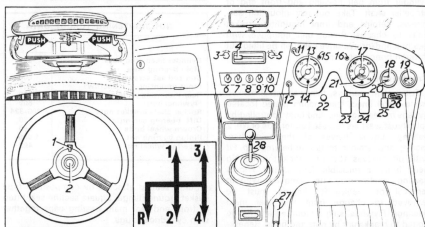

INSTRUMENTS, CONTROLS, GEAR POSITIONS AND BONNET LOCK

1. Direction indicator switch
2. Horn push
3. Air control knob
4. Heater blower motor switch and temp. control
5. Heater air control
6. Overdrive switch
7. Screenwiper switch
8. Ignition starter switch
9. Panel lights switch
10. Lighting switch
11. Choke control
12. Screenwasher control
13. Engine rpm indicator
14. Ignition warning light
15. L/h direction indicator warning light
16. R/h direction indicator warning light
17. Speedometer
18. Oil pressure gauge
19. Fuel gauge
20. Water temp. gauge
21. Headlamps main beam warning light
22. Headlamps dip switch
23. Clutch pedal
24. Brake pedal control
25. Accelerator pedal
26. Bonnet lock control
27. Handbrake
28. Gearlever

Inset upper, outer left: shows method of releasing the bonnet safety catches; below outer left: the siting of the steering wheel mounted controls; and inner left: the operative positions of the centre mounted gearlever

A range of special tools for speeding up many repair operations is marketed by the vehicle manufacturers through their dealer/distributorship network, and a list of those considered to be the more essential is included in these pages.

Threads and hexagons are, in the main, of the Unified thread series pattern and form, but in cases of doubt, it is always preferable to replace threaded parts as they were dismantled, taking care to renew those parts with stretched or damaged threads.

ENGINE

Mounting

At front, bonded rubber blocks bolted between bracket extensions from bosses on engine, and to feet bolted to box-type bracket welded to chassis side member. Additional right-angle brackets bolted up with inner brackets fitted on engine bosses, and carry smaller bonded rubber blocks at top (at right-angles to side mounting rubbers).

At rear, bonded rubber blocks are bolted up between either gearbox or overdrive extension casing and to frame member. Tighten all bolts and nuts fully.

Removal

Engine, gearbox (and/or overdrive) are best removed as unit. If gearbox is left in chassis, it may be difficult to reassemble engine.

Detach bonnet from hinges. Disconnect fan and remove radiator core (two bolts each side to wing valances). Disconnect all pipes, wires and controls, including rev. counter drive on near side, and remove carburettors, oil filter and distributor. Take weight of engine on slings behind front engine plate and below rear of bell-housing, or on lifting eyes on engine rocker cover, so that engine can be tilted sharply.

Remove metal cover over propeller shaft front joint, and detach gearbox cowl (Phillips screws to floor) and vertical scuttle plate. Disconnect overdrive wiring from solenoid and switches on off side of gearbox, also speedometer drive cable. Disconnect clutch slave cylinder from bell housing and front end of propeller shaft. Take out rear mounting setscrews, setpins and front mounting bracket bolts to chassis. Power unit complete with gearbox and/or overdrive can then be lifted out through bonnet opening.

Crankshaft

Four main bearings, thin-wall, steel-backed white-metal lined, lead-indium plated located by tabs in bearing caps. End float controlled by split thrust washers recessed either side of No. 2 bearing. Lower halves of thrust washers located and retained by tabs in bearing cap. Fit with oil grooves towards crank throws. No hand fitting permissible. Nos. 2 and 3 main bearing shells may be removed without removal of crankshaft; engine must be removed to change front and rear main bearings. Flywheel spigot mounted and flange bolted to crankshaft by nuts and bolts. Renewable bush pressed into crankshaft end, shrunk on starter ring gear fitted. Timing sprocket keyed to front end of crankshaft by Woodruff key; aligning shim abuts against inner boss of sprocket.

Renewable felt oil seal fitted into timing case cover. Dynamo and water pump drive pulley keyed to crankshaft by outer of two Woodruff keys. Oil thrower fitted between timing sprocket and pulley, torsional vibration damper in front, assembly retained by starter dog nut screw.

GENERAL DATA

Wheelbase	7ft 7$\frac{11}{16}$in
Track: front	4ft 0$\frac{3}{4}$in
rear	4ft 2in
Turning circle	35ft 7in
Ground clearance	4$\frac{1}{2}$in
Tyre size: front }	5·90—15
rear }	
Overall length	13ft 1$\frac{1}{2}$in
Overall width	5ft 0in
Overall height (hood raised)	4ft 2$\frac{1}{2}$in
Weight (dry)	2,380lb

SERVICE TOOLS

Description	Part No.
ENGINE	
Crankshaft gear and pulley remover	18G2
Crankshaft pulley replacer	18G16
Crankshaft gear replacer	18G16
Valve rocker bush remover and replacer	18G21
Valve seat cutter and pilot handle ..	18G27
Valve seat cutting tool fibre box ..	18G27B
Valve seat finishing cutter—exhaust	18G28
Valve seat glaze breaker—exhaust..	18G28A
Valve seat finishing cutter—inlet ..	18G30
Valve seat glaze breaker—inlet ..	18G30A
Valve seat narrowing cutter—top— inlet	18G30B
Valve seat narrowing cutter— bottom—inlet and exhaust ..	18G30C
Piston ring compressor	18G55A
Oil pump release valve grinding in tool	18G69
Valve seat cutter pilot	18G174D
Cylinder head spanner	18G545
TRANSMISSION	
Bevel pinion setting gauge	18G191
Differential bearing setting gauge	18G191A
Bevel pinion bearing pre-load gauge	18G207
Bevel pinion bearing outer race remover	18G264
Bevel pinion bearing outer race remover adaptor	18G264D
Adaptor for above	18G264H
REAR AXLE AND REAR SUSPENSION	
Bevel pinion inner race remover and replacer	18G285
Rear hub remover	18G304
Rear hub remover bolt adaptors (3)	18G304B
Rear hub remover thrust pad ..	18G304K
STEERING	
Steering arm remover	18G75A
Steering ball joint separator ..	18G125

NUT TIGHTENING TORQUE DATA

	lb in
Cylinder head stud nuts	900
Main bearing nuts	900
Con-rod set screws	600
Front mounting plate screws ..	200
Rear mounting plate screws ..	600
Flywheel bolts	600
Rocker shaft bracket nuts ..	300-324
Diff. bearing cap nuts	780
Crown wheel bolts	680
Pinion bearing nut	1,680
Steering wheel nut	492

Sump sealing effected by composition type gasket around flange. Square section seal fitted to front and rear main bearing caps together with cylindrical plugs.

Connecting rods

Big end bearings offset, thin-wall bearings steel backed, white metal lined, lead indium plated, located by tabs in caps and connecting rods. No hand fitting permissible. Big ends of H-section rods split horizontally for removal with piston through bores from top of engine. Gudgeon pins retained in small ends, by clamp bolts and retained by circlips in piston bosses. Tighten con-rod nuts to torque figures specified.

Pistons

Aluminium alloy, "T"-slotted with dished crowns. Oversizes available as in table of piston data; oversize dimensions marked on piston crowns. Gudgeon pin bores offset $\frac{1}{16}$in towards thrust side of pistons. Reassemble with slot in piston to non-thrust, i.e., nearside, fully floating gudgeon pins.

Top compression ring plain, second and third taper faced, and slotted scraper oil control ring all fitted above gudgeon pin.

Remove pistons with con-rods through cylinder bores, after removal of sump, etc., to gain access to con-rod bolts.

Camshaft

Double row roller, endless chain drive. Spring-loaded slipper type tensioner fitted to front engine plate by two bolts and secured with locking wire. Tensioner is secured for removal of timing chain by insertion of $\frac{1}{8}$in Allen key in tensioner body base after removal of plug cover, and engaging key in hole in base of cylinder helix.

Camshaft runs in four steel-backed white-metal lined bushes pressed into crankcase block. End float controlled by thrust plate locating on spigot on front end of shaft. When refitting timing chain and gears, set crankshaft and camshaft with keyways at approximately TDC when viewed from front. With "short" part of chain, when chain is doubled and bright links are together on right-hand side, engage camshaft sprocket tooth marked "T" with top bright link and crankshaft sprocket tooth marked with dimple with other bright link. Press on sprockets retaining their positions relative to their respective shafts.

Valves

Overhead, non-interchangeable, inlet large and of different face angle than exhaust. Split cone cotter fixing, retained by spring clips. Rubber sealing rings with retainer on valve stems below collars. Valve guides plain chamfered at each end, no shoulder, non interchangeable; exhaust guides counterbored at lower ends, and both types countersunk at top. Guides should be driven out and new guides inserted from top until upper end project $\frac{7}{8}$in from machined surface of spring seat.

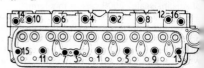

Correct sequence for tightening cylinder head nuts

Tappets and rockers

Shouldered barrel tappets sliding direct in crankcase. Access through plates in crankcase. Bushed rockers all interchangeable, work on hollow shaft carried in six pillars mounted on cylinder head. Oil is fed to rocker shaft from drillings in head and piped to No. 4 shaft pillar whence oil is delivered to each rocker through shaft drillings. Pairs of rockers for each cylinder are located either side of mounting pillars separating springs between rockers of adjacent cylinders.

Push rods can be removed after adjustment has been slackened right off. Inner rockers can be pulled aside against separate springs. End rockers may be taken off after removal of split pin, plain washer and double-coil spring washer. Note: Valve springs must be compressed before rockers can be pulled aside.

Lubrication

Gear type pump spigoted and flange bolted to bottom face and towards rear of crankcase.

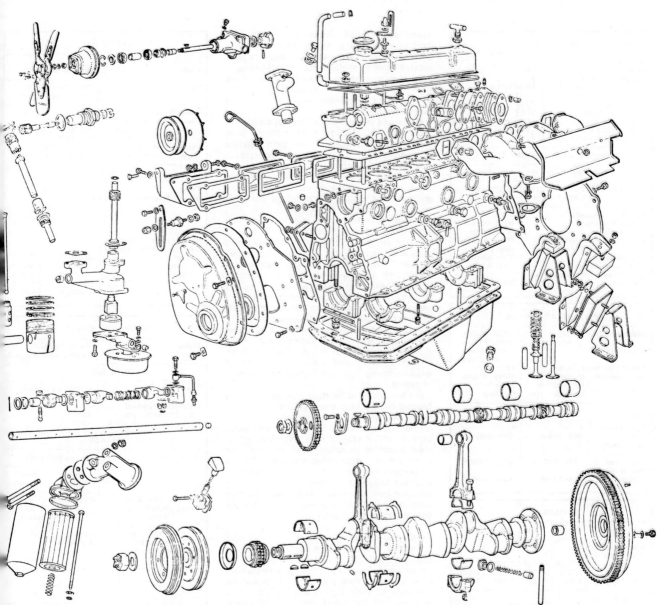

driven by slotted shaft and skew gear from rear of two gears of camshaft. Pump may be removed after taking off sump and pick-up strainer and three securing nuts. Oil pump cover gears, and driving shaft may be removed after taking out four bolts securing endplate and strainer flange pipe to pump body. Gauze intake strainer in sump.

Normal running pressure is 50lb/sq in (3·52kg/cm²) and 20lb/sq in (1·4kg/cm²) should be shown when engine is idling.

Cooling system

Pump, fan, non-adjustable bellows type thermostat retained in water outlet elbow in cylinder head. Pump spindle runs in two ball bearings and has renewable seal. Adjust fan belt until there is $\frac{1}{2}$in movement either way in vertical run of belt.

TRANSMISSION

Clutch

On later cars from Eng. No. 29F/4898, a diaphragm clutch is fitted. This unit is hydraulically operated by slave cylinder from master cylinder.

Access to clutch unit for service is obtained after removal of gearbox. No provision for pedal adjustment in service.

Gearbox

Four-speed, synchromesh on upper three ratios, central, remote control lever fitted. Overdrive, of Laycock de-Normanville pattern, fitted as optional equipment, is operative on 3rd and top gears. For full constructional details of this unit, readers are referred to Service Supplement No. 226/C1.

To remove gearbox and overdrive

Gearbox and/or overdrive unit may be removed from chassis separately from engine, or engine/gearbox and overdrive may be removed as detailed in engine "removal" section. Complete power unit/gearbox removal is to be preferred.

To dismantle gearbox

With gearbox on bench or in suitable cradle, unscrew eight short bolts and one long bolt and remove bellhousing complete with clutch operating mechanism. Take off drive gear bearing plain and spring plates. Remove oil level indicator from gearbox top cover, unscrew and remove 12 bolts, and take off cover. Note that two cover securing screws nearest gearchange lever turret are longer than rest, and ensure that detent springs (three) posi-

SHOCK ABSORBERS		
Make		Armstrong
Type		lever hydraulic
Service		replacement

STEERING BOX		
Make		Cam Gears
Type		cam and peg
Adjustments:		
column end float	}	shims
cross shaft end float		
mesh		grubscrew and locknut

FRONT-END SERVICE DATA		
Castor		2°
Camber		1°
King pin inclination ..		6½°
Toe-in		$\frac{1}{16}$-$\frac{1}{8}$in
No. of turns lock to lock ..		2¾ (approx.)
Adjustments: castor	}	Nil
camber		
toe-in ..		screwed track rod ends

Component	Model	Part No.
Battery (dry charged, export)	BTZ9A	
Steering column control (Fixed column) ..	CC1	33517
Radex reflector (Export Germany & Sweden)	RER14	57083
Starter solenoid switch (Earlier fitment) ..	28T	76464

ENGINE DATA	
General	
Type	29K
No. of cylinders	6
Bore × stroke: mm ..	83·34 × 88·9
in ..	3·281 × 3·50
Capacity: cc	2,912
cu in	177·7
Max. bmep at rpm ..	142lb/sq in at 2,700
Max. torque at rpm ..	167lb ft at 2,700
Compression ratio ..	9 : 1

CRANKSHAFT AND CON. RODS

	Main Bearings	Crankpins
Diameter ..	2·3742-2·3747in	2·0000-2·0005in
Length ..	1·495-1·505in	—

Running clearance:	
main bearings	·0013-·0028in
big ends	·002-·0035in
End float: main bearings ..	·0025-·0055in
big ends	·005-·009in
Undersizes	·010, ·020in
Con. rod centres	6·601-6·60in
No. of teeth on starter gear/ pinion	106/10

PISTONS AND RINGS

Clearance (skirt): top	·0032-·0043in
bottom ..	·0010-·0016in
Oversizes	+·010, ·020, ·030, ·040in
Weight without rings or pin ..	15oz 10dr
Gudgeon pin: diameter ..	·8748-·8750in
fit in piston ..	push fit
fit in con. rod	floating

	Compression	Oil Control
No. of rings	3	1
Gap	·009-·014in	·009-·014in
Side clear- ance in grooves ..	·0015-·0035in	·0015-·0035in
Width of rings ..	·125-·138in	·125-·138in

CAMSHAFT

	No. 1	No. 2	No. 3	No. 4
Bearing journal dia- meter (in)	1·7887-1·7892	1·7687-1·7692	1·7487-1·7492	1·7287-1·7292
length (in)	1·50	1·187	1·187	1·25

Bearing clearance	·001-·002in
End float	·003-·006in
Timing chain:	
pitch	·375in
No. of links	62

VALVES

	Inlet	Exhaust
Head diameter	1·750-1·745in	1·562-1·557in
Stem diameter	·341-·342in	·341-·342in
Face-angle	45°	45°
Seat face width	·091-·097in	·198-·217in

	Inner	Outer
Spring length:		
free	1·069in	2·047in
fitted	1·504in	1·594in
at load	26lb	55·7lb

tioned in gearbox casing under cover front edge are preserved.

To remove change speed lever from top cover, release circlip, washer and conical spring from lever turret. With small dia. punch drive two roll pins in turn into the $\frac{3}{16}$in holes on each side of lever turret. This will cause them to move into bore of lever ball, lift out lever and retrieve roll pins from ball end. Remove three detent springs, cut locking wire and remove striking fork retaining screws. Hold shifter shafts in neutral position (preventing interlock balls from operating) and withdraw 3rd and 4th speed shifter shaft, retrieving detent ball. Withdraw remaining shifter shafts, similarly preserving detent balls, and two interlock balls located between shafts at front end of casing.

To remove reverse selector plunger from reverse striking fork, extract split pin, releasing plunger and spring which, in turn, will release a detent plunger and spring.

Undo and remove propeller shaft flange nut (tool No. 18G34A) to prevent flange from turning, and withdraw flange from gearbox mainshaft splines. Unscrew speedometer pinion housing from gearbox extension casing, and remove it complete with pinion. Unscrew eight bolts, and take off rear extension casing from gearbox main casing, and withdraw mainshaft bearing plain and spring washers.

If gearbox is fitted with overdrive, unscrew eight nuts securing adaptor plate to rear of gearbox. Do not disturb joint between adaptor plate and overdrive, pull both away from gear-box and over mainshaft. Slide overdrive oil pump cam off mainshaft, exposing bearing distance collar and circlip, which may be left *in situ*. If, when dismantling mainshaft assembly, it is required to remove mainshaft bearing from shaft, it will be necessary to with-draw circlip and distance collar first. Unscrew reverse idler gear shaft locating screw, with-draw shaft and lift out reverse idler gear. Push layshaft forwards, and remove it from front of gearbox casing, lowering laygear onto bottom of casing.

Mark position of locating peg on mainshaft bearing relative to gearbox casing, so that on reassembly peg may be correctly aligned to locate in hole provided for it in rear extension, or in overdrive adaptor plate. Withdraw main-shaft assembly complete from gearbox from rear, for further dismantling if required. Extract 18 needle roller bearings from rear of drive gear, and with suitable brass drift, drive out bearing forwards from its housing, and draw drive gear assembly from front of gearbox casing. Lift out laygear and thrust washers.

To dismantle mainshaft

Remove items in following order: slide off top 3rd gear hub and interceptors from forward end. Depress plunger locating 3rd gear locking plate, rotate plate to line up splines, and slide off shaft. Extract plunger and spring and slide off 3rd speed gear with 32 rollers. Remove the small circlip retaining rear bearing to the mainshaft and press off bearing complete with locating plate and spacer. Slide off 1st/2nd speed hub, 2nd speed interceptor and 1st gear rearwards from shaft. If 1st gear is withdrawn from its hub take care to preserve balls and springs located in radial drillings in hub. Depress 2nd gear locking collar plunger and rotate collar to line up splines; slide collar from shaft and extract two halves of 2nd gear washer, retaining spring and plunger. Take off 2nd speed gear, together with 33 rollers. To dismantle primary shaft assembly, turn up lock-tab, unscrew nut and remove bearing.

To reassemble gearbox

Reverse dismantling procedure, noting following points. Fit spacer to laygear unit, with washer positioned at each end. Smear needle rollers with thick grease, and insert them in ends of laygear unit (23 each end). Assemble layshaft front and rear thrust washers and plates, position them in gearbox, tags engaging in grooves in gearcasing. Place lay-gear in box. Assemble drive gear and bearing, together with needle rollers and insert in box. Fit mainshaft assembly from rear end of box ensuring that sliding dog and interceptors are in position on 3rd/4th synchronising hub. Align mainshaft bearing housing locating peg with marks made on gearbox casing when unit

CHASSIS DATA	
Clutch	
Make	Borg & Beck
Type	From Eng. No. 29F/ 4898 diaphragm
Diameter: No	9in
Damper springs: No ..	6
colour	maroon/lt. green
load ..	110-120lb
Facing material	wound yarn
Clutch release bearing	Graphite (MY3D)

GEARBOX

Type	synchromesh
No. of forward speeds	4

		From Eng. No. 11342
Final ratios (Standard box with 3·545 : 1 axle)		
1st	10·386 : 1	10·209 : 1
2nd	7·877 : 1	7·302 : 1
3rd	4·640 : 1	4·743 : 1
4th	3·645 : 1	3·545 : 1
Rev.	13·400 : 1	13·127 : 1

PROPELLER SHAFT

Make	Hardy Spicer
Type	Needle roller brg. U.J.

FINAL DRIVE

Type	$\frac{3}{4}$-floating hypoid bevel
Crownwheel/bevel pinion teeth: std.	39/11
o'drive	43/11

BRAKES

Type	Girling hydraulic

	Front (disc)	Rear (drum)
Drum or disc diameter	11$\frac{1}{4}$in	11in
Lining: length	—	10·53in
width	—	2$\frac{1}{4}$in
(or disc pad) thickness ..	13/32in	·187in
pad area ..	4·25sq in	—
Frictional area (rear only)	—	95sq in

SPRINGS

	Front	Rear
Length (eye centres, laden)	—	36 ± $\frac{1}{8}$in
Width (or wire dia. of coils)	·531in	1$\frac{3}{4}$in
Mean dia. of coil springs	4·125in	—
No. of leaves (or coils)	7	7
Free camber (length, coil)	11·82in	4in
Loaded camber (length, coil) at load	7·375in@ 1040lb	$\frac{1}{2}$ ± $\frac{1}{8}$in neg.

was dismantled, press bearing into positior Lift laygear unit in position, insert layshaft fro front end of box, lining up thrust washers an needle rollers. Insert reverse idler gear. Wit non-overdrive box, fit mainshaft bearing plai and spring plates, with the plain plate agains bearing. Bolt gearbox rear extension int position, ensuring that rear bearing washer in position on mainshaft. Screw in speed pinion and housing. Push propeller shaft flang onto mainshaft splines, securing it with nu and washer (tool No. 18G34A).

Insert the three gear striking forks in positio Replace reverse gear shifter shaft, securing to reverse gear striking fork, making sure th dowelled end of locating screw engages wi hole in shaft. Place shifter shaft interlock ball i position between reverse gear and 1st/2n speed shifter shaft bores, at front of gearbc casing. With reverse striking fork in neutr position, insert 1st and 2nd speed shifter sha

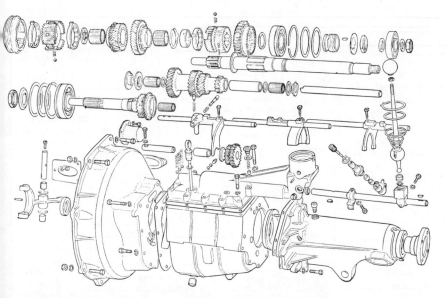

noting that shaft has an interlock pin. Fit fork locating screw, place second interlock ball in position, between 1st and 2nd speed gear and 3rd and 4th gear and the 3rd and 4th speed gear shifter shaft bores.

With 1st and 2nd speed gear striking fork in neutral position insert 3rd/4th gear shifter shaft, and fit fork locating screw. Tighten all three fork locating screws and secure with new locking wire. Refit change speed lever to gearbox top cover, and place shifter shaft detent balls into respective bores, refit top cover, locating remote control selector rod arm in striking forks, refit oil level indicator.

Turn layshaft so that stepped end engages groove in bellhousing. Position drive gear bearing plain and spring plates in recess in rear face of bellhousing (plain plate to bearing), and refit bellhousing to gearbox, ensuring that oil seal on primary shaft splines is not damaged.

Rear axle

Three-quarter floating hypoid bevel drive, rear cover welded to banjo-type housing.

To remove axle unit from car, jack up and support chassis frame side members on stands and remove rear wheels. Undo four self-locking nuts and remove bolts securing propeller shaft and pinion flanges. Disconnect handbrake cable from axle tubes by unscrewing it from link on balance lever and nut from outer casing to axle. Detach brake fluid pipes at unions and shock absorbers from links on mounting brackets. Remove self-locking nuts from "U" bolts, preserve fibre pad between axle and springs for replacement. Disconnect anti-sway bar, and with axle free, shock absorber connecting links. Remove rubber block between axle and N/S chassis frame. Axle unit may then be drawn out to off side.

Differential unit and axle should not be serviced without stock of distance-pieces and gauges. Replacement units available.

CHASSIS

Brakes

Girling hydraulic servo-assisted. Calliper and disc arrangement on front wheels, leading and trailing shoe drum brakes at rear. Front brakes are self-adjusting. Rear brake cylinders carry also wedge expanders operated by centre positioned handbrake through cable from compensator on axle.

To renew front disc brake pads, jack up car and remove road wheels. Take off spring clips locking pad retaining pins in position and take out pads. Push piston assemblies back, with suitable lever, insert new pads, refit retaining pins and spring clips.

Square ended adjusters for rear brakes. Tighten and back off two clicks, then apply brake hard to centralise shoes. No need to jack up rear wheels.

No separate adjustment for handbrake.

Rear springs

Semi-elliptic. Three zinc interleaves between upper leaves. Silentbloc bushes in spring eyes.

Sundry Equipment	Model	Part No.
Battery Master	ST330	76604
Switches	Model	Part No.
Auxiliary (overdrive not fitted)	65SA	31828
Transmission Units		
LAYCOCK		
Control switch	65SA	31828
Transmission gear solenoid	11S	76525
Rotary throttle switch	RTS1	31402
Interruption switch ..	SS10	
Relay	6AR	33213

Frame shackles brackets have flanged bronze bushes, and pins are shouldered. Nut and spring washer fit on outside, self-locking nut on inside.

Lateral link anchored in rubber between chassis frame on off side and axle bracket on near side.

Front suspension

Independent. Coil springs and double wishbone links. Inner ends of upper links pivoted on shock absorbers. Outer ends of upper links and inner ends of lower links rubber bushed. Outer ends of lower links have screwed bushes. Anti-roll bar linked to brackets bolted to front arms of lower links with spring plates.

Hubs run on taper roller self-adjusting bearings. Inner races separated by cast-iron distance-piece. Lipped oil seal pressed in behind inner bearing, lip to bearing. Tighten stub axle nuts fully (40-70lb ft).

Relay arm shaft pivoted in bracket attached to chassis frame by three set-screws inserted from outside. Shaft has flange at top, fitting in recess, and works in two plain bushes. Retaining cap flange-bolted to top of bracket with joint washer.

Steering ball points are nylon seat, sealed-for-life pattern. No maintenance required. Joints on side sections are integral with tubes.

Steering gear

Bishop cam and lever. Provision made for adjustment of inner column and cam end float by shims between lower ball race cup and cover plate; mesh of peg in cam adjusted by grub screw and locknut in top cover.

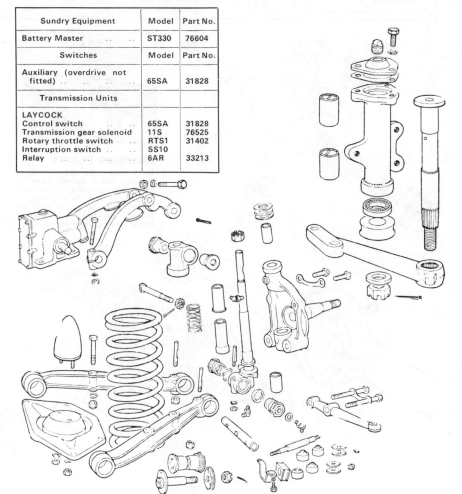

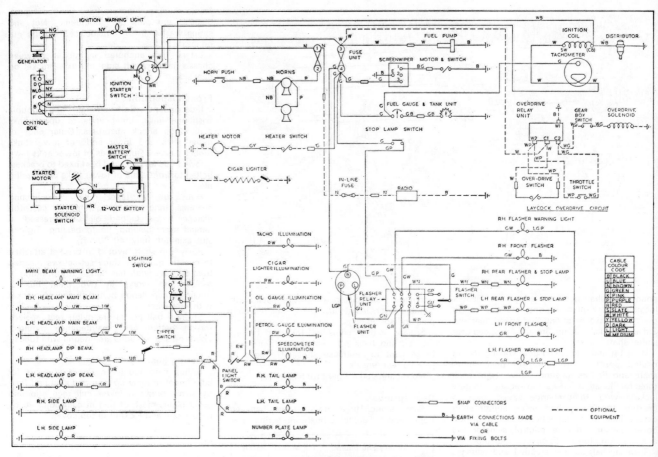

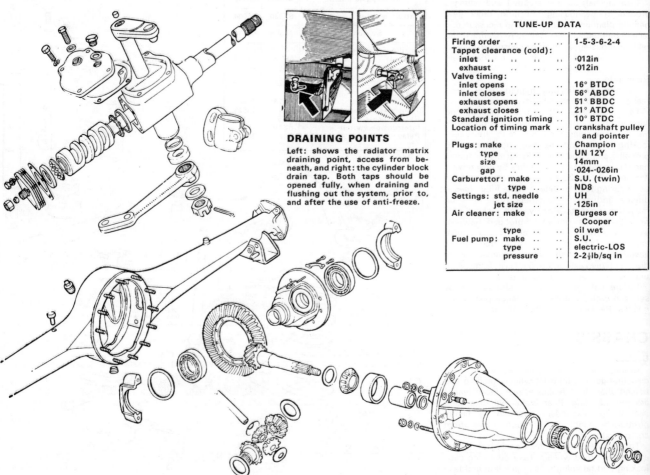

DRAINING POINTS

Left: shows the radiator matrix draining point, access from beneath, and right: the cylinder block drain tap. Both taps should be opened fully, when draining and flushing out the system, prior to, and after the use of anti-freeze.

TUNE-UP DATA		
Firing order		1-5-3-6-2-4
Tappet clearance (cold):		
inlet		·012in
exhaust		·012in
Valve timing:		
inlet opens		16° BTDC
inlet closes		56° ABDC
exhaust opens ..		51° BBDC
exhaust closes ..		21° ATDC
Standard ignition timing ..		10° BTDC
Location of timing mark ..		crankshaft pulley
		and pointer
Plugs: make		Champion
type		UN 12Y
size		14mm
gap		·024-·026in
Carburettor: make ..		S.U. (twin)
type ..		ND8
Settings: std. needle ..		UH
jet size ..		·125in
Air cleaner: make ..		Burgess or
		Cooper
type ..		oil wet
Fuel pump: make ..		S.U.
type ..		electric-LOS
pressure ..		2-2½lb/sq in

FILL-UP DATA

	Pints	Litres
Engine sump (including filter)	12¾	7·25
Gearbox	5¾	3·27
Overdrive	1½	·76
Rear axle	3	1·7
Cooling system ..	19	10·78
Fuel tank	12 galls.	54·6
Tyre pressures		
front	20lb/sq in	1·41kg/cm²
rear	25lb/sq in	1·76kg/cm²

Sundry Equipment	Model	Part No.
Suppressor (U.K. & Germany)	WS5	78106
*Reflex reflectors	RER25	57125
Flasher relay	DB10	33117

Switches	Model	Part No.
Ignition/starter	47SA	31973
*Starter solenoid	2ST	76471
Lighting	57SA	31837
Dip	103SA	34536
Stop light	HL2	31882
Panel light	65SA	31828
Wiper	57SA	34426
*Steering column control (adjustable column) ..	CC1	32984

*See also Addenda

LUCAS EQUIPMENT

*BATTERY
Model BT9A
GENERATOR
Model C42 — Part No. 22900
CONTROL BOX
Model RB340 — Part No. 37331
STARTING MOTOR
Model M418G — Part No. 25578
Drive S-Type Inboard
DISTRIBUTOR
Model 25D6 — Part No. 40966
Max. centrifugal advance (crank degrees) 34-38 at 3,200 rev. min.
No advance below 300rpm.
Centrifugal advance springs. Part No. 54416660
Max. vacuum advance (crank degrees) 14°-18° at 15in Hg
No advance below 2½in Hg.
IGNITION COIL
Model HA12 — Part No. 45102
Primary resistance 3·0-3·5 ohms.
Running current at 1,000 rpm 1·0 amp.
WINDSCREEN WIPER
Model DR3A — Part No. 75456
HORN(S)
Model 9H — Part No(s) 54068008 High Note
Part No(s) 54068009 Low Note
Type: Windtone
Current consumption 3·0-3·5 amp. (per horn).
FLASHER UNIT
Model FL5 — Part No. 35020
FUSE UNIT
Model 4FJ
Fuse ratings: 35 amp.
35 amp.

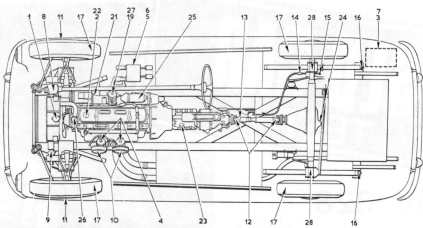

KEY TO MAINTENANCE DIAGRAM

DAILY
1. Radiator ⎱ check and top up
2. Engine sump ⎰

WEEKLY
3. Battery—check and top up

EVERY 3,000 MILES
4. Carburettor piston dampers
5. Clutch supply tank
6. Brake supply tank
7. Battery ⎱ check and top up
8. Steering box ⎰
9. Steering idler box
10. Carburettor air cleaners—clean and re-oil
11. Brakes—check and adjust, inspect disc pads
12. Propeller shaft universal joints
13. Propeller shaft sliding joint ⎱ grease gun
14. Handbrake cable
15. Handbrake compensator
16. Rear spring shackles
17. Tyre pressures—check

EVERY 6,000 MILES (as for 3,000 miles plus following):

18. *Valve rocker clearances—adjust
19. Distributor—oil shaft bearing, auto. advance mechanism smear cam with grease
20. *Front wheel alignment—check
21. Dynamo end bearing—oil can
22. Engine sump—drain and refill
23. Gearbox ⎱ check and top up
24. Rear axle ⎰
25. Engine oil filter element—renew

EVERY 9,000 MILES (as for 3,000 miles)

EVERY 12,000 MILES (as for 6,000 miles plus following):

26. Water pump—lubricate sparingly with grease
27. Distributor drive shaft—half turn of grease cap
28. Rear road spring seat bolts—check for tightness
*Not shown on diagram

Lamps	Model	Part No.	Bulb		
			Lucas No.	Wattage	Cap
Head (Home)	F700	51956	414	50/40	BPF
Head (LHD Dip Right)	F700	51966	355	42/36	BPF
Head (Export U.S.A. and Canada) ..	F700	58626	—	—	—
Head (Export France)	F700	58291	411	45/40	Unified European
Head (Export Sweden)	F700	58463	410	45/40	Unified European
Head (Export Europe)	F700	58290	410	45/40	Unified European
*Side flasher	594	52338	380	6/21	SBC
Rear flasher	594	53564	380	6/21	SBC
Number plate	467	53836	989	6	MCC
Ignition warning (bulbholder) ..	—	319408	987	2·2	MES
Main beam warning (bulbholder) ..	—	319408	987	2·2	MES
Flasher warning (bulbholder) ..	—	863511	987	2·2	MES

*See also Addenda

ADDENDA					
Lamp	Model	Part No.	Bulb		
			Lucas No.	Wattage	Cap
Side (Export Germany & Sweden)	594	52391	207	6	SCC
Front flasher (Germany & Sweden)	594	52337	382	21	SCC

RECOMMENDED LUBRICANTS

	CASTROL	ESSO	B.P.	DUCKHAM'S	MOBIL	SHELL	FILTRATE	STERNOL
Engine: All temperatures above 0°F (18°C), and Gearbox	Castrolite	Extra Motor Oil	Energol Visco-Static	Q5500	Mobiloil Special	X-100 Multigrade 10W/30	10W/30 Multigrade	Multiplic
Rear axle and steering and idler box (a)	Castrol Hypoy	Gear Oil GP 90	Energol SAE 90EP	Hypoid 90	Mobilube GX 90	Spirax 90 EP	Hypoid Gear 90	Ambroleum EP 90
Water pump and Grease points	Castrolease LM	Multi-purpose Grease H	Energrease L2	L.B. 10 Grease	Mobilgrease MP	Retinax A	Super Lithium Grease	Ambroline LHT
Oil can. SU carb. dashpot	Castrolite	Extra Motor Oil	Energol Visco-Static	Q5500	Mobiloil Special	X-100 Multigrade 10W/30	10W/30 Multigrade	Multiplic
Upper cylinder lubricant	Castrollo	Upper Cylinder Lubricant	Energol UCL	Adcoid Liquid	Upperlube	Upper Cylinder Lubricant	Petroyl	Magikoyl

(a) Rear axle and steering: For temperature below 10°F use SAE 80 Hypoid lubricant. Hydraulic brakes and clutch: Girling Crimson Brake Fluid. Shock absorbers: Armstrong Super (thin) Shock Absorber Fluid.

Note: MULTIGRADE OILS. In addition to the above recommendations, is approved the use of multigrade oil produced by the companies shown, for all climatic temperatures unless the engine is old or worn.

USED CAR TEST

No. 328

1964 Austin-Healey 3000 Mk III

PRICES

Car for sale at Sheffield at	£575
Typical trade value for same age and model in average condition	£430
Total cost of car when new including tax	£1,185
Depreciation over 7 years	£755
Annual depreciation as proportion of cost new	9 per cent

DATA

Date first registered	12 November 1964
Number of owners	4
Tax expires	30 November 1971
MoT	10 August 1972
Fuel consumption	1 9-22 mpg
Oil consumption	55 miles per pint
Mileometer reading	63,425

PERFORMANCE CHECK

(Figures in brackets are those of the original Road Test, published 12 June 1964)

0 to 30 mph	**4.5** sec.	(3.4)
0 to 40 mph	**6.6** sec	(4.8)
0 to 50 mph	**10.1** sec	(7.0)
0 to 60 mph	**13.6** sec	(9.8)
0 to 70 mph	**17.1** sec	(12.8)
0 to 80 mph	**22.1** sec	(16.2)
0 to 90 mph	**27.4** sec	(21.1)
0 to 110 mph	**—** sec	(35.3)
In top gear:		
10 to 30 mph	**9.6** sec	(—)
20 to 40 mph	**7.8** sec	(7.5)
30 to 50 mph	**7.6** sec	(6.8)
40 to 60 mph	**8.4** sec	(6.9)
50 to 70 mph	**Ω3** sec	(7.9)
60 to 80 mph	**9.6** sec	(8.1)
70 to 90 mph	**10.5** sec	(9.0)
80 to 100 mph	**15.2** sec	(9.9)
Standing ¼ mile	**18.8** sec	(17.2)
Standing km	**32.7** sec	(—)

TYRES

Size: 165SR-15 Pirelli Cinturato tubed. Approx. cost per replacement cover £13.85. Depth of original tread 9mm; remaining tread depth, 8mm right front, 5mm left front, 3mm on back and 7mm on spare.

TOOLS

Jack and wheelbrace only; no handbook

CAR FOR SALE AT:

A. B. Gelder Automobiles, 247-249, London Road, Sheffield, Yorkshire. Tel: Sheffield 53226.

Fog and spot lamps, a parking lamp, badge bar and wireless are among the obvious extra items fitted to the car, which however needs considerable restoration. Extensions have been fitted to the important switches. Underbonnet appearance, like that of the rest of the car at the time of the test, awaited the promised attention of the vendors

SEVEN years ago (in our issue of 12 June 1964 to be exact) we were not too impressed with the Mk III Austin-Healey 3000. The Road Test began with a mention of the "world of difference between those frequent winners, the former Spartan works rally cars and the over-the-counter product of today"; readers will remember the tremendous International rally successes of the red-and-white BMC works team cars, truly "hairy" machines that greatly endeared themselves to the braver drivers, like Timo Makinen and Rauno Aaltonen. Today, possibly because of those rally stories, an increasingly golden glow seems to surround the various models, as far as some sorts of car buyer are concerned. It was interesting to try one well-used example of what a 1971 "big Healey" enthusiast might start with.

Although this particular one, as explained under the Condition Summary, has suffered perhaps unusually badly from a long lay-up in obviously less-than-ideal conditions, there is still about enough of the car's original performance to make it enjoyable to drive, and encouraging enough for the man who intends to restore the car fully. From an admittedly kinder standing start than the original Road Test one, 0–60mph comes up in 13.7sec instead of 9.8sec, the ¼-mile in 18.8sec instead of 17.2, and 100mph in 36.7 instead of 25.7sec. With its still very smoothly engaging "overdrive"—really an electrically selected top gear, as on overdrive cars a lower final drive ratio was fitted—the car will still cruise at a comfortable 90mph, at 3,900 rpm; the word "comfortable" applies to the engine speed rather than to the driver's ears, which must put up with a fair amount of intake and exhaust noise which grows a little tiring on a long run.

Overdrive works on third and top, giving in effect a six-speed gearbox; as a matter of interest speeds in each gear in the original Road Test were 43 (1st), 52 (2nd), 83 (3rd), 104 (o.d.3rd), 111 (top), and 121mph mean (o.d. top). These figures illustrate the pointlessly low ratio'd 2nd gear and the welcome fact that overdrive 3rd, is, for once, not coincident with direct top. The gearbox itself appears to be in good order; the gearchange is very precise,

The battery, which appeared to be fairly new, needed fixing down in the boot. A battery master switch is standard equipment, and is one way of preventing theft

synchromesh (on all but bottom gear) is still good, and there is only a small oil leak from the tailshaft seal underneath.

The engine, with 63,000-odd miles on the mileometer, is not so good. Oil consumption on the 1964 test car was not too economical at 200 miles per pint, but on this car it is down to 55 miles per pint. Most of that seems to go down the exhaust pipes if one accelerates away again after any slowing-down, due probably to oil mist sucked up past the piston rings and down the valve guides. As on the original car, one is strongly reminded of some Vintage period machines, with little between the engine compartment and the cockpit; at all times the amount of engine heat that comes in past one's legs makes one think that the heater has been left on, and on acceleration one notices the characteristic smell of crankcase fumes due to piston blow-by. Tickover has always been lumpy on these cars, but popping and banging in the exhaust on over-run on this car, which developed during the short test period, suggests that exhaust valves are perhaps not sealing properly. Fuel consumption remains

about what one would expect.

The cam-and-peg steering never was as precise as one would wish. This example has now developed around 3in. of slop at the big-diameter steering wheel rim. The car needs a little learning in this respect, as it tends to wander somewhat particularly over poorer roads which its correspondingly poor ride does little to disguise. The vacuum servo Girling disc-drum brakes are still powerful enough for the performance for ordinary purposes; the handbrake works well, but there is some pulling to the right when slowing down at speed. A noticeable amount of pitching and screwing, seemingly at the front end, betrays dampers that have lost their virtue to varying extents at each corner of the car.

Condition Summary
Bodywork

DWE 933 B has had four owners since first registered on 12 November 1964. According to the sellers, the last owner laid the car up for 18 months, though not it would seem in a properly

ventilated dry place. As a result, some unusually deep corrosion has occurred in many places; the vendors had not been able to set matters right before we borrowed the car, but assure us that they are doing so before it will be offered for sale.

Underneath the car, underbody compound probably applied early in its life has flaked disturbingly in several places, exposing rusting or else allowing rust to take hold. On the right hand side the box member under the body sills behind the front wheel arch has lost much of its bottom part due to rust. Farther back it has been glass-fibre'd, probably quite recently. Other recent attention includes new underbody sealer applied along the sills and under the tail, and the fitting of a pretty sound-looking exhaust system; Austin-Healey 3000 exhausts need to be stronger than most, as they are very close to the ground.

Suspension and steering parts are heavily corroded both under the car and under the bonnet; the latter has to be raised carefully, as it frequently fouls at its back edge. Other items which have suffered from the long "lay-up" include the two Lucas extra lamps whose reflectors have corroded at the bottom, and the body of the brake servo. Pimpling is lifting the recent re-spray over the right front wheel arch, but the car is to be stripped and re-sprayed properly before sale. One can smell previously damp upholstery as one gets into the car. The hood is however quite good, though needing a new back window panel; the old one is a little obscured now. The driver's wind-up window mechanism needs some attention.

Equipment

The comprehensive instrumentation still works, but the offside headlamp bulb gives only a cheerful red glow, the additional parking lamp does not light, and the winkers do not self-cancel. A pair of Maserati air horns are fitted, but pressing the horn button produces an inconspicuous beep that is not their normal voice. The battery needs fixing down properly again.

Accessories

A Philips radio is in good order, though it is only reasonably audible at low speed or in a traffic jam. A flexible map lamp is fitted, and that most sensible extra instrument, an ammeter.

ABOUT THE AUSTIN-HEALEY 3000

The very attractively shaped Austin-Healey 100 first appeared at the 1952 Motor Show, using the 2.6-litre four-cylinder engine from the Austin A.90 Atlantic; in fact it was called the "Healey Hundred" at the start, becoming the Austin-Healey 100 only a little later when Austin collaborated to produce the car. In 1956 the six-cylinder Austin Westminster unit was fitted, beginning the transformation of the car from an out-and-out sports car to something a little more refined. The Mk II 3000 2.9-litre came in 1961, having triple SUs and a new camshaft and stronger valve springs. In 1962 the two-seater was discontinued, leaving the "2/4"-seater sports convertible, which had wind-up windows, swivelling quarter lights, a curved windscreen, twin SUs, and a shorter gearlever. The Mk III was introduced early in 1964, having more power, servo brakes, a locking glove box, wood veneer facia and the gearlever in the centre console. This was continued with little change up to January 1968 when the final production car was superseded by the short-lived MGC (itself introduced the previous year). ☐.

PROFILE

Austin-Healey 3000

The last of the Big Healeys: you can tell a late Mark III 3000 by the badging and the separate trafficators

THE BIG HEALEY

Charismatic, powerful and stylish, the Austin-Healey 3000 is a much loved British sports car which also did well in competition. Mark Gillies records the car's history, assesses its qualities, and offers advice to today's buyers

If any present day motor manufacturer was to produce a sports car with a macho image, elegant styling, and a big, lusty, six-cylinder engine of around 3-litres capacity, there would be little doubt that the press and public would dub it the new Big Healey. After all, that's what happened to the Datsun 240Z, another example of the he-man's sports car.

There is little chance of any modern motor manufacturer producing such a sports touring car today, as the concept has died. It was dying towards the end of the Austin-Healey 3000's life in 1967, when the car was seen as unrefined and old-fashioned, a distinct contrast to the rave reviews which had greeted the model on its introduction in 1959. There are no true sports tourers now, for today's Morgan 4/4 lacks the power to make it a true hood down tourer in the grand manner.

The subject of this profile, the Healey 3000, is

regarded by most enthusiasts as the archetyp Healey, the machine which was to be seen bein hurled down forest tracks with Timo Makinen at th wheel, or the car in which the Morley brothers coul drive at breakneck speeds for days on end over th bone-shaking roads that made up the Tulip Rally. Fo the ordinary driver, it held the promise of ope 120mph motoring for hours on end. It was the perfec car for the long continental drive or the motorin holiday round Britain, with looks and handling match its other undoubted qualities. In short, th Healey 3000 is a car with charisma, an attribute that few cars genuinely possess.

The 3000 story dates from well before i introduction in 1959. It is the direct successor to th Austin-Healey 100/4 and 100-Six, all of which owe their genesis to the vision and skill of Donald Mitche Healey.

Before the war, Donald Healey had been technic director at Triumph and was responsible for th Gloria range, and, more notoriously, for the fabulo and unsuccessful straight-eight supercharged Dol mite model. After the war, he set up the Dona Healey Motor Company Ltd to produce a sports c capable of 100mph in the mould of the pre-wa 4½-litre low chassis Invicta, but smaller in size an with better handling. This was the Healey 2. powered by the 2½-litre Riley engine and available a variety of body styles. Although fast (a saloc version covered the flying mile at 104.6mph in 1946) proved expensive, as did the Healeys produced wit Alvis and (for the American market) Nash units. 1952, an open Healey cost a whopping £2490, son £800 more than an open Jaguar XK 120.

The economical 100/4

By 1952, Healey recognised the need for a cheap alternative, to cater for the large and growing U sports car market. 'I wanted to produce a very fas everyday road car with genuine sporting character tics, capable of 100mph, which would be exception ly cheap to buy and economical to maintain.' This w the philosophy behind the Healey 100/4.

This car's chassis was to become the basis for subsequent Healeys, so it is important to deal with th model. Following an approach to Austin's Leona Lord about replacing the Riley unit with the A engine, this 2660cc ohv 'four' was mated to an A gearbox while the front suspension and rear axle a came from this source.

The 100/4's chassis was completely new a entirely conventional. The frame was formed by tw parallel 3ins square box section longerons, runni the length of the car 17ins apart, underslung at th rear. Cross-bracing was by parallel and crucifor members. Integral steel floor pressings and co structure were built up from this base.

The independent front suspension was by coils a wishbones with Girling lever arm type dampers, wh at the rear was a live axle suspended by semi-ellipt springs, with lateral location by Panhard rod. Dru brakes were fitted all round. Chassis design was combined effort by Donald Healey, son Geoffrey a Barry Bilbie, with styling by Gerry Coker.

When this sensational 103mph, 17½cwt two-sea sports car was revealed to the public, it was known the Healey 100/4. This name was soon to chang however, as the car impressed Lord, now head of t newly-formed British Motor Corporation. He w looking for a corporate sports car to follow Jaguar a MG onto the US sales patch, and this car fitted the admirably.

Austin took over the marketing and manufacture the vehicle, and Healey joined the firm on a long-te engineering and racing consultancy agreemen Production of the Austin-Healey 100/4 began in 19 with body/chassis units built by Jensen at W Bromwich, and fitment of engines and gearboxes the finished shells at Longbridge.

The Healey's character was changed totally 1956, when BMC took the decision to fit it with Corporation's C-series six-cylinder from the A1 Westminster and the car was christened the Aus Healey 100-Six. The desire to rationalise the B stock of engines to the A-series (Morris Minor a Austin A35), B-Series (MGA), and C-Series dicta this.

John Snow's beautiful Mark III is one of the finest Healeys you'll find. Details show bonnet badge, straight-six engine (good for 148bhp in this guise) and elegant wooden facia

The C-Series engine was rather curious. The cylinder head was so badly thought out that the inlet manifolding was cast in to the head in the form of a rigidly angular gallery, and in which there were only two flanges for mounting manifolds. Early six-cylinder Healeys were only producing 120bhp at 4600rpm after a great deal of development work. A late 1957 revamp saw a new six-port cylinder head, new inlet manifold, twin 1¾in SU carbs (in place of the single device on the earlier 100-Sixes), larger valves, increased compression ratio and other modifications, all of which boosted power to 117bhp at 4750rpm, and greatly increased the available torque and smoothness.

At the same time as the new 2639cc unit was

shoe-horned in, there were a number of other changes. For a start, the chassis was lengthened by 1.66ins to produce a 2+2 body, but there was no radical alteration. The C-Series four-speed and optional overdrive 'box, as fitted to late model 100/4s, was carried over, and the C-type back axle used. The doors were longer, a fixed windscreen (instead of the 100/4's folding device) became standard, and there was an improved hood and sliding side windows. Pressed steel disc wheels was also made available.

Mid-1959 saw the straight-six engine enlarged to 2913cc, in line with the rest of the BMC range, and thus was born the Healey 3000. The capacity increase required a new cylinder block with siamesed bores, giving a larger bore of 83.36mm (from 79.4mm), with

the stroke unchanged at 88.9mm. The crankcase was stiffened at the flywheel end by the addition of external webs. The compression ratio was also increased from 8.5:1 to 9.0:1, and maximum power was now 124bhp at 4600rpm, with peak torque of 162lb ft developed at 2700rpm. At first, an automatic choke was used on the two SU carbs, but this was discontinued in November of that year.

The drive line was beefed up to deal with the extra power and torque, with a larger (10ins) clutch and revised gearbox internal ratios, which effectively meant that third, first and reverse were slightly higher but second was lower. The optional overdrive had a lower ratio, while rear axle ratios were higher at 3.545:1 (non-overdrive) and 3.909:1 (overdrive).

The real innovation for the Healey, though, was the use of Girling disc brakes at the front, one of the few visible (if wire wheels were fitted) differences of the 3000 from the superseded 100-Six. Badging was also different, and the 3000 Mark 1 came in two different guises, the BT7 2+2 and the BJ7 two-seater. The new model cost £1,168 9s 2d for the two seater and £1,175 for the 2+2. Most customers specified overdrive (£66 8s 2d extra) and wire wheels (£35 8s 4d), the former of which gave extra driving pleasure, the latter adding to the aesthetics.

Overall, the main difference between the 3000 and the 100-Six was in the performance, as the 3000 proved to have a higher top speed (up 5mph on overdrive cars to 116mph, and up 10mph to 110mph on non-overdrive versions) and better mid and top range acceleration. The 30-50mph time in top came down 0.6secs to 6.8secs, and the 80-100mph time down 4.1secs to 13.9secs.

The press eulogised about the car, but complained about pedal spacing, the poor gearchange and the badly placed gearlever, cranked across to the driver on rhd versions. The late John Bolster, writing for *Autosport*, summarised the 3000 as the car 'for the driver who enjoys horsepower and finds the smaller sports cars a little too gear happy.' He was impressed 'by the sheer power of the big engine, and this feeling persists after hundreds of miles of driving. The Austin-Healey 3000 is a wonderfully effortless car.' He also remarked on the large amount of torque available, and the fact that the engine never became rough, no matter how hard the car was driven. Handling was cited as good, but without the firmness necessary for high speed driving around a race-track.

The Autocar delighted in the engine's smoothness and torque, commenting that 'the latest Austin-Healey maintains the reputation of a good quality, fast touring car which its predecessors established . . . the new performance will make it even more competitive.'

Fine handling

The Motor also praised the car for its effortlessness and excellent handling, although there were a few more quibbles from their testers. They saw the need for caution on wet and slippery roads, because injudicious use of the throttle caused vicious back end breakaway. They didn't appreciate 'the older sports car driving position', with steering wheel close to the *pilote*, and thinly cushioned seats which they felt lacked support for the small of the back.

All testers felt the new braking system an improvement, but even at this early stage the amount of cockpit heat with the hardtop fixed was noticed, as was the lack of headroom in the back, complaints that were to plague the car throughout its production life.

It didn't take long for the BMC Competitions Department to get their hands on a 3000, and right away it was competitive in International rallying. Initial modifications included a re-routed exhaust exiting from the side of the body, but twin SU carburettors were kept. Pat Moss was second on the 1959 German Rally, second on the '60 Alpine, and won the Rome-Liège-Rome that year, striking a blow for female rally drivers as well as providing a portent of things to come from the rallying Big Healeys.

Not until 1960 did the 3000 become homologated for sports car racing as a proper GT machine complete with hard top, 25 gallon fuel tank, and all-round disc brakes. Built at the Healey factory at Warwick, the trio of cars entered for the 1960 Sebring 12 Hours met with mixed success, Riley/Sears finishing third in class, another badly delayed by gearbox trouble (a fate that had befallen the Riley car), and the third having crashed. A singleton entry was made for Le Mans, but it retired through big-end failure. The basic story of the Healey 3000's competition career — rallying success with irregular racing forays taking a back seat — was therefore mapped out.

The first changes to the 3000 happened in May 1961, when the Mark II was launched. This was one of those periodic updates of which BMC were so fond, in an attempt to please American buyers as much as anything.

There was a new front grille with vertical slats, a new bonnet air intake, and different badging details. The main changes came under the bonnet, though, as

SPECIFICATION	Austin-Healey 3000 Mark III BJ8 Convertible
Engine	In-line 'six'
Capacity	2912cc
Bore/Stroke	83.36mm x 88.9mm
Valves	Pushrod OHV
Compression	9.0:1
Power	148bhp (net) @ 5250rpm
Torque	165lb ft @ 3500rpm
Transmission	4 speed manual (overdrive optional)
Final Drive	3.545:1 (3.909:1 with overdrive)
Brakes	Discs (front)/drums (rear)
Suspension Front	Coil springs and wishbones; anti roll bar; lever arm dampers
Suspension Rear	Live axle; semi-elliptic leaf springs; radius arms; lever arm dampers
Steering	Cam and peg
Body	Separate body and chassis
Tyres	5.90 - 15

DIMENSIONS	
Length	13ft 1½ins
Width	5ft 0½ins
Height	4ft 2ins
Wheelbase	7ft 8ins
Dry weight	2548lbs

PERFORMANCE	
Max speed	121mph
0-60mph	9.8secs
Standing ¼ mile	17.2secs
Fuel consumption	20.3mpg

ON THE ROAD	
Years built	Feb 1964 to Dec 1967
Numbers built	16,314
Price new	£1106 3s 9d

Mk I: Peter Ustinov occupies this lhd US market model

Mk II: vertically slatted grille and there's more power

Mk III: greater comfort, including wind-up windows

the Mark II used triple 1¼in SU carburettors on entirely new manifolds and fitted at a 30 degree semi-downdraught angle. A new camshaft profile was also used. In effect, these changes were claimed to boost power output to 124bhp at 4600rpm, but they must have been fairly lightweight horses as *The Autocar* and *The Motor* recorded inferior road test figures to the original 3000!

The triple carb set-up was notoriously tricky to keep in tune, and the installation lasted just a year before reversion to twin SUs with the Mark II BJ7 Sports Convertible. But two other events were to occur in the 3000's life before that date. First, the two-seater BJ7 model sold poorly, only 355 cars out of a Mark II production run of 5450 being in this form. The second was that, in October 1961, BMC fitted the new C-Series gearbox casing, which had the selector mechanism on top of the 'box, rather than at the side, which meant that the gear lever emerged from the centre of the transmission tunnel via a remote extension, instead of taking the form of that long, willowy and rather un-sports-car-like lever.

It was a case of mixed feelings from the press over the revisions. *The Motor* felt it incredible that, despite their large resources, BMC had failed to iron out ground clearance and cockpit heat problems after eight years of production. Moreover, they found the pedal spacing poor (again . . .), the overdrive switch too far to the right of the dashboard, and the triple carb engine suffered from poor throttle response when cold. *The Autocar*, while full of praise for the car's handling and performance, was less than enamoured with the driving position, the lack of proper jacking points, and the stiffness of the doors. Oh, and the 12 gallon tank didn't provide a great range on a car that was good for only 20mpg if pushed hard.

August '62 saw the launch of the '3000 Sports Convertible', which featured the first and only major styling change to the 3000 in its eight year history.

Wind-up windows, a new slightly wrap rou windscreen and a permanently attached hood helped to transform the car into more of a drop-he coupé than the tourer it had been. More sou deadening material was fitted in an attempt furthe refine the car.

Just as importantly, the engine reverted to Mar specification, with twin SU HS6 1¾in carburettors the original inlet manifold. There was also a n camshaft profile to ensure no loss of power. Optio extras available were a vacuum servo for the brak wire wheels, overdrive and a heater. The car retai for £1,190 7s 9d inclusive of purchase tax. This mo was sold in Britain until the Mark III appeared February 1964, by which time the Mk III had beer sale in the States since November of the previous ye illustrating just how important the American mar was. In actual fact, something like 90% of all Heal produced were exported there.

End of the line

The Mark III BJ8 was the end of the line for the Healey, for despite a number of major changes, it phased out in December '67, perhaps the last of vintage sports cars. The car was made even quic (120mph plus capability) by engine mods, includin new camshaft profile and bigger 2in SU car boosting output to 148bhp at 5250rpm, and there a re-routed exhaust system with a pair of silenc under the nearside sill, with tailpipes pla transversely across the offside of the car. transmission was strengthened, with a new 9 diaphragm clutch, and first and reverse gear ra were raised. A vacuum servo was standardised as of the braking system.

Finally, there were a number of cockpit change full width wooden facia was fitted, and the gear tunnel console featured a padded cubby box.

From mid-May 1964, one final change

introduced, which makes the later Mark III the most desirable Healey 3000. BMC at last took action to increase ground clearance at the rear. The frame member under the back axle was cut, lowered, re-boxed and strengthened to give the rear axle another 1½ins travel, and twin trailing radius arms were added to locate the axle tube in order to obviate wind-up of the new, low rate rear springs under acceleration and braking. The Panhard rod was deleted. From April '65 onwards separate flashing and side lamps were introduced in place of the earlier one piece units.

These later cars were quicker than their predecessors, with the top speed up to 117mph and a 0-60mph time of 10.4secs for the Mark II Sports Convertible, and 122.5mph and a 0-60mph time of 9.8secs for the Mark III.

The motoring press still had their doubts, because the car was quite old-fashioned by now. What prompted BMC to introduce the MGC — so similar and dated in concept — in the same year the Healey died is not known, and probably never will be. Illogic perhaps the best answer.

As well as the usual quibbles over the driving position and cockpit heat, the press criticised the lack of luggage space, while *Autocar* noticed appreciable understeer (though other critics found the car to have mild power-off understeer, easily converted into power oversteer by deft use of the throttle), a relative harshness when compared to the new generation of cars such as the 'soft' MGB, and hard and poorly padded seats.

Aerodynamic Edwardian

Car and Driver summed the vehicle up as 'an aerodynamic Edwardian with roll up windows' and went on to say that the 'ponderous nature of all the controls is a factor which lends a kind of appealing massive masculinity to the car . . . harking back to the days when men were men.'

Motor weren't enamoured with the new facia or the new gear lever position on the Mark III, but they felt that 'a little of the Healey 100 still remains; the classic looks, firm ride, only marginal ground clearance, vintage driving position and a take-off that few cars can equal regardless of price.'

It was left to *Autosport* to appraise the car in the most realistic light. It '. . . is a car for long journeys. It will go anywhere, and fast, too, without wilting under the worst conditions.'

By December 1967, the Healey 3000 was finished after an illustrious career, through which 43,017 examples were made. Not only was it the last of the true hairy sports touring cars, but it was one of the great rally cars. Pat Moss's driving in the 1960 season provided a taste of things to come. And the Morley brothers made the demanding Tulip Rally virtually their own, winning it outright from 1962 to '65, though overall victory eluded them because of the handicapping system.

The Morleys also won the 1961 and '62 Alpine Rally, an event won by Hopkirk in 1964, and Aaltonen was victor in the '64 Spa-Sofia-Liège Marathon. One major rally the big Healey failed to win, though, was our very own RAC, on which there were four second places from 1961 to '65. A big, unwieldy machine at the best of times, it wasn't best suited to the forest stages that made up the punishing event, but Makinen so nearly won the '65 event. He was overtaken on the final night by Rauno Aaltonen's Mini Cooper S, the Healey struggling for grip in the snow that had fallen overnight. That meteoric drive proved the big Healey's rallying swansong. The very special cars built for '67 RAC were never used, since the rally was cancelled owing to the outbreak of foot and mouth disease.

In rallying guise, the Healey 3000 was very different from the production car. Six branch exhaust manifolding, light alloy cylinder head, triple twin-choke Weber carbs and slight overboring (to 2968cc) pushed up to around 200bhp and there were light panels, glass-fibre boots, heavy duty (14 leaf) rear springs, larger dampers, rear disc brakes, and high anchor mounting for a re-routed exhaust among other modifications by the end of the car's competition history.

As most people like to remember the Big Healey; Timo Makinen flinging his 3000 sideways on the '65 Scottish Rally

Brutal! One of the cars prepared for the cancelled '67 RAC

By way of contrast, Healey race outings were few and far between, with 12th place in the 1963 Sebring 12 hours for Olthoff/Bucknum and second in the '65 Guards 1000 miles event at Brands for the Paddy Hopkirk/Roger Mac private entry the only highlights in a low profile racing effort.

What more could you ask for in a sports car? A competition pedigree of the highest order, traditional throttle-controlled tail-out handling, performance a-plenty, and the promise of hood-down motoring for hours on end in comfort. There isn't anything better around. . . .

Production history

While the Austin-Healey 3000 underwent many changes during its lifespan, there were relatively few running modifications between revamps. The first such modification was the re-introduction of the manual choke in November 1959, from Chassis Numbers BN7 5235 and BT7 5311 onwards. The next series of modifications came with the Mark II model, with its triple SU carburettor specification (BN7/BT7 13751 on).

From November 1961 the 3000 was fitted with the new gearbox casing with a remote control lever (from BN7 16039 and BT7 15881), the final revisions before the major styling rehash that constituted the 3000 Sports Convertible.

Out went the BN/BT7 sequence and in came BJ7 nomenclature. The first Mark II Sports Convertible was BJ7 17551. However, the last Mark IIs are BN7 18888 and BT7 19853, as there were three batches of convertibles whose chassis numbers overlapped: four cars (17551 to 17554), 36 cars (from 18017) and a further 20 cars. A diaphragm clutch was introduced from engine 29F/4398 on.

Last of the line was the Mark III, and this was given the designation BJ8; the first car was chassis BJ8 25315, and the first of the Mark IIIs with the all-important new rear suspension was phased in from BJ8 26705, from mid-May 1964.

Final change was the introduction of the separate side and indicator lamps, from Chassis Number 31336 on, in April '65. December 21, '67 was the date of the Austin-Healey's demise, the last car finished then being 43025, though two cars were finished in January '68 (43000 and 43007) with a final car constructed in March '68 (Chassis number 43026).

Buyer's spot check

It almost goes without saying that prospective buyers of a classic sports car should make sure they know what they are looking for before they buy. That applies not only to the car's condition, but also to the exact model they desire.

In the case of the Austin-Healey 3000, the most practical and desirable version is the Mark III, with its increased power, better braking, re-routed exhaust and improved ground clearance thanks to the later chassis modifications and radius arm rear suspension. However, the early Mark IIIs without the suspension mods are less coveted than the BJ7 Mark II Convertible as the early Mark IIIs had a larger exhaust system and thus less ground clearance than the later Mark IIs.

If you want a two-seater, make sure that that's what you get, but remember that the Mark II BN7, as well as being rare, has the temperamental triple carburettor set-up, one reason why the Mark 1 is a better bet for the home mechanic/enthusiast, despite its greater age.

Parts are available for all Austin-Healeys. All panels, major sub-structural and chassis sections and mechanical parts can be bought off the shelf from specialists such as Southern Carburettors, who helped us in the compilation of this article and own the Mark III pictured on the front cover.

Like most classic sports cars, the Healey 3000 is a catch-22 for the prospective buyer — you must purchase a structurally sound car, yet you can properly assess the sub-structure/chassis condition only when the wings are taken off.

A number of fundamental factors affect the life of the Healey's structure: as there is no cross-bracing on the chassis longerons until well after the bulkhead, accident damage will usually have led to some lozenging of the chassis rails; catalytic corrosion occurs where aluminium body panels bolt onto steel sub-structure; and spot welded seams lead to trapped mud causing rusting.

Austin-Healey 3000 production		
Model	**Dates**	**Numbers**
Mark I BN7 2-seat	Mar 1959-May 1961	2825
Mark I BT7 2 + 2	Mar 1959-May 1961	10,825
Mark II BN7 2-seat	Apr 1961-June 1962	355
Mark II BT7 2 + 2	Apr 1961-June 1962	5095
Mark II BJ7 Convertible	Feb 1962-Nov 1963	6113
Mark III BJ8 Convertible	Nov 1963-May 1964	1390
Mark III BJ8 Convertible	May 1964-Dec 1967	16,314
Total		**43,017**

It is most important to check that glass-fibre panels have not been fitted — this short-term measure taken when Healey values were low generally disguises horrors underneath. Similarly, avoid cars fitted with wide wheels and wheel-arch extensions — not only are they likely to have led a hard life, but wide tyres place increased stress on suspension and steering. It would be expensive and time consuming to bring the car back to original specification.

Rust is the Healey's great enemy. Unfortunately, it is difficult to detect many of the problems just from routine inspection. Sills, wing bottoms, boot floors, door pillars and the bottom/sides of front bulkheads, chassis outriggers, and front damper mounting points all give trouble. The ends of each sill can be seen by peering under each inner wing, but this may not show the true extent of corrosion. It is difficult to detect whether the chassis outriggers (which support the rear spring hangers) are badly corroded unless the car is on a ramp, but this should be done as they can cause MoT failure and are costly to repair. It is also advisable to put the car on a ramp if there is any hint of accident damage, for those vulnerable longitudinal members may be out of true. If the chassis rails kink, then leave well alone.

While the boot floor tends to suffer, it is relatively easy to get at, the panels are available at reasonable cost, and basic welding and cutting skills are all that are required here. One point to bear in mind is that a badly corroded main floor panel is a cause of MoT failure, and if sill renovation is contemplated it is as well (and relatively simple) to renew the main floor at the same time.

The front and rear door posts tend to rust badly, and you can only inspect for superficial rot — you can see the true extent of rusting when panels are off. Again, either the ability to weld, or a tame welder, is needed to renovate these sections. In the case of a really rotten front door post, it's worth replacing the whole of the bulkhead side panel, because it's likely that the rest of the section will have suffered too.

Front and rear wheel arches can also suffer from rot, which, as usual, may be disguised by underseal (though it is as well to bear in mind that some newly restored cars may use underseal for protection, not disguise). Check the solidity of the metal. Renovation here is not too expensive, except on the Mark III radius arm cars. If the rear wheel arch has gone in this case, radius arm location problems will occur, and will prove costly and time consuming to rectify.

Many of these problems are under the surface, so what appears quite a sound car may be awful once the panels have come off. One good all-round check can be made when driving the car; severe scuttle shake can indicate a poor sub-structure, though to the uninitiated, Healey scuttle shake, even on the best car in the world, might seem severe!

Mechanically, the news is far better. Usual checks for the front suspension apply — look for play in the kingpins and steering arms. The rear axle is virtually indestructible. Watch for grounding of the exhaust on a test run as this could indicate poor exhaust mountings or sagging rear springs. Front damper mountings are prone to fracture (and tend to do so in dramatic fashion), but you won't be able to check for

Concours are part of the Austin-Healey Club's activities

Sprints (here at Snetterton) are also popular club events

this. Bad repairs can lead to altered suspension geometry, by the way. Dampers have a life expectancy in the region of 20,000 miles.

Engines are superb, and have great longevity. If you can, go out for a long test drive to get the engine really hot, as it is only then that a tired but sound engine will give itself away — oil pressure should be around the 50psi mark at speed and stay there when hot. Taking an engine out is not a job for the faint of heart, because that lump is *very* heavy and will require the use of a good hoist. Even removing the head really needs two people. The triple carb set up on the Mark II BN7 is notoriously tricky to maintain in good tune.

The only major weak point mechanically is the gearbox. Signs of impending trouble are noisy first and reverse gears, so avoid cars with these grumbles. Overdrives when fitted are strong, but beware of a car with this device not engaging when hot, as this can indicate internal trouble.

The final area which can be a horror story is the bodywork, particularly where the aluminium and steel panels join. The front and rear shrouds are prone to this form of rot, and it is detectable on the panel outers. Wing bottoms, in steel, can also give trouble.

If all this sounds like our advice to the young

gentleman about to buy a Healey 3000 is don't, it is n
meant to. There are problem areas on this car, as
any classic vehicle. But with care and the attitude th
'I will buy the best car I can afford', it is possible
pick up a well maintained and generally go
condition car, especially as the car's present d
following ensures that the vehicles are mc
presentable and less likely to catch the buy
unawares. Also, make sure that you get the car y
want — perusal of the production history in t
profile should give an idea which model has whi
particular feature. And if you want wire wheels a
overdrive, make sure you get a car so equipped, as i
costly to convert to these options.

Rivals when new

One feature of the Austin-Healey 3000 was th
throughout its production life it provided an awful
of performance for its price (£1168 in 1959 and £1
in 1966). In 1959, the only car that could provide w
over 110mph, and was in the same league financial
was the Daimler SP250 Dart sports car, which sold
£1395 in 1960. A better engine (?) gave it a sligh
higher top speed and faster acceleration, but it alwa
lacked the looks and pedigree of the Healey.

Neither the Triumph TR3 nor MGA 1600 were
fast or as flexible. They were sports cars for wind
English road, much too fussy to be driven at Hea
speeds (around 90 to 100mph) over long distanc
Perhaps the Jaguar XK150 is the best comparis
faster, with better acceleration, it was also m
expensive at £1665 for the 3.4-litre variant, but
that combination of looks, and effortless performa
that sums up the Big Healey's appeal.

By 1966, the last year of serious Healey marketi
the competition was just as difficult to define.
MGB was Abingdon's wonder car, but like
predecessor, the 'A,' it never had Healey perfo
ance, yet was more refined and more in keeping w
the mid-sixties than the rather old fashioned Hea
Triumph's TR4A, again, never quite had
performance, but when Triumph installed th
2½-litre 'six' into the same chassis and called it
TR5, it was a real competitor . . . except that it
introduced in October '67, just two months before
last Healey rolled off the line. It was, with the M
much nearer in concept to the Healey, a macho spc
car with 120mph plus performance for sensi
money (£1261 for the Triumph, £1146 for the M
The Sunbeam Tiger, with a top speed of o
120mph, provided a good rival to the Healey wi
price tag of £1446, but it never sold well in Britai

In short, even by the end of its life, t
Austin-Healey 3000 was some motor car. If
wanted a true bred sports car, you had to outlay m
cash. The superlative value for money Jaguar E-t
cost £1934, but then that did provide the owner v
140mph and handling to match.

Clubs, specialists and books

There is only one club for the Austin-Healey 3
owner, and that is the Austin-Healey Club. N
extremely well established, it provides vari
services to the Healey owner, such as advice
technical aid, has a varied range of events from sc

This year sees a resurgence of A-H circuit activity, as not only is there involvement in the TR Register race series, but there are cars racing in the AMOC Thoroughbred Championship

heetings through to sprints and driving tests, and roduces a quality quarterly magazine 'Rev Counter' addition to monthly section newsletters. It also rganises the International Healey Weekend in July nd there exist registers for each separate Healey nodel. The club offers a special insurance scheme of vhich members can take advantage. Membership osts £8.50 per year, and the person to contact is Mrs . Marks, 171 Coldharbour Road, Bristol, Avon BS6 SX (tel: 0272 427166).

Coming onto specialists, there aren't that many. If 's parts that you require, then Southern Car-urettors at Unit 14, Oakwood Industrial Park, atwick Road, Crawley, Sussex RH10 2AZ (tel: 0293 17841/2) stock a vast range of solely Big Healey pares, and there's also Austin-Healey Spares at Unit , Southam Industrial Estate, Southam, Warwicks U33 0JH (tel: 0926 7181).

Restoration is carried out by Orchard Engineering, rchard House, The Avenue, Horam, Sussex (tel: loram Road 2374); Victor D.J. Smith, Unit 16, outhwall Road Industrial Estate, Deal, Kent (tel: Jeal 65510) and K and JB Restorations, The Croft, 0 Allseley Old Road, Coventry CV5 8GF (tel: 0788 3848).

Then there's Ellis and Son (Restoration) at othersthorpe Avenue, Northampton NN4 9J1 (tel: 504 67231); Monza Classic Cars at Hall Barn Works, loat Close, Doddinghurst, Brentwood, Essex CM15 NG (tel: 0277 822504); JME at 22 Penfold Close, ishops Tachbrook, Leamington Spa (tel: 0926 15587); Colin Groom at St. Luke's Road, Torquay, evon (tel: Torquay 28033) and Harold Everard at ise Terrace, Leamington Spa, Warks (tel: 0926 5038).

There are a fair number of books for the Healey iff on the market today, but there is little doubt that ie *Austin-Healey 100/6 and 3000 Workshop Manual* at .95, a reprint of the original manual, is the most tal source of information for the owner/potential vner. On a more general note, *The Big Healeys: A ollectors Guide* by Graham Robson is a useful ference work on the models from 100/4 through to e 3000s and is good value at £7.95. *Austin-Healey: he story of the Big Healeys* is straight from the horse's outh as it were, written by Geoffrey Healey and very tertaining (price £9.95) and Brooklands Books blish a useful compilation of road tests under the le *Austin-Healey 3000 1959-1967* at £4.95. Also on e market is *Healey: The Handsome Brute* by Chris arvey at £14.95, and another Brooklands tome, ustin Healey 100 and 3000 Collection No 1 — 1952-68 £3.95 which covers the 100s as well.

rices

ealey prices vary not only according to condition but cording to model. The radius arm rear suspension ark III is considered most desirable, and is thus ost expensive, while the early Mark Is fetch the west price. So few Mark II BJ7 two-seaters were ade (355) that they tend to fetch more money than e comparable Mark II BT7 2 plus 2s.

Concours cars tend to be put on the market at dicrous figures, and, according to Southern rburettors, an immaculate Mark III can have a tag up to £10,000. More sensible, therefore, is to go for e good condition, useable car that may require a tle work to make it into an excellent example, and ese generally go for around £4500. A rebuild project ll cost up to £1500, and, unless you are very keen d do all the work yourself, will be uneconomic to store. One point to remember is to check cars over ry carefully when buying. If possible get it vetted by expert before purchase.

Mark Is can fetch up to £7000 for a mint condition , with £3500 for a good condition vehicle and £1000 a restoration project. Mark II cars are usually iced between these two extremes, but remember t possibly the best buy is the Mark II Sports nvertible, not as quick as the Mark III, but noisier d with the Mark III's added refinement at a lower st today. Remember also that the first batch of Mark s had the traditional Healey ground clearance blem with its unmodified rear suspension, so ke sure that you don't pay late Mark III money for e.

John Snow talks about his superb 3000 Mk III 2A

John with the Healey he bought new back in 1965. The rack on the boot lid carries the spare wheel on trips abroad

In 1963, John Snow was looking for a new car. He approached his local branch of Caffyns and consi-dered an MGB. He wanted to look at a Healey, but Caffyns didn't have a demo model on hand, so he finished up buying the MG. Two years and 40,000 miles later he was having engine problems with the B, so decided to change it. Naturally he wasn't too keen on another B, but Caffyns took him to Abingdon for a drive in a Healey straight from the line (which turned out to be a customer car — even Abingdon didn't have a demonstrator!).

This resulted in an order from John for a 3000 Mk III 2A, Healey blue over white, with overdrive, telescopic steering column, and wire wheels. It took three months to build, and it was eventually delivered on July 16, 1965. John has owned the car ever since. He still has the original bill, for £1260, which includes £17 10s for the road fund tax!

In fact ownership started rather ominously: he only had it a week before it went back for a respray. It seemed there was something wrong with the white panels, which had little brown specks which were more than just surface deep — they went right through to the metal. The car was away for a month . . .

In spite of this John kept the car, and hasn't regretted it for a day. It has now covered 60,000 miles and is very much a cherished possession, only coming out occasionally in good weather. His insurance policy, arranged at special rates through the Club, allows him to cover 2000 miles in a year, but "I look at the annual MoT slip and find I've only done 600 miles or something like that in the year, and each time I promise myself I must drive it more!"

The Healey was John's only car for about five years, when a front-end shunt put it off the road for a while: to keep mobile he bought himself a second car, and ever since then the Healey has been kept for high days and holidays.

In all the time he's had it remarkably little has gone wrong. Obvious items like tyres (the current set are 10 years old) and — the bane of Healeys — exhaust systems have been replaced, but apart from a new clutch at 59,000 miles, and new front king pins and brake pipes at the last MoT, nothing major has had to be replaced.

Nor has he added much to it. There's a rack on the boot to take the spare wheel, and a special chromed rocker cover with a flip-up filler, but those are about all the extras on it.

There was one major change, though. At one point rust began to show in the back wings. He took the car to a local garage with the intention of having it resprayed the original colours. However, investiga-tion showed that a total respray would cost very little more, and there wouldn't be the problem of colour matching, so out came the colour swatches and today the car is a beautiful shade of dark metallic blue, which sets off the lines beautifully, and makes it a somewhat rare machine.

He's taken the car abroad many times, journeying as far as Liechtenstein. "It's superb on long fast roads, cruising at 70, 80, 90mph in overdrive top all day with no effort at all — and if you do need extra urge suddenly you just flick it out of overdrive and the power is there. And I get about 27-28mpg too: in this country it's more like 23mpg.

"Mind you, it does have its drawbacks. There's not all that much luggage room (hence the spare wheel rack), but above all it can get terribly hot! Not just the engine, but the cockpit as well! On one occasion we had to put the hood *up* to protect us from the sun . . ."

What does John find so special about the Healey? "Well, for a start, there's the looks, the appearance. To my mind it has no equal — it never has had.

Instant power

"Then there's the more than adequate power. It's a bit crazy, the amount of power compared to the size of the car, but it's very useful in an emergency, if you need to accelerate quickly. There's instant power there. And, of course, it makes lovely noises too.

"About the only drawbacks are that exhaust system — you have to be very careful where you take it, and it only just clears the ramp up to my garage! — and the steering, too, at parking speeds is very heavy: U-turns are really hard work, you've got to lug the wheel around".

Minor services John carries out himself, while for the bigger jobs he takes it to Jim Storey down at Horeham. During the winter months, however, he starts the car up occasionally, running it in and out of the garage just to make sure everything's free.

John's never thought of selling it, "even when the insured value was in the hundreds — now with this special policy it's properly covered for what I consider a reasonable sum and it's fully comprehensive even when it's in the garage in winter".

John's a member of the local branch of the Austin-Healey Club. "We've now got about 300 members in the Southern Counties Branch, and, of course, the Club is so useful for spares and so on — somebody's had your problem before, for sure!"

Looking at the admiring glances the car attracted while it was out on the road, we can see why John isn't interested in selling it. "But more than that — I really enjoy driving it." And that's what ownership of such a car is all about.

1967 Austin-Healey 3000 MKIII

by Robert C. Ackerson
photos by the author

ONLY the most optimistic observers of the British motor industry could have foreseen that the linkup of Donald Healey's small Warwick-based firm with the Austin Motor Company in 1952 to produce the Austin-Healey 100 would lead to the eventual production of over 70,000 "big Healeys." But this success had a bitter-sweet conclusion.

When Austin and its long-time rival Morris merged to become the British Motor Corporation (BMC) in 1952, the long, bumpy process leading to the creation of the British Leyland Motor Corporation in 1967 began. And by that time the fate of the Austin-Healey had gradually slipped out of the hands of its creators into a morass of government machinations, corporate in-fighting

and jealousy. Thus when the last Austin-Healey Mark III left its Abingdon Assembly line in December 1967 there was no replacement waiting in the wings. However, less than three years later the gap was nicely filled by the Datsun 240Z, and yet another British beachhead in the US car market was defaulted to the Japanese.

As an unwitting trailblazer for Nissan, BMC tailored the Austin-Healey to an expanding market for sports cars in the

United States. The Austin-Healey, beginning as a two-seater that neatly filled the performance-price gap between the MG TD and Jaguar XK 120, became over the years less Spartan, less pure sports car and more of a luxurious grand tourer. The big Healey always retained a few rough edges to remind occupants of its heritage, but its evolution typified the movement away from the "Spartan is best" attitude among sports car manufacturers to a decidedly more plushbottom outlook.

The Healey's first step in this direction took place in 1956 when Austin phased out production of its 2,660 cc four which dated back to 1949. Its replacement, a marginally larger 2,639 cc six, was first introduced in October 1954 in the Austin A90 Westminster

End of the Line

This engine, known as the BMC "C" Series, carried its camshaft on the right side of the cylinder block and was fitted with a cylinder head designed by Harry Weslake. Its use in the Austin-Healey was initially somewhat of a mixed blessing. With 102 hp at 4,600 rpm, the C engine was more powerful than the old four. Yet its torque output of 141 lb/ft at 2,400 rpm was inferior to the four's excellent 150 lb/ft at 2,000 rpm. Moreover, the new engine outweighed the four by over 100 pounds. However, progress sometimes is well disguised, and this smooth-running six had a future of substantial improvement while the four which had originated as a spin-off of a wartime, six-cylinder truck engine was ready for honorable retirement.

In comparison to the older BN2 Healey, the six-cylinder BN4 was slower from zero to 60 mph, although not by a wide margin. *Sports Cars Illustrated* (February 1957) reported an 11.6-second time for the BN4 which compared favorably both to the 11.2-second run recorded by *The Motor* (September 16, 1953) with a very early 100 that had previously competed in the 1953 LeMans race and the BN2 four-speed Healey. However, *The Autocar* (November 2, 1956) could only coax a best zero to 60 mph run of 12.9 seconds from its 100-Six; and John Bolster, an early Austin-Healey enthusiast, reported a mediocre 13.2-second time for the new Healey in *Autosport* (October 12, 1956). However, thanks to its 3.09:1 first gear, the 100-Six was a very strong car off the line and both in top speed and overall smooth-

ness superior to the original version.

Use of the six-cylinder engine required a higher hood line whose negative impact upon the Healey's appearance was minimized by the addition of a small hood scoop. Although Geoffrey Healey later reported that it actually tended to impede air flow to the engine, the scoop looked purposeful, and along with a reshaped grille with corrugated horizontal bars interspersed with thin vertical units, set the stage for the Healey's basic front end appearance for the rest of its production life. While there was considerable discussion about the aesthetic merits of these changes, far more controversial was the transformation of the Austin-Healey into a four-seater sports car. In the postwar era a number of British sports car producers ranging from Berkeley to Morgan marketed four-place versions with various degrees of success.

Since the new BN6 Austin-Healey was described by its maker as an "occasional four-seat sports tourer," when it appeared at the London Motor Show in October 1956, there were no large promises made for this configuration. A wheelbase increase of two inches to 92 inches plus wider doors allowed small rear seats to be installed that were suitable for use by two very small children or by one slender adult. When Austin-Healey later offered a two-seater as an alternative its sales were not good. for example, from July 1959 to May 1961 only 2,825 two-seaters were produced while outputs of the 2/4 seater totalled 10,825.

Austin-Healey

continued

Although a new top design was part of the revamped Austin-Healey package for 1957, it seldom evoked fond sentiments from those called upon to install it in haste. It was, to be sure, nice and snug when finally in place. But, with 14 seals to be snapped in around the rear window alone, and a fiendishly crafted frame, the top maintained the British sports car's reputation of needing a crew of experienced circus roustabouts to erect correctly.

The conversion of the Healey into a 2/4 seater required the removal of the spare tire from its perch on a ledge at the back of the trunk to the trunk floor. This change was accompanied by the removal of the fuel filler pipe from its inconvenient placement under the trunk lid to a spot high on the rear deck. Also given a new home was the Healey's battery. Previously two six-volt batteries were stowed away behind the seats where their inaccessibility encouraged owners to pay little attention to them until they dried up. On the 1957 model a single 12-volt battery was installed in the trunk. This consumed even more of the Healey's scarce storage space, but it greatly enhanced serviceability and as a bonus helped offset the six-cylinder engine's impact upon front and rear weight distribution.

The 100-Six interior carried over the older model's non-adjustable passenger seat, strangely positioned underdash

choke control, too-short-for-long-trips seat and awkwardly shaped shift lever that grew from the left side of the transmission tunnel. But at a p.o.e. price of $3,095 (up $110 from 1956) the Healey remained a great sports car bargain. Included in its base US price was overdrive, heater and defroster, wire wheels and a tonneau cover. Also new for 1957 were rigid-framed side screens with sliding Perspex panels and instrumentation with black numerals on a silver background.

No one was more aware of the 100-Six's need for added power than Geoffrey and Donald Healey, who joined the Austin partisans at BMC in a coalition demanding more from the Morris-

designed unit. Prior to any changes i the production engine, the results this effort were made evident by anothe successful Austin-Healey record-breaking venture to Bonneville in Augus 1956. Three drivers, Carroll Shelby, Ro Jackson-Moore and Tommy Wisdor were given two cars which set eve speed record in their class from one t three thousand miles. The so-calle endurance car was an older BN2 mod with streamlined front and rear se tions powered by a 100-Six engine fitte with triple, dual-throat Weber carbur tors. These exotic fuel mixers were ca ried on a cast-aluminum six-port intal manifold that was introduced on pr duction models during November 195

The second Austin-Healey, an elab rately streamlined creation with supercharged, 292-horsepower, si cylinder engine was less successful. C his first run with this car Donald Heal had reached a speed just over the 2(mph mark when the chain driving tl supercharger failed. The resultir damage to the crankshaft sprocket ar piston required a time-consuming r build which limited Healey to just tv runs through the timing lights. A though the chain came apart a secor time, Healey was able to claim a two-w average of 203.06 mph. Closer in time the introduction of a more power engine for the production 100-Six w Tommy Wisdom's entry in the 19 Mille Miglia where he averaged 75 mph to finish second in his price clas

When the Austin-Healey 100-Six w bored out to become the first of the 30(series, *Road & Track* concluded th in terms of smoothness and perform ance it was similar to the origin Jaguar XK 120. Although the only e ternal identification of the Healey 300 in either two-place (BN7) or 2/4 seat (BT7) form was a 3000 flashing on tl grille, there were plenty of technic improvements made to insure its o going popularity. The Healey's 17 cubic-inch 2,912 cc engine had a ne stronger cylinder block/crankcase a with a 9.03:1 compression ratio w

specifications

Illustrations by Russell von Sauers, The Graphic Automobile Studio

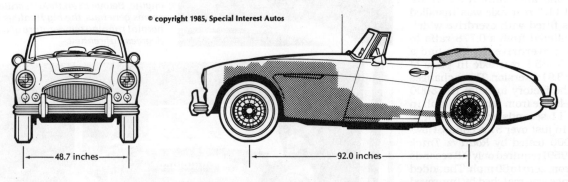

← 48.7 inches →   ← 92.0 inches →

1967 Austin-Healey 3000 MKIII

Price $3,565
Optional equipment Seat belts, tonneau cover

ENGINE
Type Overhead valves, in line, 6 cylinder
Bore and stroke 3.281 inches x 3.5 inches
Displacement 177.7 cubic inches
Max bhp @ rpm 148 @ 5,200 rpm
Max torque @ rpm 167 @ 2,700 rpm
Compression ratio 9.0:1
Induction system 2 SU model HD8 single barrel carburetors
Lubrication system Full pressure
Exhaust system Twin exhausts and resonators
Electrical system Lucas 12 volt

CLUTCH
Type Single dry plate, Borg and Beck
Diameter 9 inches
Actuation Hydraulic, foot pedal

TRANSMISSION
Type 4-speed selective, synchronized second, third, fourth gears, electrically controlled Laycock de Normanville overdrive standard on US models
Ratios: 1st 2.637:1
2nd 2.071:1
3rd 1.306:1
4th 1.00:1
Reverse 3.391:1
Overdrive (operates on 3rd and 4th gears)

DIFFERENTIAL
Type Hypoid bevel
Ratio 3.909:1 (overdrive)
Drive axle ¾ floating

STEERING
Type Cam and peg
Turns lock to lock 3.0
Ratio 15:1
Turning circle 36.0 feet

BRAKES
Type Girling hydraulic
Front Disc, 11 inch diameter
Rear Drum, one leading, one trailing shoe, 2 7/16 x 11 inches
Total swept area 383 square inches

CHASSIS AND BODY
Frame Separate ladder type
Body construction Steel and aluminum panels
Body type 2+2, convertible

SUSPENSION
Front Independent by coil springs and wishbones, Armstrong lever hydraulic shock absorbers
Rear Semi-elliptic leaf springs, Panhard rod, Armstrong lever hydraulic shock absorbers
Wheels 4J x 15 wire wheels
Tires 5.19 x 15

WEIGHTS AND MEASURES
Wheelbase 92 inches
Overall length 157 inches
Overall height 50 inches
Overall width 60 inches
Front tread 48.7 inches
Rear tread 50.0 inches
Ground clearance 4.5 inches
Shipping weight 2,380 pounds
Curb weight 2,460 pounds

CAPACITIES
Crankcase 7.5 quarts
Cooling system 10.8 quarts
Fuel tank 14.4 gallons

PERFORMANCE
Maximum speed 122 mph
Acceleration: 0-30 3.5 seconds
0-60 9.8 seconds
0-100 24.7 seconds
Standing start ¼ mile 17.0 seconds

Marque Club Austin-Healey Club of America
603 E. Euclid
Arlington Heights, IL 60004

From the original, semi-Spartan, side-curtained rough 'n ready 100-4, the Healey became a snug convertible with wrap-around windshield, roll-up side windows and a walnut-trimmed interior during its final years.

rated at 124 net horsepower at 4,500 rpm and 167 lb/ft at 2,700 rpm. To cope with this added power the gearbox innards were strengthened and a larger ten-inch instead of nine-inch diameter, single plate Borg & Beck clutch was installed. In addition, gear ratios were shifted about to provide less of a gap between second and third. A 3.91:1 instead of 4.11:1 rear axle was installed on models fitted with overdrive which was also altered from a 0.778 ratio to 0.822. Non-overdrive Healeys had a standard 3.545:1 rear axle in place of the earlier 3.91:1 version. These changes enabled the factory to claim the 3000 could accelerate from zero to 60 mph in less than 11 seconds and from rest to 100 mph in just over 31 seconds. However, a 3000 tested by *Road & Track* (August 1959) required only 9.8 seconds to speed from zero to 60 mph. The added performance was matched by improved braking capability provided by new 11.25-inch Girling front disc brakes.

The Healey still had some annoying design shortfalls such as its eternally condemned poor ground clearance, inadequate cockpit ventilation and poorly matched seat/pedals/steering relationship. To the very end of production, Healeys suffered from this last flaw. For example, Jerry Titus reported in his test of a 3000 MKII Austin-Healey *(Sports Car Graphic*, October 1961) that "a fairly short driver still finds the big steering wheel tangling with his nose if he has the seat adjusted far enough forward to reach the pedals." It also wasn't much fun to change a tire in any kind of weather with the Healey's old-fashioned screw-type jack. BMC did decide the time was opportune to update the Healey's roadster top, but the result was still far from perfect. Even *The Autocar* (August 28, 1959) had to report that its "erection during a sudden rain storm proved to be neither quick nor simple to an admittedly inexperienced crew."

Yet as a total package the Healey was hard to beat. "The best way to describe the new Austin-Healey 3000," said *Road & Track* (August 1959) "is to say that it is a real enthusiast's sports car: fun to drive, with lots of performance and good handling and braking characteristics... Dollar for dollar this is still one of the top sports cars on the market." For those who had both a few extra dollars on hand and a yearning for a 130-mph Healey 3000, K.N. Rudd (Engineers) Ltd. of Sussex, England, offered a comprehensive package of engine-chassis modifications that promised a maximum output of 178 horsepower. Rudd's use of triple SU carburetors forecast a similar arrangement introduced on the Austin-Healey 3000 MKII which debuted in May 1961. The short production run (355 two-seaters and 5,450 two-four seaters) of

Left: Airscoop in hood is functional, provides an eye-pleasing way to have a hood profile which clears the Healey's tall engine. Below: Even though grille area seems generous, the big Healeys have a normal running temperature of close to 20 degrees Fahrenheit.

The Austin-Healey in Rally Land

The Austin-Healey appeared to be a poor choice for competition in European-type rallies. Its limited ground clearance which exposed key mechanical components to all sorts of abuse, poor cockpit ventilation, relatively heavy steering and general bulk seemed good reasons enough to leave the rallying to someone else. But the Healey did have some things going for it that until the heyday of the Mini enabled it to be one of the most competitive British rally cars. The Healey's basic construction (Pat Moss described it as "built like a tank") enabled it to absorb a tremendous amount of punishment and harsh treatment; and thanks to the Laycock overdrive it was possible for the Healey driver, in the words of former BMC competitions manager Peter Browning, to keep the car "on the cam" under all road conditions.

The first major rally for the six-cylinder Healey was the 1958 Alpine, a 2,360-mile competition through the Alps and Dolomites that also required participation in hill climbs and speed runs on several race courses. The five-car Healey team which included Pat Moss (Stirling Moss's younger sister) and Ann Wisdom (daughter of long-time racing driver and Austin-Healey proponent Tommy Wisdom) acquitted itself well. Not only did one team car finish seventh overall (second in class) but in the final timed circuit test a 100-Six made the fastest time. However, team captain John Gott and his navigator weren't so fortunate. Heading towards Marseilles his car lost a rear wheel. After parting company with the Healey the wheel passed it, ran up the mountain side and then proceeded to crash down on the car. As a result of this episode,

Healeys were soon fitted with stronger rear hub assemblies. The Moss/Wisdom car also had its share of problems with a slipping clutch and low oil pressure, but it struggled on to an eighth place finish.

Later in 1958 Pat Moss and Ann Wisdom finished fourth overall out of 106 starters of the "Marathon of the Road," which had formerly been known as the Liege-Rome-Liege Rally. This was no mean achievement in one of the most grueling European rallies, and represented the best showing of both any British team and an all-female crew.

Just two years later they were the Marathon's outright winners. Their Healey was with its London taxi rear ratio capable of only an 80 mph top speed, but its acceleration (zero to 60 mph in five seconds) was phenomenal. Appropriately enough an Austin-Healey 3000 won the last Marathon (a 94-hour/3,100-mile grind that made 77 of the 98 starters non-finishers) in 1964. But beyond that point BMC placed primary emphasis upon the Mini as its rally standard bearer. However, plans were made in 1967 for the Healey to close out its long production run in a blaze of glory. With the 1967 R.A.C. Rally open to Group 6 prototype sports cars, a super Healey 3000 replete with light alloy body panels, magnesium alloy wheels and an all-aluminum engine was prepared. Slightly bored out to provide a displacement of 2,968 cc and with three Weber 45DCOE carburetors attached to a special magnesium-alloy manifold, it was reported to deliver nearly 200 horsepower to the rear wheels. Sad to say, this rally was cancelled due to (of all things) an outbreak of foot and mouth disease in England!

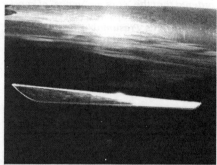

Austin-Healey

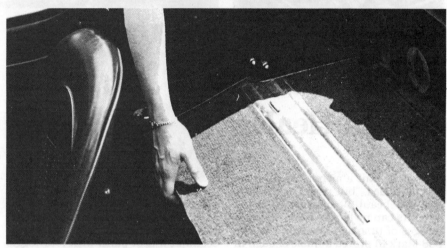

his 132-horsepower Austin-Healey nded less than a year later in March 962, when the three 1½-inch HS4 SU arburetors were replaced by two 1¾-nch versions that had been used on the riginal 3000. The use of a new cam ith slightly less dwell kept power loss o a minimum. Austin-Healey claimed he 1962 BJ7 version had 131 net orsepower at 4,700 rpm or just one less nan in 1961. Furthermore the new cam nproved both low speed flexibility and rovided a solid 158 lb/ft from 2,800 om to 3,700 rpm.

The 3000 MKII Healeys were easily istinguished by front grilles with ver-cal slats that were virtually identical to nose installed on the old 100S com-etition models. Late in their produc-on run the MKII's were also equipped ith a new centrally mounted gear shift ver in place of the old awkwardly naped creation. Also welcomed was nother BMC effort to fathom the in-icacies of modern top design. The re-ult was still a complex, time consuming peration but at least, said Jerry Titus *Sports Car Graphic,* October 1961) it as "no longer an exercise in finger-reaking."

But just short of ten years after its riginal debut the Austin-Healey in KII, BJ7 form received not only a new nvertible top but windup windows. though it couldn't completely stow vay in the body when lowered, there ere few complaints from customers ho welcomed its easy operation and cellent fit. Rounding out the Healey's finements was a curved windshield, nall quarter-vent windows and a gher stainless steel door belt line.

Regardless of these welcome changes, decade was a long time for any sports r to remain in production; and with G introducing its new B at roughly the me time as the MKII Healey, jour-

The Might-Have-Been Healeys

While the aging Healey 3000 was being criticized in the motoring press for being "over the hill," a variety of projects were pursued with varying degrees of competence and logic as possible successors to the big Healey. One of these based a new Austin-Healey upon the MGB platform. After many twists and turns through the maze of BMC product planning it eventually emerged as the MGC.

Poorly regarded by both Donald Healey and his son Geoffrey was another project, the "Fireball XL5" which involved use of a Rolls-Royce four-liter engine, a center backbone-type frame and a suspension system utilizing the hydrolastic components of the Austin 1800. In *Austin-Healey: The Story of the Big Healeys,* Geoffrey Healey lambasts this car as "a monster, consuming vast amounts of skilled labor, time and money." Far more practical, desirable and feasible in his view was an all-Healey proposal that used the Rolls-Royce engine in a widened version of the grand old Healey body. Two prototypes, with and without overdrive, were produced and a target date of January 1968 was set down. But it too was cancelled, thus leaving the ill-fated Jensen-Healey to serve as the big Healey's successor.

nalists began to gently suggest that the time was soon approaching for an all-new Austin-Healey to make an appearance. Jerry Titus (*Sports Car Graphic,* December 1962) optimistically stated that "with the updating of the Sprite in 1962, the remodeled MG in 1963, it's highly probable that this is the last year for the now-classic Healey body style." *Road & Track* (November 1962) was a bit more cutting in its review of the MKII Healey: "The Austin-Healey is going to have to sit on the same showroom floor with BMC's MG B and it is in all respects save performance substantially inferior to that model. Perhaps it is time for an Austin-Healey 'B.'"

Meanwhile back in Abingdon, where Austin-Healeys had been produced at the MG works since late 1957, events had already transpired that could have led to such an automobile. Although the MG Midget had been a successful example of badge engineering derived from the Sprite (see *SIA* #52), there had been little enthusiasm for a program to create an MGB clone to be marketed as a new "big Healey." Instead the 3000 MKII Healey gave way in February 1964 to the MKIII version. By this point the Healey's age dominated the perspective of most road testers. *The Autocar* (June 12, 1964), noting that the Healey had

Right: *Top folds up neatly into well behind rear seats.* **Below:** *The end of a familiar sight on Healeys and other British sports cars came when the safety hysterics ordered that the "ears" or "wings" of knock-on hubcaps be removed to protect pedestrians. Presumably, by the time the hapless pedestrian had gotten that close to a moving car it would have been curtains anyway.* **Below right:** *Up front, there are also two sets of small lamps on the '67s, one set for parking, one for directionals.*

Austin-Healey

continued

steadily become a more powerful automobile, added, "but now, like an aging but still beautiful dowager, repeated face lifts can no longer wholly hide the ravages of time and progress." Yet the BJ8 Mark III proved durable enough in the marketplace for a three-year, 17,703 production run. Admittedly, purchasers of MKIII's were acquiring an automobile whose character was rooted in an earlier

age, but such vintage features as a big 17-inch steering wheel were also part of a new interior with walnut veneer dash sections, a neat panel with four toggle switches and that great hulk of a six-cylinder engine that now pumped 148 horsepower at 5,250 rpm. Early in the MKIII production run, after 1,390 had

been assembled, another inch of precious ground clearance was provided by the introduction of a new dropped rear frame. At the same time twin radius arms were added at the rear along with softer leaf springs. Larger Girling Type 16 front disc brakes replaced the Type 14s previously used, and stronger front and rear spined hubs were installed. Externally these MKIII's were identified by their separate front parking and directional lights and lockable doors. And just like the old days, in spite of a rerouted exhaust system with twin transverse-mounted resonators linked to dual mufflers, the Healey still touched bottom whenever it passed over a small dip.

But the MKIII represented the swan song of the big Healey's career. Pete Browning and Les Needham describe

---

The Jensen-Healey

The big Healey easily qualified as one of the postwar cars really worthy of being described as "greatly missed." Even after they were gone the melody lingered on, and when rumors about Jensen producing a successor started circulating in early 1970, just about everyone who had owned or coveted the Healey felt their prayers for its resurrection had been answered.

In addition to producing the Healey bodies (plus those for other British marques) Jensen had produced its own line of automobiles for many years. However, Jensen's experience and facilities weren't matched by financial resources on a scale needed to launch a new sports car. Thus early in 1970 Kjell Qvale, one of California's successful purveyors of sports cars, led an "international group" in acquiring the Jensen Company.

Less than two years later, on March 7, 1972, the efforts of Donald Healey's design team of Jensen and Qvale debuted at the Geneva Motor Show in Switzerland. While production models reaching the crucial US market early in 1973 made an initially favorable impression, their reputation was seriously dulled by a tendency to

harbor rust worms, suffer from water leaks and have a lousy finish. Although these problems were resolved fairly quickly, the whole Jensen operation, which included production of the much larger Interceptor and four-wheel-drive FF models, was mortally wounded by the oil crisis and the ensuing economic downturn.

If the Jensen Healeys had been mediocre cars all of this would have mattered little. But they were, after the resolution of their initial teething pains, fine automobiles, in many ways worthy successors to the big Healeys. Many of their suspension elements came from the sporting Firenza (that sounds familiar!) version of the Vauxhall Viva. This meant the J-H had strictly conventional front A-arms, a solid rear axle and coil springs at all four wheels. Jensen did use its own specially made coil springs plus Girling shocks in place of the Vauxhall's Delco units. The results were praiseworthy. *Road & Track* regarded the Vauxhall as "one of the best suspended and handling live-axle cars in Britain," and the J-H's respectable 0.7589 lateral acceleration, quick steering and comfortable ride were all credits to its designers. While the J-H had

the same 92-inch wheelbase as the old 3000, its overall length of 160 inches was three inches longer; and at 2,150 pounds the Jensen weighed in at nearly 3,000 pounds less than the Healey.

A displacement of just 121 cubic inches suggested the Jensen-Healey might be just a bit lethargic. But its four-cylinder engine was very much a thoroughbred. Designed by Lotus with dual overhead cam, four valves per cylinder and a healthy 140 horsepower at 6,500 rpm rating, it enabled the J-H to accelerate from zero to 60 mph in under ten seconds and reach a 125 mph top speed.

The Jensen-Healey's weakest point after its mechanical and structural composition had been put in order was its appearance. Unlike that of the early Austin-Healeys, the Jensen's styling was boxy and uninspired.

Eventually Kjell Qvale bailed out of the Jensen operation, and as a last ditch effort the new owners offered a neat sports wagon version, the Jensen GT, which had a conceptual and visual similarity to the Volvo 1800ES. Alas this wasn't enough to save the day and Jensen slipped away into the netherworld of British sports cars.

the final moment in *Healeys and Austin-Healeys*: "Sadly without any ceremony, one of this country's great classic sports cars came to the end of the line."

Some 3½ years earlier *The Autocar* (June 12, 1964) had prophesied that, 'despite some dated features the big Healey is still terrific fun to drive. Tractable, capable of an immense amount of hard work with reasonable economy, it will still have its devotees long after production has ceased."

Driving Impressions

One such devotee, Jim Terzo of Bainbridge, New York, remembers the time back in 1965 when he was eager to purchase a new MKIII Healey. He was "impressed with its power," but the Healey's $3,800 price tag nudged him towards the considerably less expensive Sunbeam Alpine. But a dozen years later Terzo got his Healey. Though far from being the proverbial basket case, his 1967 MKIII with its rusted rocker panels, tatty interior and tired engine, fit with ease into that classic "restorable" category so often used by peddlers of clapped-out British sports cars to snare the unwary.

But Terzo knew what he was getting into, and five years later his Mark III had garnered a number of first place class wins in local show competitions.

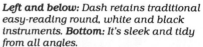

Left and below: Dash retains traditional easy-reading round, white and black instruments. Bottom: It's sleek and tidy from all angles.

Driving the Healey in 1984, if your motoring experiences include time spent with British two-seaters of days gone by, serves as an instant nostalgia trip. It's all there, the close fit of the pedals, the heat seeping out from under the dash and gearbox, the transmission's reluctance to shift from neutral to first gear without an initial visit to second. But then there's that sensation that the Healey can out-corner anything ever built around four wheels (that's actually far from reality, but that doesn't really matter). And if you switch on the wipers by mistake instead of engaging overdrive during a night run (the two are identically shaped and positioned close to each other) you can always

mutter something about the need to check out all equipment just in case it does rain.

The Healey's greater size and weight keeps it from impersonating a 1967 MGB in the turns. With only three turns lock to lock, the Healey's steering is plenty quick enough, but with a turning radius of 36 feet it lacks the maneuverability of the MGB which was less than four inches shorter than the Healey. But with three liters of punch the Healey makes a good account for itself whether it's effortlessly cruising in fourth gear overdrive or making a quick getaway from a stoplight. It doesn't have the sheer muscle of a Corvette of course, but there's enough on tap to impress most anyone except hard-core supercar enthusiasts.

Perhaps it was true that the Healey by the mid-sixties had gotten long in the tooth, and maybe we would be honest if we owned up to the fact that all that noise, those uncomfortable seats and rough ride of the Healey weren't really essential features of a modern sports car. But there was just something about taking the Healey up to about 80 mph and switching into overdrive that did all kinds of nice things for your smile muscles. At moments like that all the Healey's idiosyncrasies and antiquated ways were forgotten, and some great motoring memories were with us for a few fleeting moments. □

THE 'BIG' AUSTIN

by Dave Destler

It's been a decade now since the last of the 'big' Healeys rolled off the Abingdon production line, and the following it has maintained through the ensuing years is reaching cult status. Historically filling the price and performance gap between the MG and Jaguar sports cars, the Austin Healey 3000, which cost $3565 in 1966, is now bringing upwards of $12,500 for excellent examples, (a 3000 MkII recently sold at auction for $18,400) and looks to be a sure bet to go higher soon.

With typical British beginnings, the Austin Healey series of sports cars was originally derived from the staid Austin A90 sedan. British Motor Corporation (BMC) gave the thumbs-up to Mr. Healey to create a purposeful, aggressive roadster, and, in 1952, the Austin Healey '100', designated *BN1*, was born. Utilizing the A90's 90hp, 4-cylinder, 2660cc OHV engine and a three-speed gearbox in a chassis designed by Geoff

Healey, Donald's son, the one-ton car was a spunky performer and a nimble handler. Clothed in sleek lines conceived by Healey (he admits to being inspired by the classic Raymond Loewy-designed Coke bottle) and refined by stylist Gerry Coker, it was also an attention-getter.

A simple, crude car, it was basically a steel body wrapped around a chassis, a pair of seats, and a motor. Amenities were few; clip-on side curtains and a 'rag' top, erected over a detachable framework, were all that was provided for weather protection. This was ludicrous in the country that built it, needing perhaps the most comprehensive sheltering devices, not the most minimal. But the strongest market was the United States, as was the case with most British sports cars of the post-war years, and the enthusiasts in the eastern states put up with a few butt-numbing months out of the year, while the folks out west probably never put the top up. For those

BELOW: Dan Pendergraft's restored 1957 100-6 Rally car, now used extensively in vintage roadracing. Successes in 1986 include first place finishes at the Meadowbrook Historic Races in Michigan and the Palm Springs Vintage G.P., second at the Monterey Historic Races at Laguna Seca. Among the special factory features are: all-aluminum body (RHD), vented hardtop, bootlid 'bustle' for extra spare tire, triple Webers, four-wheel disc brakes.

Photo: Bob Dunsmore

HEALEYS

At speed in the California desert; Henning Krebs' beautiful 1967 Austin Healey 3000 MkIII.

Photo: Dayna Destler

Two-tone 100M at rest at England's famous Silverstone circuit, site of many Healey racing successes.

TOP: The Austin Healey team at Sebring, 1954. Left to right: Lance Macklin, Morris Goodall, George Huntoon, and Donald Healey.

ABOVE CENTER: Donald Healey at the Bonneville Salt Flats, 1954, driving the '100' streamliner at 192 mph.

RIGHT: Geoff and Margo Healey at a recent club gathering in England.

Photo: Paul Skilleter

who wanted even more wind in the face, the windshield could be slid down and forward into a partial layed-down position, giving the car a racey, rakish look, and the driver bugs in the teeth.

When the stock 90 hp was insufficient for competition purposes- the Sebring 12 Hour Race in particular- the '100' was re-developed in 1954, utilizing a Weslake-designed cylinder head and modified engine internals to put out 132 hp through a revised 4-speed gearbox. With an aluminum bodyshell, fitted with an abbreviated windscreen, louvered bonnet, new, smaller grille, big external 'Le Mans'-type gas cap, and devoid of bumpers, it was a purposeful sports/race car. To cope with the 125 mph speed potential, the 'special' 100 was equipped with beefed-up suspension and four-wheel disc brakes by Dunlop. This, the prototype of the 100S ('S' for Sebring) went on to take third overall and first in class in the race, driven by Lance Macklin and American George Huntoon.

It again proved its mettle at Sebring, taking its class win in '55, driven by Stirling Moss and Lance Macklin, and gave a good showing in that year's Mille Miglia 1000-mile road race. Only 50 of these hot four-bangers were built, and are prized today for their high performance and low production.

1955 also saw the '100' upgraded with a four-speed gearbox with overdrive and, to utilize readily-available BMC components, a Morris rear axle. This was the BN2. Around the same time, a breathed-upon version of the standard production car was offered for those with a need for more power, but not to the extreme of the 'S'. This was the 100M (designated BN2) of 1955 and '56, which developed 110 hp and was characterized by its two-tone paint scheme, distinctive louvered bonnet and leather strap. 1159 100Ms were built, and proved to be popular In club racing. It's short lifespan was due to the arrival of a new, more potent Austin Healey, the 100-Six.

BMC had made the corporate decision in 1955 to take the new 2.6 litre six-cylinder motor, actually 30cc smaller in displacement than the four (2660cc vs 2630cc), which first appeared in the Austin A90 and Wolseley 6/90, and stuff it into the Austin Healey. Although Donald and Geoff Healey themselves were less than enthusiastic about abandoning the faithful four-cylinder mills, Leonard Lord, Chairman of Austin (see Austin Vanden Plas Princess article this issue) had spoken, and the BN4, or 100-Six as the public knew it, was announced in late 1956. It was to begin a new era of success, both in competition and in sales, for the marque.

Although it was hardly any faster than the 100-Four (so-named ex post facto), it did produce more torque and was smoother for more liesurely around-town motoring. With the smaller grille from the 100S, featuring horizontal bars, a small additional air intake at the leading edge of the bonnet, and a fixed (instead of folding) windscreen, it was easily distinguishable from its presecessor, which is important when a manufacturer wishes to sell a new model. Furthermore, its wheelbase was increased from 90 inches to just about 92, the extra length helping to accommodate two small occasional seats behind the driver's and

RIGHT: Early and late big Healeys; the 100M and 3000 MkIII showing detail differences, yet overall similarity.

Photo: Henning Krebs

passenger's. Though becoming more refined, it still bore the clip-on side curtains deemed *de rigueur* for true sporting roadsters, and there was a choice of either disc or wire wheels.

Being a part of a large corporation like BMC has its advantages and disadvantages. If Donald Healey had not agreed to having Austin build his cars at the Longbridge works, he would have been limited to a production of perhaps 20 cars a week, never making the inroads necessary in the American market and perhaps not surviving in the process.

However, first he had to discontinue his beloved 'Four' in deference to the corporate-conceived 'Six' (which turned out to be beneficial after all), and then to see produc-

tion move from Longbridge to the MG factory in Abingdon, in the autumn of 1957. This decision, to have all BMC sports cars built there, was another part of BMC's rationalization program. So, if you visited the MG works in the late 50s, you'd have seen both MGs and Austin Healeys coming down the line.

The six's cylinder head was redesigned at the same time, and power was bumped from 102 to 117 hp. The only other big change to this model was the option to buy a 100-Six in a two-seater version, the BN6, like the old '100' model. Both two- and four-seaters were available concurrently.

Come 1959, though, the final model change was to take place with the displacement bored out to 2.9 litres, rounded off in marketing

parlance to three litres, and dubbed the Austin Healey 3000. The larger capacity engine pumped out 124 hp through a beefier clutch and gearbox, and its top speed was in the neighborhood of 112 to 115 mph. Now disc front brakes were provided as standard equipment, and virtually the only visible difference was a '3000' badge on the grille in place of the '100-Six'. The new 3000 too was offered in either two-seater (BN7) or 'two-plus-two' (BT7) configuration.

With the new model came a more diversified field of competition endeavors and successes. Now, besides sports car road races, the low-slung 3000 proved its capabilities in grueling rallies as well, taking first and third in the 1960 Marathon Rally, second in the Alpine, and third overall in the RAC Rally. At

SPECIFICATIONS

	100 (BN1)	100 (BN2)	100S (AHS)	100M (BN2)	100-6 (BN4)	100-6 (BN 6)	3000 (BN7-BT7)	3000 MkII (BT7)	3000 MkII (BJ7)	3000 MkIII (BJ8)
POWERTRAIN										
Engine (Type)	OHV 4	OHV 4	OHV 4	OHV 4	OHV 6	OHV 6	OHV 6	OHV 6	OHV 6	OHV 6
Bore X Stroke (mm)	87x111	87x111	87x111	87x111	79x88	79x88	83x88	83x88	83x88	83x88
Displacement (cc)	2660	2660	2660	2660	2630	2630	2912	2912	2912	2912
Output (BHP)	90	90	132	110	102/117	102/117	124	132	132	148
Gearbox	3 spd	4 spd/OD	4 spd/OD	4 spd/OD	4 spd/OD	4 spd/OD	4 spd/OD	4 spd/OD	4 spd/OD	4 spd/OD
DIMENSIONS										
Wheelbase (in)	90	90	90	90	92	92	92	92	92	92
Length (in)	151	151	151	151	157	157	157.5	157.5	157.5	157.5
Weight (lbs)	2015	2150	1925	2015	2425	2435	2460	2460	2550	2550
PERFORMANCE										
Top Speed (mph)	100	100	120	102	103	103	114	114	114	120
PRODUCTION										
Years Built	1952-53	1954-56	1955	1955-56	1956-59	1956-59	1959-61	1961-62	1962-64	1964-67
Amount	10,688	3924	50	1159	10,246	4150	13,650	5450	6113	17,712

HEALEY HIGHS & LOWS

For any note-worthy automobile, there are days to remember and days to forget. What makes a car a great car is when the former outnumber the latter such as it was for the 'big' Austin Healey.

Factory rally car on its way to a second in the '65 RAC Rally.

HIGHS

October 22, 1952- The 1952 Motor Show in London, where the brand-new Healey '100' is unveiled to the public and given the go-ahead by Austin boss Leonard Lord. A new marque, Austin Healey, is born.

Le Mans, France 1953- Austin Healey's debut at the 24-hour race, garnering a second and third in class.

Sebring, Florida 1954- Lance Macklin and George Huntoon take the 'special' alloy-bodied 100 to third place overall, defeating many larger, more expensive cars and encouraging the production of 50 'replicas', the '100S'.

Bonneville, Utah 1954- A supercharged, streamlined 100 screams down the Salt Flats at 192.62 mph, and sets record 12- and 24-hour high-speed runs.

Sebring, Florida 1955- The 100s sweeps their class with a 1,2,3 finish, taking sixth overall in the 12-hour event.

Italy, 1955- The grueling 1000-mile race down the length of Italy and back up is the setting for a first and second in class for the Austin Healey 100s.

England, 1956- Two 100s take first and second in class in the Autosport Production Sports Car Championship.

Bonneville, Utah 1956- Donald Healey fulfills a dream and drives his supercharged 'liner on the Salt Flats in excess of 200 mph- 203.06 to be exact.

Longbridge, August 1956- The first BMC 6-cylinder engine appears in a Healey, and the 100-6 is launched.

Italy, 1957- Another first in class in the Mille Miglia.

Abingdon, March 1959- The 100-6's displacement is increased to just under 3 litres, and the '3000' is born.

England, 1960- The new 3000 makes its mark in international rallying, with an outright win in the Marathon and a third in the RAC.

The Alps, 1961 and 1962- First place overall in the Alpine Rally both years focuses a lot of attention on the little 'big' car, making Austin Healey the one to beat.

All-over Europe, 1964- A banner year for the big Healey; winning overall the Marathon Rally, Austrian Alpine Rally, first in the GT category in the Tulip Rally, and a second each in the Alpine and RAC Rallys.

England, 1965- The Austin Healey's last official appearance in competition was that year's RAC Rally, taking second place overall.

Abingdon, February 1962- The first 'civilized' Austin Healey, the 3000 BJ7 gets roll-up windows and a easily-lowered top.

LOWS

Le Mans, France 1955- The 100S of Lance Macklin is involved in the worst racing accident in history. As Macklin passed the pit area in the rain at around 125 mph, he was overtaken by Mike Hawthorn in a D-type Jaguar, who suddenly pulled into his pit. Swerving to avoid the Jaguar, Macklin's Healey was struck from the rear by Pierre Levegh in a Mercedes, who was attempting to pass Macklin at around 155 mph. The doomed Mercedes vaulted into the pit wall and broke up in flames, sending engine, wheels, chassis parts and other heavy debris into the crowd, killing 80 spectators and injuring scores more. Macklin was shaken but unhurt. Levegh died on the scene. Hawthorne went on to win, but victory's taste was sour. No fault was put to anyone, but the tragedy caused the track to implement many changes for drivers' and spectators' safety.

Abingdon, December 1967- While not as tragic as the last account, this marked a significant point in Austin Healey history; the end of the line. The production run of the 3000 ended, killed by burgeoning U.S. safety laws and insufficient demand for the cars to warrant the extensive modifications necessary to comply. Although the Healey name continued on the tiny Sprite until 1971 (with its badge-engineered twin, the MG Midget, produced through 1979), and the Lotus-powered Jensen-Healey, announced in 1972 and discontinued in 1976, the true Healey era ended, at least to Donald's and Geoff's proponents, with that last BJ8.

Sebring that year, it took second and third in class, then went on to win its class at the Nurburgring 500. The next year, 1961, the 3000 won the Alpine Rally outright, with a second in the RAC and a third in the Acropolis Rally. It obviously won the respect of the racing world as well, earning itself ample pages in the record books, while gaining a reputation that helped to sell production models to the public.

The same year, 1961, brought more changes, and the 3000 MkII boasted eight more horses under the bonnet, as result of three SU carbs in place of the two previously used, and a new camshaft to take advantage of the improved breathing. Visibly, it was the same except for a change to vertical bars in the grille.

The next year, however, came a very important modification that opened up the 3000's market to a wider range of potential customers. The 1962 Austin Healey 3000 MkII now came with roll-up windows in place of the clip-on curtains, and a top that easily lowered down behind the seats, rather than unfastening for stowage. Only the 'four-seater' was offered in this guise, the two-seater discontinued. A return to dual carburetors with yet another camshaft revision completed the major changes.

Through the early and mid-sixties, the 'big' Healeys, so-called to avoid confusion with the Sprites and others, continued to show well in competition, with the last official appearance in November 1965, where it garnered second in the RAC Rally.

Improvements learned from the racing efforts continued to benefit the production cars, and the last update came about in 1964, with the MkIII's revised chassis and suspension yielding both improved ground clearance and a more compliant ride. Power, too, was increased, with cams, carbs, and exhaust modifications helping to produce a very respectable 148 hp. The BJ8, as the final incarnation of this handsome machine was designated, sported yet more luxuries, such as a polished wood-veneer dashboard and a modern central console.

The 3000 MkIII, the last of the line, was not only the most comfortable, but also the fastest, with a top speed of a solid 120 mph. This trend would probably not have continued anyway, even if the car had *not* been discontinued in 1967, another victim of the strict U.S. safety and emissions regulations to go into effect in '68. The now-dated design just did not lend itself to the magnitude of re-engineering and redesigning necessary to bring it into compliance with the new laws, and it was no longer feasible for BMC to build the car.

What's the attraction of the 3000, possibly Donald Healey's finest creation? Up until recently, only the devoted Healey fanatic paid much attention to the cars, the general public giving it a subtle nod of approval, but little more. Now, all of a sudden, the speculators are buying them to resell later for a profit, the sports car buff is wishing he bought one when they were still cheap, and even some owners of other marques are taking a hard look at the 'handsome brute'.

When a loyal Jaguar XK driver adds a big Healey to his garage, or the long-time owner of two MGs sells both to buy one 3000MkIII,

The 3000 MkIII's distinctive front end, with bonnet-mounted air intake.

Photos: Paul Skilleter

Donald Healey is still very active in club events worldwide.

it's obvious that what was once overlooked is now being looked over. Both these situations recently occurred, and the renewed interest in these cars is pushing the value of all the big Healeys upwards. A contributing factor to both the popularity and the increasing value of the Healeys is the availability of parts to repair or restore them. Through such companies as Moss Motors, The Austin Healey Store, Austin Healey Enterprises, Faspec, and others, parts and service are plentiful enough to make driving one of these cars on a daily basis a practical proposition.

Never built in the same high numbers as the MGs, Triumphs, or even the relatively sparse Jaguar E-type roadsters, the Austin Healeys were steady sellers to those few sports car buyers who wanted something 'better' than the MG or Triumph, but not as expensive as the Jags. Many of these people were more in tune to the racing scene than most, and bought Healeys based upon their competition performances.

Being a bit 'different', but not so esoteric that no one knew what it was, always seemed to be in the big Healey's favor, not to mention that it was very rugged, and proved itself to be a reliable, virtually unbreakable sports car.

It did have its weak points of course, such as the earlier cars' inability to keep the inclement weather outside. It was also prone to rust-out in several areas of the body that were inadvertently designed as 'traps' for moisture, wet dirt, and road salt (in the eastern states), especially behind the wheel wells and in the sills, to name the worst two. The lack of ground clearance must have surely contributed to a brisk aftermarket in exhaust systems, as it would scrape on virtually every driveway the car traversed.

Another customer complaint with the cars preceding the MkIII was noise. The loud exhaust note, while sporty and exciting, got to be a bit too much on a long run, and the loud droning tended to promote headaches, if not hearing loss! The cars would 'harmonize' and buzz with the throaty cascade of sound, and putting the top up meant sitting inside a four-wheeled resonator. The MkIII ended this problem with a quieter exhaust system, losing no power in the process, and better insulation. That insulation also helped to prevent the copious amounts of heat from the engine compartment from reaching the occupants, as was a problem in the early cars.

In effect, the MkIII took all the good points of the earlier cars, refined them, and presented them in a more comfortable package. It was a car that a 'civilized' person could live with, without too much of the 'pain' of British sports car ownership. Because of this, the 3000 MkIII is the most sought-after Healey (aside from the rare competition models) by collectors and enthusiasts, as well as being the one sold in the greatest numbers.

Driving the MkIII is quite enjoyable- almost surprisingly so. It has a far more supply ride than one would expect of such a light car, with more compliance than the earlier models due to the revised rear suspension. The handling is quick and responsive, due to the short 92-inch wheelbase and well-engineered suspension, yet very stable and confidence-inspiring as a result of the very low center of gravity (although not as low as the earlier cars) and the big fifteen-inch tires.

The long-stroke 2.9 litre motor produces abundant torque right from the lowest revs, and in fact makes taking off from rest in

second gear easy and convenient in stop-and-go traffic. However, the car wasn't built for such sedate use; the winding hills and mountain roads are where it shows what it does best. The silver-blue MkIII pictured here, owned by Henning Krebs, is a superb example of what a big Healey should look like and what it can do.

While scouting out possible photo locations in the Topanga hills of Southern California, we had the opportunity to put the BJ8 through its paces. Having owned the car since 1981, taking a year to restore it, Henning is very familiar with it, which was evident by the smoothness with which he drove it fast.

Using mostly third gear, occasionally flicking the overdrive switch on (which works on third or fourth gear), the blue roadster pulled its way strongly from 1500 rpm on up to 5000, showing the flexibility of the Austin six. The low-end torque gives the impression of more horsepower than there really is, which allows an easy, relaxed driving style. The handling, which Henning has further improved with the addition of an anti-sway bar, is quite impressive for such a 'dated' design. The fat Dunlop 185/70-15s gave nary a chirp as we dove into corners without a touch of the brakes, powering out with a good shove back in the sheepskin-covered seats (a necessity under the hot California sun).

The Healey howl out back harmonized with the rather prominent intake hiss up front, providing a pleasing, but not offensive auditory experience. The car, with the top down, was relatively draft-free, and wind noise was minimal.

Whether the car was parked or in motion, people of all ages showed a great deal of interest, the public's awareness of the car seeming in excess of what you would expect for a rather scarce car that's been out of production for twenty years. It's obviously a handsome, rugged-looking car, but not a flashy one, and the attention says a lot for the original basic body design that Donald Healey laid down thirty-five years ago.

The 'big' Austin Healeys, though not the fastest, quickest, nimblest, or best in any respect of the classic British sports cars, do score high enough in *all* these categories, though, to rank up there as one of the greatest British sports cars of all time. □

Modern History

Seemingly, the Healey 3500 MkIV has it all, with traditional 1960s feel, 1980s levels of performance, and style by the hamperful. Just as British in its own way as the Healey, Prescott's hillclimb course proved to be the ideal location for **Brian Laban** to find out if this specialist car is worth the hefty price

Ettore's Bend, on the loop of the long course of the Bugatti Owners Club's famous hillclimb at Prescott, is a tricky little number, especially when it is still drying patchily in the sun from another short, sharp April shower.

The approach from the left-hand sweep of Orchard Corner – as the course gets into its stride from the start line, down by the gate on the Cheltenham to Winchcombe road – is quick and generously wide for a hillclimb course, and there will never be anyone in your way, which only makes it the more frustrating for a novice.

Brake firmly, change down into second, staying well over to the left on the approach, and turn in where instinct says you should for the tight right-handed hairpin. It's not a particularly quick corner, but if you were tackling the course in anger it would be a very important one in terms of shaving the hundredths of seconds by which hillclimbs are won and lost – the first building block for the rest of the hill, out to Pardon Hairpin and the steep rush up through the trees to the Esses, through the daunting Semi-Circle with its seemingly bottomless drop past your left shoulder, and onto the last, flat-out blast to the finish line.

But Ettore's is just Prescott's first little strand of deception. As the black car turns into what feels like the apex, cresting the small rise with a big handful of understeer and the rear haunches rising on their springs, the power goes down and the back end steps out of line as ordered, the inside wheel chirping slightly as the roll lifts it gently from the inside camber of the track. Feed in more and more power and the appropriate opposite lock to line the car up for the exit to the corner and then discover, ignominiously, that the corner has tightened viciously towards its end, and what should have been a smooth, clean drift onto the short curve to Pardon has turned into a clumsy rumble over the bump strips, and a lurid, over-correcting slide towards the outside grassy verge.

Never mind, it's not for real, it's only for the first action pics of the big, black Healey; we'll get it right on the next run. Or maybe we won't; try again and just keep talking yourself into getting deeper and deeper into the corner before you even begin to turn, let alone feed in the glorious, whooping power of the hairy chested sports car. And again; and again, deeper every time, staying over on the outside until you can see the metaphorical whites of Pardon's eyes, *then* turn hard in *past* the jaws of the corner, and start the opposite lock slide down towards the old course, with the power hard on and the Healey accelerating in a massive rush of sound and fury.

Then you only have to learn the rest of the tricky 1127 yards, and as soon as Bill Goodman's Prescott Hillclimb Driver School can fit us in, we will.

This is terribly English – the hill, the Healey, the April showers – but one small element isn't quite what it seems; the car is just a bit of an impostor. It isn't the concours last-of-the-line 1968 Austin Healey 3000 MkIII that anyone who saw it on the way up to Prescott might have thought it was; it is a brand new Healey 3500 MkIV, and it is sensationally good.

We saw it first a few weeks ago, with degree of scepticism, having seen pictures and the brief announcement that it was about to go into production in rural Gloucestershire. But with a penny in the bank for every time we hear of another fabulous recreation of a classic car, we could retire tomorrow – almost as soon, in fact, as the majority of such projects fall apart at the seams. Or the cars do.

This one won't.

Drive as hard as this in most 'specialist' cars and it is simply a matter of what will break and when, rather than if. But the Healey 3500 Mk IV never so much as creaked or fluffed, never complained or hesitated or faltered – it just got better and better the more we grew to understand it. And you do need to understand it to

degree, because, good as it is, it doesn't set out to be a next generation sports car, but more a sensible and sensitive updating of a tradition. The tradition was one of Britain's finest, the 'big' Healey, which went out of production in 1968, as a 3-litre Mk III model, when Austin (who built it) dropped the Healey line in favour of MG. It was a great car then and it is a better car now, which is some compliment.

Its new specification apart, the single most impressive aspect of the Mk IV is its engineering. All too often the beginning of the end for a project like this is the small aside at the unveiling that says 'of course, the dash will change before the customer cars', or 'well, we won't actually be using these wheels or this engine but otherwise it will be more or less the same'. . . and so on, *ad nauseam*.

The new Healey has clearly been totally thought through and finished in every detail. The body is glassfibre, though you'd be hard pushed to tell, and although no panel is precisely the same as the originals on which they're based, the car is pure 3000 in looks. It is genuinely difficult to fault the finish, and all the chrome has that lovely, deep, almost black look of

quality. The cockpit is superbly trimmed, the underbonnet as neat as any production model – with never a loose wire or an unsightly run of hose. Even such tiny details as the bullet hinges for the quarter lights are absolutely right – while the big knock-on wire wheels look perfectly proportioned, and are in fact 15-inch diameter, as original.

It all has to reflect Graham Holmes' background as an aeronautical engineer, and brother Peter's longtime background as a classic car restorer, with a formal engineering training encompassing design, prototype production and testing.

And the final seal of approval comes with Geoffrey Healey, son of the late

founder Donald, as the third director of the new Healey Motor Company – which was founded as a direct result of the collaboration over this project by the Holmes' company Harrier Cars, and Geoffrey's Healey Automobile Consultants.

The aim was an updated version of the 3000; a low volume, high-spec sports car, with 2 + 2 seating and more refinement in all areas than the original, to make it a practical car for everyday use.

Well, every day might be stretching it a bit far, but the 3500 Mk IV is certainly fun. Free of the nagging doubts that it is going to break, you couldn't help but love it, from the moment you climb in.

The seats are black, the dash is walnut; the instruments are comprehensive and traditional, and the controls are light and modern. The driving position is low but not so low as on the original, so the small, leather-rimmed wheel, though adjustable for height and reach, can still foul your knees slightly, and the space around the pedals is on the tight side of adequate. The top fits superbly and folds fairly easily under a clip-on tonneau, which is where it stayed while we had the car, April showers or no.

Underneath, there is a tubular backbone chassis where the original had a cross-braced ladder, and independent

Although none of new Healey's glassfibre body panels, above, are shaped as original 3000, it has classic look. Wire wheels are original 15-inch size, which helps

ont view, above, is unmistakably Healey. Handling is predictable, with taut, solid chassis, and there is ample grip from 195/65VR15 Avon Turbospeed tyres

rear suspension where the original had cart springs. That is now by semi-trailing wishbones and the front is by unequal length wishbones, with coil springs and adjustable gas dampers all round. Steering is rack and pinion, there are ventilated discs on the front, solid discs on the back – and there is 190bhp and 209lb ft of torque from an injected Rover V8, driving through a five-speed all-syncro gearbox.

All of which adds up to a car which belies its 1960s looks with sharp-end 1980s performance. The V8 starts with a burble and revs with a glorious, musical whoop, giving the Healey quite *serious* urge, across the board. From a standstill it is claimed to reach 60mph in 6.1 seconds, 70 in 8 seconds and 100 in 15, and it feels capable of at least that and maybe even better; with a kerb weight of only 2700lb and bags of traction from 195/65VR15 Avon Turbospeed tyres, there's no reason why it shouldn't. And beyond outright power and performance, the huge advantage of the V8 is its wonderful flexibility, which with five gears and a long-legged 25.6mph in top makes this a car for virtually any kind of road.

Up and down Prescott, on varied A- and B-roads, and even on the M5, we tried it on pretty well everything without ever catching it out, yet with a lot of the ori-

ginal, strong character shining through.

The feel is a mixture of traditional and modern; the chassis feels taut and solid but definitely alive – a 'proper' sports car feeling, not a fault. The steering feels heavy at first after any modern power assisted system, and dead around the straight ahead position, but with tremendous feedback and accuracy once you adapt to it. The ride is firm and uncompromisingly stiff but never jarring, even on the worst potholes, there's enough suspension travel to counter that, and the brakes are powerful and delicate at the same time.

The grip and handling, too, are so consistent and predictable that you can use all the Healey's considerable power in both wet and dry without hesitation. It won't run rings round a modern hatchback or a

modern sports car, but it won't give much away either, and with the top down and the V8 howling away you can have three guesses as to who's having the fun. With so much power and with your backside so close to the rear wheels you can power slide it with abandon and always catch it neatly, or you can behave yourself and drive it on this side of its limits grabbing just as much reward from the point-and-squirt side of its nature.

It's as hard to fault it dynamically, given its brief, as it is to fault its build quality.

And although quality does cost money, the new Healey isn't outrageously expensive for something so unique; the very up-spec 3500 MkIV Convertible version that we drove, with electric windows and mirrors, heater, radio/casette player and very comprehensive equipment levels will be around £35,000, while the mechanically similar but much more basically equipped Silverstone 3500 Roadster will be £24,000. Production is due to start in June and the initial target is a couple of hundred cars a year.

For once, that deserves to come true.

Hood, above, slips neatly into clip-on cover or, when erected, gives snug, watertight fit. An equally tight fit, flexible Rover V8 engine, bottom right, gives 190bhp

Superbly-finished exterior quality is carried through to interior. Traditional-looking instruments set in walnut dash and low driving position, above, are pure 3000